HOMESPUN

HOMESPUN

Tales from America's Favorite Storytellers

Edited by Jimmy Neil Smith

Crown Publishers, Inc., New York

Published by Crown Publishers, Inc., 225 Park Avenue South, New York, New York 10003 and represented in Canada by the Canadian MANDA Group.
CROWN is a trademark of Crown Publishers, Inc.
Manufactured in the United States of America
Book design by Dana Sloan

Library of Congress Cataloging-in-Publication Data
Homespun: tales from America's favorite storytellers
   Bibliography: p.
   1. Tales—United States.   2. Storytellers—United
States.   I. Smith, Jimmy Neil.   II. Title: Homespun
GR105.5.A48   1988   398.2'0973   87-32989

ISBN 0-517-56936-1
10 9 8 7 6 5 4 3 2 1
First Edition

To

Jean G. Smith, my wife

Eric L. Smith, my son

Dorothy J. Smith, my mother

Pearl N. Jackson, my grandmother

With love

Contents

ACKNOWLEDGMENTS

There have been many individuals who have helped inspire *Home-spun* and give it life. I owe them my sincerest appreciation.

Homespun would not be a reality today had it not been for Trish Todd, my agent, and Mark Gompertz, my editor, who believed in me and America's storytelling revival. Throughout the book's writing, they advised me, encouraged me, and nudged me to keep on track.

It was Greta Hedburg-Talton who assisted me in bringing structure to a seemingly boundless topic, helped me refine and polish my writing skills, and gave me encouragement to overcome a passel of difficult obstacles.

The constant writing of *Homespun* required hours of typing and re-typing, which was successfully performed without complaint by Helen Jones and Beckie Fields, my assistants. They were jewels.

Lorena Cradduck, Beckie Fields, Sharon Johnson, Helen Jones, Carla Papy, and Greta Hedburg-Talton—the capable staff of the National Association for the Preservation and Perpetuation of Storytelling—gave me moral support and, at the drop of a hat, would read any passage and comment endlessly on it.

Members of the Board of Directors of NAPPS—Donald Davis, Gay Ducey, Clare Cuddy, Milbre Burch, Beth Horner, Ed Stivender, and Cathryn Wellner—endorsed the project, allowing me the opportunity to write this volume.

But when I think of *Homespun*, I first think of those whose lives have given cause for its writing. They are among those who have inspired America's storytelling renaissance.

I thank you—Brother Blue, Donald Davis, Elizabeth Ellis, The Folktellers, Spalding Gray, Ray Hicks, David Holt, Doc McConnell, Waddie Mitchell, Jay O'Callahan, Maggi Peirce, Lee Pennington, Gayle Ross, Laura Simms, Mary Carter Smith, Ed Stivender, Gioia Timpanelli, Jackie Torrence, Kathryn Windham, and Diane Wolkstein

Introduction

When I was eleven years old, I began raising chickens so I could sell eggs to families in the neighborhood where I lived. With money I had saved, I bought thirty White Leghorn pullets, and each morning before I went to school, and each afternoon when I returned, I dutifully cared for my flock. When they began laying eggs, I had a supply far greater than our family's needs, and my career as an entrepreneur was launched. One Saturday morning, I packed my extra eggs into cartons, stacked them carefully in a peach basket, and set out to sell them up and down my street.

But I was a shy child. As soon as I stepped onto the front porch, the screen door slamming behind me, I was overcome with fear. I couldn't go door-to-door selling eggs, facing the neighbors with my timid query. A few minutes later, my mother discovered me on the stoop, my head in my hands, the peach basket filled with eggs sitting forlornly beside me. While I don't remember distinctly what she said, I do recall vividly my mother's encouragement, her nudging me to face the challenge. And I remember setting off down the street, my basket in hand, calling first on one house and then the next. An hour later, I returned home with an empty basket.

Even today when I'm encountering a difficult challenge, my mother —still ever so wise—prompts me, "Remember the day you sat on the porch with your basket of eggs?" And she recounts the story, jogging my memory of that long-ago agony and bringing into the present a lesson from the past.

There is nothing extraordinary about my experience. Such moments are faced by all of us as we wend our way through childhood. But in her retelling of this brief tale, my mother is doing something very human. For since the beginning of mankind, we have *all* told stories—sometimes simple anecdotal tales, those cut from the fabric of life, and others, spun from the limitless world of our imagination. Yet whatever their nature, stories begin, and have always begun, quite simply: with a moment, an experience, a feeling. Whether a thousand years ago or in our highly mechanized society, tales have been told for basically the same reasons—to educate and entertain, to explain the unexplainable, to honor the past and its people, and to record the simple, seemingly unimportant moments of human existence.

Throughout the world, in every culture, people have told stories—at home and at work, when the harvest was taken in, the fish were caught, the wood was cut and carted, the wool was woven. And while the folk were telling their stories, so too were the bards and the minstrels, the *griots* and troubadours, who were the poets, singers, and guardians of a people's history.

Today, we still enjoy stories—listening to them, telling them—as deeply as did our ancestors, for our lives are bound together with stories: the tales, perhaps ever so ordinary, that seem to catch us up and in some obscure, almost magical way help us make sense of our world. And since our lives are still intertwined with stories, it would seem that the art of storytelling should have a forever-unchanging place of honor in our history and culture. Yet this is not so. Despite its ageless power and importance, this ancient folk art has, until recently, been forgotten— lost in a sea of print, film, and videotape that is testimony to the media's skill at filling us up with images and ideas that were once the province of the oral tradition.

But during the late 1960s and early 1970s, there emerged throughout America a realization that we were losing our connection to the genuine, one-on-one communication of the told tale. The seeds for a reawakening of interest in the oral tradition were being sown. And in 1973, in a tiny Tennessee town, something happened that rekindled our national appreciation of the told story and became the spark plug for a major cultural movement—the rebirth of the art of storytelling.

It began serendipitously in Jonesborough, Tennessee, a 200-year-old town in the heart of the Southern Appalachian Mountains. If you were to wander into Jonesborough, you would descend one of two long hills —one leading from the east, the other from the west. Traverse them both, down one and up the other, and you will have seen the heart of Tennessee's oldest town. That's Main Street, lined in brick and cobblestone, with stately buildings where history is crammed door-to-door. At the heart of the village is the courthouse, solemn and imposing, with its tower jutting skyward and its clock—more often wrong than right— keeping score of the passing generations. And it was here that Andy Jackson—red-haired and fiery—was licensed to practice law, fought his first duel with a distinguished but feisty North Carolina barrister, and helped douse a fire at a local tavern, wearing only his nightshirt.

Though much quieter since the day when the impetuous Jackson galloped westward to become the hero of the Battle of New Orleans and president of the United States, Jonesborough still thrives. Its shops, tucked storefront to storefront along the town's narrow street, are filled to overflowing. And with the coming of autumn, when the harvest is in, there are pumpkins—plump and brilliant orange—gooseneck squash, and apples, bushels of apples, lining our streets.

And every October since 1973, thousands of travelers, making their way down one hill or the other, have visited this tiny Tennessee town. They come for one purpose: to hear stories, and to tell them, at the National Storytelling Festival—a celebration of America's rich and varied storytelling tradition. The festival, founded in 1973, is the oldest and most respected gathering devoted exclusively to the art of storytelling anywhere in America, and this unique event has in turn spawned a national revival of this venerable art.

Despite its central role, Jonesborough's place in the national storytelling renaissance came into being by accident in the late 1960s when, after a long and distinguished history, Tennessee's first town began to decay and seemed destined to become just another dying Southern wayside. The malls and strip centers in nearby Johnson City had lured Jonesborough's customers away, and the town's economy—based for generations upon serving its residents and those living in the surrounding countryside—began to erode. Businesses along the town's historic Main Street were forced to close their doors. Shops were soon empty, and buildings were falling into disrepair.

Jonesborough's leaders were not content to allow the deterioration to go unchecked, and in a dramatic move—one far wiser and insightful than ever imagined—they devised a plan to reverse the decline. They surmised that Jonesborough's future must lie in its past and, by the early 1970s, had developed a plan to preserve the old town, restore its historic Main Street, and eventually, build a new economy based on tourism.

To spearhead this renewal, the town's leaders founded the Jonesborough Civic Trust, and within two years the infant organization had sponsored Historic Jonesborough Days—a weekend-long festival celebrating Jonesborough's history and heritage. The celebration became so popular that people in Jonesborough began thinking about staging other activities, perhaps one for each season of the year. Everyone began to cast about for just the right event, and then, in 1972, the idea—a perfect idea, disguised almost as an afterthought—came to me.

Though I lived in Jonesborough, I taught journalism at Science Hill High School in Johnson City. One day, I was driving with some of my students to a nearby town to print the school newspaper. We were laughing and talking, keeping an ear to the car radio, when storyteller Jerry Clower launched into a tale about coon hunting in Mississippi. We began to listen. And as we listened, we began to chuckle and nudge each other and slap our knees. In the wake of the laughter, I turned to my students: "Wouldn't it be nice if we could bring storytellers to Jonesborough from throughout the United States to tell stories together?" My words went unnoticed. My thoughts turned elsewhere. But we had been amused and entertained by the simple telling of a tale. The experience teased me, wouldn't let me alone. Storytelling? A storytelling *festival?* So in January of 1973, I proposed the idea to the Jonesborough Civic Trust.

"Well, why not?" one person said.

"Now, *you* do it," said another.

I had helped plan Historic Jonesborough Days, but I knew nothing about organizing a storytelling festival. There were no manuals, no models, no set of instructions. But I began—I had to begin—tentatively at first, making my own way, learning to trust myself. Slowly, the festival took shape—save for one important detail.

What should we call it? Name after name came to me, but each seemed lacking. "How about the Bugaboo Springs Storytelling Festival?" I questioned. It was catchy and certainly paid tribute to a legendary spring near Jonesborough where perhaps all manner of good stories had been shared over the years. But I hesitated. Then I began to dream. Why not name it something like . . . like . . . the *National* Storytelling Festival. I turned to a friend I trusted.

"Do you think it's too presumptuous to name our festival the *National* Storytelling Festival?" I asked, testing my notion against her good judgment.

"Well," she said, "is there anything like it anywhere else?"

"As far as I know," I assured her, "there's nothing quite like this festival anywhere in America."

She grinned. "Then let's be presumptuous."

On the second Saturday night in October in 1973, Jerry Clower— that same Mississippi coon hunter and storyteller—leapt to the stage in a hot, jammed high school gymnasium and told tales to over a thousand East Tennesseans. They had come for some side-splitting humor—the tales that had made Clower a household name throughout the Deep South. The crowd stomped and cheered, and they didn't leave disappointed.

The following afternoon, we pulled an old farm wagon into Courthouse Square—in the shadow of the clock tower—and from that wagon, under a warm October sun, we told stories. They were there, the storytellers. A former Arkansas congressman. A Tennessee banker. A college professor. A western North Carolina farmer. They told their tales, and they breathed life into the first National Storytelling Festival. And for the small group of people who sat listening—in chairs, on the curbs, cross-legged on the grassy green—there was a bond, a special connection between us and all who live and have ever lived. There were stories about people we had never met, times we had never known, places we had never been. Yet for those few magical hours, we did know them, we did go there.

Something had happened, and even as we sat listening, we knew we would return the next year and the next. It was as if an ancient memory had been jogged—of people throughout time, sitting together, hearing stories: a congregation of listeners. We were taken back to a time when the story, transmitted orally, was all there was. How had we wandered so far from the oral tradition? What had pulled us away?

Perhaps it all began with Johannes Gutenberg, a pioneer German printer, who, during the 1440s, invented the type mold which made printing from movable type practical for the first time. With his invention, printing became cost effective, and no longer would stories be only orally transmitted. The world began to depend not upon the spoken but upon the printed word. And during the centuries that followed, stories lived in books—in the collections of Jacob and Wilhelm Grimm and Hans Christian Andersen and thousands of others who have collected and written tales. Though both the oral and printed storytelling traditions continued to coexist, the role of the storyteller began to fade.

The decline went unchecked until the late 1890s when librarians began to realize the value of using the told story as a way of introducing children to reading. Gradually, storytimes appeared at libraries in Pittsburgh, New York, and Buffalo. But it was Marie Shedlock, a teacher in a girls' school in London, England, who paved the way for storytelling in library programs throughout the United States and helped lay the foundation for America's storytelling renaissance.

In 1900, Miss Shedlock was invited to tell stories in New York City—to share the literary tales of Hans Christian Andersen. Her performance was captivating—skilled, polished—and she told again and again at libraries throughout the United States, inspiring others to practice the ancient art and create times within the library's program for stories to be told.

Miss Shedlock's mission was strengthened by the emergence of the National Story League, an organization founded in 1903 by Richard T.

Wyche and a bevy of teachers attending summer school at the University of Tennessee in Knoxville. Armed with an undying devotion to the storytelling art, the league's growing number of members devoted hours to recounting the tales and keeping the stories alive in libraries and schools throughout the United States—a mission they still fervently pursue.

Today, the legacy of these early storytelling pioneers still lives in the hearts of America's librarians and teachers who, for almost a century, have made it possible for children to enjoy and cherish good stories, both read and told. And what splendid stories they have been!

With the discovery of the Americas during the 1490s, people from throughout the world began immigrating to the North American continent, and when they came, they brought with them their tales. America became a melting pot for storytelling. The stories came from everywhere, and united with the myths and legends of our Native Americans, a new world rich with stories was born—stories as divergent as the people themselves. It is a world that has given us the likes of the wily Brer Rabbit, the adventuresome Jack, and a host of other characters that people our tales and bring to life the wonderful, rich diversity of American storytelling.

Yet, while storytelling was being harbored and fostered in America's libraries and classrooms as a children's activity, storytelling as a folk art—an activity of the *people*—continued to vanish. Through America's love affair with radio and television, the death knell was struck. Storytelling was being lost, for we had surrendered our ability to entertain ourselves to the disembodied voice and image of the electronic media.

But of course there have always been storytellers—solitary tellers—telling stories, keeping them alive. They were inspired not by a groundswell for storytelling, for until now there was no revival, but simply because there was within them a need to tell. They are the storytellers who have been at the vanguard of the cultural movement that has begun to sweep America.

There is Ray Hicks, a western North Carolina farmer who has lived in the same unpainted house on the slopes of Beech Mountain where he was born sixty-six years ago. As a child, perched on his grandfather's knee, he heard Jack tales—stories of an adventuresome, imaginary mountain boy who encountered all manner of trouble. Throughout his life, Ray has recounted the old tales he heard from his grandfather—stories handed down from generation to generation. "I started tellin' tales to the little children. Them tales'd keep the youngins quiet. I've had youngins come up on my knees to watch my mouth work jist to git the understandin' of it. I've had three on each leg." And during the first National Storytelling Festival in 1973, Ray climbed aboard the old farm wagon in Courthouse Square and recounted his tales of Jack with un-questioned authority. Today, as Ray retells these ancient tales, he rares back, slaps his knees, and laughs. For you see, there's something in Ray that loves Jack, and he gets enormous pleasure from telling about him, seeing his listeners enjoy Jack's antics as much as he does.

Connie Regan-Blake and Barbara Freeman, both librarians and story-tellers at the Chattanooga Public Library in Tennessee, were drawn to that first National Storytelling Festival, and when given the chance, each rose from her chair, boarded the old farm wagon, and told a story. Later, in 1975, they both left the security of their library jobs and, with less than $2,000 in their collective pocket, set out across America to hear and tell stories. As The Folktellers, Connie and Barbara began performing in tandem—creating their own unique storytelling style. But they were listening more to their hearts than their heads, for there was no summons for the storyteller—no beckoning for tales. Yet from that time until now—as they still are exploring the perimeters of story-telling with an original two-act play based on their art—Connie and Barbara have been central to the rebirth of storytelling in America.

Sitting in the audience at the first National Storytelling Festival on that warm October day was Doc McConnell, a bewhiskered hospital maintenance supervisor from Rogersville, Tennessee. Charmed by the folklore of his native Southern Appalachian Mountains—especially the old-time medicine shows he saw as a child—Doc, during his free time, had begun traveling the countryside re-creating his own old-fashioned medicine show. Wearing a long black coat with tails, a checkered vest, and a top hat, Doc peddled bottles of his medicinal tonic and dispensed hefty doses of cornball stories, songs, and one-liners. But as he listened during the first festival, he realized that he was more than a jokester, a funnyman, a barker—he was also a storyteller. In 1974, Doc performed his old-time medicine show as a highlight of the National Storytelling Festival, and today he continues to tell the tales mined from his heri-tage of growing up in Tucker's Knob in the heart of the Southern Appa-lachians.

And there is Kathryn Windham, a feisty Alabama journalist who, at the age of twenty-two, became the first woman police reporter for a major daily newspaper anywhere in the South. In 1966, a ghostly pres-ence in her Selma home stirred her curiosity in the supernatural, and soon she had written and published half a dozen collections of stories about famous Southern ghosts. In 1974, while working as an administrator for a regional planning agency, Kathryn received a telephone call. "Mrs. Windham, we know you *write* ghost stories," I explained. "But would you come to the National Storytelling Festival in October and *tell* your stories?" Kathryn was startled. "Don't you want my daughter?" Kathryn asked. "She's the actress." But in 1974, at the second National Storytelling Festival, Kathryn took the stage to share the ghostly legends she had collected throughout the South. We sat in amazement. And today, Kathryn travels throughout America recounting her eerie tales of the supernatural.

In 1972, Jackie Torrence was a reference librarian for the High Point Public Library in North Carolina. Bribed by her library director with the promise of an extra hour for lunch, she reluctantly substituted for an absent storyteller. Telling a tale she had heard as a child, Jackie quickly discovered within herself a reservoir of storytelling talent. She was affectionately called The Story Lady, and for four years, she told stories at the library and after hours at parties in High Point, Greensboro, and Winston-Salem. When she was asked to quit her free-lance telling, Jackie refused, and she was fired from her library job. With nowhere to turn, she became a full-time professional storyteller overnight. Performances were few, and Jackie's storytelling career was slow to jell. But in 1976, I stumbled upon a crumpled newspaper clipping about The Story Lady, and a year later, Jackie appeared at the National Storytelling Festival where she recounted many of the tales she had heard as a child, growing up in the tiny farm settlement of Second Creek. She continues to share a mixed repertoire of tales with audiences throughout America.

Jay O'Callahan, an aspiring writer, quit his job as dean of his parents' secretarial school in 1971 to devote all of his time to writing. While his wife worked as director of the YWCA in Marshfield, Massachusetts, Jay served as the custodian. During his free time, he wrote tirelessly, producing two novels but finding a publisher for neither. But at bedtime, Jay would create and tell stories for his two young children. Soon he discovered it was the stories he told, not those he had written, that leapt forward and came to life. There was something in him that must not only create stories but also tell them, so in 1980, Jay brought his own creative brand of storytelling to the National Storytelling Festival. And today, he continues to perform the stories he has forged from a measured blend of truth and fantasy.

After thirty-one years as a teacher and librarian in the inner-city schools of Baltimore, Mary Carter Smith ended her career as an educator in 1973 and began to sing the songs and tell the stories of her Mother Africa to break down the barriers between people separated by race and nationality, age and religion. Diane Wolkstein, as the first full-time storyteller for the New York City Parks Department, walked alone through the streets of Harlem, sharing stories—both English and African folktales sparked with songs and improvisation. And near Boston, Hugh Morgan Hill, better known as Brother Blue, adorned himself in a patchwork of ribbons, bows, balloons, and butterflies while chanting his concoction of poetry, stories, and songs throughout America— sometimes just barefooted in the streets. Waddie Mitchell, a real buckaroo, spent long, lonely days on the vast Nevada range, and as he roped cattle and branded calves, he told tales—story-poems, homespun yarns in rhythm and rhyme, handed down from cowboy to cowboy for generations. And Spalding Gray, who after performing more than a decade in experimental theater in New York City, grew tired of being cooped up in a "windowless art house" and, curious about the world outside him, chronicled his life in a series of monologues he has performed to critical acclaim in theaters throughout the world.

These are the storytellers who are among the architects of America's storytelling revival. Single voices at first, they soon were joined by others who were also attracted to the power and humanity of the storytelling art. The professional storyteller, once a fixture in earlier times and cultures, has reappeared, and as in the days of old, is again an institution. Today, there are hundreds of professional storytellers traveling throughout the United States, sharing their timeless tales—and, yes, thousands more who are teachers, librarians, ministers, lawyers, salesmen, therapists, and others who are using storytelling as an integral part of their lives and work.

Since the first National Storytelling Festival in 1973, scores of festivals and conferences have sprung up throughout America. Storytelling organizations, even libraries and centers, have been organized nationwide. And at the heart of this growing revival is the National Association for the Preservation and Perpetuation of Storytelling, a nonprofit organization founded in 1975 to help promote the practice, uses, and applications of the storytelling art. Headquartered in Jonesborough, NAPPS publishes a newsletter, journal, and directory, offers America's largest selection of storytelling resources, provides an extensive program of storytelling education, and now sponsors the National Storytelling Festival each year in Jonesborough.

Looking back, we were not presumptuous at all. Since its serendipitous beginning in 1973, the National Storytelling Festival has become America's foremost storytelling showcase, and it has nurtured and nourished a national rebirth of storytelling—one which has grown to such depth and breadth that no single volume could fully contain it. While I can only give you a sampling—a mere fraction—of the storytellers, stories, and storytelling traditions of our vast country, perhaps this simple offering will provide a delicious taste of the variety of America's stories, an introduction to those who tell them, and an exploration of the rich and diverse traditions they represent.

In this volume, you will meet twenty-one of America's best-loved and respected storytellers. They have been plying their art for years, some for almost a lifetime, and in recognition of their work, they have all appeared at the National Storytelling Festival—each representing in his or her own way the exciting diversity of America's storytelling heritage. You will hear them speak of themselves, their affection for storytelling, and the role this venerable art has played in their lives. And they will share their stories—not in a literary way, but simply, as the tales are told, re-created in print directly from the oral tradition.

And as you explore the stories in the lives of others, I hope you will discover those in your own life—the family stories, the folktales, legends, and lore you heard as a child, the stories within us, and those that unfold around us as we live. I hope you will be drawn to them, will want to tell them—at home or school, church or club meetings, or just among friends—for in them are lessons, histories, and shared moments that can be passed on in no other way.

When I think back to the storytelling in my life, I recall my grandfather. He was a tall man, broad-shouldered, with big, knotty hands and skin as rough as sandpaper. He was a horse trader, farmer, and logger, and oh, the stories he could tell. But on a cold, snowy January day in 1980, he died. He was eighty-four. And in our loss and grief, my grandmother called us to her.

"There was once a man who lay dying," she began. "He called for his children to come to his bedside.

"'Each of you bring me a stick,' he ordered. And they did.

"The man took one stick into his hands and snapped it into pieces.

"'I can break one stick,' he told them.

"Then the old man gathered the sticks from his children, one by one, placed them in a bundle, and tried to break them. He couldn't.

"'So like this bundle of sticks,' the old man told his children, 'stay together, work together, and our family will always remain strong and not be broken.'"

And as more of us discover and tell the stories in our own lives, that bond—our connection with the genuine, one-on-one communication of the told story—will always remain strong and unbroken and allow us to give back to our world something as precious, and treasured, as life itself.

JIMMY NEIL SMITH
Jonesborough, Tennessee

Stories
of the
Southern
Appalachian
Mountains

Ray Hicks

The other boys wanted to go places, but
I jist wanted to sit and hear my
grandfather tell stories. He'd git me up on
his lap a-tellin' them tales. . . . When
it would hit 'im jist right, he'd tell 'em and
jist laugh, and it looked like his whole
body was laughin'. Then us kids would laugh
'cause he was a-laughin'. And oh, what a
good feelin' that was.

3

* * *

RAY HICKS was just a young boy when the nationally acclaimed folklore collector Richard Chase wound his way through the Appalachian Mountains and found the likes of Ben Hicks, Ray's grandfather. From Ben and others who made their home in the shadow of Beech Mountain in western North Carolina, Chase collected Jack tales—long, meandering stories about an imaginary mountain boy named Jack who, though best known for chopping down the beanstalk, encountered all manner of adventures. Jack did battle with giants and dragons, suffered through the trials and tribulations of seeking life's fortune, and luckily for him, triumphed over them all.

These old tales of Jack originated in Europe, were brought to America by Irish and Scottish settlers, and have since been harbored along the ridges and in the coves of the Southern mountains. Chase's stories were published in *Jack Tales*, a classic story collection, but nobody tells them better than Ray Hicks, a fount of old-time mountain wisdom who heard the stories while perched on his grandfather's knee.

Ray was born in 1922 in the same unpainted house on the slopes of Beech Mountain in western North Carolina where he has lived all of his sixty-six years. "When I was a-growin' up, that's all the entertainment we'd have, a-tellin' stories. When us youngins would git together and git a little rough, somebody would start one of them tales. One would take a part, then another would take a part, and all of us kids would quiet down and you could hear a pin drop." For Ray, sharing tales is as natural as getting a suntan.

"My grandfather knew a lot of old tales. The other boys wanted to go places, but I jist wanted to sit and hear my grandfather tell stories. He'd git me up on his lap a-tellin' them tales—Jack tales, mostly. 'The Heifer Hide' and 'The Old Fire Dragon' and 'Hardy Hardhead.' When it would hit 'im jist right, he'd tell 'em and jist laugh, and it looked like his whole body was laughin'. Then us kids would laugh 'cause he was a-laughin'. And oh, what a good feelin' that was."

But there were others who told Ray stories—the old tales of the mountains—stories he heard from his neighbors who shared their tales as freely as they shared the warmth of their fire. "There was a family of

4

Indians that lived way down in the holler. And they had a little girl, and I loved 'er. If I could jist hear her voice it would make me feel good. So finally one fall, 'long about the last of October or the first of November, I begged my mama to let me go down to see 'er.

"I had no shoes and I had to go barefooted, but my feet were so crusty and tough that I could crack chestnuts with my heels. And my mama had made me a little ol' pair of britches with a little blouse that hung over 'em.

"Mama didn't want me to go, but she said, 'You're a-goin' to go or die, ain't ye?'

"I said, 'It's a-killin' me. I've got to see that little girl and hear 'er talk.'

"So she said, 'You ain't a-goin' to let me alone, so go on.'

"I took off down the holler and soon got there, a-wearin' this little ol' blouse and my little britches.

"The little girl was bashful. She'd sit over in one corner of their old log cabin, head down, with her hand over her face, and maybe she'd giggle a little, now and then, you know, and peep out when her mother wasn't lookin'.

"Directly, it started snowin'—them was the purttiest snowflakes— and I thought I'd better hit it home. But her mother said, 'Wait 'til my husband comes in and see what he says.'

"So, directly, he come in. He was probably out choppin' wood for that old mud fireplace, and it was a-gittin' purtty late.

"And she said, 'This little Hicks boy is a-wantin' to take off in this storm. He's bare-footed and a-wearin' jist these little ol' short britches with a little blouse. He might die. And we love 'im.'

"And the husband said, 'No, son, you can't go. You'll have to stay with us now.'

"So we sat down there at that old fireplace and they got to tellin' Jack tales and ghost tales and stories about the Indians. And I loved listenin' to them tales.

"Directly, it was time to retire and they put me in a little ol' bunk 'side the wall. I was a-layin' there, and the mud had fell out between those logs right where my head was a-layin', and, God, I hated to name it to 'em, but snow was a-pepperin' in on my face, and I knew I wouldn't live 'til mornin'. So I happened to think of my britches, and I stuffed 'em in the hole between the logs where the mud had fell out and that fixed it.

"The next mornin', I grabbed for my britches, and they was gone. An old cow, outside that cabin, had ate up my britches. I'd had it.

There I was with no britches, only a-wearin' this little ol' blouse. I couldn't git outa bed, so I played off sick.

"I told 'em, 'I'm a little puny. I don't believe I can git up.' So they went to brewin' up some medicine, and they made me drink a pint of that juice. I turned 'er up and got 'er down, and I thought to myself if nothin's wrong with me that stuff's liable to kill me deader than the dickens.

"The daddy went off a-cuttin' wood, and the mama and the little girl went to milk the cow. Directly, while I was a-layin' there, they come in with the milk in a bucket and sat it down on a little table. They had forgot the strainer at the springhouse, so they took off to go to the spring. I didn't know how fer it was to the spring, but I thought I'd have time to git up and drink a little of that milk even if it wasn't strained. And so, I was a-drinkin' it, a-lappin' it up dog-style, with the pail over my head and with no britches on, and they came in on me. It startled me so bad that when I lifted my head up, I caught the handle of that bucket 'round my neck.

"When I seen what I had done, I come to myself and made a dive for the bed. That milk, a little over half up, tilted me over and I went under the bed and spilt the milk all over the floor. And then I made for the cabin door, and as I was leavin', I caught my foot in the handle of a slop bucket sittin' on the floor and drug it out the door.

"It'd snowed two feet that night—some of the purttiest white, fluffy snow I've ever seen—and I'd come home in that snow a-runnin' as hard as I could and hadn't noticed that bucket hangin' 'round my neck. Mama said, 'Where you been with your britches gone and that bucket 'round your neck?' I told her I'd got trapped. And you know, my daddy tried to make me take that bucket back. But there was one thing for sure: Ray wasn't gonna face 'em to take no bucket back. So my daddy took it back for me. I never did see that little girl no more, and, oh God, what tales I could've learnt."

Throughout Ray's life, stories have been his constant companions, and even as a child, he began to retell the old tales he had heard. His friends began to beseech him. "Git the blues off, Ray. Tell us a story." And he would.

"When we was boys, me and my brother would go out to see my aunt's children, and we'd be out a-playin' under a rock cliff. We'd take us some 'taters and a pan and build us a fire and fry them 'taters, and in the fall, we'd roast us some roastin' ears in the shucks. And I'd have somethin' a-goin' with the boys, a-tellin' 'em tales. Linville—him and me was 'bout the same age—said, 'I knowed Ray had somethin' the other boys didn't have. We'd be down in the dumps and he'd tell somethin' to git us to laugh. He was tellin' stories young up.' Jack tales. Haint tales. Ghost tales. Yeah, I knowed a lot of 'em. I've heerd stories 'bout all my life."

Even in school, Ray heard—and told—stories. "I started to school when I was seven years old, and I got to tellin' 'Jack and the Beantree' outa the schoolbook, and we would see who could tell it the best. And while I told the stories, I tried to learn my lessons, but back in them days, it was rough for a boy growin' up in the mountains.

"We had an old cast-iron heater to heat our schoolhouse. But them little kids in there, in that little ol' cold schoolroom in the winter, the poor little things was froze blue. Ruby, my teacher, would grumble and gouge the fire in that ol' heater. She had her wood so close together it wouldn't draw.

"Finally, I got to helpin' Ruby with the fire. I'd go in, walkin', and it cold, with my britches legs froze up, a big snow, a-walkin' in it. And I'd git it red hot in jist a few minutes. From then on, she kept me a-firin' the stove and wouldn't git on to me 'bout my lessons. When it come time for me to pass the seventh grade, I got my test and I didn't know much to do. Ruby came 'round directly and said, 'Ray, can't you fill yours out?'

"And I said, 'No, Ruby, I fired that stove too much. I ain't learnt nothing.' She sat down and filled it out for me and passed me anyhow. I know yet how to build a fire. And I wound up a-tellin' the stories."

At the end of the seventh grade, Ray "got to the age that a boy had to git out and make his own livin'. So I quit school and hit the mountains a-gatherin' herbs and a-pickin' up chestnuts and a-farmin'. And directly, a boy like I was with the trainin' I had, they'd work me, and I got a job a-cuttin' spool wood.

"One day I got sick on my job and the bossman said, 'Ray, I knows you're sick. You don't give up like the others. See, son, if you can git home.'

"I walked down that road, a-pushin' my body. Just staggerin'. I got to Daddy's ten acres. It was in two flat fields up on the top of that mountain. I got there lame. It was as fer as I could go on two legs. So I crawled from there down offa that mountain on my hands and knees to git home.

"Nobody couldn't hear me to holler. I woulda died layin' there all night. There was snow on the ground, a little chilly. I finally got to the house, to the sittin' room door. I crawled in and jist give up on the floor.

"Mama asked me what was wrong, and I said, 'I don't know. There's somethin' got me. Right now.'

"Directly, my daddy come in and he said, 'When Ray gives up, he's got.' He sniffed my nose and said, 'Measles. I smell 'em.' He jist turned and walked outa the room. He come back with a half-pint of that pure corn likker, the kind that's jist heaven to your intestines.

"'Raise up, Ray, and drink this. If you can drink it, you'll be well by mornin', back cuttin' spool wood,' he said. Now, I liked the taste of it. I turned up that half-pint and emptied it. And in thirty minutes, I was singin' 'John Henry Was a Steel-Drivin' Man.'

These stories—the tales Ray heard as a child, those he lived as the very essence of a true mountain man—forever bubbled over from inside him. They were meant to be told. And in 1951, in the Cove Creek School near his home, Ray told stories of the adventures of Jack for the first time in public.

"I went to the road to my mailbox one day, and there was a card in the box from Jenny Love, the Cove Creek teacher. It said, 'Ray, I'm a-teachin' my class outa the *Jack Tales* book. We're a-havin' lessons on storytellin', and they's a-likin' it. Would you come and tell us a few Jack tales?'

"I was a-runnin' an ol' '39 Chevrolet car I'd bought for $45, was married, had them children and they was in school, and I was seein' it rough. But I drove over there and went into the school and told 'em who I was, and she come in, took me into her class, got me sit down, and I told.

"It went on a little while, and I got another card. It said, 'Ray, I want you to come back agin.' So, I told agin. When I got through a-tellin', she come out and said, 'Ray, I knowed you's up agin it.' So, she pulled three dollars from her purse to buy gas with. Then she asked me agin, and this time she gave me three dollars and a *Jack Tales* book. And I've got it yet.

"About that time, the other classes in the school come in and said to Miss Love, 'We're a-goin' to have a war here. It ain't fair for you to git Mr. Hicks to tell in your class alla the time and not in our'n. We're a-goin' to have a war.'

"So Miss Love said, 'Ray, your voice, will it hold up? Are you willin' to tell to all you can?'

"I said, 'I'll try.' I told through the whole class, and that's what got it a-goin'."

Ray has been telling tales ever since—not professionally, but quietly, to friends and others who wander up the narrow road that snakes its way to Ray's isolated mountain home. And once each October, every year, Ray comes to Jonesborough to the National Storytelling Festival where, as America's master traditional storyteller, he regales his listeners with his ancient tales—those he heard on his grandfather's knee, handed down from generation to generation, and truly told out of the oral tradition.

Whickety-Whack, into My Sack

Though the Jack tales can most widely be found in the Southern Appalachians, for Ray, these old mountain tales belong to all of us. "Ever'body can be Jack, the way I've heerd it. I'm Jack. And since we've all got our faults, our let-down ways, Jack is jist 'bout as good as anybody." "Whickety-Whack, into My Sack," the only Jack tale in which Jack dies, is a story Ray learned from his grandfather, Ben Hicks, and others who called Beech Mountain home. The tale is also known as "Soldier Jack."

WELL, JACK went into the army and stayed thirty years. And at that time, all you got when they discharged you was two loaves of bread. And when they discharged Jack, they give 'im two loaves of bread, and he headed off into the woods, tryin' to git home.

When he got into a little old town, he met a beggar who was a-beggin' fer somethin' to eat. So Jack—he was what they called good-hearted—give 'im one of them loaves of bread.

Jack went on and hadn't went but jist a little ways 'til he met another beggar, and he was a-beggin' for somethin' to eat. So Jack took out the second loaf, cut it in half, and give it to the second beggar.

Well, Jack went on down the road a little ways and got to studyin' that he'd cheated that last beggar. He'd give the first beggar a whole loaf. So Jack run back and overtook 'im and says, "I cheated you. I met a beggar before you and I had two loaves, and I give 'im a whole loaf. Here's the other half of yours."

So the beggar took it and thanked 'im. "Being you're so honest," the beggar says, "I'm a-goin' to give you somethin'." And he pulled out a sack. "Take this sack with you. If anything gits to botherin' you or you need anything, just say, 'Whickety-whack, into my sack.'"

And then he says, "Here's a drinkin' glass. Take it along. If anybody is sick, git the glass a third or half full of water. If the blubbers goes to the bottom, that person's a-goin' to die. If they come to the top, he's a-goin' to live."

Jack thanked 'im and went on his way. But he hadn't walked too fer outa town 'til he come to some woods, and he seed twelve wild turkeys a-sittin' up in a tree.

"Bedad," he says, "right here is a good time to try this sack out."

So Jack eased as close as he could—them turkeys were awful wild— and he got the sack between his legs, a-holdin' it, and he looked up at those turkeys and said, "Whickety-whack, into my sack."

And he said it was a sight to watch them twelve turkeys crowd down into that sack. Twelve big ones. And he shet it up, slung it across his back, and went on down the road 'til he came to another little old town. It was a-gittin' late up into the night, he was hungry and tired, and he seed he had to stay over.

So Jack went into a hotel and showed them folks the turkeys, and he made a deal with 'em. They kept 'im all night for them turkeys, and Jack got fifteen cents to boot.

Well, the next mornin', he started out and purtty soon made it home. He went to a-workin' on his cabin, repairin' his old home place, to live in it 'til he got to where he could do better.

In a few days, he heerd that there was a man in that settlement who had a big farm, and it was hainted. Ghosts were 'bout to run 'im off his place. So the farmer put the word out that if there was any man in that country that could whip them ghosts, he'd deed 'im the house and land, give 'im a clear title to it.

So Jack went out the next day, inquirin' and findin' out about it, and finally he found the man. Jack took 'im up on it, and the man gave Jack a fryin' pan and some vittles. Jack got settled in at the house, and when it got dark, he fixed 'im some supper and eat and laid down aside the fireplace to take 'im a nap.

He hadn't laid there but jist a few minutes 'til he heerd somethin' a-comin' down the stairs. He shook his head and said, "What do you reckon that is?" And directly, they come down and it was six little black devils and each had a sword apiece, a bag of money apiece, and a deck of playin' cards apiece. They rousted Jack up and begin to beggin' 'im to play cards.

Well, they got to playin', and finally at three games, Jack had lost all but a nickel of the fifteen cents he got in his boot fer them twelve wild turkeys on his way home from the army. But Jack watched careful and purtty soon got one pot, and he begin to gain, and directly, Jack broke them six little black devils. He had all of their money in his pocket.

So them little devils said, "We'll jist kill you and take it back." So, they got to makin' at Jack with their swords, and Jack was dodgin' 'em. And they thought they had 'im, but Jack happened to think of his sack. So when them little devils got to puffin' for wind and begin to give down a little, Jack grabbed his sack, jerked it open—it had a drawstring on it—and said, "Whickety-whack, into my sack."

Jack said it was somethin' to see them six little devils stuff themselves down in that sack. He jist shet it up, throwed it over in the corner, and laid down to finish his nap.

The next mornin', the farmer come up, jist a-knowin' certain that Jack was gone. He'd done buried fifty men who'd tried. "You're a-livin' and they ain't a scratch on ya," the man said. "What happened here last night?"

Jack says, "It's a-layin' over there in that sack. It's six little black devils shet up in there."

The man says, "As much trouble as them devils have been to me, I won't be satisfied until I see 'em beat up on a blacksmith's anvil. There's a fellow down yonder in the holler who runs a blacksmith shop. Will you go with me?"

Jack says, "Yes, I'll go."

So him and Jack went down there and got the man that run the blacksmith shop to hammer them devils up on the anvil. And when he begin to hammer, so many sparks flew outa them little devils that it set the blacksmith shop on fire and burnt it down.

Well, anyhow, Jack got the deed to the land and begin to stay there and work on the place.

But then, the king's daughter got sick and death was on 'er. And he'd had all of the doctors beheaded 'cause they couldn't cure his daughter. So the king put out an advertisement that if any man, just any community country man, could cure 'er, the money, the gold and silver, wouldn't be a-lackin'.

So Jack took that drinkin' glass and his sack and begin to hunt up the old king to see 'im and see if he could do 'er some good. So he went to the king's house and hollered 'im out.

And the king says, "What're ya here for?"

Jack says, "I hear that you had out word that if any man could cure your daughter the money wasn't a-lackin', and if he couldn't cure 'er, you'd behead 'im."

And so the king says, "Yeah, but you don't look like you could do a job like that."

"Well, bedad," Jack says, "I might look like that, but you said *anybody.*"

So the king says, "That's right. I'll have to give ya a try."

Well, they took Jack into the room where the king's daughter lay sick, and Jack sent the king to git his special glass a third or half filled with water. And the king brought it to 'im, and Jack looked, and, sure enough, the blubbers went to the bottom. Death was on 'er.

So Jack got his sack down beside 'er bed and said, "Whickety-whack, come into my sack." And Death went down in that sack, and Jack shet it up. And the girl, the king's daughter, went to jumpin' over the floor, a-praisin'.

The king offered to pay Jack, but he wouldn't take nothin'. He said, "I didn't come for wealth. I come to save your daughter."

Jack went on back home and got some boys to climb a tree, a big poplar in the yard, and take that sack with Death in it and tie it way up on a big limb.

Well, years passed and one day, Jack decided he'd take a little walk down the road. And he hadn't went but a little ways 'til he heerd somethin' a-comin' 'round the turn. Rickety-rack. Bumpety-bump. Rickety-rack. Bumpety-bump. And he looked beyond the curve, and he saw it was an old woman who'd jist went to bones and hide. Her bones was a-creakin' as she walked, and her nose was a-bumpin' her knees.

Jack says, "Howdy do, ma'am."

"Howdy do," she says. "Law me, I can't git around no more. I'm so poor. I've jist went to bones and hide. It seems like I've been a-livin' a million years. And I can't die. I've heerd that some rascal has Death tied up in a sack, and we can't die."

Well, that made Jack think. And after a while, he went back home and tried to climb that poplar tree to git the sack. But he had gotten so poor 'imself that he had to git a younger boy to go up that poplar. So that boy got that sack and brought it down to Jack, and they said when Jack opened it, he was the first one that fell dead.

And that was the end of Jack in that tale.

Elizabeth Ellis

*I don't really understand the magic
of storytelling. I don't know how it happens;
I only know how to invite it. And when
the magic occurs, I'm always frightened
that it may never come again.
Yet, it always does.*

14

* * *

ONE NIGHT in a crowded bar in Wichita Falls, David Ruthstrum—a folksinger from Dallas—was performing. The bar was packed with people, talking and laughing, and Elizabeth Ellis was in the audience, listening to the music. At the close of one of his songs, David—much to Elizabeth's surprise and dismay—paused and introduced her. He wanted her to tell a story.

A librarian at the Dallas Public Library, Elizabeth loved folk music, and whenever David performed in clubs near Dallas, she went to hear him. The two had become close friends. "During our quiet times together, I told David some of the stories I told at the library. They were children's stories, the only ones I really knew well enough to tell, but he had never heard stories as a child and he loved them, and storytelling became an important part of what we did when we were together." But when David introduced Elizabeth that night and asked her to tell a story, she was horrified.

"It was totally unplanned, unrehearsed. I had never told a story to anyone other than children—and David—but the eyes of the audience were upon me. How could I refuse? David asked me to tell *Caps for Sale,* a children's storybook by Esphyr Slobodkina, that I had told him earlier that afternoon. And during the telling, the audience stopped talking and everyone in the room listened intently to every word. It was a magical moment for me."

Elizabeth was born in 1943 in Winchester, Kentucky, and throughout her childhood, she recognized and loved the inherent power and magic of language. Though Elizabeth grew up in the Tennessee mountains, she returned to Kentucky during the summers to visit her grandparents, and there, she heard stories—usually old mountain tales—and she reveled in them, soaked them in. It was her grandfather, Isaac Gabbard, who first introduced Elizabeth to this special, magical realm of storytelling.

"My grandfather had been a circuit-riding preacher—they called him Preacher Ike—and for years he had done the marrying, the burying, and everything else that needed tending to in several different communities throughout the mountains. As a circuit-riding preacher, he would often travel far away from home, and when nightfall came, members of his various churches would invite him to their houses to spend the

night. As they all sat talking after supper—often late into the evening
—they would tell stories.

"When I was a child, I helped my grandfather work—stringing beans
or peeling apples or shucking corn—and as we worked, he would tell
me stories to keep me on the task. Sometimes the ones he told were
stories he had created, but many of the tales he entertained me with
were those he'd heard while sitting around a fire in the home of one of
his parishioners.

"He'd tell me about the snake that bit the hoe handle and how the
handle swelled so big they sawed enough lumber from it to build a
chicken house, or of the time a deer was shot in his mouth with a peach
seed and a tree grew out of his head, or of the dog that ran into a buzz
saw, was sliced in two, and how when the dog was put back together,
two of his legs were on the bottom and two were on the top.

"And he'd tell tales of adventure, of giants and dragons and seeking
life's fortunes, but these weren't Jack tales—mountain stories about
Jack—they were 'Ike tales,' for they were centered around the imaginary exploits of my grandfather."

As Elizabeth heard her grandfather weave his magical tales, she just
knew they were *his* stories—tales that belonged to her grandfather and
no one else—for they seemed to dwell in him so completely. She reveled in the old tales, took them in as if they belonged to her. But as she
grew older, Elizabeth discovered that the stories she had heard were
universal, that they belong to all of us. This concerned her not one
whit, and hearing her grandfather's old tales further stimulated Elizabeth's vivid imagination.

"As a young girl, I would create stories of my own, and occasionally
my imagination got the best of me and I got into trouble for lying. I
could tell the difference between fact and fantasy, but I couldn't figure
out why the difference was so important. Not until I was in the fourth
grade did I find a way to channel my creativity, and then it was only
through the understanding of my teacher, Sue Price.

"'Elizabeth,' Miss Price said, 'it really upsets people when you tell
them things that they think are true when they're not. Instead of telling
stories all day long, do you think you could tell stories only one time
each day?'

"I thought about her proposal, and I was intrigued. So every day after
lunch, Miss Price allowed me to tell my stories to the whole class at one
time. I soon discovered that I didn't want to waste my good stories on
two or three kids on the playground when I could have an audience of
twenty-five of my schoolmates, sitting in front of me and listening at-

tentively. The only hitch came when Miss Price insisted I write my stories after I had told them."

Both the writing and the telling of the tales helped nurture a talent that could have been lost. Fortunately, Miss Price saw in Elizabeth a reckless stream of creativity that needed only a clear-cut outlet, and she helped Elizabeth reroute the flow and transform her imaginative exploits into a positive activity. And through her teacher's efforts, Elizabeth became a better person—and a better storyteller.

"As I created and told my stories, I thought of my grandfather. Like him, I often took traditional themes—the Jack tales, Aesop's fables, a folktale—and built stories around them, spicing these old tales with bits and pieces of contemporary life. Through the telling, I felt the physical sensation of power—of making people laugh, giving them joy."

From her grandfather, Elizabeth gained an appreciation of language and story gleaned from the oral tradition—something natural and spontaneous—but she soon encountered another world, the companion world of literature, through a man named Reverend Orvel Crowder.

"Just across the street from our home in Tennessee was the Hopwood Christian Church, a little stone church house with a beautiful stained-glass window. As a child, I thought it was the loveliest thing I had ever seen. It showed a likeness of Jesus with a lamb held in His arms, surrounded by a flock of sheep, but most important to me was the brass plaque at the bottom of the window. It read: 'In loving memory of Elizabeth Ellis.'

"That was my grandmother, and though she had died many years before, we had shared the same name since I was born. I was sure that she wouldn't mind our also sharing this beautiful stained-glass window. So I would run across the street, quietly enter the church, and sit and gaze at our window for hours. I loved to watch the light filter through the glass and how it changed, hour by hour, during the day. But the minister, who didn't like my being in the church house alone, began escorting me out of the sanctuary, and eventually he locked all of the doors to the church.

"I loved those moments of solitude, gazing at *our* window, and I was not to be denied the pleasure. Within two weeks, I had discovered the coal chute, and with a tiny little push, I could slip through the chute and into the church. Once again, I could sit for hours gazing at the stained-glass window. I could come and go as I wished, night or day, without anyone ever knowing that I was there.

"When I visited my grandparents in Kentucky that summer, I was unable to see the window for almost three months. So upon my return, as soon as my mother drove into the driveway, I threw open the car door and ran across the lawn to the church. Quickly, I pulled open the coal chute and began to slide through, but during the summer my body had betrayed me and I had grown too big to fit. I found to my dismay that I was firmly stuck.

"My head was hanging down into the blackness of the cellar, and my feet were sticking up into the brilliance of the sunlight. And despite the fact that it would mean alerting the minister who was forever excusing me from the premises, I was forced to call for help. I began to scream. Within minutes, I felt a pair of hands tugging at my ankles. Then, as I emerged from the coal chute—blinking my eyes and wiping coal dust from my face—I saw someone I had never seen before.

"'What are you doing?' he asked.

"It seemed to me to be a reasonable question, but at the time, I didn't have an answer. He took me by my hand, and we walked to the back door of the church. He told me that he was Reverend Orvel Crowder, the new minister, and I told him the story of the stained-glass window. He poured us two glasses of grape juice, and together, we sat in the sanctuary, drank juice, and gazed at the beautiful stained glass. The door of *his* church was never locked, he said. So every day after school, I would run to the church, enter properly through the door, sit in a pew, and look at the window for as long as I wanted.

"One day, I heard typing in Reverend Crowder's office, and I went in. The office was lined with books—on all four walls, floor to ceiling. They were everywhere. I had never seen that many books in my young life.

"He looked up from his work and said, 'Hello. Nice to see you.'

"And I murmured, 'Booooooooks...'

"He waved his hand and said, 'Look around. If you see anything that you like, take it home with you and read it. Just take care of it and bring it back.'

"So I carefully looked through his library, and I saw books on theology and religion and history and literature. But then I noticed a small blue book. So I pulled it from the shelf, stepped to his desk, and said, 'I'd like to have this one.'

"He ran his finger along the binding and nodded gravely. 'Good choice. A lot of people read Kierkegaard.'

"I took the book home, and within moments, I realized that Kierkegaard and I would never be friends. I kept the book for a week, a respectable period of time, and then I returned it, trembling in fear that the reverend would ask me how I liked it.

"He didn't. He just said, 'Are you finished with it?'

"I said, 'Yes.'

"He said, 'Then look for another one.'

"As I began to search, I discovered a gray-and-lavender book with a picture of a wardrobe on the front. It looked exactly like the wardrobe I had at home. So I brought the book to his desk and said, 'I'd like to read this one.'

"He looked up from his work and said, 'A good choice. A lot of people read C. S. Lewis.'

"I came again and again, reading book after book. And each time I had read one, he would always say, 'Just keep looking. You'll find another one you'll enjoy.' And I did. I read the stories of Hans Christian Andersen and the Grimm brothers, *Treasure Island*, and *Black Beauty*— books I discovered in Reverend Crowder's personal library. I was a grown woman before I realized that as I grew up and changed, the books in Reverend Crowder's library also changed. Through his kindness and interest, I was provided with an opportunity I would never have had otherwise—to enter into the world of story through the printed word."

Elizabeth's early encounter with the world of literature stood her in good stead. For after her first performance in that Wichita Falls bar, she began telling stories during all of David's performances. And as she began performing more for adults, she began looking for new tales— those for a more mature audience. Elizabeth first remembered some of the tales her grandfather had told her. They were stories that had filled her early life with magic. Then she discovered a host of others equally powerful, and gradually, she built a solid repertoire of stories for all ages.

Today, Elizabeth tells both stories from the oral tradition—tales she heard growing up in the Kentucky mountains—and those gleaned from the world of literature. Yet even after her many years of living with stories, and telling them, Elizabeth still marvels at the sheer wonder of a good tale, well told. "I don't really understand the magic of storytelling. I don't know how it happens; I only know how to invite it. And when the magic occurs, I'm always frightened that it may never come again. Yet, it always does."

The Peddler's Dream

Elizabeth remembers her grandfather, sitting on the front porch with a day-old newspaper on his lap, stringing beans or peeling apples—and telling stories. One of his favorites was "The Peddler's Dream," an Irish tale about the importance of following one's dreams, of being willing to risk the known for the unknown.

A LONG time ago, there was a peddler. And back in those days, if you wanted to buy something, you would buy it from him. He would carry his big pack to a fair or market where people had gathered, open it up, and show them what he had to sell.

Every once in a while, a little boy would come by and pick up a knife and say, "How much is the knife?"

The peddler would say, "It's fifty cents."

When the little boy would hear this, his face would fall because that was more money than he had. But when the peddler would see the child's face, he would say, "Take it on, son, and put it in your pocket. It'll be lighter there than it was in the bottom of my pack." And the boy would run off to show his new knife to his friends.

Or sometimes a little girl would come by, and picking up a handful of bright, pretty ribbons, she would say, "How much are the ribbons?"

The peddler would answer, "They're fifty cents."

When the little girl would hear this, her face would fall because her father would never allow her to spend that much money on something he considered just plain foolish. But when the peddler would see her face, he would say, "Oh, take them on and wear them in your hair. They'll be prettier in your hair than they ever were in the bottom of my pack." And the girl—maybe she had her eye on some fellow—would tie the ribbons in her hair and run off to see if she could find him.

The people would just look at each other as the peddler went by and they would always say, "The fool and his money are soon parted, and that peddler is a fool. He gives away more than he sells."

The peddler lived in a little cabin. Just outside the cabin was a big garden, and in the middle of that garden was an enormous cherry tree. Every night, the peddler would watch from his back porch as the raccoons and possums came out of the woods and into the garden to eat his vegetables, or he would watch as the mockingbirds swooped down on the cherry tree to pick off the ripe fruit. His neighbors would always say, "Why don't you shoo away those thieving birds and animals? They'll rob you blind."

The peddler would always say, "They don't steal from me. What they take is a payment, for I love to watch the animals at night. They're company for a lonesome man, and there's no place on earth that the mockingbirds sing as sweet as they sing in the top of my tree."

And all the people would say to the peddler, "You just wait. The day will come when you'll be outside our back door begging for a handout."

As people feared, the contents of the peddler's pack became smaller and smaller, until finally, the day did come when the peddler had given away everything he owned. On that night, he went to bed hungry; and a hungry man is going to dream.

In the middle of the night, the peddler thought he saw an angel standing at the foot of his bed. And the angel said, "Peddler, follow the road into town. Stand in front of the courthouse. You'll see what you're to see and hear what you're to hear." But when the peddler woke up, an empty stomach seemed like a very poor traveling companion, so he didn't go to town.

That night, when the peddler fell asleep, the angel appeared again, saying, "Peddler, follow the road to town. Stand in front of the courthouse. You'll see what you're to see and hear what you're to hear." But when the peddler woke up, he was so weak from hunger that once more, he didn't go to town.

But the peddler dreamed of the angel for the third time, and finally, the next morning, he walked all the way to town, where he stood in front of the courthouse as the angel had instructed. And as everyone went by, he watched them and listened to them, but nobody spoke to him at all.

At the end of the day as the sun was going down, the peddler, who was now weak and hungry, wrapped himself in his old coat and began walking toward a lonely alley—to lie down, perhaps to starve to death. He said to himself, "I'll never make it home again. I'm just too weak."

But as he was walking across the courthouse square, an innkeeper came out of his inn across the street. He said, "I've been watching you, and you've been standing there all day and nobody has spoken to you. I want to know what's going on." But then the man saw how weak from hunger the old peddler was, and said, "Come into the inn and have a meal. To satisfy my curiosity, I can satisfy your hunger."

And so the peddler went into the inn with him, sat down, and ate a better meal than he had eaten in many a day. When he had finished, the innkeeper pulled up a chair next to the table and said, "Now, I want to hear your story."

The peddler said, "I dreamed a dream."

"What?"

"I dreamed a dream."

"You mean to tell me that you've been standing out there in that ice-cold wind in your ragged coat all day long because you dreamed a dream?'"

The peddler nodded.

The man said, "I dream dreams too, but I don't pay any attention to the things I dream. I stay here and tend to business like a sensible person. Why, just last night, I dreamed that an angel appeared and told me that if I followed the road out into the countryside I would come to a cabin, and outside the cabin there would be a big garden, and in the middle of the garden, an enormous cherry tree. And if I dug underneath the roots of that cherry tree, I would find gold. Where would I be if I paid attention to what I dream?"

The peddler thanked the man for the meal and walked home, and when he reached his little cabin, he went into the garden, and there, underneath the roots of that enormous cherry tree, he began to dig. Before long, he had unearthed an old wooden box, and when the box was opened, it was filled to overflowing with gold. And the good he did in the spending of it, I haven't the time to tell you.

Like Meat Loves Salt

During the hot summers when Elizabeth was a child, her Aunt Ida Moore would lie on the bed beside her, fan her with a magazine, and tell her stories until she fell asleep. Elizabeth remembers her telling "Like Meat Loves Salt," a powerful story about forgiveness, and when Elizabeth retells it today, the story never fails to move her—again and again.

THERE WAS once an old king who had three daughters, and one by one, he called them to him and said, "What would you have me bring you when I go to town?"

The oldest daughter said, "I want a bright, flashing red dress."

The middle daughter said, "I want a dark, flashing green dress."

And the youngest daughter said, "Bring me a dress of solid white."

The old king went into town and bought the three dresses for his daughters, and he folded them carefully and laid them in the bottom of his saddlebags. Then he rode home. As he was riding down a mountain trail, he found the low-growing branch of a maple in his path, and so that it wouldn't knock off his crown, he reached up and broke off the limb. When it was broken, he found it was covered with beautiful white roses. So the king laid the branch before him on his saddle horn and rode home with it.

One by one, he called his daughters to him again, and he asked, "How much do you love me?"

The oldest daughter said, "I love you more than all of the gold and jewels in the whole world," for that was what she had on her mind. The old king liked her answer, so he broke off one of the white roses, laid it on her bright, flashing red dress, and gave it to his daughter. Then she went off to make herself ready for a dance.

Next, the king asked the middle daughter, "How much do *you* love me?"

And she replied, "I love you more than all of the boyfriends and sweethearts I could ever have," for that was what she had on her mind. The old king liked her answer, so he broke off one of the white roses, laid it on her dark, flashing green dress, and gave it to his daughter. Then she went to make herself ready for a dance.

Finally, the youngest daughter came to the king. She had always been the one that he had loved most, so he was eager for her answer. He said, "How much do you love me?"

But she shook her head. "I don't have an answer for a question like that."

"No?" the king asked. "But I must know. How much do you love me?"

"I just love you," said the daughter. "That's all. I love you like meat loves salt."

"What?" said the old king.

"I love you like meat loves salt."

The old king flew into a terrible rage at her answer. He threw the white dress on the floor, grabbed his youngest daughter, and locked her in a high tower where she saw no one—except one old woman who cooked for her and brought her water. And there she stayed for many years.

One day, as the youngest daughter was sitting in the tower window combing her long hair and letting her tears flow freely, the Duke of England came riding across the land. When he looked up and saw the girl sitting in the tower window, he felt he must speak to her, and grasping the grapevine that grew on the tower's wall, he climbed up to the window. Then the duke helped the girl down from the tower, sat her on his horse, and rode away. They went to England, where he married her, and they lived very happily together.

As time went by, the king's other two daughters married as well, and they went to live with their own husbands. When the old king grew too old to rule and could no longer care for himself, he was sent to live with his oldest daughter. But she sold for her own pleasure all of the beautiful things her father had brought from his home, so he knew that she really didn't love him.

Then he went to live with his middle daughter. But her husband didn't like the old king, and his daughter was ashamed of her father. So she made him eat in the kitchen and sleep among the servants. In his anger and pride, he wandered away. Nobody even cared enough about him to see where he had gone.

As more time passed, the husbands of the king's two oldest daughters began making war against the Duke of England, and the duke, his troops, his ships, and his wife came to fight the war.

When his wife reached her own country again, she turned to her husband and said, "I've lived with you a long time and we've been happy together, but I'm anxious to be in the place where I lived when I was a child. I want to go there and see my old home, and after I've seen it, I will come back to you."

When the youngest daughter came to the place where her old home had stood, there was nothing there except burned and charred ruins. The old king, her father, was there wandering among them, wearing a crown of blackberry briers he had made for himself. As he walked along, he muttered quietly.

When his daughter saw him, all the years she had spent in the tower fell away from her, and all she saw then was her father, old and sick, who needed her. So she went to him, and although he didn't recognize her, he let her lead him away. She brought him to her husband, the duke, and when the war was won, they sailed back to England. And in her home, the king's daughter made beautiful quarters for her father, and she saw that he would never want for anything.

One night, she went into the kitchen and said to the cook, "Tonight when you fix the meal, I want you to cook the meat without one grain of salt."

"I don't want to do that," said the cook. "The meat won't taste right."

"Never mind," said the daughter. "You do what I bid you."

And so that night, when the meal was placed on the table, the meat was served without one grain of salt. And when the old king tasted his food, he put his face in his hands and began to weep bitterly.

He said, "I had a daughter, and I asked her how much she loved me. She said she loved me like meat loves salt. But I was very cruel to her because I didn't try to understand. I don't even know what's become of her now."

"Father?" said the daughter.

When the old king raised his face from his hands, standing before him was his youngest daughter. When he saw her, his mind came back to him and his sadness was replaced with joy. He sent a servant across the ocean to get the white dress that he had promised to give to her so long ago. When the dress was brought, on it lay a spray of beautiful white roses. And they were as fresh and as fragrant as the day they were picked.

The Folktellers
Connie Regan-Blake and Barbara Freeman

*For me, storytelling is a natural vehicle for genuine
communication—both the telling and the listening—and
I have always felt that to be a good teller one must
also be a good listener. I truly believe that to be
able to tell stories you must have an ear for the story,
an ability to take in people's emotions, especially
those feelings you haven't experienced yourself.*

Connie Regan-Blake

*I enjoy making people laugh. And while all stories
aren't about funny things, I still try as a storyteller to
create delight—even from stories of grief and sadness. For
if a story is well told, the listener opens up the little
pockets in his heart and, by so doing, experiences a special kind
of joy—simply for being alive and for experiencing life.*

Barbara Freeman

* * *

ON A CLEAR summer day in 1975, two young women pulled their yellow Datsun pickup into a downtown parking lot in Hartford, Connecticut. As the pair began unloading puppets, books, and musical instruments from the back of the truck, children who had been playing across the street began edging over to watch.

"What's all of this?" the children asked. "Who are you?"

"We're storytellers," the women replied, as the sock puppet each was now wearing on her hand nibbled at the children's fingers. Lowering the tailgate, the two women sat down to face their growing, curious audience, and then one of them launched into "Three Billygoats Gruff." The kids loved it.

Connie Regan-Blake and Barbara Freeman loved it too. Only weeks before they had left the security of their jobs as librarians at the Chattanooga Public Library in Tennessee, and with less than $2,000 in their collective pocket, begun traveling throughout America to listen to stories, tell stories, and live as storytellers. Now they sat in downtown Hartford, doing what they had set out to do and, at that moment, about to make the serendipitous discovery which would lead them to create the unique style of tandem storytelling.

As soon as Connie had concluded her story about the three billygoats, one of the children piped up, "Tell us *Where the Wild Things Are.*" Both women hesitated. Though time and time again they had told the story—from the children's book by Maurice Sendak—they had never recounted it without the book in front of them.

But they recalled that Marilyn Garrison, a library aide and storyteller who had worked with Barbara at the Chattanooga Public Library, always began her telling of the story with a special ritual designed to get the kids involved and participating. So in the middle of that parking lot in downtown Hartford, Connie and Barbara asked the young children to "stand up, open your closet door, take out your wolf suit, and try out your wolf's roar."

Then Barbara said, "That night Max wore *his* wolf suit . . ."

And Connie chimed in, ". . . and made mischief of one kind . . ."

And Barbara added, ". . . and another."

27

Some lines were repeated alone, and since the two didn't know who was going to say what, some lines were said together. This was not their usual style—they had never told a story together before—but Connie and Barbara spontaneously swapped lines or chorused them, each taking her cue from the other and from an intuitive sense of the story itself.

Less than a week later, in a concert on a college campus, Connie and Barbara asked a thousand people to rise from their seats, open up their closets, take out their wolf suits, and try out their wolf's roar. And the audience did. The listeners were all adults, and Connie and Barbara knew at that moment that they were doing something very special. For the first time in actual performance, the two women told in tandem—refining the technique they had happened upon just a few short days before, a technique that was to become the hallmark of their professional storytelling. As they told, it came to them as never before how strongly they were touching people—not only children but adults—catching them up in the mystery and magic of language through storytelling.

Calling themselves The Folktellers, Connie and Barbara continued telling stories, their travels leading them to performances at coffeehouses, festivals, libraries, schools, and conventions throughout the United States. "We didn't use music, we didn't sing ballads, we simply told stories." But there had been no summons of the storyteller, no beckoning for a tale. Yet their storytelling performances met with receptive audiences throughout America, and they played a major role in inspiring a national rekindling of interest in the oral tradition and the power of the told story. As The Folktellers told stories throughout the United States, the duo forged new paths that other storytellers have trod for more than a decade.

Connie and Barbara are cousins, and their love of storytelling began when they were children growing up in the South amid relatives who told jokes, stories, and family tales—handed down generation to generation. Although Connie and Barbara lived apart, the two cousins spent their summers together—riding horses and exploring the vast fields and woods on an uncle's farm in Florida, laughing, talking, and all the while making up stories to tell. Even then, each was developing her own style, her own unique notion of what stories could do.

Barbara was born in 1944 in Nashville, Tennessee, and for as long as she can remember, she has enjoyed hearing and telling stories. "When I was growing up in Nashville, a boy named Billy Greer lived just up the street. His family had a garage that was built into the hillside, so the roof was almost on the same level as the ground. As children, we would sit on that garage—it was like a stage because the roof was flat—and perform. I would entertain the neighborhood kids on that stage, telling ghost stories, scary tales. The scarier, the better."

But Barbara's penchant would be humor. As a child, she and her neighborhood friends would show old movies and perform in front of the screen—becoming the characters, acting out the roles—and they would just roar with laughter. "Being funny just ran in the family, I guess. I can remember how people gathered around my dad. He was forever telling stories, usually old jokes, and everyone would always laugh and say, 'Tell us another one.' And he would." Then one day, Barbara saw comedienne Martha Raye on television, and she began to realize, "That's what I want to do with my life. I want to make people laugh."

Barbara's first public storytelling performance came at an early age. For an elementary school talent contest, she dressed in a pair of ragged bib overalls and a long raccoon coat and won first place reciting Andy Griffith's then-popular monologue, "What It Was Was Football." Since she didn't have a record player, Barbara had learned the story from the radio, listening over and over again until she knew the monologue by heart.

In high school, Barbara continued to exercise her love of humor and wit, earning accolades for her performances—both on and off stage. "Though I was told by the school's registrars that I had a high IQ, one of my teachers had always seen me joking and clowning around at school, and she recommended that I not try to go to college. She just *knew* that I wasn't going to assert myself and make good grades." But Barbara went to college, earned excellent grades, served as the student government historian, was even chosen for "Who's Who," and graduated with a degree in history while working as a dorm hostess during the night, a cafeteria worker during the morning, and reading for a blind teacher during her spare time.

After two years of teaching in Chattanooga during the troubled Sixties—the only white teacher in an all-black junior high school—Barbara earned a master's degree in library science at the University of Tennessee in Knoxville, and by 1971, she had become head of the children's and young adult departments at the Chattanooga Public Library. It was here that she and her cousin Connie first conceived the idea of a joint storytelling venture and began their journey across the country to explore the breadth of storytelling nationwide. And throughout their travels, Barbara, the humorist, has always been the funny one.

"I enjoy making people laugh. And while all stories aren't about funny things, I still try as a storyteller to create delight—even within stories of grief and sadness. For if a story is well told, the listener opens up the little pockets in his heart and, by so doing, experiences a special kind of joy—simply for being alive and for experiencing life."

While Barbara uses her hands, her body, her voice, to create her characters—to garner the guffaws which forever accompany her performances—Connie's delivery is more reserved, intense, and always powerful. Her voice rises and falls in cadence with the tale, and her words are precise, and measured, and filled with imagery.

Born in 1947 in Mobile, Alabama, Connie grew up listening to her father tell stories. As a child, it was the magic of his words, the clarity of his speech, that Connie found comforting, nourishing. "We lived in Birmingham, and when I was a little girl, my daddy would take us out in our backyard—a big yard that backed up against Red Top Mountain— and spread a quilt, and we would lie there, look up at the stars, and talk. And I have such a memory of my daddy's words on those starry nights. He was able to breathe life into his words, to give us, as listeners, a vision as he spoke, and we knew and understood all the shades of meaning." Connie remembers as a child always wanting to have that same measured powerfulness, and clarity, and hint of humor when she spoke.

After graduating in 1969 from Loyola University in New Orleans with a degree in political science, Connie, still unclear about her future, began to follow her heart's desire. With only a backpack and tent, she traveled throughout Europe—living on pennies a day but soaking in the culture, feeling the rhythm of life, and hearing the stories, the flow of words. Within two years, Connie returned to America and visited Barbara in Chattanooga, and more by chance than design, she accepted a job as a storyteller at the Chattanooga Public Library. "I vividly remember telling my first story from a picture book—Gene Zion's *Harry, the Dirty Dog*— sitting there with this frozen little smile on my face and almost talking through my teeth."

Known as Ms. Daisy, Connie took puppets, films, tales, and lots of love to disadvantaged children at day-care centers throughout Chattanooga—to children who didn't have books in their homes and weren't readers. She wanted to foster in them a love of reading and literature through storytelling. It was there, within the comforts of storytelling, that Connie discovered she was happiest. "While growing up, I would never have thought of myself as a performer, but once I began telling stories, I knew this was what I should be doing with my life." Four years

later, Connie and Barbara had combined their talents to become The
Folktellers, and the power and intensity of Connie's voice—the wisdom
and strength it conveyed—found a larger forum.

"For me, storytelling is a natural vehicle for genuine communication
—both the telling and the listening—and I have always felt deeply that
to be a good teller one must also be a good listener. I truly believe that
to be able to tell stories you must have an ear for the story, an ability to
take in people's emotions, especially those feelings you haven't experienced yourself. Though I'd never really thought of this as good training
for a storyteller, I have, all through my life, been someone who other
people come to with their problems. And I'm sure that in the stories I
tell—especially those encompassing a depth of emotion—the empathy
I have with that story has been nurtured by the empathy I have experienced in my life."

In the years since The Folktellers set off across America to hear and
learn stories, they have performed throughout the United States, Europe, and the Far East. They have been among the first to bring storytelling into the spotlight at some of the most prestigious folk festivals in
the United States and Canada. And in their extensive workshops on
the creative uses of storytelling, Connie and Barbara have also shared
their stories and the techniques of storytelling with teachers and librarians, helping them to learn how to foster in others an appreciation of
words, language, and reading—conveying the love and excitement of
the storytelling art.

But whether they are telling tales or teaching others to tell, it's the
stories Connie and Barbara treasure: listening to them, sharing them,
keeping alive the oral tradition. And through their travels, they have
continued to herald the art of storytelling throughout the world as well
as at home in the Southern mountains.

No News

In the 1950s, Marshall Dodge began swapping Down East stories with Robert Bryan—re-creating the humor, warmth, and accent of Maine's people. In the years that followed, Marshall's reputation as a storyteller grew, and when he was killed in a hit-and-run accident in 1982 while bicycling in Hawaii, he was at the height of his popularity as one of America's premier storytellers.

During the late 1970s, Connie and Barbara of The Folktellers often told stories with Marshall at festivals throughout America, and they heard him tell "No News"—a story told years earlier by popular entertainer and recording artist Nat M. Wills. Connie and Barbara were taken by Marshall's retelling of this delightful old story, and Marshall urged them to tell it. Today, the Folktellers perform the story in tandem—Barbara as "a certain Southern lady" and Connie as her evasive friend—as they keep the tale alive and pay tribute to its legacy.

A CERTAIN Southern lady was returning home after recuperating in the mountains for three months. Her friend Georgeanne met her at the railway station.

"Georgeanne, has there been any news while I've been away?"

"Oh, no, there's no news."

"No news? Surely something has occurred in my absence. Why, I've been gone for nearly three months, and I'm anxious for any little bit of news you may have."

"Oh, now, since you mentioned it—'course it don't amount to much—but since you've been away, your dog died."

"My dog died? How did my dog die?"

"He ate some of the burnt horseflesh, and that's what killed the dog."

"Burnt horseflesh?"

"Well, after the fire cooled off, the dog ate some of the burnt horseflesh, and that's what killed the dog."

"Fire cooled off?"

"Well, the barn burned down, burned up all of the cows and horses, and when the fire cooled down, the dog ate some of the burnt horseflesh, and that's what killed the dog."

"My barn burned down? How did my barn burn down?"

"Oh, it was a spark from the house. Blew over, lit the roof of the barn, burned down the barn, burned up all the cows and horses, and when the fire cooled off, the dog ate some of the burnt horseflesh, and that's what killed the dog."

"A spark from the house?"

"Oh, yes, now that's completely burned down."

"But how did my house burn down?"

"It was the candle flame that lit the curtains, shot up the side of the wall, and burned down the house; a spark flew over on the roof of the barn, burned down the barn, burned up all of the cows and horses, and when the fire cooled off, the dog ate some of the burnt horseflesh, and that's what killed the dog."

"Candles? I don't even allow candles in my house. How did the candles get into my house?"

"Oh, they were around the coffin."

"Coffin? Who died?"

"Oh, now you needn't worry about that. Since you've been away, your mother-in-law died."

"Oh, my mother-in-law. What a pity. How did she die?"

"Well, some folks say that it was the shock of hearing that your husband had run away with the choir leader. But other than that, there ain't been no news."

Old Dry Frye

When Richard Chase was roaming through the Southern Appalachian Mountains during the 1940s listening to old songs and tales, he heard a story about old Dry Frye—a preacher man who preached for revival collections and all the fried chicken he could eat. Chase included this time-worn story and two dozen more in Grandfather Tales, a collection of Southern Appalachian yarns that has become a storytelling classic.

Barbara remembers listening to the misadventures of the old mountain preacher when her friend Phil Wolfe read to her from Chase's storybook. It charmed her, and Barbara now retells this traditional mountain tale of wit and humor—enlivening its telling by introducing us to old Dry Frye through a handed-down story about a real preacher who loved chicken and an old joke about a lost bicycle.

I WANT to tell you about a man down in my community, and I'm sure you all must remember 'im, 'cause everybody knows old Dry Frye. But for those of you who aren't rememberin' 'im right away, I'll refresh your memory.

Old Dry Frye was this old preacher man, but all he ever preached for at revivals was the collection and all the fried chicken he could eat. Dry Frye just loved chicken, and he liked to mooch offa folks whenever he could git 'imself a free dinner.

Once old Dry Frye was at this church picnic, and he got to talkin' so fast that his false teeth came out of his mouth and dropped right into a mud hole. Ever'body wanted to help old Dry Frye fish out his teeth, but nobody was willin' to put his hand down in that hole.

Well, that's when little Jennie Johnson got a bright idea. She went over to a picnic basket and pulled out a big piece of fried chicken, brought that chicken over to the mud hole, tied a string to it, and dangled it over those false teeth for bait. And sure enough, those old teeth came up out of that mud hole and latched on to that piece of chicken, and Jennie just ripped 'em away, rinsed 'em off in some lemonade, and gave 'em back to old Dry Frye. And he was as good as new.

Well, I know you're startin' to remember 'im, 'cause ever'body knows old Dry Frye.

One day, old Dry Frye got mighty upset 'cause somebody had stole his bicycle, and he was complainin' that he didn't have a way to git to the church meetin's. Then a fellow told 'im, "Dry Frye, if you're so upset about the loss of your bicycle, why don't you just wait 'til the next meetin', get up there and take them Commandments one by one, and when you git to the one that says, "Thou shalt not steal," just give a frozen look over the congregation. And the one that breaks out in the worst bead of sweat, well, that's the one who got your bicycle."

So old Dry Frye thought that was a real good idea, and at the next meetin', he took them Commandments one by one—just mixin' 'em up, just sayin' 'em as they come to his mind—and when he got to the one that said, "Thou shalt not covet thy neighbor's wife," he remembered where he'd left his bicycle.

Well, I know you're surely startin' to remember 'im, 'cause ever'body knows old Dry Frye. And now I'm a-goin' to tell you what happened to 'im.

One night, old Dry Frye was at a farmer's house havin' supper and he got to eatin' fried chicken so fast that he got a bone caught in his throat and he just choked and died. That farmer looked across the table and said, "Law me, ain't nobody goin' to believe old Dry Frye didn't know how to put down a piece of fried chicken. Ever'body is goin' to think I kilt 'im, and I'm a-goin' to git hung for murder. I've got to git shet of 'im."

So that farmer drug old Dry Frye out the back door and down the road 'til he came to a big bush, and he just hunkered down old Dry Frye over in that bush and then turned around and went back home.

There was a big moon out that night, so naturally there were two lovers out under it and they came strollin' down the lane a-holdin' hands. Suddenly, one of them two lovebirds stopped and said, "Look! Look up there! Somebody's up there in that bush."

The other one said, "I bet you that it's one of them highway robbers a-layin' low for us and gonna steal from us when we come by. We'd better git him before he gits us."

So they reached down, picked up some big rocks, and began throwin' the rocks into the bush, and one of them big rocks hit old Dry Frye and knocked 'im flat out into the middle of the road. So they ran up to see who it was.

"Law me, it's old Dry Frye." Ever'body knows old Dry Frye. "Why, we've kilt 'im, and we're a-goin' to git hung for murder. We've got to git shet of 'im."

So they drug old Dry Frye up the hillside 'til they came to a farmer's big corncrib, and they jist leaned old Dry Frye up against that crib.

The farmer who lived there was up before the crack of dawn, washin' his face with cold water and gittin' ready for the day. Folks had been stealin' from 'im, and he wasn't a-goin' to let it happen again. He looked out his window, and he thought he saw somebody up at his corncrib.

So he opened up his window and gave a holler: "You git away from there or I'll shoot."

He reached for his shotgun, and when he fired, that old preacher man hit the ground, and the farmer ran up there to see who it was.

"Law me, it's old Dry Frye." Ever'body knows old Dry Frye. "I've kilt 'im, and I'm a-goin' to git hung for murder. I've got to git shet of 'im."

He drug old Dry Frye into the corncrib 'til it got dark. And as soon as darkness came, he stuffed that old preacher man into a big burlap sack, put it over his shoulder, and started down this country lane a-tryin' to find a place to hide 'im.

While that old farmer was a-walkin' down the lane, he didn't see the two thieves on the other side of the hill. They'd been out stealin' that night, and each one had 'im a big sack of hog meat on his shoulders. But when they saw somebody a-comin' down the road, they dropped those sacks of hog meat so as not to weight 'em down and they ran whippity-cut into the woods as fast as they could go.

Well, that farmer didn't know nothin' 'cause he's got his nose stuck up in the sky jist a-comin' along, a-bumpin' and a-dumpin' old Dry Frye. When the old farmer spied them sacks a-layin' along the road, he sat old Dry Frye down, opened one of them sacks, and saw it was filled with hog meat. So he just sorta looked over each shoulder and traded old Dry Frye for one of them sacks of hog meat, put it up on his back, and headed home.

The two crooks came outa the woods and found their sacks still a-layin' along the road. So they put 'em on their shoulders, carried 'em home, and hung 'em in the smokehouse.

Early the next mornin', the wife of one of them two thieves got her butcher knife and went out to the smokehouse to git her some hog meat for breakfast. She looked at those sacks of hog meat a-hangin' there, and finally, she cut a long rip into one of the sacks. And out fell old Dry Frye.

She went a-screamin' out of that smokehouse, and those two thieves came to see what was a-happenin'. And hangin' outa one of them sacks was that old preacher man.

"Law me, it's old Dry Frye." Ever'body knows old Dry Frye. "With all our troubles with the law, ever'body goin' to think that we've kilt 'im and we're a-goin' to git hung for murder. But we know how to git shet of 'im."

They went out into the woods and found themselves a horse—not a normal horse, but a horse that had steam a-comin' outa its eyes and ears, its nose and throat, and all four hooves at the same time. In the barn, they found a no-good saddle and a piece of a bridle.

They put old Dry Frye on that horse, strapped 'im to the bellyband, and tied his hands to the saddle horn. Then they put a big old hat on the top of his head. The two thieves wound up their wrists and gave that horse a pop you could hear all the way into town, and he went a-tearin' down the road with that old preacher man a-bouncin', first to one side and then the other.

The two thieves ran behind the horse a-yellin' as loud as they could. "Horse thief! Horse thief! Stop that man! He's stole our horse!"

When folks in the community heard the commotion, they began to throw rocks and fire their guns at old Dry Frye. But that horse had built up such steam that nobody could catch 'im, and he headed out toward the mountains. And I want you to know that that horse has been spotted in the Black Mountains of North Carolina and all the way up in the White Mountains of New Hampshire, and some say they've even seen that old horse as far away as California. And as he gallops by, I'm sure you can just hear what folks are a-sayin'.

"Law me, didn't that look like old Dry Frye?" 'Cause, ever'body knows old Dry Frye.

Two White Horses

"*Two White Horses,*" *a strange and chilling tale of the Southern Appalachians, was written by Elizabeth Seaman—a mountain woman who has pioneered a homestead on Tumblin' Creek in the East Tennessee mountains for years. Elizabeth heard the tale from Clare Bailey, whose mother had told it to her children on Coffee Ridge back in the days when people sat around the fire on wintry evenings, roasting hickory nuts and telling stories.*

When Connie first read "Two White Horses," it was the most haunting, powerful story she had ever read. While she was primarily telling stories for children, she was drawn to the tale and realized that the story's sensitive approach to death was really meant to be shared with an adult audience. When Connie first told "Two White Horses" before an audience—one primarily composed of adults—she knew right at that moment that she was truly a storyteller. Connie recounts this Southern Appalachian legend with power and intensity.

AMANDA JANE fixed me with her big roun' eyes. "Mama'll be home tomorrow, won't she, Jenny?" She held tight to her rag doll.

I almost said, "Mama won't never be back, Mandy," but I choked back the words. How could you tell that to such a little youngin'? When the neighbor women came to get Mama ready for the buryin', they took Mandy and little Joey over to the McMinns' house.

Nells Woodsby brought the box to lay Mama in, and we put on her best taffeta dress, the one with the stand-up collar that she only wore to church on Sundays. Grandma Turner's brooch was pinned to her blouse. And on Mama's hand was her wide gold wedding band and the ring Papa gave her with the real diamond set in it.

We all walked to the graveyard. Bird and Dock, our two white horses, pulled the wagon, slow like, with the buckets of flowers in it, and Mama's coffin. Mama always loved the view from Graveyard Hill. You could look out over most of Greenup County with the rivers windin' below. Meadowlarks were singin' and I could smell honeysuckle on the warm air. But I had a cold, drizzly feelin' inside and the sunshine seemed all wrong.

Preacher Gorge made a long sermon sayin' what a fine woman Mama was and tellin' things from the Bible. But I wished he wouldn't talk so long. I was afraid Papa was goin' to break down and cry. He looked so sad and stern.

Charlene Moss and Leslie Crunk sang, "You got to walk that lonesome valley, you gotta walk it all alone." I could just see Mama, dressed in white, walkin' down a dark, lonesome valley all by herself. At the end, Papa asked them to sing her favorite hymn, "Precious Memories."

I almost smothered when they shut down that coffin. I could see Mama through the little window in the lid. She looked like she was just asleep. When they commenced to shovelin' in the dirt, I ran down the hill and waited with Bird and Dock. Everybody left the graveyard, and we all walked home.

The house seemed so empty and quiet, the old clock tickin' on the mantle. I missed Mama. She was always 'round the house, and the kitchen had always smelled good from the things she'd cooked. She'd call me to go carry a bucket of water from the well or go hunt the guinea's nest.

But she was gone now. It seemed like it took me a long time to get supper ready. The cornmeal mash had lumps in it, and it tasted kind of scorched. Papa said it was real good, and he was proud of me.

When bedtime came, Little Joey hollered for Mama. He was terrible fussy 'cause he hadn't had his nap on account of the buryin'. I could hardly get him into his trundle bed. Didn't have no trouble with Mandy, though. She sleeps with me. Papa blew out the lamp and climbed into the big four-poster bed in the corner, alone.

A huge moon came out behind the barn, makin' dark shadows across the yard. The chickens that perched on the butternut tree were already on their roostin' limb. And Papa's gun was on its rack over the door, ready in case anything bad should happen.

I couldn't get to sleep—I kept thinkin' about Mama up there in that graveyard with all those dead people. The little Carter boy who died with the thrash was near her. Grass hadn't growed back over his grave yet. Over by the stone wall was ol' Miss Crower. She got so heavy she couldn't get up out of her chair. She died of heart dropsy.

Outside the crickets were chirpin'. I wondered if they were chirpin' up at the graveyard, too. Ol' Yellowthroat gave a few clucks from over in the blackberry briers. Sometimes he sings at night, 'specially if there's a big moon a-shinin'.

The dog at the McMinn farm began to howl. I felt all shivery. Then I heard somethin' else. Slow footsteps came draggin' across the front porch. There was a knock at the front door. Papa's bed creaked as he sat up and reached for his clothes. "Who's there?"

"Open the door, Clint. It's me, Althea," Mama's voice answered. It sounded weak and far away. "I've come home from the grave."

"No, no, go away!" Papa almost shouted. "Your ghost has come to trouble me. Ohhh, I'm wretched enough, Althea. My heart is wrung with sorrow."

"Open the door, Clint. Let me in."

"No, Althea! It's the moon that's got you awake. Moon's so big and strange tonight and the shadows are so dark. Go back to your grave and sleep in peace."

"No! Never! Let me in!"

"No, Althea! It's the moonlight that's made you restless. Last night it shone through the window on your pale face, and you a corpse a-waitin' for the buryin'. They say if it shines on your face and you're asleep, it'll drive you mad. Maybe even the dead."

"Ohhhhh, but I wasn't dead, Clint. I must've been in a deep, dark sleep. Believe me, truly, I'm alive. Ohhh, let me in before it's too late."

The voice drifted away. The little ones were so scared they hid under their covers. I was scared, too.

"Children," Papa said, "look to the barnyard. If our two horses have their heads out of the stall windows a-lookin' the way they do when someone comes, then I'll know for sure it's your mother."

We ran up the shade. "They're there. Bird and Dock have their heads out. Did you hear Dock nicker?"

Papa hastened to the door, and threw it open. He caught Mama in his arms, just as she was about to fall. He carried her over to the bed and laid her across it. "Jenny, run and make Mama a cup of hot tea. She's so cold.

"Althea, I saw Nells Woodsby nail down that coffin lid and dirt shoveled in on it. How'd you escape?"

Mama took a deep breath. "Well, a grave robber dug up my coffin, and pried off the lid. He tried but couldn't get my rings off. He was tryin' to cut away my fingers."

"Lordy me, Mama, then what?"

"Well, the pain got me awake. When I sat up and screamed, that ol' man hollered, too. Dropped his knife and went hoppin' away across those graves. Why, it was that strange Ralph Zenion that lives back in the swamps."

I tugged at Mama's sleeve. "Mama, how'd you get all the way home?"

She stroked my hair. "Well, I pulled myself up out of the coffin and walked home. Moon was so bright, it lit up the fields. I came by the crossroads and took the old mill road to the foot of our lane. Ohhh, it was soooo far, sooooo far."

Papa drove his fist in his hand. "That dirty Zenion, stealin' from the dead. I'll stomp him."

"Why, Clint, if it hadn't been for that ol' scalf, I'd still be up on Graveyard Hill, in my coffin, buried alive. Ohhh, pray God, I might never have gotten awake."

The next day, Papa took a wide board and sawed out two horses' heads. He painted them white like Bird and Dock and nailed them to the side of their stall window, so's we'd never forget how it was those horses that knew it was Mama that night in the moonlight when she knocked at our door.

Stories
of Humor
and Wit

Jackie Torrence

I pastored that little church for six months,
and the attendance began to grow, and since I was paid by
those who came, I kept food on our tables
and clothes on our back. But when I told the congregation
a Bible story, I thought I was preaching.
I didn't know—didn't have no idea under the sun—
that I was storytelling.

45

J OEL CHANDLER HARRIS collected for us our most endearing and enduring stories of America's heartland: the tales of Brer Rabbit, Brer Fox, Brer Coon, and a parade of homespun characters who have delighted us in our childhoods for generations. Harris, an American author and journalist, learned the old tales from slaves as he worked in a print shop on a Southern plantation. He created the imaginary Uncle Remus—an elderly black servant—and through him retold these stories of America's black heritage in *Uncle Remus: His Songs and Sayings*, a storytelling classic since the late 1800s. These are the stories Jackie Torrence heard—and cherished—as a child.

Though Jackie's life is laced with an abundance of stories, ranging from mountain legends to tales of the supernatural, it's her renditions of these old slave tales that are probably her best. Reflecting the richness of her black tradition, these stories that she heard as a child nurtured and nourished her. As she says, "You dance with the one who brung ya."

Now a professional storyteller, Jackie weaves gesture, facial expression, vocal sound effects, and, above all, the poetry of her words to create a kaleidoscope world inhabited by giants, wily rabbits, ghosts, and some "ordinary" folks who find themselves in some extraordinary circumstances. As she tells of their antics, her eyes, wide and bulging, flash with delight, her arms wave rhythmically in time with the tale, her face twists as it becomes a frightened frog or sneaky snake or troubled raccoon.

Jackie was born in Chicago in 1944, but she spent much of her time on Second Creek, a farm settlement near Salisbury, North Carolina, where she lived with her grandparents and was "surrounded by a family who told lovely old stories." Her fondest memories are of her grandfather—Jim Carson, the son of a slave—who, though sick and weakened, told her stories.

"I remember my grandfather. We called him Mister Jim. He walked with a cane, and I would hold tightly to it as he walked, running to keep up with him. One day, we were walking out to the big road and down by Aunt Sally's house when we came to a hillside covered with wheat. Hovering over the wheat field were puffs of purple smoke.

"I asked, 'What's that smoke, Mister Jim?'"

"He didn't blink, he didn't pause. 'That's the smoke comin' from Mammy Bammy Big Money's house.'"

"And I asked, 'Where's the house?'"

"'It's in the ground. Mammy Bammy Big Money lives in the ground.'"

Though the purple smoke was only a swarm of gnats, it was the hint of a story, a fragment borrowed from a tale of Brer Rabbit—Jackie's first introduction to that cast of characters who people the stories she now tells.

Throughout her childhood, Jackie heard many of the old tales from her grandmother as she baked the weekly bread in an old wood cook-stove. "I was curious, full of questions, and to keep me busy, my grandma sat me in the corner, gave me a big ball of dough, and as the bread rose, she told me stories." Jackie boasts playfully, "I know stories Uncle Remus never heard of.

"Though my life was filled with old tales, it was also plagued with sadness—and loneliness. You see, I was a fat child, had no daddy, and felt unattractive. And when I was old enough to go to school, I moved from Second Creek to Salisbury to live with my Aunt Mildred who, bless her dear soul, was unmarried, had no children, and didn't know nothing under God's sun about little girls. Then, in the fifth grade, I realized I didn't talk like everyone else. I had a speech impediment.

"Pauline Pharr, my fifth-grade teacher, always had us write stories and stand in front of the class and read them aloud. But whenever I began to talk, it sounded as though I had rocks in my mouth, and the other kids laughed at me. I was shattered. One day, Miss Pharr came to me.

"'Jackie,' she said, 'if *you* will write the stories, *I* will read them.'

"Miss Pharr had seen my plight, and I was elated. I didn't have to stand in front of the class, I didn't have to read aloud, and I didn't have to be laughed at anymore. And I began to write."

The first story Jackie wrote for Miss Pharr was a smidgen of a tale about her curious, unspoken friendship with a ragman she called Mister Henry.

"During the summer, when I was out of school, I stayed at Aunt Mildred's alone. I wasn't allowed to venture outside of our yard, so I often sat on our porch, dreaming. About ten o'clock every morning, every summer day, an old man with a mule and wagon came down Lloyd Street. The mule always wore a funny little straw hat with a fringe of balls. Well, every day when the old man and his mule got to our house, he looked at me and yelled, 'Rags.' It became a game with me. Every

morning I would rush to get dressed, run to the steps along the side-
walk, and wait for the old man to come by. I called him Mister Henry.

"I wrote about Mister Henry and his old mule, and Miss Pharr loved
it, and she read it to the class. The more I wrote, the more she read.
Soon Miss Pharr and I were going to the library, reading stories, writing
scripts, and, while I made papier-mâché masks, the other kids acted out
my stories.

"Four years later, the mystery of my speech impediment unraveled
when my mother and stepfather and their young son came to live with
me and Aunt Mildred. One morning, I gave my brother some Coke in a
bottle, and for whatever reason, he gave it back to me—across the
room and through the air—and the bottle hit me right in the mouth.
My lips swelled, and my teeth gradually turned black. When they took
me to the dentist, he discovered impacted teeth: a complete set of extra
teeth in my mouth that was keeping me from talking plain. Nobody had
ever looked into my mouth before. All of my teeth were removed, and
at thirteen years old, I was given false teeth."

As a student in high school, Jackie met Abna Aggrey Lancaster, an
English teacher who also recognized her talents, and for four years,
every day after school, she worked with Jackie to help her develop
better speech patterns. "Mrs. Lancaster gave me the courage to stand in
front of an audience and say what I wanted to say and do what I wanted
to do." For Jackie, this marked the beginning of a love for an audience
—the yearn to perform—and throughout high school, she read the
Scripture in every assembly program.

"When I graduated from high school, I entered Livingstone College,
a small black school in Salisbury, to become a teacher. I couldn't join a
sorority because it was too expensive. And since the only organization
on campus that didn't cost anything to join was the Drama Club, I
signed up—knowing that I could write scripts, make costumes and
masks, and even build sets.

"The first play was A Raisin in the Sun, and all of us in the Drama
Club were asked to do something. I volunteered for backstage work. But
W. Clyde Williams, the new faculty advisor, asked me to try out for the
part of the young mother. And I did. When I had completed my read-
ing, everyone at the audition stood up and applauded. I was shocked.
And I got the part.

"The play ran for two months. On closing night, I came offstage and
the ministerial student I was dating met me in my dressing room. I fell
into his arms, crying, and I cried for twenty minutes.

"He kept saying to me, 'What's wrong? Has something happened?'"

"But I couldn't tell him. I was overcome. I hadn't made the masks or sewn the costumes or built the sets. I had *performed*. It was a moment to cherish, to savor. And now that the play had closed, I thought I would never hear that applause again."

Jackie married the ministerial student, dropped out of school, and began traveling throughout the South from community to community, church to church. Her husband's first church was in Rockingham, North Carolina—just eighty miles from Salisbury. But within less than eight years, he had pastored churches in Georgia, Mississippi, Arkansas, Oklahoma, and Texas. They were always backwoods churches, some with only dirt floors. When it rained, the members of the congregation brought cardboard—carried it under their arms—to place under their feet during the service.

"Eventually, we found ourselves in Little Rock, Arkansas, where my husband spent so much time away from home that he began neglecting me and our newborn baby daughter, Lori. When he wasn't there to preach, I'd get up in the pulpit, read the Scripture, and give the pastoral prayer. And then I would always tell a Bible story.

"I pastored that little church for six months, and the attendance began to grow, and since I was paid by those who came, I kept food on our table and clothes on our back. But when I told the congregation a Bible story, I thought I was teaching. I didn't know—didn't have no idea under the sun—that I was *storytelling*."

Confused and unhappy, Jackie began to realize that her marriage was over, and in Little Rock, she made the decision to come home to North Carolina. Almost penniless, Jackie left Lori with her mother at her home at Granite Quarry and went to High Point to find work. Soon she landed a job as a reference librarian at the High Point Public Library, and then, quite by chance, Jackie the storyteller emerged.

"When the library director was in trouble and needed help, he would always hook his thumbs in his vest pockets. Well, one day, after I had been there for a few months, he came to me with his thumbs in his vest pockets, and I knew something was wrong.

"He said, 'The storyteller's not here. There's nobody to tell stories, and the children are yellin' and screamin'. Will you tell 'em a story?'

"I was a reference librarian. I had never told a story at the library before, so I told him, 'No, I have a stack of questions to answer and telephone calls to make.'

"But he begged me. Then he bribed me. 'I'll give you an extra hour off, any time you choose, if you'll just do it for me.'

"So, reluctantly, I went into the children's department. Before me were four young ones, three and four years old, whose parents had left them at the library for storytime. I was terrified.

"'How about "Little Red Riding Hood"?'

"'Don't do that one. We know that one.'

"'How about, "The Three Little Pigs"?'

"'No, we've heard that one too.'

"'Well, I know. How about "Three Billygoats Gruff"?'

"'No, we've heard that one.'

"I was stumped. What do you tell three- and four-year-old children who've heard every story in the book? I thought and thought and then remembered Corrine Thomas, the librarian who had told us stories when I was in elementary school. One of her favorites—and mine— was 'Sody Sallyraytus.' And though I hadn't heard that story in years, I began to tell it."

> One day, this old woman went into her kitchen to make some bread, but when she looked in the cupboard, she didn't have any sody sallyraytus.

"And I explained that sody sallyraytus was nothing more than plain old baking soda and the old woman had to have some if she was going to make some bread."

> So she sent her little boy to the store. And as he goes down the mountain to the store, he's singin', "Sody, Sody, Sody Sallyraytus. Sody, Sody, Sody Sallyraytus."

"And the kids chimed in, and they sang for ten minutes."

> And finally, he gets to the store and buys some sody sally- raytus.

"'How much was it?'

"'Twenty-five cents.'

"'How far was the store?'

"'Two miles.'

"And I tried to continue the story."

> Out from behind the bridge jumps a big bear.

"'What color was he?'

"'Black.'

"The more I told, the more enthralled with the story the children became. Before we knew it, that old bear had eaten up all the library books and all of the librarians, and the kids were rolling in the floor with laughter."

Jackie's young audience was delighted, and since she didn't introduce herself, the children affectionately called her The Story Lady. Week after week, story after story, the scene was repeated, and Jackie soon became the full-time storyteller of the High Point Public Library. For four years, people from throughout High Point and the surrounding countryside crowded into the library to hear Jackie Torrence tell stories. As her repertoire grew, Jackie began telling stories after hours—during the evenings and on weekends—at private parties in High Point and nearby Greensboro and Winston-Salem. But when she was told to quit her free-lance performances, Jackie refused, and she was fired from her library job. She now had no choice: Jackie Torrence became a full-time professional storyteller and began to depend upon her free-lance work to sustain her and her young daughter. It was not an easy path to tread. But slowly, her way was marked with growing achievement and recognition, and today, Jackie receives international acclaim for preserving an art for which she has an undying devotion.

"I love storytelling, and I'm having a good time. And I want everybody to enjoy my stories as much as I do. There's no better way to explain that than to tell a little story about a dear friend of mine.

"You see, I belong to the White Rock AME Zion Church at Granite Quarry, where I now live. Though my friend was an alcoholic for thirty years, he's dry now and a very religious man. When we have revivals, the preacher calls us up to testify, and eventually, my friend gets up in the pulpit.

"'When I was a drinkin' man,' he tells us, 'I'd git the bottle and pass it around to ever'body I was a-drinkin' with. You see, I was havin' such a good time that I wanted ever'body to have a good time too. But now that I've found God, I want to pass that around too, 'cause I want ever'body to feel like I feel.'

"If I never tell another story, I'll at least be satisfied that I, like my friend, have 'passed it around.' And when I go back home to Second Creek and drive through the country, I always remember that hillside of wheat and the puff of purple smoke that I, as a child, saw rising from Mammy Bammy Big Money's house. And I keep thinking: I just might see it again. Someday."

Brer Possum's Dilemma

For Jackie, stories have always comforted her—eased her disappointments, healed her hurt feelings, and mended her broken heart.

"When I was in high school, my best friend promised for months to buy me a sweater. 'I'm goin' to git you that sweater for Christmas,' she told me. 'I've done laid it away.' Her mother was a teacher and her father was a professional band director, and I knew that she could afford to buy me the sweater.

"Then she took me shopping downtown and showed me a bracelet and ring that she wanted. Since she had promised me the sweater, I knew that I had to give her something just as nice. The bracelet and ring cost $25, and I begged Aunt Mildred to help me buy it for my friend for Christmas. We were poor, and Aunt Mildred refused.

"'I've got to get that bracelet for her!'

"Aunt Mildred just said, 'I know her and I know her mama, and she's not goin' to git you that sweater. She's jist talkin'.'

"I spent nights awake wondering where I was going to get the money to buy that jewelry, and finally, I persuaded my Uncle Nesbit to give me $25. And I bought the bracelet and ring.

"Christmas came, and I couldn't wait to get my sweater. Sure enough, my friend called.

"'I'm comin' to see you with your Christmas present.'

"I said, 'That's great, 'cause I've got your present too.'

"But when she walked into my house, I didn't see a box. I looked at her, puzzled.

"She said, 'I've got your gift right here.'

"And from her purse, she pulled a little box and gave it to me. I ripped it open, and instead of the sweater, I found rocks glued to a piece of paper—something you could buy for fifty cents.

"I gave her the bracelet and ring. And when she left, I cried. But Aunt Mildred took me into her arms and said, 'I warned you of her nature.' And she told me this story."

BACK IN the days when the animals could talk, there lived ol' Brer Possum. He was a fine feller. Why, he never liked to see no critters in trouble. He was always helpin' out, a-doin' somethin' for others.

Ever' night, ol' Brer Possum climbed into a persimmon tree, hung by

52

his tail, and slept all night long. And each mornin', he climbed outa the tree and walked down the road to sun 'imself.

One mornin' as he walked, he come to a big hole in the middle of the road. Now, ol' Brer Possum was kind and gentle, but he was also nosey, so he went over to the hole and looked in. All at once, he stepped back, 'cause layin' in the bottom of that hole was ol' Brer Snake with a brick on his back.

Brer Possum said to 'imself, "I best git on outa here, 'cause ol' Brer Snake is mean and evil and low-down, and if I git to stayin' around 'im, he jist might git to bitin' me."

So Brer Possum went on down the road.

But Brer Snake had seen Brer Possum, and he commenced to callin' for 'im.

"Help me, Brer Possum."

Brer Possum stopped and turned around. He said to 'imself, "That's ol' Brer Snake a-callin' me. What do you reckon he wants?"

Well, ol' Brer Possum was kindhearted, so he went back down the road to the hole, stood at the edge, and looked down at Brer Snake.

"Was that you a-callin' me? What do you want?"

Brer Snake looked up and said, "I've been down here in this hole for a mighty long time with this brick on my back. Won't you help git it offa me?"

Brer Possum thought.

"Now listen here, Brer Snake. I knows you. You's mean and evil and low-down, and if'n I was to git down in that hole and git to liftin' that brick offa your back, you wouldn't do nothin' but bite me."

Ol' Brer Snake just hissed.

"Maybe not. Maybe not. Maaaaaaaybe not."

Brer Possum said, "I ain't sure 'bout you at all. I jist don't know. You're a-goin' to have to let me think about it."

So ol' Brer Possum thought—he thought high, and he thought low —and jist as he was thinkin', he looked up into a tree and saw a dead limb a-hangin' down. He climbed into the tree, broke off the limb, and with that ol' stick, pushed that brick offa Brer Snake's back. Then he took off down the road.

Brer Possum thought he was away from ol' Brer Snake when all at once he heard somethin'.

"Help me, Brer Possum."

Brer Possum said, "Oh, no, that's him agin."

But bein' so kindhearted, Brer Possum turned around, went back to the hole, and stood at the edge.

"Brer Snake, was that you a-callin' me? What do you want now?"

Ol' Brer Snake looked up outa the hole and hissed.

"I've been down here for a mighty long time, and I've gotten a little weak, and the sides of this ol' hole are too slick for me to climb. Do you think you can lift me outa here?"

Brer Possum thought.

"Now, you jist wait a minute. If'n I was to git down into that hole and lift you outa there, you wouldn't do nothin' but bite me."

Brer Snake hissed.

"Maybe not. Maybe not. Maaaaaaaybe not."

Brer Possum said, "I jist don't know. You're a-goin' to have to give me time to think about this."

So ol' Brer Possum thought.

And as he thought, he jist happened to look down there in that hole and see that ol' dead limb. So he pushed the limb underneath ol' Brer Snake and he lifted 'im outa the hole, way up into the air, and throwed 'im into the high grass.

Brer Possum took off a-runnin' down the road.

Well, he thought he was away from ol' Brer Snake when all at once he heard somethin'.

"Help me, Brer Possum."

Brer Possum thought, "That's him agin."

But bein' so kindhearted, he turned around, went back to the hole, and stood there a-lookin' for Brer Snake. Brer Snake crawled outa the high grass just as slow as he could, stretched 'imself out across the road, rared up, and looked at ol' Brer Possum.

Then he hissed. "I've been down there in that ol' hole for a mighty long time, and I've gotten a little cold 'cause the sun didn't shine. Do you think you could put me in your pocket and git me warm?"

Brer Possum said, "Now you listen here, Brer Snake. I knows you. You's mean and evil and low-down, and if'n I put you in my pocket you wouldn't do nothin' but bite me."

Brer Snake hissed.

"Maybe not. Maybe not. Maaaaaaaybe not."

"No, sireee, Brer Snake. I knows you. I jist ain't a-goin' to do it."

But jist as Brer Possum was talkin' to Brer Snake, he happened to git a real good look at 'im. He was a-layin' there lookin' so pitiful, and Brer Possum's great big heart began to feel sorry for ol' Brer Snake.

"All right," said Brer Possum. "You must be cold. So jist this once I'm a-goin' to put you in my pocket."

So ol' Brer Snake coiled up jist as little as he could, and Brer Possum picked 'im up and put 'im in his pocket.

Brer Snake laid quiet and still—so quiet and still that Brer Possum even forgot that he was a-carryin' 'im around. But all of a sudden, Brer Snake commenced to crawlin' out, and he turned and faced Brer Possum and hissed.

"I'm a-goin' to bite you."

But Brer Possum said, "Now wait a minute. Why are you a-goin' to bite me? I done took that brick offa your back, I got you outa that hole, and I put you in my pocket to git you warm. Why are you a-goin' to bite me?"

Brer Snake hissed.

"You knowed I was a snake before you put me in your pocket."

And when you're mindin' your own business and you spot trouble, don't never trouble trouble 'til trouble troubles you.

How Brer Rabbit Outsmarted the Frogs

Jackie's best audience has always been her daughter, Lori. She was there when Jackie told her first stories at the High Point Public Library, and when Jackie was trying to succeed as a full-time professional storyteller and times got tough, Lori always told her, "Don't worry. I'll listen to your stories."

Every night when Jackie tucked Lori into bed and tried reading her a story, Lori would wrap her feet in her bedcovers and put them on top of the book. "Don't read any more," she pleaded. "Tell me a story." Then one night, Lori said to her, "Tell me where I come from."

Jackie thought for a moment.

"Do you want the truth or a fairy tale?"

"A fairy tale," she said.

Jackie was relieved, and she began her story.

"One day, I read in the newspaper that there were babies on sale at the hospital. The babies were overstocked and were going cheap. I knew how much babies cost, and since I didn't have much money, I went to the sale.

"I looked at all the babies. Some were white, some black, some yellow, some brown. They were all real cute, but I didn't see a single baby that I really liked.

"So finally, I told the clerk in the baby shop that I didn't see anything that I wanted. 'Do you have any babies in the stockroom?'

"She whispered, 'Well, we've got one baby in the stockroom that we've never been able to sell. We took it out of stock because we didn't think anybody would buy it.'

"And I said, 'What's wrong with it?'

"'Well,' she said, 'it has a little mole on its bottom. I'll bring it out and let you see it.'

"So out of a tattered old shoe box came this beautiful little baby with a tiny mole on its bottom—a mole that was the shape of a star."

Lori kept asking, "Was it me? Was it me? Was it me?"

"From all of those little babies," Jackie told her, "I liked you the best. And I brought you home with me."

Lori, satisfied with her mother's story, soon fell asleep. But the next day, Jackie received a call from Lori's teacher. She got right to the point. "Mrs.

Torrence, if you're going to teach your daughter the facts of life," she suggested, "I have a book I'd like for you to read."

Lori is now twenty, and even today when she brings a new friend home for a visit, she always introduces her mother and says, "Tell her about the shoe box." And Jackie tells that little tale again and again, and the story still lives.

Jackie has told Lori "a zillion stories," but the one she enjoys most has always been "How Brer Rabbit Outsmarted the Frogs"—a story her grandma told her.

OL' BRER Rabbit lived near the pond, and he was a good fisherman. Ever' mornin', he'd drop his hook into the pond. Five or ten minutes later, he had about fifteen or twenty fish layin' right there on the bank. He was a good fisherman.

But Brer Rabbit had a good friend named Brer Raccoon—he called him Brer Coon for short—and Brer Coon couldn't fish at all. He didn't like fish. He liked frogs. But the frogs didn't care too much for Brer Coon.

Ever' mornin', Brer Coon got his sack, headed down to the river, filled that ol' sack with frogs, dragged it home, and throwed it up on the porch. His wife saw them sacks full of frogs and she said, "Wooooooo, hee, hee, hee! Frogs!" She liked frogs, too. Brer Coon and his wife were eatin' up the frog population.

Well, sir, the frogs finally called a big meetin'.

"What are we a-goin' to do 'bout Brer Coon catchin' us?" asked one of the frogs.

They talked for hours, and they soon decided they needed a lookout frog to sit on the bank of the pond and watch for Brer Coon.

They needed a frog with big eyes to see 'im when he was a-comin', big ears to hear 'im when he was a-comin', and a big mouth to warn 'em when he got there. The only frog that had them qualifications was the bullfrog, and they sent him down to the bank to watch. When Brer Coon got within a half mile of the river, the bullfrog saw 'im, heard 'im, and then he commenced to warnin'.

"Heeeeeeere he comes. Heeeeeeere he comes. Heeeeeeere he comes."

And the little frogs would echo what the bullfrog had said. "Here he comes. Here he comes. Here he comes."

By the time Brer Coon got to the pond, all of the frogs was in the water and Brer Coon couldn't swim. So as the days went by, it started gittin' real slim at home for ol' Brer Coon. The food was goin' quickly, and try as he might, Brer Coon wasn't replenishin' it.

His wife said, "Where's the frogs? Do you know that we can starve to death? You'd better go out there and catch some frogs."

And Brer Coon answered, "Now wait a minute. Them frogs has done got too wild to catch. I done been down there and ever'time I come within a half mile, all you can hear is 'Here he comes. Here he comes. Here he comes.' And I can't catch 'em."

Well, that made her so mad she went to the corner, got the broomstick, and hit 'im on the head.

"Ooooooohhhh," Brer Coon cried. "Why'd you do that?"

"We's all goin' to starve to death. Now you get out of here and find them frogs."

He said, "Now, I done told you . . ."

"You want me to hit you on the other side?"

"All right. I'm a-goin'. I'm a-goin'. I'm a-goin'."

Well, sir, Brer Coon left one mornin' before the sun come up. He had his ol' sack, and he was walkin' down the road talkin' to 'imself. "I can't catch them frogs. I done tried. All I hear is 'Here he comes. Here he comes. Here he comes.'"

When he looked up, ol' Brer Rabbit was comin' toward 'im. Brer Rabbit saw his best friend and said, "Hideeee there, Brer Coon. How you a-doin'?"

Brer Coon said, "I ain't doin' too well."

Brer Rabbit said, "Why, you looks right down in the mouth."

Brer Coon said, "It ain't my mouth I'm down in. You see this knot on my head?"

"Yeah," Brer Rabbit said. "Where'd you git it?"

"My wife gave it to me with the broomstick. I can't catch them frogs. I done tried. Ever'time . . ."

"Oh, wait a minute," Brer Rabbit said. "There's a thousand frogs on one side of that river alone. Why can't you catch 'em?"

He said, "Ever'time I git within half a mile of the river, all you can hear is 'Here he comes. Here he comes. Here he comes.' And when I git there, they's all in the water and I can't catch 'em."

Brer Rabbit said, "You need a plan to catch them frogs."

Brer Coon said, "I don't know nothin' about no plan."

Brer Rabbit said, "That's all right. You done come to the right place. I'm the best planner that ever planned a plan. I gotta think you up one."

So, Brer Rabbit tossed his string of fish that he had caught over a limb on a tree, sat down on his hind legs in the middle of the road, and throwed his ears up in the air. He scratched one ear with one hind leg, and he scratched his other ear with his other hind leg. And all of a sudden, he jumped up and said, "Wooooooo, hee, hee, hee! Gotcha a plan!"

Brer Coon said, "What is it?"

"This here's your plan," said Brer Rabbit. "Go down to the river. When you git to the river, fall dead."

Brer Coon said, "Do what?"

Brer Rabbit said, "Sssshhhhhhh. Go down to the river. When you gits to the river, fall dead."

Brer Coon said, "But I don't want to die."

Brer Rabbit said, "Sssshhhhhhh. I don't mean die. I mean play dead."

Brer Coon said, "Wheeeew. That be better. Now when I play dead, what do I do after that?"

Brer Rabbit said, "You don't do nothin'. You just lay there. Lay there until I tell you when to move."

"Hee, hee, hee," Brer Coon said. "I don't know what the plan is, but it sounds like a good one."

So, he picked up his ol' sack and headed toward the river, and when he got to within a half a mile of the river, he heard it. "Here he comes. Here he comes. Here he comes." And he commenced to dyin'. "Oooohhhh. Oooohhhh." He fell on his back and kicked his legs up in the air.

Well, the sun came out and it was hot. It shown right directly down on Brer Coon. He wanted so bad to roll up under a shade tree, but Brer Rabbit had told him not to move. So, he jist laid there and took it. After a while, the flies come in, sat down on his face, crawled in and out of his ears, walked up his nose, and sure enough, he wanted to move. But he didn't. He jist laid there. The sun went down, and the flies flew off.

Down through the woods come Brer Rabbit. He looked out to see if the frogs was there, and sure enough, they were, a-waitin'. Brer Rabbit stood on the edge of the river and commenced to cryin'.

The bullfrog climbed up on the bank, looked at Brer Rabbit, and said, "What's the matter with you? What's the matter with you? What's the matter with yoooou?"

The little frogs said, "What's the matter with you? What's the matter with you? What's the matter with yoooou?"

Brer Rabbit said, "Oooooooohhh. Don't you know? My best friend here done fell dead. He done fell dead. Brer Coon is dead, dead, deeaad."

The bullfrog said, "Good, good, goooooood."

The little frogs said, "That be good. That be good. That be goooooood."

Brer Rabbit said, "I promised my friend here years ago that when he passed away I was gonna dig 'im a grave right here at the place he loved the best. I was gonna dig him a grave right here. Dig him a grave right here on the river. Gonna dig it right heeeere."

The bullfrog said, "Let us dig it. Let us dig it. Let *us* dig it."

The little frogs said, "Let us dig it. Let us dig it. Let *us* dig it."

Brer Rabbit said, "Well, seein' as how I'm so tore up with grief and all, I'm goin' to let you dig it. But I'm goin' to stand right back here under this tree and tell you how deep to dig the grave."

Well, sir, the frogs was all gathered 'round Brer Coon and they got out their frog shovels and they commenced to diggin'. It was a curious sight. Brer Coon was layin' there dead, the frogs was a-diggin' his grave right from under 'im, and Brer Rabbit was standin' out under the tree a-watchin'.

The grave got deeper and deeper. As Brer Coon went down in the grave, the frogs went down in the grave with 'im. The dirt was flyin'. The grave was seven feet deep and the frogs was still a-diggin'. The bullfrog thought that that was enough.

Leapin' upon Brer Coon's chest, he hollered up to Brer Rabbit. "Is it deep enough? Is it deep enough? Is it deeeep enough?"

The little frogs said, "Is it deep enough? Is it deep enough? Is it deeeep enough?"

Brer Rabbit run over to the grave and said, "Well, can you jump out?"

And the bullfrog looked up to see. "Yes we can. Yes we can. *Yes* we can."

The little frogs said, "Yes we can. Yes we can. *Yes* we can."

Brer Rabbit said, "Well, it ain't deep enough. Dig it deeper."

The frogs was a-gittin' mighty tired, but they kept a-diggin'. And they dug. And they dug. The grave was twelve feet deep, and the frogs was still a-diggin'. The bullfrog thought that that was enough.

He leapt upon Brer Coon's chest and hollered up out of the grave. "Is it deep enough? Is it deep enough? Is it deeeep enough?"

The little frogs said, "Is it deep enough? Is it deep enough? Is it deeeep enough?"

Brer Rabbit said, "Well, can you jump out?"

And the bullfrog looked up to see. "Believe we can. Believe we can. *Believe* we can."

The little frogs said, "Believe we can. Believe we can. *Believe* we can."

Brer Rabbit said, "It ain't deep enough. Dig it deeper."

Well, the frogs kept a-diggin'. They was mighty tired. Their little ol' arms was gittin' weak. They commenced to lay down all over Brer Coon, and he started to turn a little green. But Brer Coon jist laid there. He never moved. The grave was twenty feet deep, and the bull-frog thought that that was enough.

He leapt upon Brer Coon's head, looked up, and said, "Is it deep enough? Is it deep enough? Is it deeeep enough?"

The little frogs said, "Is it deep enough? Is it deep enough? Is it deeeep enough?"

Brer Rabbit said, "Well, can you jump out?"

The bullfrog looked up to see. "No, we can't. No, we can't. *No,* we can't."

The little frogs said, "No, we can't. No, we can't. *No,* we can't."

Brer Rabbit said, "Git up there, Brer Coon, and grab your groceries. They's too tired to jump out of the hole."

And ol' Brer Coon had enough frogs to do 'im this year and next year too.

Ed Stivender

As I began telling "Jack and the Robbers" and
other traditional tales, more and more I grounded the
stories in common experience. Through
frequent, usually humorous references to everyday life—
to those things we all know and understand—
I bring the story home to my listeners
and create a communion between the story and the listener
and all of his experiences.

*　　*　　*

E D STIVENDER, his slim frame slightly bent forward, stood alone facing a room filled with children in an Episcopal day-care center in Hartford, Connecticut. He was The Storyteller.

"Hi, I'm Jack," Ed declared proudly, convincingly, as he jumped quickly into a story about Jack—that imaginary mountain boy who takes on the likes of giants and dragons and evil spirits and always, almost always, wins out. "I'd like to tell you a story about the time I went out to seek my fortune."

> I said to my mama, "I'm going out to seek my fortune."
> She said, "You be careful, Jack. Don't talk to any strangers on the road."
> I said, "Don't worry about me, Mama. I'll be all right."
> So I went on down the road to seek my fortune.

Ed shuffled his feet, walking in place, his arms and legs moving in the rhythm, as the children, sitting crossed-legged on the carpeted floor, began their imaginary journey with Jack.

> I had traveled about a mile or so when all of a sudden, I heard a terrible, mournful sound.

Ed brayed like a mule.

> I turned the corner, and sure enough, standing by the side of the road, with his head hung low, was an old mule feeling sorry for himself.

Ed moaned, then groaned, and looked at his young listeners with the saddest of sad eyes.

> I said, "Howdy, Mr. Mule. What seems to be the problem this morning?"
> Mister Mule looked at me with his sad gray eyes and said, "Oh, Jack. My master says I'm too old to be of any use to him, so tomorrow he's going to take me to the glue factory and have me made into glue."
> I said, "Mister Mule, we can't let that happen to you. I've got a great idea. I'm going to seek my fortune, and if you have a mind to, you can come too."

63

Ed stood erect, his sad eyes now wide with delight, and he marched down the imaginary road. Jack and Mister Mule were off to seek their fortune. And on that road, Jack met others—Mister Dog, and Mizzus Cat, and Mister Rooster—and they too, no longer useful to their masters, joined Jack on his adventure.

As Ed told of Jack's journey, Ed became Jack—getting inside of him —and both Ed, as the storyteller, and his young listeners saw the story unfold through Jack's eyes. As Jack encountered his new animal friends, Ed became them too—howling like a dog, purring like a cat, cackling like a rooster. He spread his rooster wings, and twitched his cat whiskers, and wagged his dog tail.

The children laughed uproariously. Through Ed's kinetic telling of this classic story, his young audience became involved—ever so wrapped up—in the tale, and the richness of our Southern Appalachian heritage continued to be preserved—and enhanced—and shared.

But Ed wasn't born in the Southern Appalachians where this tale and others of Jack's adventures have been told, and retold, by the mountain folk who have lived there for more than two centuries. Nor had he even seen these lush green mountains until 1976, when he became intrigued with the storytelling art and attended his first National Storytelling Festival. There, he met Ray Hicks—a western North Carolina farmer and herb collector who first heard the Jack tales while perched on his grandfather's knee at his family's rustic home on the slopes of Beech Mountain. Ray recounted many of the Jack tales he had learned as a child, and Ed was captivated, both by the storyteller and by his stories. Ed's penchant for storytelling and performance—an inclination that began as a child—was heightened.

Having a Protestant father from South Carolina and a Catholic mother from Pennsylvania, Ed has often said that the Mason-Dixon Line runs through his chromosomes. Yet despite the diversity in Ed's family heritage, his mother's influence prevailed. His parents settled in Philadelphia, and Ed grew up in a strict Catholic home. Storytelling— and especially performance—was always an important ingredient in his life.

"After dinner with the family, it was my Aunt Bet's job to take all of us children into the bedroom upstairs and tell us stories—usually spooky tales. Some of my cousins even called her Aunt Spooky. That was my first awareness of storytelling. But my first recollection of performing was on Sunday afternoons after dinner when the children in my family, my sisters and I, would perform—singing, playing the piano, juggling—and I vividly remember playing 'Swanee River' on a toy piano when I was six years old."

Ed's opportunities for performance expanded during elementary school when, in the third grade, he had his first experience performing before a large audience. "It was for the Saint Patrick's Day play in 1954, and when it came time to choose the cast, Sister Mary looked around the classroom and said, 'We need somebody to be in the play as the virtuous Irish shamrock grower.' Her eyes rested on me. Since I was the best reader in the class, I got the job, and that began my addiction to applause." But it wasn't until 1971, when Ed graduated from Notre Dame with a master's degree in theology, that he discovered there was a *serious* performance aspect to his life.

"I was teaching a freshman Bible class in a Catholic high school in Hartford, Connecticut. While telling my students about Jacob going to see his new bride, Rachel—how he came across the desert riding a camel—I acted out the scene, becoming Jacob, riding a camel. The kids roared with laughter, and I found myself *performing* in the classroom more and more often. I reveled in the experience, and in 1971, I re-signed my teaching job and joined the Plum Cake Players—a children's theater troupe that performed throughout New England.

"After our performances, a teacher would inevitably come up to us, her eyes glowing, with the look of someone who was giving a real compliment, and say, 'You really held their attention.' Though it was difficult to accept, I realized that holding their attention was our most important function—not artistry, entertainment, learning, but holding their attention. I decided that I could baby-sit more economically than the six-man Plum Cake Players. If six people could do it, I could do it alone, so I quit the Players and began performing solo.

"Within a month of my break with the Players, both the Players and I, as a solo act, were scheduled to perform at the same time at the same event. The Players drew everyone, the entire audience, and my show was canceled. I watched the Plum Cake Players from the back row."

Ed persisted, however, and for the next two years, from 1977 to 1979, he lived and worked as a performance artist in Hartford, honing his performance skills in street theater—a potpourri of acting, movement, improvisation, comedy, and storytelling. It was then that Ed realized that "baby-sitting" wasn't enough upon which to build a career as a performer—a storyteller. Looking back upon his visit to the National Storytelling Festival, Ed began consciously developing stories—ranging from his ever-popular Jack tales and other stories of the Southern Appalachians to religious comedy, revised fairy tales, and improvisational

storytelling. As he learned stories, he learned style—techniques borrowed from his street-theater experiences that colored his delivery and
created for him a style unique to contemporary storytelling.

Through telling "Jack and the Robbers," Ed discovered that the classic old mountain tales were successful with his audiences—especially
young audiences—because of their repetition, their strong element of
structure, and their audience-participation activities. "I found the old
tales easy to tell and easy for an audience to listen to, to appreciate and
enjoy." But more, Ed discovered the traditional Southern Appalachian
stories were perfect vehicles for his newly emerging storytelling style.
The realization came suddenly, but as the fruition of years of study and
performance.

"One day, I was sitting in my wicker chair in my apartment in Hartford, reading the story of 'Jack and the Robbers.' I looked into a mirror
and said, "Hi! I'm Jack. I want to tell you a story. . .' It was natural and
spontaneous. That was the first time I ever told a story in first person,
and since then, I've never told 'Jack and the Robbers' any other way.
For telling the story in the first person allows both the teller and the
listener to become Jack, to be there when the story unfolds.

"I also thought back to my high school teaching days and remembered how I acted out the scene of Jacob, riding a camel, going across
the desert to see his bride, Rachel. And because it seemed natural, I
began to act out 'Jack and the Robbers'—actually being Jack and his
animal friends. Because the story is acted out, it becomes more than just
an oral event; it evolves into a total experience for the listeners as they
become wrapped up in the story ever more completely."

The hallmark of Ed's unique style—spicing his stories with frequent,
often comic references to everyday life—came from those days in street
theater, out of the improvisation that usually closed his performances.
One night in Martha's Vineyard, Ed told "The Three Little Pigs"—a
simple children's tale he speckled with references to life in Martha's
Vineyard. That night, the audience—both children and adults—listened, and listened attentively, because they didn't know when they
would hear something that they knew, something important in their
lives, become a part of the story.

"As I began telling 'Jack and the Robbers' and other traditional tales,
more and more I grounded the stories in common experience. Through
frequent, usually humorous references to everyday life—to those things
we all know and understand—I bring the story home to my listeners
and create a communion between the story and the listener and all of
his experiences."

During the decade since Ed's performance in that Hartford day-care center—his first as a storyteller—his lively and highly kinetic storytelling style has won him accolades from audiences throughout the United States. Through his retelling of the classic tales, Ed breathes new life into the old stories, allowing them to be heard and seen anew, giving his listeners a new appreciation for storytelling and a realization that the art is both as old as mankind yet as contemporary as today's newspaper headlines.

Jack and the Robbers

A traditional Southern Appalachian story, "Jack and the Robbers" is the *first story Ed ever told, and more than a decade later it remains his most popular. Ed tells this classic old tale of the Southern mountains in first person, and, through Jack's eyes, he recounts the story as it unfolds. While acting out the story, Ed becomes Jack as he marches down the road to seek his fortune, and as Jack encounters his new animal friends, Ed becomes the old mule, and the floppy-eared dog, and the sad-eyed cat, and the downtrodden old rooster. Through Ed's telling, the story and its characters come to life as we, the listeners, follow in his footsteps.*

MY NAME'S Jack, and I'd like to tell you a story about the time I went out to seek my fortune.

I said to my mama, "I'm going out to seek my fortune."

She said, "You be careful, Jack. Don't talk to any strangers on the road."

I replied, "Don't worry about me, Mama. I'll be all right."

So I went down the road to seek my fortune. I had traveled about a mile or so when all of a sudden, I heard a terrible, mournful sound. "Hee-haw. Hee-haw." I turned the corner, and sure enough, standing by the side of the road, with his head hung low, was an old mule feeling sorry for himself.

I said, "Howdy, Mr. Mule. What seems to be the problem this morning?"

Mister Mule looked at me with his sad gray eyes and said, "Oh, Jack, my master says I'm too old to be of any use to him, so tomorrow, he's going to take me to the glue factory and have me made into glue."

I said, "Mister Mule, we can't let that happen to you. I've got a great idea. I'm going out to seek my fortune, and if you've a mind to, you can come too."

Well, old Mister Mule perked up his eyes, perked up his ears, and came along with me. So, now there were two of us walking down that road to seek our fortune. I was in the front, followed by the old mule. "Hee-haw. Hee-haw." We had traveled about a mile or so when all of a sudden we heard another mournful sound. "Arrh. Arrh. Arrhooooooh."

I turned the corner, and sure enough, sitting by the side of the road with his head on his paws was an old dog feeling sorry for himself.

I said, "Howdy, Mister Dog. What seems to be the problem with you this morning?"

Mister Dog looked up at me with his sad brown eyes and said, "Oh, Jack, my master says I'm too old to be of any use to him, so tomorrow, he's going to take me to the Humane Society and there ain't nothing humane about that."

I said, "Mister Dog, we can't let that happen to you. I've got a great idea. I'm going out to seek my fortune. Mister Mule is going with me, and if you've a mind to, you can come too."

Well, Mister Dog perked up his eyes, perked up his ears, and came along with us. So, now there were three of us walking down that road to seek our fortune. I was in the front, followed by Mister Mule and Mister Dog. "Hee-haw. Hee-haw. Arrh. Arrh."

We had traveled about a mile or so when all of a sudden we heard another mournful sound. "Meow. Meow. Meoooowwwww."

We turned the corner, and sure enough, sitting up in a tree was old Mizzus Cat looking down at us.

I said, "Howdy, Mizzus Cat. What seems to be the problem with you this morning?"

Mizzus Cat looked down at me with her sad green eyes and said, "Well, Jack, my master says I'm too old to be of any use to him, so tomorrow, he's going to put me in a burlap bag with some stones in it and drop me to the bottom of the river."

I said, "Mizzus Cat, we can't let that happen to you. I've got a great idea. I'm going out to seek my fortune. Mister Mule's going with me, Mister Dog's going with me, and if you've a mind to, you can come too."

Well, old Mizzus Cat jumped down from her tree and came along with us. So now there were four of us walking down that road to seek our fortune. I was in the front, followed by Mister Mule, Mister Dog, and Mizzus Cat. "Hee-haw. Hee-haw. Arrh. Arrh. Meow. Meow."

We had traveled about a mile or so when all of a sudden we heard another mournful sound. "Cock-a-doodle-boo-hoo-hoo."

We turned the corner, and sure enough, standing on a fence post by the side of the road was old Mister Rooster, feeling sorry for himself.

I said, "Howdy, Mister Rooster. What seems to be the problem with you this morning?"

Mister Rooster looked up at me with his big beady eyes and said, "Oh, Jack, my master says I'm too old to be of any use to him, so tomorrow, he's going to have rooster stew for dinner and I think I'm invited."

I said, "Mister Rooster, we can't let that happen to you. I've got a great idea. I'm going out to seek my fortune. Mister Mule's going with me, Mister Dog's going with me, Mizzus Cat's going with me, and if you've a mind to, you can come too."

Old Mister Rooster jumped off the fence post and came along with us. So, now there were five of us walking down that road to seek our fortune. I was in the front, followed by Mister Mule, Mister Dog, Mizzus Cat, and Mister Rooster. "Hee-haw. Hee-haw. Arrh. Arrh. Meow. Meow. Cock-a-doodle-ya-hoo. Cock-a-doodle-ya-hoo."

We had gone down that road about a mile or so when all of a sudden everything started getting real dark. The moss was hanging off the trees and in our faces. The path was getting smaller and smaller. And all of a sudden, we came upon an old ramshackle house by the side of the forest. We sneaked up, looked in the window, and saw on the kitchen table a pile of gold coins all the way to the ceiling.

I said to my friends, "Quick! This must be the house of some robbers who've gone back downtown to rob some more. Let's go inside to see how much money they've got."

So we sneaked around to the front door, opened it, went inside, and started counting the money. We had that money about half counted when all of a sudden we heard another mournful sound. "We are the robbers. We're very, very mean. We're the meanest robbers that you've ever seen. When we find someone that we don't like, we kick them in the stomach and we steal their bike."

I looked out the window, and coming up the path were ten of the meanest, ugliest robbers I'd ever seen in my life. The shortest one of them was eight foot eight. The tallest one was thirteen foot three and a quarter inches, and he was so mean and ugly his face looked like hamburger.

I said, "Mizzus Cat, I think we're in big trouble. Would you hide in the fireplace?" And she did.

"Mister Dog, would you hide in the cupboard?" And he did.

"Mister Mule, would you stand by the front door?" And he did.

"Mister Rooster, would you get inside the chimney?" And he did.

I stood back in the dark corner to see what would happen, and the meanest, ugliest-looking robber of all came into the shack. It was too dark for him to see anything, so he walked over to the fireplace to blow on the old embers, and he blew right into Mizzus Cat's face.

Mizzus Cat opened her eyes. And when the robber saw her eyes glowing in the dark, he figured it was the glowing embers, and he blew twice as hard. She couldn't take it any longer, so she took out her claws and went for his eyes.

Just then, Mister Dog jumped out from the cupboard and began to chew on the robber's legs. And when the robber headed for the door, Mister Mule kicked him right in the seat of his pants. Down the path he went as Mister Rooster said, "Cock-a-doodle-wooooo. Cock-a-doodle-wooooo."

The old robber gathered up his nine friends, and they kept running, and we ain't seen hide nor hair of them since.

Me and my four friends walked back inside the house, divided the money five ways, and I took my share home to my mama. We had a real good Christmas that year.

My four friends decided they'd stay at the old shack in the forest, and they went to fixing up the place, and pretty soon, they'd made themselves a real nice farm. In fact, they're still there. And if you ever get up early in the morning, you just might be able to hear old Mister Rooster.

"Cock-a-doodle-ya-hooooooo. . . ."

Doc McConnell

I like to tell stories that depict my background,
my heritage, my family, my home, and who I am and
what I stand for. For me, the stories I
tell—though borrowed from the story tradition—have
become personal experiences, and
that makes them more believable and more tellable.
People often say to me, "You're excited
about telling your stories, aren't you? You're having a
good time tellin' 'em." And I am. They're my stories
now, because to me the stories I tell could actually
have been a part of my own personal experiences.

72

* * *

Doc McConnell's eyes twinkled, he smiled a smile, though ever so slight, and took a long, deliberate puff on his pipe. "Tucker's Knob may be the coldest place on earth. Why, back in 1937, it got a hundred and sixty-five degrees below zero." There was a thoughtful pause and another long puff on his pipe. "It was so cold that sound wouldn't even travel through the air. If you went outside and said anything, you wouldn't hear a word. Just total silence. You'd have to grab a handful of words and sentences and take them in by the fire and thaw them out before you could hear what anybody said." Doc's smile turned sly, then into a wide grin that swept across his whiskered face. "And that's the truth!"

Tucker's Knob, a tiny Tennessee community in the Southern Appalachian Mountains, is a real place with real people. And to Doc McConnell, who was born there in a hand-hewn log cabin sixty years ago, telling tales was just a part of everyday life. "We had very few books. We read the Bible, and once in a while, we saw a two-day-old copy of the *Knoxville Journal* down at John Mauk's General Store. But if we wanted to be entertained and informed, we told stories." Doc, now a professional storyteller, places Tucker's Knob clearly at the heart of his mountain tall tales, lies, and yarns.

Doc's life is deep-rooted in the cultural treasures of the Southern Appalachians, and he tells the traditional mountain stories of his region. But they are tales he has personalized, given a measured dose of realism, and tailored to reflect his world as a youngster, growing up at Tucker's Knob. Although there *is* a distinction between fact and fantasy in Doc's tales, it's slight and subtle, and for his listeners—laughing uproariously at each concocted episode—it's of no importance.

For Doc, storytelling began as a child, when his father and mother told him stories, usually about the family, and he vividly remembers his mother singing old ballads and hymns while she went about her work in their mountain cabin. His childhood was filled with humor and youthful adventure.

"I remember most my dad tellin' us about his old blind horse. We heard that story time and time again and marveled at a horse so well trained he could cope with his unfortunate affliction. My mother told

73

me and my brothers, Steamer and Tom, that we should always be thankful—for our health, good food to eat, a warm place to sleep, clothes to wear, and—for our good sight. I was just a young boy then, but I thought to myself, 'If I ever went blind, I sure would be in a fix.' I thought about bein' blind, what I would do if I was ever blind, and how I would get along, especially gettin' from one place to another. So I began to memorize my environment.

"I spent hours walkin' with my eyes closed so that if I ever went blind I would be practiced up and know my way around the farm. I would walk down the bank from our house, across the road, over the stile, down through the garden, and to the chicken house—feelin' my way, my arms wavin' in front of me. I soon learned to find my way around the farm.

"One day, I closed my eyes and went down the bank from our house and I thought to myself, 'Wouldn't it be great if I could learn to run when I'm blind?' So I began to pick up speed, and I commenced to trottin' down the pasture field toward the garden and the chicken house. When I came to the fence post at the corner of the garden, I hit that post so hard that I saw stars for hours. That was the last time I ever tried to be blind."

To Doc, growing up in Tucker's Knob, entertainment meant creating the mischief and then living to *tell* about it.

"I was flyin' before most people in Tucker's Knob ever thought of it. I'd seen pictures of airplanes and read about flyin', and I had learned that for any kind of flyin' machine to actually get off the ground, it had to have wings and some wheels on the bottom. So I began to scrape around in the sheds on the farm and found a long, wide wooden board about two inches thick and probably weighin' sixty to seventy-five pounds. Nice and long and wide. I built an airplane usin' the board as wings, and I made two old homemade wooden wheels and tacked them to the bottom. I was ready for my first airplane flight.

"It took all the energy I could muster to drag my airplane across the road, down the valley, over the creek, and to the top of the highest hill on our farm. I was plannin' to take off from that hill and fly across the creek, over the valley, and land near my house—surprisin' my mother. I got astraddle that old homemade airplane with those thick, heavy wings, kicked myself off, and begun to roll down that hill. Was I thrilled! The farther down the hill I went, the faster I went. I was pickin' up speed. I was sittin' on top of that plane, holdin' on for dear life, and I thought, 'Here's my chance. I'm goin' to fly.' And finally, the plane rolled over a hump, and when it came off of that hump, there wasn't anything on that plane touchin' the ground. I was airborne. I flew fifteen, maybe eighteen inches, and suddenly, my airplane hit the ground and went tumblin' and rollin' down that hill on top of me. Before the plane came to a stop, it had knocked me out cold. That was my first airplane flight, but it ended my flyin' career."

Doc rared back to laugh, enormously pleased he'd remembered so vividly this little vignette of life at Tucker's Knob, but more, he reveled in the story's humor, its likeness to the naive adventures we've all had as children. And it's this life—the simple, carefree world he knew as a child—that has become the setting for the tales Doc tells. For Doc, storytelling has been natural, always spontaneous, even as a child. But it was a youthful exploration into a nearby town that brought him face to face with a remnant of Americana, one which eventually led him to a personal discovery of storytelling and a professional career in the art.

"As a young boy, I didn't know what was happenin' in the outside world—a world *beyond* Tucker's Knob—but occasionally, I would walk or ride a wagon two miles down the road to Surgoinsville, the nearest town. One day, I stopped at Spark Vaughn's blacksmith shop, and on the street near his shop was a medicine show. I was curious, so I slowly edged closer—through the crowd gathered there—to see the show. A man was sellin' a tooth dentifrice, a powder that not only cleaned the teeth but strengthened them.

"As I watched, a young man walked out on stage carryin' an iron bar, and as he strutted around, he flexed his muscles, showin' us his strength. He passed the iron bar among the crowd, and everyone examined it to assure themselves it was made of solid iron. Finally, he pulled a white handkerchief from his pocket, wrapped it around the bar, flexed his muscles again, and with the strength of his teeth—after usin' the good doctor's tooth dentifrice—he bent the iron bar into a U shape.

"I had never seen a medicine show before. But now that I had heard the barker's pitch, I was fascinated. I became intrigued with them—the pitchmen, the barkers—I loved their stories. And as I grew into manhood, I realized I too had a gift for gab, a fondness for showin' off, and it was natural for me to stand in front of an audience and say, 'You know, folks, I had a funny thing happen to me today...'"

Because Doc always remembered the old stories he'd heard—those he'd learned from his parents while growing up in the Southern Appalachians, tales told around the potbellied stove at John Mauk's General Store, and the chant of the medicine show barker—he never lacked for a tale to tell.

Once grown, Doc moved to nearby Rogersville, just a stone's throw

from Tucker's Knob, where he worked for twenty-one years as a maintenance director at the county hospital and, later, for the county school
system. And whenever the need arose, Doc served as emcee for the
local charity show or country music concert or talent search—for he
could always be relied upon to have a story or two to share.

Gradually, Doc became more aware of his rich cultural heritage and
the folklore of the Southern Appalachian Mountains, and in 1971, he
attended the Folklife Festival of the Smokies at Cosby, Tennessee. One
night, around a campfire, the conversation turned to medicine shows,
and those gathered there bemoaned their passing into American history.
Intrigued, Doc thought back to the old medicine shows he'd seen as a
child, and he returned home and went to work. Over the next few
months, he borrowed an old wagon, unearthed a checkered vest, a long
black coat with tails, and a top hat, brewed sassafras roots for tonic, and
began rehearsing the banter he'd heard while growing up—and Doc
re-created an old-time medicine show. He was soon extolling the virtues
of his famed Rootin' Tootin' medicine and dispensing hefty doses of
old-time medicinal mayhem—cornball stories, songs, and one-liners—
at the folk festival in Cosby and at other festivals and fairs throughout
the United States.

"Now, ladies and gentlemen," Doc proclaimed earnestly, "you've
heard of Louis Pasteur, and Jonas Salk, and the other great medical
giants of our world." His voice climbed in octaves, grew louder, more
resolute. "Well, dear friends, *now* you've heard of Doc McConnell and
his famous medical cure—my popular Rootin' Tootin' tonic." Doc
thrust forward a bottle, tightly fisted, and in a single sweeping motion,
gave the entire crowd an opportunity to see firsthand his famous bottled
healer. "It's all bound and balled together into one compound made of
roots and herbs, sparks and kerosene, morphine, golden seal and wild
cherry, buckeye and sarsaparilla, and yes sireeeee, good for *anything* that
ails ya.

"Why, my dear friends, it's even good for a lazy liver. My grandmother developed a chronic liver ailment from the day she was thirty-
three years old—a mere bride—and she lived to the ripe old age of one
hundred and three. That's seventy more happy years—thanks to my
Rootin' Tootin' tonic. She had such a good liver that on the night she
died, the undertaker had to take her liver out and beat it to death with
a stick . . . but thank goodness, we were able to save the baby."

In 1974, Doc was invited to perform his old-time medicine show at
the National Storytelling Festival, and it was then that he realized he
was not just a jokester, funnyman, pitchman—he was also a *storyteller.*

In the years that followed, Doc began telling the old traditional stories he knew, expanding beyond his medicine show wit, and today he travels around the United States spinning yarns and telling tall tales and lies from back home at Tucker's Knob.

"I like to tell stories that depict my background, my heritage, my family, my home, and who I am and what I stand for. For me, the stories I tell—though borrowed from the story tradition—have become personal experiences, and that makes them more believable and more tellable. People often say to me, 'You're excited about telling your stories, aren't you? You're having a good time tellin' 'em.' And I am. They're my stories now, because to me the stories I tell could actually have been a part of my own personal experiences."

And whether he's telling tales or reeling off his medicine show spiel, Doc is revisiting old memories, old times, old places. For his retelling of those well-traveled mountain tales seems as natural and familiar to him as sharing the stories from his own days growing up on Tucker's Knob. "Stories, good stories, survive through time. It doesn't make any difference who tells them, how often they're told, or how they're told; good stories survive."

The Snake-Bit Hoe Handle

One Saturday morning, Doc's father gave Doc and his brother Tom a sack of corn kernels and sent them to a newly plowed field to plant corn. He told the boys that when they finished their task they could "go to town"—a quick jaunt to nearby Surgoinsville or Rogersville. So Doc and Tom began their work. Row by row, Doc would dig a hole and Tom would drop in two or three grains of corn and cover them up. But soon, the two boys became impatient.

"It got to lookin' like we were goin' to be plantin' corn all day and into the night. And if we didn't finish plantin' that corn, we wouldn't get to go to town that afternoon. So ever' time me and Tom came to the end of a row, we would pitch a handful of corn into the bushes. Pretty soon, we had emptied the whole bag of corn seed. So we went to the house, cleaned up, and headed to town.

"Well, everything was fine for two weeks, but one day, Daddy hollered for me and Tom. 'You boys come out here to the corn patch. I wanna show you somethin'.' So we walked through the cornfield, and sure enough, tiny, tender, green stalks of corn were comin' out of the ground. When we got to the end of those rows of corn—where me and Tom had pitched those extra corn kernels —we saw that the end of that cornfield was standin' full of bright, green, shiny cornstalks. I bet we didn't go to town again for the rest of the summer."

It was in that same corn patch that Doc met a contrary old "copperheaded rattlesnake" in a traditional story that Doc makes his own.

WHEN I was growin' up, it seemed like all I ever done was hoe corn. I'd hoe corn from mornin' to night. One day, I was out in the field a-hoein' corn and, as I was lookin' outa the corner of one eye, there in that corn patch was a great big ol' copperheaded rattlesnake. You'd never seen such a snake in your life. He rared back at me, and I rared back at him with my hoe. I took a swing at that ol' snake, missed 'im, and hit a rock and broke the hoe outa the end of my hoe handle. That ol' rattlesnake sunk them teeth into the grain of that hoe handle and held on for dear life. Down through the cornfield we went. I would shake him awhile, and he would shake me awhile. We got clear down to the end of the corn patch before I finally shook that ol' snake offa the end of my hoe handle.

I ran to the house, throwed that ol' hoe handle down at the garden fence, and said, "Pa, you won't believe what's happened to me out there

78

in the cornfield. I jist seen the biggest snake up there on that ridge as you've ever seen. He bit my hoe handle, and I hit a rock and broke my hoe offa the end of my hoe handle, and I ain't a-goin' back into that cornfield no more."

Pa said, "Son, I know what you're a-tryin' to do. You're jist tryin' to git outa hoein' corn. You jist go out there and git that hoe handle and bring it to me and I'll put you a new hoe on the end of that handle."

Well, I went out to the garden fence and started to pick up that hoe handle, and you ain't a-goin' to believe this. Where that snake's poison had soaked into the grain of the wood of that ol' hoe handle, it had done started swellin' up. It commenced to swellin' and swellin' and swellin' from the poison until that hoe handle was as big 'round as a baseball bat—and ten feet long. I couldn't believe it.

So, I took that ol' hoe handle to show Pa and he said, "Why, we'll jist have to make some kindlin' wood outa that hoe handle. Run out and git the axe."

By the time I got back, the hoe handle had kept a-swellin' and a-swellin' and a-swellin' so that it was as big 'round as a water bucket.

Pa said, "We'll jist have to saw that ol' hoe handle up for firewood. Git the crosscut saw."

So I went over to the woodshed to git the saw, and by the time I got back, that hoe handle was as big as a wagon wheel—and over seventy-two feet long.

"Why," Pa said, "there ain't nothin' to do now but to take that hoe handle down there to the sawmill and have it sawed up for lumber."

It was so big now that we could barely git it in our wagon. And as that ol' team of mules pulled that log to the mill, that hoe handle drug a big trench right down the middle of the road.

Well, they sawed all day Friday and 'til dinner on Saturday. And when they was done, they had sawed 746,362 board feet of lumber from that ol' hoe handle. It jist kept on a-swellin' and a-swellin', and by the time we got that lumber stacked up, we had twenty-two wagonloads of lumber. We hauled that lumber home, and Pa sat out there and looked at that pile of lumber and thought and thought.

Finally on Monday mornin', he said, "You boys git outa bed. We're a-goin' to build a chicken house."

Well, we commenced to sawin' and hammerin' them boards, and when we was done, we had one of the finest chicken houses in Tucker's Knob. It was a purtty structure—twenty-two foot long, seventeen foot deep, and nine foot high in the front. We had boxes for layin', and little poles for roostin'. It was a nice-lookin' building.

And as we were standin' back admirin' our new chicken house that afternoon, Pa said, "Son, that chicken house needs one thing before we've completed our job. We need to put a good coat of paint on our new chicken house. Run and git us some paint."

So I went down to John Mauk's store and bought five gallons of the purttiest striped paint that you've ever seen. We commenced to paintin' that chicken house, and we painted way up into the evenin' 'til it was jist gittin' dusky dark. And when we finished, we stood back to admire our work, and all of a sudden, we heard this creakin' and moanin' and groanin' and that chicken house commenced to shakin' and movin' 'round.

You see, I had mixed some turpentine in that paint, and that turpentine that I'd used to thin the paint was such good medicine that it started takin' the swellin' outa that lumber. And that chicken house went to shrinkin' and shrinkin' and shrinkin'. And when it got done shrinkin', it wasn't no bigger than a shoe box. And it's a good thing we hadn't put our chickens in it, 'cause they'd ever' one been killed, I know.

The Mule Egg

Burt Christian's wife was expecting a child. Burt, one of Doc's neighbors at Tucker's Knob, called for Doc's father to find the doctor. And while he looked for the community's physician, Doc's mother, being a midwife, went to the Christian home to help deliver the baby.

"Mama and my brother Steamer walked to the Christians' house. And after the baby was born, Mama stayed with the mother and child, but she sent Steamer walkin' home by 'imself after dark. Steamer was wearin' a pair of new, big-legged corduroy knee pants.

"As Steamer walked home—through the old graveyard near the Christians' house—he got to hearin' a strange sound. But ever' time Steamer stopped walkin', the sound stopped. Then, ever' time he'd take another step, he'd hear the sound again. When he'd walk faster, the sound got faster; and when he'd walk slower, the sound got slower.

"Steamer just knew that somethin' was after 'im in that spooky ol' graveyard, so he started runnin' home—faster and faster. And the faster he ran, the faster the sound came. Steamer had gotten all the way home before he realized that the sound he was hearin' was comin' from them new, big-legged corduroy pants rubbin' together."

Doc often tells tales about Steamer—traditional stories that he personalizes, placing his older brother at the heart of the tale. In Doc's version of this traditional mountain story, Steamer buys a "mule egg" at John Mauk's General Store.

I'D LIKE to tell you a story about my brother Steamer. Now, ol' Steamer liked a lot of different things. Vienna sausage. Frog legs. Girls. Goin' to town. But best of all, he liked mules. He said that a mule was all a mountain boy should ever need.

He said, "Why, a mule'll plow all day long. He won't talk back. You can't push 'im off a bluff. He don't eat much, and he don't cost much to keep. Any man needs 'im a good mule."

Steamer would take any kind of mule.

He said, "If I could jist git me a little baby mule, I'd even take the runt of the litter. Jist a little ol' mule about twelve inches long with nice floppy ears, soft, fluffy fur, big, strong hind legs. Why, if I had me a little baby mule, I'd feed it and take care of it. And when it'd git up about waist high, I'd put my little harness on it, hook it up to my toy plow, and I'd plow ever' corn patch in Tucker's Knob."

That's all Steamer would ever talk about. He even begged Mama and Daddy to put 'im a baby mule in his sock at Christmastime.

Well, one day Steamer went down to John Mauk's General Store and begun to look around. John asked 'im, "Steamer, did ya ever find yourself a little baby mule?"

Steamer said, "No, I didn't. You don't know anybody that's got any little baby mules, do ya?"

John said, "No, I don't know nobody that's got a baby mule, but . . ."

And about that time, Steamer looked over on the shelf and saw John's shipment of big, ol', brown, round, hairy coconuts, a whole basketful of 'em. Steamer looked at them things and said, "John, what in the world are those big, ol', brown, round, hairy things over there?"

He said, "Why, Steamer, them things is mule eggs. Ain't you never seen a mule egg before?"

Steamer said, "A mule egg?"

John said, "Yeah, you know how an ol' hen sits on a hen egg and hatches out little baby chickens? Well, these old mare mules sit on them big nests full of mule eggs, and that's where you git little baby mules."

And ol' Steamer says, "Where in the world did you ever find that many?"

John said, "Well, there was an old mare mule that had a nest down there in the brier patch, and we gathered 'em up this mornin'. Folks is always askin' for a good mule egg. You need one of them mule eggs, Steamer."

"You mean I could hatch it out myself?"

John said, "Why, Lordy, yes, son. You could hatch it yourself. Jist fix yourself a little nest, and sit on that ol' mule egg for 'bout two weeks, jist like an ol' hen. But don't ever let the egg git cold. You have to keep it warm all the time, or it won't hatch. Just sit on that egg for two weeks, don't ever git offa it, and when two weeks is up, that mule egg will pop open and there'll be a little ol', hairy, long-eared baby mule jist like you've always wanted."

Well, ol' Steamer was excited. "What will you take for one of them mule eggs?"

John said, "I'd have to have thirty-five cents for one, I guess."

So ol' Steamer picked up some pop bottles and pumped a little gas for ol' John and he gave 'im one of them mule eggs. Steamer carefully carried it home and showed it to Mama.

Well, Mama went along with Steamer—helpin' 'im git an ol' tobacco basket and some straw, settin' up Steamer's nest in our woodshed behind the house.

Ol' Steamer laid that mule egg right on top of that pile of straw, climbed on top, and sat down. And Mama brought Steamer an ol' quilt because she jist knew he was a-goin' to git chilly sittin' out there in the shed for two weeks.

Well, ol' Steamer started sittin' on that ol' coconut, thinkin' it was a mule egg, and he started countin' the days. One, two, three . . . And when Steamer would git hungry, Mama would bring his meals out to 'im. Four, five, six, seven, and finally, eight days had passed. Ol' Steamer was gittin' excited 'cause it wasn't goin' to be long 'til that mule was a-goin' to hatch out and he was a-goin' to have 'im a nice, fluffy, long-eared, baby mule.

Steamer counted the days. Nine, ten, eleven, twelve, thirteen, fourteen, fifteen, and finally, eighteen days come and went. Two weeks had already passed and no baby mule. He couldn't figure out why that baby mule hadn't kicked open that shell, so he held it up to his ear to see if he could hear 'im kickin' inside. He didn't hear a sound.

Well, Steamer got mad, and out there behind that woodshed he threw that ol' mule egg as hard as he could down into the brier patch— hopin' it would bust open and, if there was a baby mule inside, it would git out.

Well, sittin' out there in that brier patch was a floppy-eared jackrabbit. And that ol' mule egg hit that jackrabbit on the side of the head, addled 'im, and that rabbit jumped from the brier patch and commenced to runnin' 'round in circles and, finally, run off across the cabbage field.

When Steamer saw that ol' floppy-eared jackrabbit, he thought it was his baby mule and commenced to chasin' it, hollerin', "Come back! Come back! I'm your mammy! And your pappy, too!"

Steamer chased that ol' jackrabbit 'til he was jist give out, and he watched 'im run over the hill and out of sight.

"Oh, go on then," yelled Steamer. "I don't want ya. I can't plow that fast nohow."

Stories of Faraway Times and Places

Laura Simms

There is a continuous wisdom that we share
with people of every culture. And for me, storytelling is
a means of experiencing this knowledge in
a powerful and entertaining manner so
we can gain a deeper, richer sense of ourselves
and the world we live in.

*   *   *

STORYTELLER Laura Simms stood alone in New York City's Bryant Park. She was preparing to tell stories. But there was no stage, no one to introduce her, and her only audience was the street people lingering around the park fountain.

"I'll tell them a funny story and go home quickly," she thought.

Then Laura looked at her audience. A bare-chested black man eating ice cream as pink as a neon light stared curiously at her. If anyone needed a story, Laura thought, he did, so instead of telling the humorous tale, she began recounting the ancient Egyptian story of "The Black Prince."

Her tale was about a lazy boy who played the flute, and who sold his soul and his flute to a magician so he could become handsome and fearless and, ultimately, marry the girl with whom he had fallen in love. In the end, he loses her, and he learns that she actually loved that foolish and ugly boy. But it is too late, for he has sold his soul.

As Laura told her story, more and more of the street people began to gather. And when it was over, the man eating the pink ice cream walked over to her.

"Are you coming back tomorrow?" he asked.

"No," she said, "I was only hired for today."

Then he whispered urgently, "Why did the boy do it?"

"When he sold his soul," Laura explained, "the magician told him that he could never change it back again."

The man looked at Laura with his piercing eyes and said, "Damn it, lady, that's like real life."

The ancient stories, shaped centuries ago in other times and cultures, preserve wisdoms that are just as relevant today as they were generations ago. For Laura, stories create a timeless bridge between each listener and his own imagination and everyone who has ever lived. While the listener often thinks of himself as listening to a story that happened a long time ago, he is actually living that story, psychologically, in the present.

"There is a continuous wisdom that we share with people of every culture. And for me, storytelling is a means of experiencing this knowledge in a powerful and entertaining manner so we can gain a deeper, richer sense of ourselves and the world we live in. As a storyteller, I'm not re-creating museum pieces. It is just the opposite. Myths and stories reveal archetypal patterns of psychological truths which are timeless, and while delving into these stories and recomposing them for performance, I am making a genuine, modern storytelling theater.

"Ever since I was a child, I have been fascinated with the meaning of life. My first memory is waking up in a stroller on the back porch and looking across the yard to a neighbor's house. I had a startling perception. Simultaneously, I saw the difference and the similarity between stars in the night sky and the lights in the windows in the distant houses. This image still haunts me. In my life, I have been searching for and feel I have found, through stories, a way of expressing two truths, seemingly opposite, at the same time: death and life, evil and good, magic and ordinary events, the inner world of the psyche and the outer world of relationships and nature. Through storytelling, they arise coemergent and dynamic as life itself.

"My life as a storyteller has been like descending into a darkened cellar or crawling into a sunlit attic or turning the corner on a city street and being in a vast space and finding unexpected treasures. I bring them into the light with words. Oftentimes, the treasure I've discovered is the most ordinary thing, or event, or person I've encountered. In the end, however, the discovery has not been as important as the serendipitous search, for the path itself is the meaning, and sometimes, when I think I have really come to some ultimate find or feel that the story is complete and understood, I tell it again, and something else pushes up out of the words and, once more, the search is awakened. The same story fascinates me anew."

Storybooks were kept in a linen closet near her bedroom, remembers Laura, recalling her childhood fascination with storytelling in her home in Brooklyn, where she was born in 1947. "I remember sneaking into the hallway at night to take a book. I loved to sit in my bed, under the covers, with a flashlight, and enter the world of the fairy tale. When I was nine or ten, I would play in my backyard, enacting long stories, making the garden my tableau. Later, in my room, when I began to write, I would compose fairy tales and true-life stories almost in a trance—for hours at a time. I would read them to my friends at school. And since I always found it hard to do my homework when I was in junior high school, my father would have to sit with me, like an anchor, for a single image from any book would set my mind off on a journey." It has always been easy to stir Laura's imagination.

After high school and college, Laura intended to pursue a master's degree in medieval literature, but she left graduate school after three days, deciding instead to return to New York City to study theater and the philosophy of art. To help pay for her studies, Laura taught theater to children. And since she didn't know very much about technique at the time, she began having her students create and act out stories.

"As a part of my class, the students presented a program in Central Park, which turned out to be shorter than expected. During intermission, the kids said to me, 'Let's keep the audience here longer. You do something.'

"I said, 'Ah, I don't have anything to do.'

"They said, 'Do a monologue. You've got to do *something*.'

"So I thought, 'I'll just go out there and see what happens.'

"As I was standing in front of the audience, I remembered a Russian fairy tale I had heard a few years earlier from a wonderful, white-haired lady in a library. I told the story in intricate detail, becoming all of the characters, and, during my performance, I realized that all of the things I had looked for in theater were happening in this single, solo performance of a story. When I returned home that night, I decided I would be a storyteller.

"At first, I mainly told stories I was writing, but I became fascinated with the power of myth and fairy tale and decided to learn about them. That detour has lasted nineteen years. It will probably last my whole life. I am reaping the fruits of my study."

Laura spent years in the library at the American Museum of Natural History, voraciously reading everything of myth and ritual, anthropology and psychology, that she could find. She attended workshops and lectures. For Laura, it became an exploration—the "process of searching, the enjoyment of discovering how dynamic that quality of being alive is, and how constantly unfolding phenomena are the realm of the storyteller." Soon, Laura was telling stories throughout New York City —at the Museum of Natural History, in the halls of the Metropolitan Museum of Art, for the Children's Aid Society, and even in the parks where often only the street people were her audiences. Wherever Laura has performed, she has seen the potency of storytelling again and again.

"Several years ago, I entered a schoolroom where I was to perform. Two boys were fighting, the teacher was enraged, and the other children were frozen at their desks. The air was thick with anger.

"The teacher asked, 'Who are you?'

"'I'm the storyteller,' I answered. Feeling a little like a doctor arriving in the emergency room, I walked slowly toward the front of the class. 'I came to tell you a story,' I said.

"The children scurried to their seats, even the two who had been fighting. And after a moment, the fidgeting settled and all eyes were focused on me. As I began to speak, the children slowly entered the world of story. Even the teacher sat down to listen. The air in the room mellowed and the anger dissolved. The children relaxed into the rhythm of the words and their own imaginative creation of the tale."

This is the magic of the story, for "whether one is listening to a contemporary tale, a family legend, or an ancient myth, the listener—child or adult—drops his self-conscious and conceptual thinking and begins to imagine. He is drawn into a more immediate form of dynamic listening. The audience is the artist.

"Between teller and listener, there is a potent connection of the minds, a connection that stimulates the listener to create the story himself from within, see characters and vivid landscapes, transparent, one upon another. It is then that the real tentacles of the story reach out and grab the listener and they become engaged at a very deep, personal level—a moment when he actually *lives* the story while he is imagining it, when he becomes so involved in the story that he ultimately forgets about me, the teller, and the story becomes his more than it is mine."

But good storytelling—and good stories—don't just happen. For Laura, good storytelling comes from the willingness to experience one's life directly, live the story, allow the images to prick, and unnerve, and excite us. And through her search—finding the essence beneath the words—good stories emerge.

"A few years ago, I went to Anquilla in the West Indies. My trip to the island was a nauseating ride aboard a rickety boat, powered by a small motor, carrying eight native merchants, a dog, and a friend. When we arrived, we passed through customs—a table that blocked a narrow doorway.

"We decided that we would walk very slowly and unobtrusively through the town and look for interesting people. We were looking for ghost stories. But because we were the only tourists to arrive that morning, every taxicab driver on the island was vying for our attention.

"'Hey! Come with me! Taxi ride! Good price! Show you things!'

"We waved them off. The best way to find a story is to happen upon one. But every taxicab in Anguilla followed us down the street. We became a parade. We were anything but unobtrusive. This was *not* the way to find a story.

"I stopped, turned around, and looked at each driver. I've always thought that I have a good intuition, so I wanted to intuitively choose one—the driver who looked the most interesting, the one who would take me somewhere and maybe tell me a great ghost story. I spotted a toothless old woman with bare feet, whose hands were knotted by arthritis. She had wild hair like Medusa. We climbed into the backseat of her cab, and she revved up her engine and took off. She never asked us where we wanted to go, but it didn't even strike us at the moment that that was odd or expensive.

"As we drove through the island, the driver suddenly came to a screeching halt, practically tumbling us off the road, and said, 'You look at that house. That house very strange. The old man in that house, one day he come downstairs and he dead.' There was a pause, and then she revved up her engine again and took off.

"Soon we came to another house—an old, dilapidated pastel-painted shack—and she said, 'This house, this house really strange. A young lady, one day wake up, then . . . dead.' And again, she took off.

"Then, inspired by my good fortune and obviously brilliant intuition, I leaned forward and said, 'Do you know any *ghost* stories? I'm looking for ghost stories—spirits, demons, corpses.'

"She said, 'Oh, yeah, coming right up.'

"And again she sped down the road, soon stopping in front of a small house. Since I have always thought it best to never ask questions in the beginning when collecting stories, but to just allow the process to evolve, we sat quietly in the backseat of the cab.

"After a few moments, she charged off down the road, farther inland, and soon we stopped at another building. Again, we sat quietly.

"As we stopped at each nondescript house or shop, it slowly dawned on us that she was giving us a tour of all of the *grocery* stores on the island.

"We jumped from the taxi. But the old woman had jacked up the price, and when I refused to pay, she took off, leaving us four miles from where our trip had begun.

"I thought at the time my trip had been futile. But to tell the truth, this story—the search for ghost stories on the island of Anguilla—is a story in itself. I didn't find what I was looking for, but I did find something else."

Laura's search for stories and her desire to understand her art form in the modern age have taken her on journeys across three continents. She has performed in theaters, schools, libraries, festivals, and conferences. But regardless of what she is telling—a true-life story or an ancient myth—she wants her stories to provoke her audience, reach into our minds and awake a treasure-house of imagination and memory that belongs to us all.

The Seal Maiden

When Laura was eleven years old, her mother—a Rumanian-born concert pianist—suffered a crippling stroke. She never played the piano again. "I would go into her room to dress her in the mornings and she would often whisper to me, 'Last night I dreamed I was running.'"

From the time Laura's mother was twenty-one years old, she wore an ankle-length sealskin coat her father had made for her. But when she became ill, she had it altered to a short jacket. Her mother died in 1969, and Laura continued to wear the jacket for ten years until it became unrepairable.

Since 1979, Laura has been telling "The Seal Maiden," an intriguing story based on an ancient Scottish legend—a classic tale about a creature, half human and half animal, who is captured against her will by a fisherman. The seal maiden marries him, but later returns to the sea.

"From the beginning, my listeners have responded very strongly to 'The Seal Maiden' because the story is so contemporary. It speaks both to the feminist who is aware of the role of women today and to anyone who has ever felt the poignancy and pain of being torn away from their childhood or caught in a situation which denies them their true inner nature. It may be couched in the language of an old story, but it speaks directly to our own experience."

Laura was recently telling stories in Nova Scotia, and while there, she wandered into a secondhand clothing store. On a lark, she went over to the sales clerk and asked, "Do you have a seal coat?"

"No," the clerk confidently replied.

But Laura turned, went to the rear of the store, and began rummaging through the clothing, and there on a rack was an ankle-length, dark-skinned seal coat selling for $20. She bought it, had it repaired and cleaned, and today, it is like new.

THERE WAS a fisherman in Northern Scotland who was the handsomest man in his village. He was a friendly man and a good fisherman, but he couldn't find a woman beautiful enough to wed. When all his friends chose wives and would spend their evenings around the hearth fire with their young brides and new families, he would row out to sea alone and dream about the woman whom he would marry.

One evening, the fisherman was rowing out much farther than he had ever gone before when he came to a strange place in the sea. The water went around in whirlpools and the full moon shed a silver path to a huge gray stone jutting out of the ocean. Then he heard an eerie sound and he saw a row of female seals swimming one behind the other. Their voices made a high-pitched ululation. One by one, they pulled themselves onto the stone and stood erect, facing the full moon.

It's an odd thing for female seals to swim alone, and the fisherman shivered at the sight of them. But what he saw next was stranger still. The seals let their sleek black skins slide from their backs, and then standing before him were the most beautiful women he had ever seen.

The fisherman dove into the water and swam, as silent as a ghost, until he looked up into their faces. "Now, here's a woman I would like to marry," he thought, looking at the maiden who stood before all the others. "What kind of a life is it to live in the sea? She would be better off as my wife." So he stole her skin and swam back to his boat. The women were unaware of him.

When the moon was high, they raised their arms above their heads and, swaying back and forth, they began to sing. Their eerie song echoed over the sea. And they sang until dawn. Then, one at a time, they pulled on their black skins and dove into the ocean, except for the one that had stood before the others. She began to search for her skin, trembling fearfully. And then she saw the fisherman, holding it in his arms.

"Give me back my skin," she cried. "I have a husband and children in the sea. What good is it to you?"

The fisherman explained that it was far better to live as a human on earth than as an animal in the sea. When she tried to throw herself off the stone, he caught her and dragged her into the boat. She shuddered. Then she sat up tall, and looking straight ahead, said not another word.

The fisherman took her to his home, and he married her in silence at the church. All the people agreed that indeed she was more beautiful than any woman they had ever seen. But, "She is strange," they whispered to each other. They noted that she never went down to the sea in the evenings to greet her husband when he returned from fishing. Nor did they smell fish cooking in her house. In fact, they rarely saw her, and the shutters of the house that faced the ocean remained closed. Yet, she seemed a good wife. She bore the fisherman seven children and they never heard him complain.

Years passed and the village people grew accustomed to her and soon forgot about her strange ways. The fisherman himself was certain that she was happy with her life and had forgotten her years in the sea. And perhaps she had.

When all but one of the children had grown, their father took them traveling. The youngest girl was left at home with her mother. At first, during his absence, the fisherman's wife did everything that she always did. But late in the afternoon, she grew restless. She longed to smell the sea. So, she threw open the shutters that faced the ocean and breathed deep the cool, fresh sea air. Tears fell from her eyes.

Her little girl said, "Mother, I have never seen you so sad. Why do you weep?"

She said softly, "My daughter, I weep because I lost something that I loved. Once, I was walking by the shore and I found a thick, dark skin of a seal in the moonlight. I took it home to make boots and gloves for you and your brothers and sisters. But I cannot find the skin."

The little girl took hold of her mother's hand. "I know where it is. Sometimes at night, father comes into the room when he thinks I am sleeping. He pulls back a board in the ceiling and takes into his arms the skin of a seal. He sits by the candlelight and quietly caresses it. Mother, it smells of the sea."

"Show it to me."

She went into her daughter's room, and the little girl brought a chair and set it beside her bed. The seal maiden stood on the chair and drew back the board in the ceiling. Then, she took her own skin in her arms and held it to her breast, and it smelled like the sea.

The little girl, smiling, climbed into the bed with her mother seated beside her. The seal maiden drew the blanket close to her daughter's chin and kissed her tenderly, saying, "You must never forget that I love you and your brothers and sisters with all my heart." And the little girl closed her eyes.

The seal maiden told her daughter story after story about the lives of the seals in the sea. And just as the little girl drifted into sleep, she whispered, "If ever you wake and find me gone, do not be sad. Go down to the shore and watch how the seals cavort and play among themselves. And should you be lonely, go to the shore on a full-moon night and listen to the sound of the female seals and be comforted."

Waiting until the little girl was fast asleep, the seal maiden went outside for a walk. And as she walked, she turned down toward the sea. In truth, she did not intend to leave that night, but when she put her feet in the water, it was so cool and so familiar that the seal maiden could not help herself. There was a full moon in the night sky and in the distance she could hear the silkies cry. So she drew on her skin and dove into the sea.

As she touched the water, she heard her daughter's footsteps on the sand and her voice call out, "Mother, wait for me."

But it was too late.

When the fisherman returned, his wife and daughter were gone. He knew what had happened, for the skin was missing from the ceiling and the house was unbearably silent. Night after night, he went down to the shore and waited for the seals, hoping they would return. But no seals came to that beach ever again.

The children grew and married. They moved away from their father's house and begged him to go away with them. But the fisherman wouldn't leave. He always hoped that his wife and child would come back. They never did, and he grew old alone.

At first the villagers tried to comfort the fisherman and bring him to their homes, to their families. But the old man wanted to be by himself. He spent his hours thinking about the past.

Late one spring, on a full-moon night, the fisherman rowed out to sea. He rowed slowly and painstakingly until he could no longer see the hills of his village or the wooden houses in the distance. He rowed farther and farther until he came to that strange place again where the water went around in whirlpools and the moon shed a silver path along the water to a huge gray stone.

He waited and they appeared: a line of female seals swimming in the moonlight, incanting their uncanny song. Just as before, they climbed upon the stone, took down their skins, and faced the moon, swaying their arms aloft, singing.

He was an old man now. His face was wrinkled and his body was weary. But he swam, as silent as a cloud, to the edge of the stone and looked upon his wife's face. She was as young as the day he had first seen her.

"I'm an old man," he said. "Won't you come back and live with me until I die?"

The seal maiden answered, "Did I not bear you seven children? Did I not love you as best I could? I told you my life is in the sea."

The fisherman swam slowly back to his boat and rowed home. They say that he died soon after that, alone. Some say the daughter died the night she tried to follow her mother into the sea. Others say that she ran away and lived alone somewhere in Scotland. And still others say that the seals took care of her, and it was her song you could hear on a full-moon night.

Savitri

One night when Laura was telling stories, a friend, who had suffered the tragic death of her young husband, came to hear her. Laura wanted to tell something special for her friend, but the only story that came to her mind was "Savitri"—a North Indian tale about a young princess who, through her love and devotion, brings her husband back from death.

"At first, I thought I couldn't tell 'Savitri,' for though the story was beautiful and I enjoyed the teachings woven into it, the tale seemed untrue. People don't return from the dead, and perhaps telling the story could cause my friend even greater sorrow. But for me, intuition is often more intelligent than logic, so I told the story of 'Savitri.' At the close of the program, my friend beamed with happiness. She reminded me that, indeed, the story of 'Savitri' is true, for she knew that death is real, and yet, even in death, there is continuous life, vivid and intimate and invisible."

Laura enjoys telling "Savitri," for the story embodies a quest for true knowledge. "Just as Savitri follows the Lord of Death to bring her husband back to life, so can we, through stories, journey far into the frontier of our own spirit to reawaken genuine goodness and revitalize our lives."

IN INDIA, there was a king named Asvapati, which means Lord of Horses. He was a great ruler whose country and subjects flourished. In his kingdom, there was peace and happiness. However, he and his queen had no child. So, there was no heir to the throne.

For many years, Asvapati and his wife prayed intensely for a son. Then, they repeated the mantra of the Goddess Savitri one hundred thousand times and asked for her aid, for she was the "stimulator of energy, the bestower of long life," and one of the consorts of the Great Lord Brahma, Lord of Knowledge.

At last, their prayers were answered and the queen became pregnant and soon gave birth to a girl. In appreciation of the goddess, they named the child Savitri. And as she grew up, she equaled her name. She was graceful and beautiful and she excelled in goodness and intelligence. The young woman's accomplishments were such that no young man came to ask for her hand in marriage because each feared that she was a goddess incarnate.

Thus, one day the king called his daughter to his court and told her to go out into the world and find a husband.

"How will I know if a man is worthy to be king?" asked his daughter. Asvapati answered, "The man you choose must seem as good to you as you are to me. You shall know."

So, Savitri left the kingdom with her courtiers and a trusted minister to find herself a husband.

Many months passed. Savitri traveled far. Then, one day she returned. Her face was glowing with a mixture of shyness and excitement. The king was sitting in his court discoursing with the sage Nerada. Nerada was renowned for his realizations and yogic feats. He was said to know the past, the present, and the future.

"I can see from your face that you have made a choice," said her father happily.

Savitri answered, "I have found the man who will be my husband. His name is Satyavan." She paused. "I did not meet him in a palace. I met him in a forest hermitage. He is living with his father and mother. His father is a great king named Dumyatsen.

"The old man was blinded by a strange accident at the time of his son's birth, and an enemy took advantage of him and defeated his kingdom. He is in exile. Satyavan cares for his father and mother."

The sage Nerada stood up. "Your daughter has chosen well. Satyavan is the son of the king of Salwa. He is brilliant and accomplished. The young man is unequaled in strength and grace and generosity." At these words, Savitri smiled with pleasure. Then, Nerada said, "But she must choose another, for it is destined that Satyavan will die in one year."

Savitri trembled, but standing tall, she looked calmly at her father and the sage and said, "I can think of no one else as my husband. I will marry Satyavan, for my mind is made up. You have taught me that time is nothing at all. What is one week, or one year, or one lifetime, if you love truly?"

Pleased with her answer, Nerada said to the king, "Your daughter's love is stronger than Death. Let her marry Satyavan."

King Dumyatsen at first denied his son's marriage to Savitri. He told Asvapati that the life in a hermitage was lonely and difficult, that a princess would not be happy living in the forest. But Savitri's father simply stated that his daughter would marry no one but Satyavan, and the blind king admitted that indeed his son had said he would marry no other.

The wedding was held in the hermitage. Savitri took off her jeweled crown, her golden bracelets, and her silken robes. But in truth, Satyavan and Savitri knew wealth in their love. Every day they grew to know each other better and they experienced supreme joy. As a wife, Savitri

was generous and dutiful. She helped care for Satyavan's parents without hesitation. As a husband, Satyavan was devoted and kind. Their
days in the forest were happy.

But beneath her happiness, Savitri was sorrowful, for she alone knew
that with each day her husband's life grew shorter. So when it was four
days before his destined death, Savitri began to fast and meditate without interruption. Satyavan respected her wishes to give thanks to the
goddess who had brought them such joy, but he looked forward to the
end of her four days of austerities.

On the fourth morning, Satyavan said he would go out and gather
fruit and chop wood to build a fire now that her fast was nearly ended.
As he set off for the forest alone, his wife said, "Let me go with you. I
am refreshed by my devotion and would like to walk among the trees."
She had never asked for anything before, so the old king and queen and
their son, who all feared she was too weak to travel, granted her wish.

Satyavan walked cheerfully, pointing out all the new blossoms in the
forest. Savitri walked beside him silently. She never took her eyes off his
face. They gathered fruits, and then stopped to chop wood. She sat on
the ground and watched her young and virile husband wield an axe.
And the sound of the axe echoed among the trees.

Suddenly, the axe fell from his hands. "I have a headache," he said.
Fighting back her tears, Savitri whispered, "Put your head on my knees
and rest. It will pass." And he lay down and closed his eyes. She gently
caressed him as the color faded slowly from his face.

As she comforted him, she felt a presence, and looking up, she saw
standing before her a tall figure dressed in red. His hair was tied in a
topknot. And in his right hand he held a noose.

"Who are you and what do you want?" she asked.

"Young woman, you must be extraordinarily sensitive to see me. Few
see me and fewer less speak to me, although everyone knows who I am.
My name is Yama. I am Lord of Death."

"Why did you come? Don't you usually send your messengers?"

Yama answered, "Your husband's nature is possessed of such goodness
that I came myself."

Then the Lord of Death took his noose and extracted the life essence
from Satyavan, and turning, began to walk south. Savitri lifted up her
husband's head and set his body carefully on the earth. Then, she
turned and quickly walked after Death.

"Young woman," he said, "the living do not go where I am going. You
must prepare a funeral for your husband. Turn around. Follow me no
farther."

"I go where my husband goes," answered Savitri. "Sir, is it not true that a wife can be faithful to her husband even after he is dead?"

Yama stopped and shook his head. "Yes. Even after death a wife can be faithful. But you cannot enter the land of the dead." He grew thoughtful. "You are interesting. What you say pleases me. I will grant you one boon, but ask not for the life of your husband and follow me no farther."

"Could you return the eyesight of my father-in-law?"

"It is done," spoke Death, and he continued walking south. But Savitri followed after him.

"It is cold where I am going. Go no farther," he commanded.

"Excuse me for my disobedience, but it is so rare to have the opportunity to speak to someone of your virtue. May I not ask you several questions?"

Yama was pleased. "Ask me your questions."

"Sir, you are Lord of Death. Does that not mean that you are Lord of Life as well?"

"Yes, I am Lord of Life. You speak well. So many misunderstand and see me as evil."

She continued, "I have often thought about the true nature of compassion. Most people consider that one should be kind only to one's friends and family. But does not true compassion mean that one is kind even to one's enemies?"

"If this truth were understood, great happiness would be felt among people," he said. "You speak intelligently. Ask for one more boon, but ask not for the life of your husband."

So Savitri requested that her father-in-law's kingdom be returned to him, and Yama agreed. Then, Death turned and walked south again. And once again, Savitri followed behind him.

"Young woman, you will tire quickly. You cannot follow me."

"It is so hard to turn and leave when I can partake of the feast of your knowledge."

And Yama was pleased again and listened to her questions. They stood and talked for a long time. Yama answered many of her questions, and he was content with her knowledge and offered her one more boon.

"My father and mother wanted a son but had none. Would you grant me fifteen sons in my lifetime?"

"Certainly," he replied. "You shall have fifteen valiant and strong sons. But you have come too far. You must turn back."

This time, she followed his instructions and did not move any closer. However, she called after him. And he stopped again. "Your voice is beautiful," said Yama. "It is hard to resist you. I revere your understanding. Yet, have I not answered all your questions or do you desire one more boon?"

"Sir, did you not say that a wife can be faithful to her husband even after death? And if that be so, I ask you to return my husband's life so that I can give birth to fifteen sons."

And the Lord of Death smiled and did what he had never done before: he gave back life, the life of Satyavan. Savitri bowed low before him, touching all seven places of her body on the earth in gratitude, knowing that her love and devotion had won back her husband's life.

Swiftly she returned to the clearing and held Satyavan's head on her lap, and as she caressed him, slowly the color came back to his face.

He awoke startled, for it had begun to grow dark. "I slept so long. I am feeling better. We had best return to my parents quickly or they will think something has happened to us. I had a strange dream. I saw Yama standing beside me."

Savitri said, "The dream has come and gone." They walked home through the forest.

In the meantime, the eyesight of the king of Salwa miraculously returned. His blindness was cured. And not long after that, messengers came to tell him that his enemies were vanquished and he could return to his kingdom. The days of hermitage were gone, and he took this as an auspicious sign that Savitri and his son were in no danger.

At long last, when the couple returned, Dumyatsen and his venerable wife asked, "What took you so long?"

And Savitri answered, "We journeyed much farther than we expected."

Gioia Timpanelli

Stories are being returned to the adult world,
not as an archaic literature, but as something significant,
enduring, from which we recognize things we dimly saw
before but did not name . . . yet the analysis
of our stories must not be too rigid. For if it is,
we run the risk of not meeting the story—and its life—
directly, of not continuing our journey,
never meeting the deer unexpectedly in the pine forest,
never praising the mountain for itself.

FOR MORE than twenty years, Gioia Timpanelli has told stories—
tales learned from an oral tradition, deeply rooted in ancient
Europe, and those she has written or re-created from aged written texts. Her pursuit of both the oral, collective tale and the
written, literary story has been the foundation of her storytelling career.
Considered by many as the dean of America's professional storytellers,
Gioia was born in 1936 in New York City and grew up with her Sicilian
grandparents and English-speaking parents in a Jewish-Italian neighborhood. Since childhood, she has shared both the oral and literary traditions.

"I have always considered myself fortunate to be born into a family
that spanned three living generations, two countries, two cultures, and
two East Coast landscapes—the ocean and the mountain foothills. And
although my grandparents spoke and wrote Italian and lived in an
American neighborhood, they preferred to speak Sicilian at home. As a
child, I was surrounded by a rich body of traditional stories and songs
that everyone in my family knew—stories and songs I learned in Sicilian from each of them.

"When asked, my mother told me stories of her life as a child, of her
days working at Hattie Carnegie, and my father—who still sings ballads—read to me and created adventure tales every night. My father's
brother, my godfather Alphonse, loves music, and opera, and had memorized as a child in Sicily long Sicilian poems and, even today, can tell
dramatically any number of narratives. Then there is my Aunt Frances,
who was like a mother to me and told me stories of her grandmother,
Alice Lamb, and her own childhood growing up in Baltimore, and my
Uncle Salvatore who retold folktales about San Pietru learned from my
great-grandmother, and my Aunt Connie who remembers vividly the
way our neighborhood was before the land was all eaten up, and the last
great vegetable farms gave way to concrete, and a stretch of sandy race-
track became endless row houses.

"Much of my childhood was spent visiting with Nanna Filippa, my
great-grandmother, and my grand-aunts and -uncles who lived in a large
and comfortable house where an ancient clock chimed on the hour and
where, on feast days, the entire family sat around a large dining room

table covered with handspun linen and set with old china, and where marvelous Sicilian dinners were served. It was here that my family celebrated the great feasts of the year and where I heard my first Sicilian fairy tale—a story told to me by my youngest aunt, La Zia Mariuzza. The tale was a mysterious story like nothing I had ever heard, and even today, I can still hear my aunt's voice and remember the delight on her face when the story was happily resolved—as if it had just happened.

"For you see, in my family, it was natural to tell stories. It was never considered an art. No one ever said, 'Let's continue this tradition.' It was just a part of the ordinary business of life."

As Gioia soaked in the stories, the tales that surrounded and enchanted her, Gioia's mother taught her to read English as a game in front of the fireplace. At five, her grandfather read her Dante. And soon, Gioia was reading stories and creating long, rambling praise poems to her cat while the two of them sat under the dining room table and later, in school, falling in love with the old poets and their poetry and memorizing poems for her teachers. Gioia developed early an appreciation for language, literature, and books, and there emerged within her a natural penchant for the literary, the lettered world.

"When I was fourteen and a student at Hunter College High School, I spent the afternoons after school in the quiet rooms of the museums of New York City. One day, while at the Frick looking at a Vermeer painting, all of a sudden I noticed for the first time the way Vermeer had painted a string of pearls. I was awestruck. What drew me to the painting was not its beauty, nor its meaning, but how Vermeer painted the pearls. It was the doing of it, the form being a true partner of creation, that interested me, excited me.

"Later, while I was in college, I studied English literature—reading poems and stories, studying their possible meanings, learning more about the different forms and styles that were being created and re-created. I became fascinated with the great writers, philosophers and scholars, critics, and brilliant thinkers—those who plant seeds and reap, those who illuminate and show ways of seeing and appreciating, those who create new ideas and ways of thinking, those who add to the possibilities. I was inspired to read, and read carefully, and appreciate differences."

Gioia graduated in 1957 from New York University with a degree in English and, a year later, earned a master's degree in English language and literature from the University of Michigan. But she didn't pursue a doctorate degree and a career in college teaching as she had intended. Instead, Gioia became inspired by the masters whose works she admired as a child and, later, through a course in drawing with respected artist Philip Guston, and she turned to painting as the potential form for her creativity. Gioia returned to New York City to study art, and to support her work, she began teaching English in a secondary school in the city. Within a few years, however, she was asked to audition for a job as host of a program on New York City's educational television system, and Gioia found a new forum for her artistic expression.

In the twelve years that followed, Gioia's career in television challenged her creative spirit. While she had learned form through art, her new pursuit forced her to create, to shape, to make something with form in words and pictures. She wrote, produced, and presented one program a week. The result was seven complete series. One of the seven, *Stories from My House,* was devoted to storytelling, and for the first time, Gioia told stories—recounting tales of many times and cultures, giving the stories new life in the world of the electronic media. The series won two Emmy citations.

Then, in 1975, with New York City facing economic peril, the television station's production department was closed. All programs were canceled, the crew disbanded, and Gioia was without a job. Her colleagues at the station returned to teaching and secure salaries, but Gioia continued to tell stories—recapturing the tales she had heard as a child and recounting those she had created from her lettered world. She became one of America's first full-time professional free-lance storytellers, and she began to travel through the United States performing to adult audiences at colleges, festivals, art galleries, and museums—wherever there were those eager to hear stories.

Many of the tales Gioia tells come from her childhood, from her experiences growing up amid a loving, devoted family and hearing tales of people and places in faraway Sicily. Gioia remembers sitting on the sun porch after school with her grandmother as she told stories, describing their ancestral home in such detail that Gioia could "walk" through the village as her grandmother recounted the tale. Gioia carried a topographical map of the town in her mind, and as the story was being told, she could see her ancestral home as if she had lived there, grown up there.

"I was once asked to tell stories at an Italian folk concert at Hunter College in New York City. Everyone sat on folding chairs in neat rows, and most of the audience were older people who had come from the far reaches of the city to hear and experience once again some of their old songs. I decided that it might be my only chance to tell the story of the Madonna from my town.

"I began the story in Sicilian, and finding that most people understood me, I told the story in my native language, using English only at crucial moments. For me, at the heart of the story is the place, that sacred place, where the story ends, and although I had never mentioned my town by name, I described the topography in minute detail.

"Suddenly a man in the audience jumped up, threw out his arms, and spoke to me in Sicilian in an excited voice. 'Where are you from?' he asked. 'No, I know! I know! You're from Pietraperzia! Dear sister! Dear sister! I'm from Barrafranca!' The next town, just a few miles away from my ancestral home. We embraced. The story had brought us home. .

"But sometimes, telling stories involves hard work and serious study —searching out journals and books and references. For me, it's a marvelous journey. There's nothing more exciting, more playful, than questioning and coming up with possibilities—not rigid answers but views which make further study possible.

"I remember the joyous afternoons I spent searching after word meanings with my grandfather, returning again and again to the encyclopedias and reference books and dictionaries that he had brought from Sicily. In our home, and later at my godfather's, there were never many discussions that didn't send us to look up something in books. Even today, I revel in the marvelous study of stories, and I search our old tales until I either can go no further, or I am satisfied for the moment.

"But most of all I go back to the story, for it's the bringing of life to a story, whether it's old or new, oral or written, that I love. Whenever I'm retelling tales from my tradition or those from other times and cultures, I always follow the bones of the story—the essential narrative as it was given to me—and then I compose an extempore piece of prose, using rhythm and language that I can create at the moment that best carries the story's images and sounds. In this way, I hope the old story is alive for us today.

"Telling the story extemporaneously means that I never tell it in the same way twice. While I do repeat certain phrases, there is no fixed text, and no matter how many times I tell a story, it is always a challenge for me to create it again. This process comes naturally to me: the oral composing within the limits of form. It feels right.

"When a story is told in an alive, present way, it's always more than we can completely understand. For the story's base is life itself, something which cannot be explained away or reduced to labels. If the old stories, rich in their meanings and simple in their structure, teach anything, it is usually something we felt we knew already, but the story has reminded us in such a splendid way."

Today, Gioia is writing most of her stories—usually about growing up in her old Jewish-Italian neighborhood, about people, and places, and animals. For these stories, one doesn't have to know many languages, gather bibliographies, or go to many lectures. One only has to discover what is already known. When one tells a story about one's family, one goes to one's roots, one's beginnings, and when one tells a tale about fox or coyote or owl, one goes to the fox or coyote or owl. And they will tell you a great deal about themselves, their relatives, about their essential stories.

"To me, one of the great joys of storytelling is how truly universal the stories are and, at the same time, how specific to culture, language, and place they can be. To some, this might appear a statement of opposites. To me, it is not. It's the very essence, the very heart of storytelling. I will never forget hearing Reuven Gold tell Hasidic tales. Though these stories do not appear to be a part of my background, my culture, I found in his marvelous tales a kinship, a haven—something I immediately recognized and loved.

"Stories are being returned to the adult world, not as an archaic literature, but as something significant, enduring, from which we recognize things we dimly saw before but did not name . . . yet the analysis of our stories must not be too rigid. For if it is, we run the risk of not meeting the story—and its life—directly, of not continuing our journey, never meeting the deer unexpectedly in the pine forest, never praising the mountain for itself.

"For me, sharing both the world of the oral tradition and the world of our written literature is a journey. One represents the more difficult journey, the constant, unknown searching in stories, and the other, the understanding and knowledge we already have within us without leaving home."

The Unwilling Magician

Gioia had been telling stories professionally for only a short time when Uncle Alphonse, her godfather and a physician and clinical professor, came to see her perform. After the program, he rushed up to her, beaming with joy, clasping her hands in his.

"You're just like La Nanna Angelina," he told her. "She told stories in our town in Italy, and people from throughout the village came to hear her. She'd gather everybody around and tell stories on winter evenings."

He paused briefly. "You know," he said, "it's just in the genes."

La Nanna Angelina was Gioia's great-grandmother, a woman she never met but one who passed on to her the love of stories and a treasure-house of tales handed down, generation to generation. Throughout her life, Gioia has shared La Nanna Angelina's destiny with stories.

"For years, people have told stories about everything they have done, experienced, wished for, understood. Some are retold, some are not, and some are still not accessible to us. Some are simply waiting for someone to search for them, bring them to light."

On a warm spring afternoon, Gioia and Elizabeth Kelly, a friend and artist, heard the Venerable Bardor Tulku Rinpoche tell stories—first in Tibetan, then translated into English. From a recording of the Rinpoche's telling, Gioia wrote this delightful version of an ancient Tibetan tale, and it appears in Tales from the Roof of the World— a collection of Tibetan stories.

ONCE UPON a time, a long time ago, there lived at the top of the world a king and his sister, a wise princess. Their palace was so magnificent that strangers traveled from faraway places to get just a glimpse of it. Now it happened that a foreign merchant was passing through their land, and since he had finished his business, he decided to visit the royal palace. It was one of those very hot days when two suns seemed to be shining, and the merchant soon tired of walking through the palace's public gardens. He found himself a quiet, cool spot off the path, where the low branches of a large willow tree made a hidden bed for him just right for a short nap.

While the merchant slept, the king's own chef stepped out into the courtyard. Like many important people, he was absorbed in his work, which he set about doing in his usual quick and skillful manner. The clanging of the great pan and the sizzling of the yak butter startled the merchant awake, and in his lackadaisical way he watched the chef make pancake after pancake after pancake.

Hmmm, what a splendid meal someone is going to have, the merchant thought. How I wish I could have just one of those pancakes.

When he saw the last pancake cooking, the scraped bowl being cleaned, and all the signs of a job almost finished, the merchant knew he had better act quickly before cook, pan, and stack of lovely pancakes disappeared forever. So he quickly left his hiding place under the willow and carefully crawled behind two sallow thorn bushes until he was out of the cook's sight. Then he straightened up and walked back to the courtyard, where the chef was just checking the last pancake in the pan.

"Aha. Greetings, honored sir. What is this splendid aroma that fills the air?" asked the merchant in a cheerful voice.

"You smell the king's lunch, merchant. Your nose is your guide, I see, and our pancakes must be especially pleasing to you, for they have pulled you a long way from the visitors' gardens into the royal quarters."

"Yes, it is true that the aroma is especially enchanting, and now that I see the pancakes are made by the royal chef himself, I understand better my nose's boldness. But do you think, kind sir, that my noisy stomach might join in this dialogue?"

"Well, it depends. I tell you what. I will give you this last pancake here in the pan if you can tell me the exact number of pancakes I have cooked," said the chef with a sly smile.

"I believe you have just made fifty-nine pancakes—that is, not counting my kurta, which is now in the pan. With that one it would be sixty," replied the merchant with confidence.

"That is incredible," said the chef. "You could not have known that by guessing, for I have many empty pans and covered plates here. How do you do it?"

The merchant smiled. (Or was it his stomach that smiled?) Without saying another word, he held out his hand, and the chef, shaking his head and laughing, handed over the last pancake to him. And it was as good as it smelled.

Now the chef went inside and announced to all in the kitchen that he had just met a merchant with magical powers. Everyone knows how these rumors travel: from kitchen to stairwell to room after room up to the top story until...

"A true seer for sure," reported a minister importantly into the king's ear an hour later. (The princess had already been discussing the matter with interest for a full half hour.)

"A clairvoyant happens to be just what we need—a magical person who can see where my great turquoise is right at this moment. This merchant is exactly the person to find the missing treasure."

So the king sent some ministers to find the merchant, and when they found him with bag in hand ready to leave the kingdom, they said:

"Our king asks you to find his lost turquoise. To encourage you in your pursuit, he asks us to tell you that if you choose not to help him, you will be brought to court, where we will be forced to sit in judgment over you. You have until tomorrow morning to tell us where the stone is hidden. Do not hesitate to call on us at any hour of the night."

And after saying this, they put him into a bedroom, shut the door, and left him there alone with his fear.

The poor man could not sleep. He could not think how to get out of this terrible situation. He paced back and forth. Finally, at four in the morning, he reached the darkest place in his heart, and in despair he called out his father's name:

"Ohhhh, Wahsa, Wahsa, Wahsa. Where are you? Wahsa, Wahsa, Wahsa . . ."

Over and over he called, for just saying his good father's name brought him some comfort.

"Wahsa, Wahsa, Wahsa . . ."

One of the king's ministers, who had also been unable to sleep, crept up to the merchant's door just in time to hear "Wahsa, Wahsa, Wahsa . . ." said in such a strange and terrifying tone that the minister shook with fear, for it was his name that the merchant was calling over and over like that.

"He has found me out. The seer has found me out," moaned the minister. And he did the only thing he could do.

"Your Excellency," he cried to the merchant, "you are right. It is I, Wahsa, who has stolen the king's turquoise. If I give it back to you right now, please do not say that I am a thief. I have never stolen before, and I have learned a bitter lesson and promise you I have learned it forever."

"Well, well, I am glad you have come forth, Wahsa. I will return the turquoise to the king and see that you are not blamed."

Now it was impossible to keep word of the merchant's powers within the palace. It spread throughout the countryside, and soon the story of the merchant and his special powers was on everyone's lips.

Not long after this it was discovered that the king's own horse was missing from its paddock. A messenger was sent immediately to the merchant's quarters, and once again he was commanded to use his exceptional powers to see exactly where the horse had been taken. The poor man could not believe he would be so lucky this time, and he sadly lamented his new reputation. This time he became ill with worry and again could not sleep. In the dark of the night he arose and went to the narrow window and looked out over the moonlit fields. There, to his surprise, were not one, not two, but three moving shadows coming closer and closer to the house.

"Could it be that the net of fear has caught three thieves?" And with that thought the merchant threw down from his window handfuls of small white feathers onto the hunched forms looking in his first-story window.

The next day the merchant called for a large gathering of all the people living in the countryside thereabouts. Everyone was ordered to attend, and when he spied his tiny feathers lodged in the creases of two sheepskin coats and one fox-skin hat, he knew who the thieves were.

"Here are the thieves," called out the merchant, pointing to the three.

Thus accused by the supposed seer, the thieves panicked and confessed, and soon the beautiful horse was back in its place. After many appreciative words from the king, the weary merchant went home.

By now the merchant was the king's own psychic. Not long afterward, a traveling caravan lost all its donkeys.

This time I am done for, thought the merchant. Certainly the thieves will not find me again, so this time I shall run away from all this. Running away is the only way to save myself.

And with hardly more than the clothes on his back, the poor man left in the cold, dark night. As luck would have it, on the very same lonely road the merchant saw a man ahead of him also traveling at great speed.

Since I am alone, the merchant thought, and that man ahead of me is also leaving the kingdom at this late hour, it would be good for us to travel together.

With this in mind, the merchant hurried along the dark road to catch up with the unknown man. But the man, without looking behind him, heard the sound of hurrying footsteps and hurried all the more. Now the merchant started to run and call out. At this, the traveler, who was indeed the donkey thief, stopped in great fear, believing himself caught.

"Please, please," begged the thief, walking toward the merchant. "If I show where I've hidden the donkeys on this road, will you please let me go?"

Now the donkeys of the foreign caravan were returned, and the merchant's good deeds in the service of all the people were loudly proclaimed. His fame spread, and his reputation was now solid as stone. So when the wise princess asked to meet the merchant, and when the king, her brother, announced the wedding of the Great Princess and the Wizard Merchant, no one in the kingdom was surprised in the least. There was only the wonderful wedding feast to go to, and the *chung* and *ara* to drink, and plenty of *kurta* to eat.

The merchant himself had a wonderful time, drinking a good deal of *chung* wine. And at the time when he forgot how many cupfuls he had already drunk, and when it was past the time to wonder whether he should drink another cupful, he began to sing in a loud voice.

At first the princess laughed. He was so spirited. Before, she had seen him only in a serious mood, and this was a nice surprise. But then she listened more carefully to the words of the song he was composing as the spirit moved him:

> I am a lucky man
> Who has no magic plan.
> Count pancakes from a tree,
> You'll see what I can see.
> I found the names the same,
> Then feathers brought me fame.
> Caught a thief ahead of me.
> That's all that I can see.

The princess understood all, while the others laughed.

Is that so? she mused. We shall see what you know and what you don't know. And she whispered her findings to the king, who immediately called the ministers, who immediately called the merchant, who on hearing he was up for trial again, immediately became sober.

Now the princess and her brother devised a clever trial for the merchant. They put a bee inside five silken scarves and placed it inside the thickest pot in the land and then placed it before the merchant.

"What is inside this pot?" the princess urged.

"Hurry," ordered the king.

And remembering his dear mother, who, when she caught him in mischief, called him Buzzing Bee, the merchant sang out.

> Little Buzzing Bee,
> All is lost for thee.
> Little Buzzing Bee,
> Nothing can you see.

"What?" cried the king.

"Ah, is that so," said the princess.

"Yes."

"Yes."

"Yes," sang out the ministers. "There is a bee inside."

"Thank you, dear Mother," muttered the merchant to himself. And so, of course, the poor merchant married the princess, and I heard that the sun of happiness shone on the mountaintop and that the staff of misery was washed away in the river.

Diane Wolkstein

Stories let us peep into the cracks of life,
the invisible things, the thoughts within thoughts, those
things that go by so quickly we don't even
realize them. During the telling, those little cracks often
open up. As a person, I see with two eyes,
but as a storyteller, I have the possibilities of seeing with
hundreds of eyes, the eyes of all who are
listening and perceiving.

FOR GENERATIONS, children as well as adults have treasured the stories of Danish writer Hans Christian Andersen. During the 1950s, Baroness Alma Dahlerup, who knew Andersen when she was a child, conceived the idea of erecting a statue to him in New York City's Central Park. Through her efforts, children throughout the world contributed pennies and shillings to help. Ida-Gro Dahlerup, the baroness's daughter, suggested surrounding the statue with benches so that stories, both Danish and American, could be told. And in 1956, the statue of Hans Christian Andersen was unveiled.

For twenty-one years, Diane Wolkstein—a professional storyteller living in New York City—has told stories at Andersen's statue on Saturday mornings from June to October. "For me, this haven of magic binds children and parents together, year after year, if only for an hour each summer Saturday." Thousands have heard Diane's renditions of Andersen's treasured tales, told and retold in the shadow of his statue, and each year her listeners return to savor again the stories and the telling.

Diane was born in 1942 in Maplewood, New Jersey, and she remembers her first childhood fascination and wonder with storytelling. She was seven, her brother, Martin, two. At night, Diane's mother would tell stories about what happened during the day when Martin and his girl friend, Harriet, played together in the sandbox. Her mother re-created their conversations, and Diane loved the stories and wanted them to go on and on.

"And then I remember when I was older and in high school seeing a man moving across the stage, reciting a monologue, and I don't even remember how old he was or how he looked. I don't remember breathing. I just remember being transported. I was no longer a high school girl with all the worries a high school girl has: Do my clothes match? Is my hair all right? No, I was in my self which was my best self, my potential, imaginative self, the self that creates along with the storyteller. There was a magic, something I didn't understand was happening, and I was glad to be there. I was grateful to that person for taking me to that glorious place."

At Smith College, Diane studied drama, and upon graduation, she went to Paris to study pantomime with Etienne Decroux, a French

115

mime. To help finance her schooling, she taught Sunday School at Temple Copernic. "Since I never had a very didactic nature, I didn't want to tell the children how to act or what to believe. But I needed to do something to earn money. So each week I would prepare—I would carefully memorize with all the details—a series of verses from the Bible. I would tell them half in English, half in French, and then the children and I would talk about the text. They had lots of questions, often the same ones I had had when I was preparing the lesson." For Diane, it was exciting, and she realized that she wanted to find a way to continue telling stories.

Diane returned to America in 1967 and earned her master's in education at Bank Street College of Education, hoping that the degree would help her find a job that would allow her to tell stories full-time. And in the meantime, on Sunday mornings, she told ecumenical stories to the young children at the Unitarian Church on 77th Street and Lexington Avenue. Then, in the spring, Diane's fiancé mentioned to her that when he was young he had heard stories in the park, and thinking this might be an opportunity, she went to the New York City Parks Department to find a job as a storyteller. There was no position as Storyteller, she was told, but she could work as a temporary recreation director— and tell stories.

"Since I wanted to tell stories more than anything else, even though the pay was only $40 a week, I took the job. I told stories twice a day, five times a week, in Harlem, Bedford-Stuyvesant, the Bronx—in all five boroughs of New York City. I had no training, no one to escort me, just a schedule and a subway map. Neither my master's in education nor my degree from Smith College could speak for me when I appeared on the streets of Harlem.

"At my first telling, I stood in McCray Park in Harlem in front of two hundred children from two to fifteen years old, with their transistor radios blaring and BB guns popping. I abandoned my carefully memorized rendition of 'Peter Rabbit' and began instead the African tale of 'Fattest of All.' 'Once there was a girl who was very, very, very, very, very. . .' By the eighteenth 'very,' the radios were turned down, the guns were laid aside, and the kids wanted to know: very, very, very *what?* Fat! Ah. And then what? So they listened and, at the end, hooted and yelled for more. I had brought them into another world, and they had joined so full-heartedly that we all were *there.*

"After several weeks when the children saw me on the street, they'd meet me at the subway and walk with me to the park. I learned to be quick, to be flexible, to stop memorizing and to adjust the stories to the kids who were there. They began to have favorites. 'Tell "Bracelets,"' one kid would shout. 'Tell "Fattest of Them All,"' another child would yell. 'I like your hair,' another one said."

Diane's storytelling garnered the attention of *The New York Times* and other news media, and her reputation as a storyteller began to grow. So the New York City Parks Department offered Diane a full-time job telling stories, and she became the first person to be employed by the city to work all year preparing and telling stories. For five years, she told stories at day-care centers, senior-citizen centers, and any elementary school, hospital, or park that requested her. In 1968, Diane began her radio program, "Stories from Many Lands with Diane Wolkstein," on WNYC-Radio, and it would continue for twelve years.

"During the summer that I began telling stories in New York City's parks, I also auditioned to perform at Hans Christian Andersen's statue in Central Park. And as I prepared to tell 'The Tinder Box,' I stood silently in front of the statue, and Baroness Dahlerup and a group of young children sat in small chairs in front of me. I was nervous, but I could feel the quiet of Hans Christian Andersen behind me. I turned and looked at the statue. In one hand, Andersen held a book of stories, and upon the book words from 'The Ugly Duckling' were inscribed: 'It was beautiful in the country—it was summer. The wheat fields were golden and the oats were green. . . .' But Andersen wasn't looking at the book. His gaze was both outward and inward—outward to the audience, inward to the spirit. I turned to my audience and began my story."

Since the time Diane began telling stories at Andersen's statue, she has had some wonderful, and unexpected, experiences. In 1969, she was awarded a Marshall Fellowship to study Danish and visit Odense, Andersen's hometown, and the manor houses and castles where he often stayed. In 1976, she was given a Lithgow-Osborne Fellowship by the American-Scandinavian Foundation to tour fifteen American cities, telling Andersen's stories to adults. And that summer a special visitor sat in the first row of seats at the statue—Queen Margrethe of Denmark. For the occasion, Diane told Andersen's bittersweet tale "The Daisy," and after the telling, the queen expressed her pleasure. "It was not saccharine," she said to Diane, "but just right." The following summer, the queen's sister, Princess Benedikte, came to the statue, and Diane recounted the roisterous tale "The Most Wonderful Thing of All." But the most momentous ten minutes for Diane came when her daughter, Rachel, told her first story there. She was only five.

"Rachel had often accompanied me to the statue, and she knew that I often invited my storytelling students to tell during my hour. One summer day, Rachel suddenly began tugging at my dress. She whispered, 'Mommy, I want to tell a story.'

"I whispered, 'Now?'

"'Now!'

"'What are you going to tell?'

" '*Squirrel's Song.*'

"'All right. But tell it loud.'

"My heart was pounding. But despite my fear that I was unfairly imposing upon the audience, I introduced Rachel.

"'We have a surprise storyteller today. A new one. She's five years old. Rachel Zucker.'

"Rachel stood up. There was a hush in the audience. She told *Squirrel's Song* faultlessly, but she never took her eyes off the ground nor did she raise her voice above a whisper. But when she finished, there was great applause. Rachel, startled by it all, sat down quickly.

"I was more startled than anyone. I had sat in agony throughout her entire telling. And though she had broken the two unbreakable laws of storytelling—to look at the audience and to let them hear you—she had stolen their hearts. She had told the story perfectly and from the *inside.*

"Each summer, on the last Saturday that I tell stories at the statue, I tell Eleanor Farjeon's 'Elsie Piddock Skips in Her Sleep.' This is the story of tiny Elsie Piddock who, at 109 years old, returns to her village in order to save a small plot of land—the Skipping Ground—for the children.

"For me, this small oasis in the heart of New York City—the statue of Hans Christian Andersen—has the same kind of magic as the Skipping Ground, a haven of enchantment. And Andersen's presence lends a special depth to all of the tellings. His stories are like fine wines— they grow better with age. Each year that I tell them, I understand more his subleties of wit, irony, poignancy, sweetness, and survival."

Despite Diane's love of the classic tales of Andersen, it was not until a visit to Haiti in 1972 that she experienced the simple primitive power of storytelling. Here was a different kind of storytelling, one she had never known, which used not only words but sound and gesture and dance. This was the flesh and blood of the art she loved.

Diane had been in Haiti on vacation, and through a series of introductions, she found herself the last evening of her visit on the porch of Jeanne Philippe—a Haitian country doctor, psychoanalyst, and lover of stories. Gathering there were peasants from the Haitian countryside, and they told stories for hours.

"I had never seen such enthusiasm for storytelling. There before me were Haitian peasants—none of whom could read or write—and they were totally caught up in the spirit and magic of storytelling. They would jump up, each one in their time, and tell a story, and those who listened were excited, laughing.

"All of the stories were told in Creole, and I couldn't understand a word. But I was wrapped up in the energy of the telling. They told in such a natural, spontaneous, eager way; and I was as excited about the response of the listeners as I was in hearing the storyteller. I was singing and carrying on as if I understood every word.

"I had never before been in a country where everyone told and enjoyed stories. I had come into my own land—the storytelling experience I had never had. So I decided to stay another week in Haiti. Over the next five years, I returned to Haiti six times."

As she listened to the Haitian stories, Diane felt a growing urge to share with the storytellers the stories *she* knew. On her third trip to Haiti, at the sugarcane plantation of Masson, Diane's urge to tell overcame her fears.

"When a storyteller in Haiti wants to tell a story, the teller calls out, 'Cric?' And if the audience wants the storyteller to begin, they respond, 'Crac!' Such a response is a pledge, a commitment, of support and encouragement.

"As soon as Elmir Innocent had finished her wonderful telling of the story of "Horse and Toad," I suddenly jumped up and cried, '*Cric?*' From the audience came a loud '*Crac!*' I was astonished. But there I was, standing before a group of lively and eager peasants.

"In Haiti, any storyteller who receives a *Crac!* starts off at a lively trot. And though I had learned Creole, my use of the language moved slowly, word by word. Yet the fire and spark of the storytelling captured me, and I began telling Mirra Ginsburg's Russian tale of an old man and woman who had a bet as to which could remain silent the longest. They both became ill, and when the mayor offered the old woman's coat to anyone who would take care of the poor, weak couple, the old woman immediately sat up and shouted, 'What? Not *my* new coat.'

"I used more pantomime than words. I jumped and leapt through the air, waving my arms. The audience was wide-eyed, laughing, and watching intently. When I finished my story, everyone clapped. I sat down, shaking, sweating, my heart thumping. And soon I began to hear: '*Li conté bien. Li conté bien.*' 'She tells stories very well.' And I was pleased. I *knew* I was at home."

Perhaps Diane's most significant storytelling pursuit came in 1983, when, after three years of intensive research, she and Professor Samuel Noah Kramer published *Inanna, Queen of Heaven and Earth*. Written in cuneiform on baked clay tablets, the ancient Sumerian story of the great goddess of love and fertility is the world's first written story. "I wanted to let people today know what was thought and felt five thousand years ago, two thousand years before the Bible. And Inanna's story—her adolescence, courtship, queenship, descent into the underworld, and rebirth—has relevance for each of us. The Sumerians, with their wide-eyed cultic statues, had a glimpse into the world of the spirit that can hopefully broaden and lift all of our views."

Whether it is recounting the literary tales of Andersen or the traditional tales from Haiti or stories collected from around the world, storytelling has a double pleasure for Diane. "I enjoy the telling and I equally enjoy the research and preparation for the telling. I spend hours reading about the cultures that give us our stories—reading about the history, archeology, art, literature, and music of the culture—talking with scholars, discovering comparable stories. I may read an entire book only to find the meaning of just one line in a story." For Diane, the process is a worthwhile search.

"Stories let us peep into the cracks of life, the invisible things, the thoughts within thoughts, those things which go by so quickly we don't even realize them. During the telling, those little cracks often open up to us. As a person, I see with two eyes, but as a storyteller, I have the possibilities of seeing with hundreds of eyes, the eyes of all who are listening and perceiving."

Throughout her career as a storyteller, Diane has collected and told a wealth of tales from around the world. She is the author of twelve books of stories, and each story that has become a book was premiered at the statue of Hans Christian Andersen on those magical Saturday mornings every summer. Now, after twenty-one years, many of Diane's past listeners at the statue are bringing their own children to hear the fairy lady of their childhood. And equally to Diane's delight, her storytelling students—those with whom she has shared the power and joys of stories—are also performing at the statue, sharing their stories with hundreds of children in New York City and around the world.

The Nightingale

Hans Christian Andersen, one of the world's most celebrated writers and storytellers, was born in 1805 in Denmark, the son of a poor washerwoman and a shoemaker. As a child, Hans listened to his father read the Bible, Shakespeare, and the Arabian Nights. And on Sundays, he would visit the town's mental hospital with his grandmother and listen to the old stories and folktales told by the patients.

Hans first gained a reputation in Denmark as a playwright and novelist, but when he was thirty years old, he wrote his first fairy tale. The Danish, however, condemned him, saying his tales were unworthy of his talents. Yet Hans persisted, and when he died forty years later, he had written over 150 fairy tales—many of them based on the stories he had heard as a child.

While Hans's plays are no longer produced and his novels are seldom read outside of his homeland, his fairy tales have become classics—treasured by both children and adults throughout the world. And since 1967, Diane has told Andersen's stories in New York City's Central Park in the shadow of the statue erected in honor of the Danish author. Every year, Diane tells Andersen's poignant story of "The Nightingale."

IN CHINA, the Emperor, as you well know, is Chinese and so are all his subjects. This story happened a long time ago but all the better that you hear it now so you will not forget it . . .

The Emperor's palace was the finest in the world. Made entirely of delicate porcelain, it was so fragile that you had to be very careful how you touched anything. Outside the palace, the Emperor's garden was filled with lovely flowers. On the rarest flowers hung tiny silver bells which tinkled, so you could not possibly pass by without noticing them.

The garden was very large. In fact, not even the gardener knew how large it was. But if you kept on walking you found yourself in a beautiful forest with tall trees and deep lakes and then farther on you would come to the sea. Large ships could pull up under the trees by its shore, and there in a branch of a tree lived the Nightingale.

Her singing was the most beautiful in the world. Every night, when the fishermen took in their nets, they would hear her sing and stop and say, "My word, that is lovely." And then they would go on with their work. But the next night when they would be taking in their nets and hear her sing, they would again stop and say, "My word, that is lovely."

From many countries travelers came to China, and they marveled at the Emperor's palace and garden, but when they heard the Nightingale sing, they all agreed, "That is the best of all."

One day, the Emperor of China was sitting on his golden throne, reading a book written about his kingdom. When he came to the sentence "The loveliest thing in China is the Nightingale," he snapped the book shut. "What's this? Why have I never heard of her?"

He called for the gentleman-in-waiting. "It says here that we have a most remarkable bird in our kingdom called the Nightingale. Why haven't I been informed of it?"

"Your majesty must not believe everything he reads in books," said the gentleman-in-waiting.

"This book," said the Emperor, "was written by the Emperor of Japan, so it must be true. I *will* have the Nightingale sing for me tonight, and if she fails to appear, I shall punch every courtier in the stomach directly after supper."

Nobody wanted that. So when the gentleman-in-waiting ran upstairs and downstairs and through the rooms and passages, half the court ran with him, asking, "Have you seen the Nightingale? Have *you* seen the Nightingale?"

"I know where the Nightingale is," said the little kitchen maid.

"Where?" they all asked her.

"Every evening I'm allowed to take food home to my sick mother who lives by the sea. I always stop and listen to the Nightingale sing. Her song brings tears to my eyes like my mother's kisses."

"Kitchen maid," said the gentleman-in-waiting, "you shall be given a permanent position and be allowed to watch the Emperor eat his dinner if you will only show us where the Nightingale is."

"Gladly," she said.

So they all set out for the woods, and after they had gone a little while, they heard, "*Moooooo. Moooooo.*"

"Oh, she's quite large, isn't she?" said the gentleman-in-waiting.

"That's a cow!" said the kitchen maid. "That's not the Nightingale."

They went a little farther and they heard, "*Croooak. Croooak.*"

"I didn't expect it to be green," he said.

"That's a frog! Come. Come on now. Look," said the kitchen maid. "There she is on that branch."

They all looked up.

"Oh, how common she looks. How ordinary—she's gray."

But when the bird sang, the gentleman-in-waiting said, "Lovely! Just like glass bells. My excellent little Nightingale, it is my pleasure to summon you to a concert tonight at the palace where you will enchant the Emperor with your singing."

"I sing much better in the open woods, but if he wishes, I will be glad to sing for him."

At the palace, the china walls and floors were polished until they shone. The rarest flowers, fastened to silver bells, were set in vases and there was such a wind from the hurrying to and fro that the bells kept ringing, and you couldn't hear a word that was said.

In the middle of the hall sat the Emperor on his golden throne. Next to him was the Nightingale on her golden perch. All the court was present, including the kitchen maid, who was allowed to watch. Then the Emperor nodded to the little gray bird to begin, and the Nightingale sang so beautifully that tears came to the Emperor's eyes and ran down his cheeks.

"Little Nightingale," the Emperor said, "I shall give you my golden slipper."

"No, no," she said, "I've already been rewarded by the tears in your eyes."

But now she was given a cage of her own and allowed to go for a walk—twice in the morning and once at night—with twelve attendants, and it wasn't much fun. The whole city began to talk about the Nightingale. When two people met on the street, one would say, "Night," and the other, "gale."

One day, a parcel arrived for the Emperor of China with the word "Nightingale" written on it. It wasn't a book but an artificial Nightingale that looked just like the live one, only it was covered with rubies and sapphires and diamonds, and if you wound it up, it could sing one of the songs that the real Nightingale sang. Tied around its neck was a ribbon which said, "The Emperor of Japan's Nightingale is poor compared to the one of the Emperor of China."

"Oh, how delightful," everyone said.

"They must sing a duet," someone said.

So the two birds had to sing together. But it wasn't a success, for the real Nightingale sang this way and that way. She never sang exactly the same way. So the real Nightingale was hushed while the artificial Nightingale sang and sang and sang, always exactly the same thing, and the people cheered her to go on and on for she was covered with diamonds and rubies and so very pretty.

After thirty-three times, however, the Emperor remembered the real

Nightingale and turned to her, but she was gone. No one had noticed that she had flown out the open window to her home in the green woods.

"How ungrateful," said the Emperor.

And the people agreed.

"But we have the better bird," they said.

The artificial Nightingale was given the title of Imperial Minstrel and provided a place to sleep at night on a silk pillow by the Emperor's bedside. But after a year, while the Emperor was sitting in bed and the Nightingale was singing, he suddenly heard a strange noise. The bird stopped singing.

Quickly he jumped out of bed and sent for the doctor. But what could the doctor do? So the Emperor sent for the watchmaker, and the watchmaker examined the bird. The springs were worn out, he said, and new ones could not be replaced without interfering with the music. So the Nightingale would now only be allowed to sing once a year.

Five years went by and the whole country was filled with sorrow, for the Emperor was ill and lay dying. The people were very fond of him, as he had been a good Emperor. The courtiers went to see the man who had been chosen to be the next Emperor, and the old Emperor was left alone.

The Emperor lay in his bed, stiff and cold. He could scarcely breathe, and he felt something sitting on his chest. When he opened his eyes, he saw Death on his chest wearing his golden crown, holding his golden sword in one hand and his banner in the other. And then, from all sides of the room strange faces appeared—some were hideous and ugly, some were kind and gentle. They were the Emperor's good and evil deeds which had come to speak to him now that Death was sitting on his heart.

"Do you remember this? Do you remember that? Do you remember what you did?" they said.

"Stop! Stop!" cried the Emperor. "Music! Music! Golden bird, sing for me!"

But the artificial bird could not sing without being wound up, and the Emperor was too weak to wind it. Then suddenly, from the open window, the most beautiful singing was heard. It was the live Nightingale come to sing for the Emperor. She had heard that he was ill, and she had flown to his window to bring him hope and comfort. As she sang, the faces faded, and Death said, "Sing, Nightingale, sing."

"Yes," she said, "if you give me the Emperor's banner. Yes, if you give me his sword. Yes, if you give me his crown." And Death gave up each of his treasures for a song.

The Nightingale went on singing. She sang of a quiet churchyard where the white roses bloomed. She sang of the fresh green grass, watered by the tears of those left behind. Death began to long for his garden, and he floated out the window like a pale, cold mist.

"Oh, heavenly bird," the Emperor said, "how can I repay you?"

"You have already repaid me," she said. "When I sang to you the first time, I saw tears in your eyes, and those are the jewels a singer wishes for. Now close your eyes and sleep, and I will sing to you so that you may wake up well and strong."

The Nightingale sang, and the Emperor fell into a deep sleep. When he woke up, the courtiers weren't there, but the Nightingale was still singing.

"Oh, bird, you must never leave me. You will be my *only* bird, and I shall break the artificial bird into a thousand pieces."

"No, no, don't do that," said the Nightingale. "It did what it could, and I can't live at court. Let me come when I wish and sit on the branch outside your window and sing to you of all that is happening in your kingdom. I will sing to you of those who are happy and those who are sad. I will sing to you of those who have and those who are in need. I will tell you everything, but promise me one thing."

"Anything," said the Emperor.

"Promise me you will never tell anyone there is a little bird who tells you everything."

And with those words, the Nightingale flew away.

When the servants came into the room expecting to find the Emperor dead, how surprised they were to find him standing before them, bidding them, "Good morning! Good morning!"

Owl

On her third of six trips to Haiti, Diane heard Rosemarie Masse tell stories. Rosemarie was a Haitian teller, thin and muscular, about fifty years old.

"Cric?" she said.

"Crac!" the audience responded.

Rosemarie rose from her seat, walked to the center of the audience, and stood erect—proud in her faded blue dress. And then she began to tell "Owl," a story about the importance of trusting in oneself and trusting in another's love of that self.

"I watched in awe as Rosemarie began to sing and dance, holding herself straight, moving her hips and chest, her arms outspread. As she danced, everyone joined in—clapping and singing and dancing in place. It was thrilling. It was the most exciting storytelling I had ever seen. I was so moved by the experience that I decided I would gather the Haitian stories I had heard into a book and write about Owl and Rosemarie Masse so they would live for others as they had for me."

The Magic Orange Tree and Other Haitian Folktales was born, Diane's seventh book and considered by many a modern storytelling classic for its interweaving of storytellers and stories.

OWL THOUGHT he was very ugly. But one evening he met a girl and talked with her and she liked him. "If it had been day," Owl thought, "and she had seen my face, she never would have liked me." But still she had liked him.

So Owl went to her house the next night. And the next. And the night after that. Every evening he would arrive at the girl's house at seven, and they would sit outside on the porch steps, talking together politely.

Then one evening after Owl had left, the girl's mother said to her, "Why doesn't your fiancé come and visit you during the day?"

"But Mama, he's explained that to me. He works during the day. Then he must go home and change and he cannot get here before seven."

"Still, I would like to see his face before the marriage," the mother said. "Let's invite him to our house for a dance this Sunday afternoon. Surely he doesn't work on Sunday."

Owl was very pleased with the invitation: a dance in his honor. But he was also very frightened. He told his cousin, Rooster, about the girl and asked that he accompany him to the dance. But that Sunday afternoon, as Owl and Rooster were riding on their horses to the party, Owl glanced over at Rooster. Rooster held himself with such assurance, he was so elegantly and fashionably dressed, that Owl imagined the girl seeing the two of them and was filled with shame.

"I can't go on," he choked. "You go and tell them I've had an accident and will be there later."

Rooster rode to the dance. "Tsk tsk, poor Owl," he explained. "He has had an accident, and he has asked me to let you know that he will be here later."

When it was quite dark, Owl tied his horse a good distance from the dance and stumbled up to the porch steps.

"Pssst," he whispered to a young man sitting on the steps. "Is Rooster here?"

"Well now, I don't know."

"Go and look. Tell him a friend is waiting for him by the *mapou* tree."

Rooster came out. "Owl!"

"Shhhhhhh—"

"Owl!"

"Shhhh—"

"Owl, what are you wearing over your head—I mean your face?"

"It's a hat. Haven't you ever seen a hat before? Look, tell them anything. Tell them I scratched my eyes on a branch as I was riding here and the light—even the light from a lamp—hurts them. And you must be certain to watch for the day for me, and to crow as soon as you see the light, so we can leave."

"Yes, yes," Rooster said. "Come in and I shall introduce you to the girl's relatives."

Rooster introduced Owl to everyone, explaining Owl's predicament. Owl went around shaking hands, his hat hung down almost completely covering his face. Owl then tried to retreat into a corner, but the girl came over.

"Come into the yard and let's dance," she said.

Dong ga da, Dong ga da, Dong ga da, Dong.
Dong ga da, Dong. Eh-ee-oh.

Owl danced. And Owl could dance well. The girl was proud of Owl. Even if he wore his hat strangely and had sensitive eyes, he *could* dance.

Dong ga da, Dong ga da, Dong ga da, Dong.
Dong ga da, Dong. Eh-ee-oh.

Rooster was dancing too. When Owl noticed that Rooster was dancing, instead of watching for the day, Owl was afraid that Rooster would
forget to warn him, and he excused himself to the girl. He ran out of
the yard, past the houses, to a clearing where he could see the horizon.
No, it was still night. Owl came back.

Dong ga da, Dong ga da, Dong ga da, Dong.
Dong ga da, Dong. Eh-ee-oh.

Owl motioned to Rooster, but Rooster was lost in the dance. Owl
excused himself again to the girl, ran to the clearing; no, it was still
night. Owl returned.

Dong ga da, Dong ga da, Dong ga da, Dong.
Dong ga da, Dong. Eh-ee-oh.

Owl tried to excuse himself again, but the girl held on to him. "Yes,
stay with me," she said. And so they danced and danced and danced.

Dong ga da, Dong ga da, Dong ga da, Dong.
Dong ga da, Dong. Eh-ee-oh.

The sun moved up in the sky, higher and higher, until it filled the
house and the yard with light.

"Now—let us see your fiancé's face!" the mother said.

"*Kokioko!*" Rooster crowed.

And before Owl could hide, she reached out and pulled the hat from
his face.

"My eyes!" Owl cried, and covering his face with his hands, he ran
for his horse.

"Wait, Owl!" the girl called.

"*Kokioko!*" Rooster crowed.

"Wait, Owl, wait."

And as Owl put his hands down to untie his horse, the girl saw his
face. It was striking and fierce, and the girl thought it was the most
handsome face she had ever seen.

"Owl—"

But Owl was already on his horse, riding away, farther and farther away.

Owl never came back.

The girl waited. Then she married Rooster. She was happy, except sometimes in the morning when Rooster would crow, "Kokioko-o-o." Then she would think about Owl and wonder where he was.

White Wave

Often in its telling, a story takes on special meaning, and Diane finds herself wanting to share her story with the widest possible audience. For Diane, it often becomes a book. So it was with White Wave, derived from a Chinese story of change and transformation from the Taoist tradition.

"When I select a story to write and tell, it's because there is something mysterious about it—an image to which I want to get closer—and I'm touched by it. In White Wave, it's the changing symbol: the shell which becomes a stone which becomes a goddess which becomes a stone which becomes a story. Through the young boy who picks up the shell and would hold on to it forever, we learn that all we know is in flux, in continual transformation."

Diane is the author of twelve books of stories, mostly for children, and they include The Magic Wings, Squirrel's Song, The Cool Ride in the Sky, The Banza, *and her most recent,* The Legend of Sleepy Hollow. *A prolific writer, Diane is recognized throughout the United States as one of our most respected authors of children's books.*

IN THE hills of southern China, there once stood a shrine. It was made of stones—beautiful white, pink, and gray stones—and was built as a house for a goddess.

Now the stones lie scattered on the hillside. If you, who are listening, should happen to find one, remember this story . . . of the shrine and the stones, and of the goddess, White Wave.

Long ago, in the time of mysteries, a young man was walking home in the evening. He walked slowly, for he was not eager to return to his house. His parents had died two years before. He was too poor to marry and too shy to speak with a girl.

As he passed through a small forest, he saw a stone gleaming in the moonlight, a beautiful white stone. He bent over to look at it. It wasn't white. It was every color in the rainbow. And when he held it in his hands, he saw it wasn't a stone at all, but a snail, a moon snail. And what was the most wonderful good fortune—it was alive.

He carried the snail gently home and placed it in an earthenware jar. Then, before fixing his own dinner, he went out again and gathered fresh leaves for the snail.

The next morning the first thing he did was to look for the jar. The leaves were gone. The snail had eaten them. He picked four more leaves and went off to the fields to work.

When he came home that evening, he found his dinner waiting for him on the table: a bowl of cooked rice, a cup of hot tea, and vegetables.

He looked around the room. No one was there. He went to the door and looked out into the night. No one. Still he left the door open, hoping that whoever had prepared his dinner might join him.

The next evening his dinner was again waiting for him—and this time there was a branch of wild peach set in a vase on the table. The young man asked in the village if strangers had arrived. No one knew of any.

Every morning he left leaves for his snail. Every evening his dinner was waiting, and always there was a wildflower in the vase.

One morning he woke up earlier than usual and started off as if he were going to the fields. Instead, he circled back to his house and stood outside the window, listening. It was quiet. There was no sound. Then, as the first light of the day touched the earth, he heard a noise.

He looked inside and saw, rising from the jar, a tiny white hand. It rose higher and higher. A second hand came up from the jar, and out leapt a beautiful girl.

She was pure light. Her dress was of silk. As she moved, her dress rippled, changing from silver to white to gold. Wherever she stepped in the room, the room shone.

The young man knew, though no one had told him, that she was a moon goddess. And he knew, though no one had told him, that he must never try to touch her. The next morning he watched her, and the next.

From the time she came to live with him, the man's loneliness disappeared. He skipped to the fields in the morning, and ran home in the evening. His dinner was always waiting. His house was shining. The air was sweet. And his heart was full.

Many days passed. Then one morning, as he watched her through the window, a great longing came upon him. He wanted to touch her hair. It burst upon him so strongly and quickly that he forgot what he knew. He opened the door and rushed into the room.

"Do not move," she said.

"Who are you?" he asked.

"I am White Wave, the moon goddess. But now I must leave you, for you have forgotten what you knew."

"No! No!" he cried.

"Good farmer," she said, "if you can hold yourself still and count for me, I will leave you a gift. Let me hear you count. Count to five."

"One," he said softly.

She crossed in front of him and walked toward the open door.

"Two," he said.

"I'll leave you my shell."

"Three," he said more strongly.

"If ever you are in great need, call me by my name, White Wave, and I will come to you."

"Four," he said.

There was a streak of lightning and a great roll of thunder.

"Five."

A huge wind came and swept the goddess into the air. He ran outside, but the rain poured down so fast that he could not see her.

He stood there a long time. Then he went back into the house. It was empty. The snail shell was there, but no living creature was inside.

He went to the fields, but he did not think of his work. He thought only of White Wave and of how to bring her back.

The farmer decided he would build a shrine for her—a beautiful house in which she might live. He spent more time choosing the stones for her house than working in the fields. When the harvest came, it was very small. He ate the little there was. He ate the supplies he had stored, and after that, he lived on berries and wild grass.

One evening he was so weak with hunger, he could barely walk. He stumbled into the house and tripped over the earthenware jar. The shell fell out. Quickly he picked it up, and as he held it, he remembered the words of the goddess, "If ever you are in great need, call me by my name, White Wave . . ."

He held the shell in front of him. Then he raised it in the air, and with his last strength he cried: "White Wave, I need you!"

Slowly he turned the shell toward him, and a wave of rice, gleaming white rice, cascaded out of the shell and onto the floor. He dipped his hands into it. The rice was solid and firm. It was enough to last him to the next harvest.

That was the last time he called her name, for he was never again in great need. With the flowing of the rice, a new strength came to him. He worked hard in the fields. The rice grew. The vegetables flourished. He married and had children. But he did not forget White Wave.

He told his wife about her, and when his children were old enough, he told them the story of White Wave. The children liked to hold the shell in their hands as they listened to the story.

The shrine was now complete and stood on the hill above their house. The children often went there in the early morning and evening, hoping to see White Wave. They never did.

When the old man died, the shell was lost. In time, the shrine, too, disappeared. All that remained was the story.

But that is how it is with all of us: When we die, all that remains is the story.

Stories

of the

Supernatural

Kathryn Windham

For you don't have to believe in ghosts
to enjoy a good ghost story. You just have to wonder.
Could it really have happened?
Can it really be?

KATHRYN WINDHAM likes ghost stories. She has been intrigued with tales of the supernatural all of her life, but her fascination with ghostly affairs—the unexplained and the unexplainable—intensified in 1966 when something she calls Jeffrey came to live in her home in Selma, Alabama. She can't say with certainty that Jeffrey is a ghost—no one has ever seen him—but strange things did go on in her house, occurrences that made her believe a playful poltergeist had taken up residence. The sound of footsteps, empty chairs that rock, heavy furniture that moves mysteriously—all stirred Kathryn's interest and led her on a search for tales of the supernatural, first in Alabama and later throughout the South.

As Kathryn collects and tells the stories, she grieves that the old tales are slipping away, falling into oblivion, and with them a wellspring of knowledge and wisdom—and strength. It is a reverence for the past, of things that have come before, that's at the heart of her unswerving desire to preserve our heritage—a feeling that Kathryn, born in 1918, likely acquired growing up in a close-knit family during the Depression in the small town of Thomasville, tucked away in the southwestern corner of Alabama.

"When I was growing up, we never had any money. I don't think I can recall our house ever being painted in my entire life. But we had books. Wherever my daddy went, he always came home with books. Though he had only three months of formal education, he had learned to read and appreciated the value of reading.

"I remember going down to the depot when Daddy would be coming home from Mobile or Birmingham, and he'd get off the train and his arms would be stacked with books. The ones on top were mine. So I'd get my books and stumble down the road behind Daddy—holding them, feeling them, opening their pages—and I would be eager to get home to read these treasures my father had brought me.

"I can recall climbing into my tree house in the backyard and reading for hours, devouring every word, but my fondest memories are of my daddy, the story*teller*. He was the finest storyteller I ever listened to—a natural yarn spinner. He loved people, he loved listening to them, and he would draw out wonderful old tales which he shared with us over the supper table every night.

"Daddy was a good historian, and he knew where historical events had taken place and how they affected the people he knew. He'd often show me someone on the street and say, 'Now one of these days, I'm goin' to tell you a tale about *his* grandfather.' So I came to realize that history wasn't just something that happened long ago, but that it reached into the lives of people *I* knew, right in the present time.

"I remember one day when I was a young girl, Daddy and I were walking in the woods south of Thomasville. We sat on a log for a rest, and he began telling me stories about things that took place as long ago as the Indian Wars of 1813.

"'You see that spot over there?' he asked. 'There near that clump of trees? That's where the old Kimball house stood.' And Daddy began a tale."

He told Kathryn of the Prophet Francis, a cruel Indian chief who was scouting the countryside, and how he and his warriors came upon this isolated spot—the old Kimball house—where they scalped and left for dead the women and children who had gathered there for protection. Among them were Sarah Merrill and her tiny, year-old baby. He told how Sarah was scalped and thrown from the house into the yard and how a gentle rain came during the night and revived her. Without a light, a torch or a lantern, Sarah crawled around in the dark among the bodies, feeling for her child, and she discovered the little baby—and he too was still alive.

"As Daddy told me his story, it became real to me. He made me feel as if I had been there when it happened. I could actually *be* Sarah Merrill, weak and bloody, searching among the bodies for her baby. I could feel her terror and pain and moment of thanksgiving, finding her child still alive. There was nobody there on that lonely spot that day but my daddy and me, yet he knew what had happened and described it to me in detail. My daddy cared enough to tell me a story—to share in his knowledge. It was the finest of history lessons."

Kathryn's father instilled in her a love of words and a respect for the power they encompass, and as early as she can remember, she wanted to be a writer—a newspaper reporter. Even as a young girl, Kathryn wrote. Having no money—allowances were unknown in her family—she would gather bouquets of flowers from her backyard and write poems and give them to her mother. And when she was older, Kathryn often spent her summer afternoons at the office of the Thomasville weekly newspaper. For her cousin Earl Tucker, the editor, she wrote movie reviews in exchange for free passes to the picture show. These were childhood experiences that fueled Kathryn's desire to become a journalist, and as soon as she graduated from high school, she enrolled in Huntingdon College in Montgomery to pursue a writing career. It was there she met Dr. Rhoda Ellison, an English teacher who taught Kathryn how to write and developed in her an acute demand for accuracy and a keen eye for detail—qualities that even today characterize the stories Kathryn tells.

"I came from a small, country high school, and I had so much to learn. Just before the Christmas holidays during my freshman year, Dr. Ellison asked me to write about Christmas. So I wrote about snowy fields and icicles hanging from the fir trees—a glorious wintry scene. But Dr. Ellison returned my paper and asked, 'How many Christmases has it snowed in Thomasville?' Well, it had *never* snowed in Thomasville on Christmas. So she asked me to write my paper again. 'What was Christmas *really* like in Thomasville?'

"This time I wrote about Omah, who would come with his wagon piled high with holly and smilax and our cedar tree. Mother and I would put up the tree in the living room and decorate the house, tucking the holly behind every picture. And we'd make fruitcakes. The whole family would sit around the fire, cracking pecans and walnuts, laughing and enjoying each other and telling stories all the while. That was the Christmas I knew, and that was the Christmas I wrote about.

"The first thing I ever wrote that really received praise was a story my daddy told me about a little country church near Thomasville. One of the church's most faithful members had died, and because the church had never had stained-glass windows, the members decided to install one in memory of the deceased. The congregation met one Sunday afternoon to decide upon an inscription for the window. My daddy recounted how they searched through the Bible, half of Shakespeare, and all of the poetry anyone knew for just the right words, but no two members could agree. It was hot, and the hour was late, and they were tired of trying to decide.

"Finally, one good old country soul stood up and said, 'Why don't we jist put, "Thar's whur he sot." And Daddy would tell that story and laugh and laugh.

"It was my first A in English composition in college, and I was thrilled. Dr. Ellison wrote a little note on my paper: 'Write more about the things you know.' And I did. As I wrote, Dr. Ellison would always ask, 'Is that *really* the way he felt? Is that *really* the way it looked? Is that *really* the way he heard it?'"

Dr. Ellison's firm insistence on accuracy marked for Kathryn the beginnings of a writer's consciousness—of writing about what she knew
best and writing about it truthfully. And though Kathryn didn't know it
then, she was developing a way of viewing and recounting the past, its
knowledge and wisdom, that augured the birth of a storyteller.

During college, Kathryn became a prolific writer, serving as editor of
the student newspaper and often providing articles for newspapers
throughout Alabama. It was not surprising that when she graduated in
1939, Kathryn began her search for a full-time job as a reporter—a
search, however, that was plagued with obstacles.

"I'll never forget Hartwell Hatton, the city editor of the *Montgomery
Advertiser*. He was a gruff man, always chewing a pipe which he held
tightly between his teeth as he talked.

"One day, I paid him a visit. 'I would surely like to work for the
Advertiser, Mr. Hatton.'

"With that pipe clenched between his teeth, he looked at me and
said, 'I've read your stuff, and you can write. I'd hire you if you were a
man. But I'm not going to have any women on my staff.'

"The door was closed. And I was shocked. It had never occurred to
me that being a woman would be a liability. I grew up thinking that I
could do anything that anyone else could do. I could shoot and fish and
tie a knot and climb a tree and hit a baseball as well as the boys, and I
never expected that I would be denied the right of doing something I
wanted to do, something I did well, simply because I was a woman."

Despite her disappointment, Kathryn didn't abandon her dream. She
returned to Thomasville to help her mother sell insurance, and she
continued to write. And finally, her patience was rewarded. One day,
Kathryn received a telegram from the editor of the *Alabama Journal*, the
Advertiser's chief competitior. Allen Rankin, their police reporter and
feature writer, had been drafted for service in World War II. They
needed someone to take his place, and they wanted Kathryn. Finally,
they *had* to have her, female though she was, and Kathryn went to work
for the *Journal* as probably the first woman police reporter on a major
daily newspaper anywhere in the South.

In 1946, while reporting for the *Birmingham News*, Kathryn married a
fellow newspaperman, Amasa Windham, quit her career in favor of
motherhood, and moved to Selma—the place of Kathryn's birth. Ten
years later, her husband was dead and, at thirty-seven, Kathryn was a
widow with three small children. As soon as her youngest child entered
school, Kathryn returned to the work that for years had sustained and
challenged her. She became a reporter for the *Selma Times-Journal*.

"It was then that my curiosity about things supernatural was piqued, and I vividly remember the day that I had my first encounter with... what? I can't be sure. I remember that sunny afternoon when I was sitting in a rocking chair in my den, reading, and I heard footsteps in the hallway. Then I heard the door to my son Ben's room open and slam closed. Though I wasn't expecting him, I thought maybe Ben had come home from college. I called for him, but he didn't answer. And when I went to see why he hadn't responded, I discovered that nobody was in the house. I was sure that I had heard footsteps, and I was sure that I had heard the door open and slam closed, but I didn't tell anyone.

"Several days later, my daughter Dilcy and I were in the den, rocking and reading, and our cat, Hornblower, was asleep in the wicker chair nearby. Again, I heard footsteps. No one else was there but us. I looked at Dilcy, and she looked back at me with big, round, startled eyes. Hornblower, terrified, shrieked and leapt from the chair, then ran from the room. *Something* was there.

"Several years later, Ben came home for a visit. He was preparing to leave, and he had packed his suitcase and laid it on top of his bed. We were standing in the doorway, talking and looking at the bed, when Ben's suitcase jumped off the mattress, cut a flip in the air, and landed on the floor, upright, with its handle ready to be picked up. Ben turned pale. *Something* was there."

Kathryn and her family accepted this ghostly presence in their home and named it Jeffrey. He became the family ghost, and because of him, Kathryn found herself wanting to know more about the supernatural world—a study that began with Margaret Gillis Figh, a folklore teacher at Huntingdon College. Kathryn told her the ghostly things that she had heard and seen, and she even bragged about having her own ghost.

The more they talked, the more excited the two women became, and they decided to write a book about Alabama's most famous ghosts—a book they called *13 Alabama Ghosts and Jeffrey*. They chose stories with definite events, definite names, definite places—ones that involved real people. As they researched and wrote, Kathryn discovered that ghost stories existed in every Southern town—stories just waiting to be listened to, researched, and retold. The supply was endless, and she never knew when she would come upon a truly great tale of the supernatural.

"One of my most curious tales came when I was working for the *Selma Times-Journal*. We had received many reports about a ghostly light in the neighboring county, but I wasn't very interested in the reportings. Ghost lights are often rather easy to explain. But the calls kept coming, so I decided to investigate. I learned that not far from the community of Maplesville there was once a settlement called Jumbo. When I visited this abandoned spot, there was nothing left except a dilapidated house so overgrown that I could barely see the old structure from the road.

"According to local legend, a man who had lived in the house had worked at a sawmill a good distance away. One night he worked late and missed his ride and, unhappy about walking through the dark woods at night, he borrowed a lantern from the night watchman. Then he made his way toward home, carrying the lantern high so that it would light his steps. But accidentally, he came upon some moonshiners working at a still in the woods. Having seen the light coming toward them, one of the moonshiners thought it was the sheriff coming to arrest them, so he fired his rifle. The man with the lantern never completed his journey home.

"Soon after his death, the people who lived in the Jumbo area began telling about seeing what appeared to be a lantern, carried high, that moved down the road toward the house where the sawmill worker had lived. I became more intrigued and sent Watson Rogers, our staff photographer, to see if he could photograph the mysterious light. As one might suspect, Watson thought it was a silly assignment, because he knew there was no such thing as a ghost light, and even if there were, it couldn't be photographed. But he went anyway, taking his wife and their next-door neighbors.

"They found the lonely spot where the light had been seen. Watson put his camera on the hood of his car with the lens open and focused down the road so it could catch any movement of light that might come. Then all of them waited in the miserable heat. Suddenly, they became clammy cold, so cold they broke out in goose bumps. And with the cold came a deadly silence. Then down that lonely road came a light, swinging along as though a tall man were carrying a lantern. Watson was terrified. He snatched his camera, snapped a picture, and the four of them jumped into the car and rushed home.

"When that roll of film was developed the next morning in our newspaper office, it showed quite distinctly a pattern of light moving down the dark road. But the strangest thing about this picture was that right in front, leading the trail of light, were two big shoes, heavy work shoes, stepping along with nobody in them. That afternoon, we printed the photograph, half-page size, in the *Times-Journal.*"

For eight years, Kathryn collected and wrote about the ghosts of America's Southland—becoming a recognized authority on Southern ghost lore. Then, in 1974, Kathryn was invited to *tell* her tales of the supernatural at the second National Storytelling Festival—her first public storytelling performance. Since then, she has shared her tales of ghostly affairs, of the unexplained and unexplainable, throughout the United States, bringing to life the stories of the supernatural world she once only reserved for the printed page. "For you don't have to believe in ghosts to enjoy a good ghost story," she says, smiling. "You just have to wonder. Could it *really* have happened? Can it *really* be?"

The Locket

Once, during a gala Christmas party, a young woman came up to Kathryn, introduced herself, and said, "I've read and enjoyed your ghost stories so much. I wish you knew my mother. She has a ghost photograph."

Kathryn thought, "Uh-huh. Sure. A ghost photograph." But she answered, "Oh, I would like to meet her. When I'm near where she lives, I'll go by and see the photograph. Where does she live?"

"Lanett, Alabama."

Lanett is all the way across the state from Selma, and Kathryn was sure she would never go to Lanett, but she said, "Well, give me her name and telephone number and I'll call her the next time I'm there." Kathryn jotted down the information on a piece of paper, dropped it into her purse, and promptly forgot the friendly exchange.

Several months later, she was speaking to a church group in Opelika and had finished earlier than expected. Realizing that she was close to Lanett, Kathryn, on a whim, dug down into the bottom of her purse and, sure enough, found the name and telephone number of the Lanett woman who had the ghost photograph.

When Kathryn called, the woman graciously invited her to come to her home. And after chatting awhile, she turned to Kathryn and said, "I know you've come to see the ghost photograph."

Kathryn smiled and nodded.

"Before I show you the photograph, I want you to hear the story behind it." Then she began to tell Kathryn of Harvey Hammer: a boy who returned from the grave so his father could photograph him.

IN THE late 1800s, Jacob Hammer moved from Indiana to Talladega County, Alabama. He had taught school and operated a small store in Indiana, but Jacob had never prospered, so he thought his fortune would change with a new beginning. He purchased a small farm near the little community of Renfro and began farming.

Jacob met Martha Hicks, a young woman living in Renfro, and they married and had five children. They were active in the church, supporters of the school, good neighbors, and everyone liked and respected the Hammer family.

Within a few years, a sixth child was born to Jacob and his wife. He was a beautiful baby boy with big blue eyes and curly blond hair—the sweet, affectionate kind of baby that everyone loves, the kind that enjoys being held and cuddled. They named him Harvey.

His older sister Cassandra—they called her Cassie—was given the pleasant task of caring for her baby brother. She enjoyed it, and spent much of her time with Harvey.

Cassie always wore a little, heart-shaped gold locket—a gift her father had given her for making good marks in the fifth grade. As she carried little Harvey around in her arms, the baby would reach up and play with the locket. And when he grew older and was cutting teeth, Harvey chewed on the locket and left his tiny tooth marks imbedded in it. As he grew even older—toddling and talking a bit—he begged Cassie to allow him to wear the locket.

She laughed and said, "Oh, Harvey, boys don't wear jewelry." And they didn't then.

One bitter cold night, little Harvey Hammer took the croup and died. The whole community was saddened by his death; the family was heartbroken. But Harvey's mother was especially sad because in the years that Harvey lived she had never had his photograph taken.

She wept, "Oh, if I had just taken a picture of my baby. If only I had something I could hold and look at to remember him by."

Hoping to ease her grief, Jacob sent word to Talladega, the nearest town, and asked that W. H. McMillan, a photographer, come to photograph the dead child.

The men in the community built a pine coffin for little Harvey, and the women dressed him in a burial gown made of soft, white cloth and lace and laid him in the casket. But when they dressed the baby's body in the gown, they discovered it was too big in the neck and fell around Harvey's shoulders. They didn't worry, though. They just tucked the fullness under the baby, saying the fact it didn't fit him would never be noticed. And Harvey was beautiful, even in death.

For several days before the baby had died, and while preparations were being made for his burial, it had rained steadily. The roads were now too muddy for travel, and it was impossible for the photographer to make the journey to the Hammer home. Despite his mother's wishes, Harvey was buried without a photograph ever having been taken of him.

But before the coffin lid was nailed closed, Cassie took one last look at her dead baby brother, and she remembered how he had always loved her locket. Almost without thinking, she reached up, unclasped the chain, and placed it around Harvey's neck. He was buried wearing her heart-shaped locket.

Oh, it was a sad day for Jacob Hammer and his family.

About six weeks after Harvey's death, Jacob was working in a remote section of his farm—several miles away from home—and it took a great deal of time to come and go each day. He noticed that nearby was an abandoned schoolhouse, so he set up camp there—with an old potbellied stove for cooking and keeping warm, and a cot to sleep upon.

He had worked hard on the first day, and after cooking himself a hearty supper, he soon fell asleep. Sometime during the night, Jacob Hammer was awakened by a brilliant flash of light.

His first thought was that the schoolhouse had caught fire and he should hurry from the building to safety, but as he jumped from his cot, he realized it was not a fire. Standing in the corner of the room was his son Harvey, bathed in a brilliant light and holding a burning candle. When Jacob stared at his son, the young boy blew out the candle and vanished.

Naturally, the experience upset Jacob. "It must have been a dream," he said to himself. But then he reconsidered. "No, it was not a dream. I was awake and I saw him."

During the next day as he worked in the fields, Jacob was haunted by the appearance of his dead son. He wished he had someone to talk to about it, but he was alone.

During the next night, after he had cooked supper and fallen asleep, Jacob Hammer was again awakened by a brilliant light and again he saw his young son, holding a flickering candle and standing in the corner of the room. Again, the young boy blew out the candle and vanished when Jacob approached him.

After Harvey's second appearance, Jacob wondered. Was the child's spirit so upset by the grief of his mother over not having a photograph of him that he was returning so a picture could be taken? Instead of going to work in the fields the next morning, Jacob went into Talladega to borrow a camera from McMillan, the photographer.

Not wanting to appear foolish, Jacob didn't mention seeing the ghost of his son Harvey. Instead, he told the photographer there was something he wanted to get a picture of on his farm.

McMillan was happy to lend Jacob his camera and show him how to use it.

Jacob returned to the old schoolhouse, set up the camera near his cot, and focused on the corner where his son had appeared on the two previous nights. After darkness came, he sat on the edge of his cot and waited, quietly and patiently.

Hours passed, but nothing happened.

"Oh, why should I have been so foolish as to think I saw my dead child? Surely I didn't see him. Surely it was just a trick of my imagination."

Then suddenly, the brilliant light came again—just as it had come before—and Harvey appeared. Jacob quickly clicked the shutter of the camera, and the figure blew out the candle and disappeared.

As soon as it was daylight, Jacob returned the camera to McMillan.

"I took only one photograph," he said. "I'd surely appreciate it if you would develop it for me as soon as possible."

Turning toward the darkroom, McMillan answered, "Well, it's very early and nobody is waiting. If you'll wait, I'll develop it for you now."

Jacob Hammer waited—and wondered. Within a few minutes, the photographer emerged from the darkroom, and he held the glass plate, dripping with chemicals.

"I thought you didn't have a picture of your baby?"

"We don't."

"Oh, yes you do. I knew Harvey, and he is—in this photograph."

As McMillan held the plate up for Jacob to see, Harvey was there—with his wistful blue eyes, his blond curls, an aura of light behind his head. The little burial gown, too large for him, had fallen over his shoulders, and around his neck hung Cassie's heart-shaped locket.

Jacob Hammer didn't go to work that day. Instead, he hurried home to show his wife the photograph he had taken. When he arrived, he—unable to speak—handed her the glass plate. And as she looked upon the image of her dead son Harvey, she broke into tears.

"It's my baby. It's my baby. It's Harvey."

During that afternoon in Lanett, Kathryn's new friend led her into a bedroom, opened up a round-topped trunk, and brought out a package wrapped in blue tissue. She handed it to Kathryn, and Kathryn unwrapped it, and there in her hands was the photograph of little Harvey Hammer—that solemn child with his wistful eyes and an aura of light behind his blond curls, and a heart-shaped locket around his neck.

David Holt

I was surrounded with stories, wonderful stories, and I
always loved hearing them. But growing up,
it really never occurred to me that storytelling was
anything other than what we did when our family got
together for Thanksgiving dinner. I've since learned that
it's that, and much more. . . . Though a story doesn't
always seek to be true to fact, it always seeks to be true to
the heart. And I soon discovered that
while I could hold children riveted for fifteen minutes with
a story, I could hardly hold them for three
minutes with only a song.

*   *   *

DAVID HOLT stood nervously backstage at the world-famous Grand Ole Opry in Nashville, Tennessee, dressed completely in white, his broad-rimmed hat slightly shadowing his face. David, an accomplished musician, had distinguished himself in the mountains of western North Carolina by collecting, preserving, and performing the traditional music of the Southern Appalachians. And now, he was performing for the first time on the stage of the Grand Ole Opry, America's mecca for country music.

A few years before, David had helped found the Appalachian Music Program at Warren-Wilson College in Swannanoa—the only program of its kind where students can study, collect, and learn traditional music. It was here in the Southern Appalachians that David had learned to play more than a dozen musical instruments—ranging from a banjo to the fiddle—and now he was sharing his love of America's rich folk music heritage with young people from throughout America.

"As a learning experience for one of my classes, I took some of my students to the Grand Ole Opry. And as I sat there listening, I realized that there was very little old-time music on the Opry any more. When I returned home, I called the folks at the Opry and told them that I thought they should have a little more traditional music and that if they thought so too, I knew I was just the man for the job. They invited me to Nashville, I auditioned, and they scheduled me for the next show. I was in shock. I couldn't believe it.

"I was incredibly nervous, wondering what I was going to play. I thought maybe I'd perform an old Uncle Dave Macon tune. I knew I had to do something different from what everyone else was going to do in order to make an impression, because there was no easy way to impress Nashville musicians. They'd seen it all.

"As I waited for my turn to perform, Little Jimmy Dickens came out on stage and sang 'May the Bird of Paradise Fly Up Your Nose.' Then Billy Walker sang 'It Ain't Love, but It Ain't Bad,' and George Hamilton IV, backed up by the entire fifteen-piece Opry Orchestra, did 'I'm So Miserable When You're Gone, It's Like Having You Here.' And I realized even more the need for something special in my performance.

"I had learned how to play the paper bag from a mountain fiddler named Bill Gosnell, and I remembered that I had a bag in my banjo case. So I decided to play my paper bag on the stage of the Grand Ole Opry—striking the bag with my hand, in time to a harmonica tune. And it worked. They loved it. Word got around Nashville about the guy who played the paper bag on the Opry. I've been invited back, and I've played traditional music at the Opry ever since."

David was born in 1946 in the tiny Texas town of Gatesville, but he spent much of his early childhood in Garland, Texas. In 1957, when he was eleven years old, David moved with his family to California, where he finished high school and, in 1964, began attending San Francisco State University. It was then that David made the discovery which sent him on an eighteen-year odyssey—one that has led him to a personal fulfillment through a love and appreciation of America's traditional music. And through his journey, David has discovered both the songs and stories of America—a blend that has become the hallmark of his career.

"My parents had always expected me to become a lawyer. But it soon became clear to me that I didn't want to be a lawyer; instead, I thought I should be a teacher. After going to school for two years, I dropped out of college and took a job at a private elementary school near Martinez, California. I had just turned twenty-one.

"It was my first night there, and my girl friend and I were staying at the school until they found us each a place to live. It was way out in the country, no one was around but us, and I was standing in front of the building, just looking up at the stars. Except for the stars, it was completely dark, and I was thinking about how big the universe was and how small I was and how the brightness coming at me from those stars was actually ten million years old.

"Suddenly a car pulled up, its headlights glaring, and three men jumped out and ran toward me. I had never been at the school before, and I knew they didn't know me. But when I realized they meant trouble, I turned and began to run. It was too late. They caught me, grabbed my shoulders, turned me around, and all I remember is seeing three fists coming toward me at the same time, right into my jaw. I tried to yell out at them, 'You've made a big mistake. You must be looking for someone else.' But nothing came out. I fell to the ground, they kicked me, and then they went into the school and began to tear it apart.

"As I lay there, I felt no fear, no pain. I was at complete peace. My girl friend, who had hidden in the laundry room, called the police. The next thing I remember was waking up in the hospital, opening my eyes, and looking up at a policeman. It was the happiest I've ever been to see one. I reached up, grabbed his arm, and began to speak. But I couldn't. My jaw had been broken in two places, and it was wired shut. I spent weeks in the hospital, had several operations, and for months had to eat through a straw. I never knew why I had been attacked, and at that point, I was feeling incredibly small and basic. I wanted to lie back and let the world go.

"But during my recovery, I visited a friend and he played for me an old 78rpm recording of Carl Sandburg singing 'Old Paint,' a traditional Western ballad."

> I ride an old paint, and I lead an old dam,
> I'm going to Montana for to throw the houlihan.
> They feed in the coulees and water in the draw;
> Their tails are all matted, and their backs are all raw.
>
> Old Bill Jones had two daughters and a song,
> One went to Denver and the other went wrong.
> His wife she died in a poolroom fight,
> But still he sings from morning 'til night.
>
> *Chorus:*
> Git along, you little dogies, git along there slow,
> For the fiery and the snuffy are a-raring to go.

"It was so simple, with no flourish. It was exactly how I was feeling, and Sandburg was singing about something I felt I needed to know more about. Old Bill Jones had lost his wife and daughters, but he was still able to sing from morning to night."

David began rummaging through archives of cowboy music, and there he discovered a 78rpm recording of Carl Sprague, the first recorded singing cowboy. Fascinated by the simplicity and strength of Sprague's music, David—having heard that Sprague was still living—began to search for him. He found the cowboy singer in Bryan, Texas, where Sprague taught David to play the harmonica and introduced him to the excitement of learning from the source: the old-time musicians themselves.

David, enamored with traditional American music, soon discovered there was a wealth of it in the Southern Appalachians. And in 1969, he began roaming these mountains, learning and collecting songs from the descendants of those who had brought the music to the Appalachians generations earlier.

"I remember Old John. He lived in Tooloose, Kentucky, a place so remote that they had built a road into that community only four years earlier. Until then, you had to either walk or ride a horse into the mountain cove, following a dried-up creek bed.

"I had stopped along the way to see if any musicians lived in Tooloose. And everybody said, 'You need to see Old John. He's the best musician anywhere around.' They said he lived in the first log cabin on the right going up the new road. And sure enough, there was his little log cabin, and Old John was sitting on the front porch. His seven children were playing with their seven old dogs in the front yard.

"The cabin was shingled with Prince Albert Tobacco cans that Old John had opened up, flattened out, and nailed to the logs. On the left side, the cans were rusty where they had been up for years, but toward the right they got redder and redder as he kept adding new ones.

"Old John met me on his front porch, welcomed me in, and offered me some supper. Over in the corner of their little cabin were a wood stove, a table with four chairs, a dresser, and a bed—nine feet wide— where the whole family slept. And that was all that was in Old John's mountain cabin.

"After supper, I went out to my truck and got my guitar. And Old John reached under the bed and pulled out an old-time mountain banjo, completely handmade long years ago. He laughed and told me it was made with catgut strings—house cats to make the high-pitched strings and wildcats to make the low-pitched ones.

"When he began to play 'Sourwood Mountain,' I knew I had found the real thing. We played for hours. And then suddenly, right in the middle of a tune, he stopped playing and said, 'I'm sorry, son, but we're goin' to have to quit now.' I was stunned. I thought I had done something wrong. But no, his youngest daughter reached under the bed, pulled out a black-and-white television, set it on the top of the dresser, plugged it in, and the whole family set in rapt attention watching their favorite television show—*The Beverly Hillbillies*.

"I fell in love with the people and the music of the Southern Appalachians. I went back to California, finished college, and told my parents I wanted to be a banjo player. And when my grandmother died and left me $2,000 and a ten-year-old car, I packed everything I owned into that old car and moved to Asheville, North Carolina, to live in the mountains and pursue my love of mountain music."

As David collected and played the songs of the Southern Appalachians, he also began to collect and tell the stories—the old mountain tales—for he had come to realize "just how powerful storytelling can be." Perhaps David has always sensed his connection to our stories, for his love—and respect—for our American heritage began as a child. As a true son of the Texas frontier, he grew up hearing stories about his pioneer Texas relatives—simple, often amusing tales of a family's personal saga. They are the stories we all possess and seldom share.

"I was surrounded with stories, wonderful stories, and I always loved hearing them. But growing up, it really never occurred to me that storytelling was anything other than what we did when our family got together for Thanksgiving dinner. I've since learned that it's that, and much more."

While David can play a dozen musical instruments—from the banjo to the paper bag—and has performed his old-time music at the legendary Grand Ole Opry, his love of storytelling is never overshadowed. "Though a story doesn't always seek to be true to fact, it *always* seeks to be true to the heart. And I soon discovered that while I could hold children riveted for fifteen minutes with a story, I could hardly hold them for three minutes with only a song." Today, David's performances of old-time music are always laced with stories—the tales that are at the heart of our American heritage, passed along orally from generation to generation of natural-born tellers.

Tailybone

When David Holt was a child, his father played the bones—handed down within his family from generation to generation. When held in the right hands, they can be used to strike a beat and keep time to a down-home fiddle or a banjo tune. But it wasn't until later that David discovered within himself his own musical talents, and he was launched on a study of traditional American music in the mountains of Southern Appalachia. "I love mountain music. To me, it's old-time wisdom bound up in melody and song. You play it, and it becomes a part of you." Today, David performs throughout the United States and the world, playing a unique assortment of musical instruments—including his father's musical bones.

As David was learning the music of Southern Appalachia, he discovered a wealth of mountain tales, including "Tailybone," a traditional story he had first heard as a child growing up in Texas. It is known traditionally as "Tailypo" and is still being recounted in the Southern mountains. While "Tailybone" is told without musical accompaniment, David punctuates his telling by using a variety of musical instruments to give the story rhythm, create a setting and mood, and produce sound effects that give life to the tale.

ONCE, A long time ago, down in the big woods of Tennessee, an old man lived in a log cabin all by himself. That cabin had one room, and at one end was a big stone fireplace. Every evening the old man would come in and cook whatever he had caught on that open fire. But if he didn't catch any meat, he would just cook himself a big pot of beans.

One cold, dark, and windy night, the old man was sittin' up by that fireplace, cookin' a pot of beans and listenin' to the wind howl through the trees outside. He was lost in his thoughts, watchin' those beans begin to boil and that fire burn down low, when all of a sudden, he looked down and saw an animal's paw begin to come up through a hole in the floorboards of the cabin. That was the hole he should have fixed last summer; but too late now, the animal was squeezin' more and more of itself up through the floor. And finally, it was all the way into the room.

It had big, long, pointy teeth and big, fiery, red eyes, and why, it was as big as a dog but had a tail like, well, like nothin' he'd ever seen before. The old man reached down for a little hatchet by the fireplace and raised it up over his head. And when that thing came into the room, he chopped at it, and he chopped its tail off. It let out an awful yell and went runnin' out between the floorboards of the cabin.

The old man had lived in those woods his whole life and had never seen a creature like that before, but there was its old tail, still lyin' on the floor, wigglin'. He reached down, picked up that old tail, and realizing he didn't have any meat for those beans, dropped the tail into the pot and cooked it. And then, like a fool, he ate it. Well, it tasted pretty good to him. In fact, he ate every bean in the pot.

It was gettin' late, so the old man crawled into his bed, pulled the covers up around his shoulders, and put his head on his pillow. He was just about to fall asleep when he heard a scratchin' sound at the side of his cabin.

He raised up and said, "Now, go on and get out of here! Get out of here!"

But all he heard was, "Tailybone. Tailybone. I want my tailybone."

The old man thought that someone was tryin' to play a trick on him, so he said, "Now go on and get out of here, whoever you are. Just go back home."

But all he heard was, "Tailybone. Tailybone. I want my tailybone."

The old man called his dogs that lived under the cabin.

"Ino. Uno. Cumptico-Calico. Get that thing!" And those dogs ran out from under the cabin and into the darkness.

The old man went to the door and listened, and he could hear the dogs barkin' way down in the woods. He knew they were mean dogs, so he didn't worry. He just closed the door, crawled into his bed, and went right to sleep. But he hadn't been asleep long when he was awakened by a scratchin' sound at the door. Something was tryin' to come in.

He sat up in bed and said, "Now, I told you to get out of here. Just go on! Get out of here! Go!"

But all he heard was, "Tailybone. Tailybone. I want my tailybone."

The old man called his dogs again.

"Ino. Uno. Cumptico-Calico. Get rid of that thing!"

Out from under the cabin they ran, almost tearing down the front-yard fence.

The old man went to the door and listened, and way down in the woods he could hear those dogs barkin'. But suddenly, they stopped. It worried him, that silence, but he thought maybe they had chased something down into a hole and he couldn't hear them. So he crawled back into bed, and though he tossed and turned for a while, he finally went to sleep.

But about midnight, he was awakened by what he thought was the sound of the wind. He sat up in bed, and way down in the woods he could hear, "Tailybone. Tailybone. I'll get my tailybone."

And once more the old man called, "Ino. Uno. Cumptico-Calico. Get that thing!"

But all he heard was the sound of the wind.

He called again. "Ino. Uno. Cumptico-Calico."

But something or someone had taken them dogs down in the woods and lost them—or killed them. The old man was scared.

He got out of bed, closed the shutters and windows and barred them shut, and built up a big fire in the fireplace so nothing would come down the chimney. Then he remembered the crack in the floorboards where that strange animal had come in earlier that night, and he stuffed some old rags in the hole, and placed the big rock he used for a doorstop over the top of those rags so it wouldn't come up through the floor again. Then he picked up that little hatchet and began walkin' around the room. Waitin'. Watchin'. Listenin'. Walkin'.

But as the sun was comin' up, the old man felt safe. And he was so tired that he fell into his bed. Then just as he was pullin' the cover up around his shoulders, he heard a strange sound at the foot of the bed.

It said, "Tailybone..."

"I ain't got your old tailybone!" the old man yelled.

But it answered, "You've got my tailybone!"

That thing jumped on that old man and scratched him to pieces, and some folks say that it finally did get its tailybone.

You can go down to those big woods of Tennessee to this very day. You won't see the cabin any more. It's long gone. All that's left is the old chimney standin' alone in a field. But sometimes, late at night, when the moon is full and the wind is howlin' in the trees, they say you can still hear it: "Tailybone. Tailybone. I *got* my tailybone."

Lee Pennington

*I grew up in a time and place where stories
were the bloodline, and the people the heart. I now
sometimes wonder how we could have survived
had it not been for the yarns which entertained us,
sustained us, made us laugh and cry,
and enriched our lives.*

158

J AMES T. and his wife, Aunt Lina, lived just down the winding, narrow road from Lee Pennington in the hollow where Lee grew up in the mountains of eastern Kentucky. Everyone called him James T. Just James T. And even as late as the 1950s, Lee remembers him driving his mules hitched to a wagon full of vegetables up to Portsmouth, Ohio, where he sold his goods on the street.

James T. had a long blacksnake whip, and every day, the old man would sit on his porch and clip the tops of ragweeds in the yard. Lee remembers the swish, the rifle-sharp crack, and the ragweed heads flying off. James T. was a good spitter, too: He could hit crawling bugs thirty or forty feet away. His real pride was a two-headed snake he had found, preserved in alcohol, and he showed it off every chance he could get. But most of all, Lee recalls, James T. was a spinner of yarns—maybe a few he had heard, but mostly ones he created right on the spot.

There was the time that James T. fought in World War II though he never joined the army, or when he killed sixteen squirrels with a slingshot and marbles, or the time he smoked out a squirrel, a rabbit, and a groundhog from the same tree, or even the day he found a spy map from the "Rooshins" dropped from an airplane on his little hillside farm.

"It's no wonder I'm a storyteller. I grew up in a time and place where stories were the bloodline, and the people the heart. I now sometimes wonder how we could have survived had it not been for the yarns which entertained us, sustained us, made us laugh and cry, and enriched our lives."

Lee was born in 1939 at the head of one of Kentucky's many hollows in a place called White Oak, one of eleven children. Though the family lived briefly in Baltimore where Lee's father worked in the shipyards during the early days of World War II, they returned to Kentucky in 1942 and bought a farm for $260—a log house, a good well, and thirty-two acres of steep hillside.

"When I was growing up, we lived as far north as you could go and as far east as you could go and still be in Kentucky—West Virginia on one side, the Ohio River on the other, and more Kentucky stretching south and west. Our neighbors were close, both physically and spiritually. I could stand in our front yard and shout to the wind and another could hear me, yet from the same spot we couldn't see one house from another. Oh, sometimes in the winter when the wood stoves were going, you could see smoke rising into the gray sky, and then we always knew our neighbors were up and around.

"In such a place and at such a time, you would expect to hear old English ballads and Jack tales galore. Yet in my growing up in Greenup County—with the possible exception of 'Barbara Allen' or 'Jack and the Beanstalk'—I never heard such songs and tales. But don't get me wrong. It was indeed a land of storytellers, a land peopled with yarn spinners, *natural* storytellers. And so close were we to the ancient art that we made little or no separation between what was fact and what we imagined might have happened.

"Our family was composed of tellers of tales, and the concept of family extended into the community. In the next house lived the Allens, and in the next the Coles, and to the right, in the lower end of the valley, the Atkinses. On beyond were the Coomers and the Hamptons. And all of them were tellers of tales. Nobody called himself a storyteller—probably wouldn't have answered to the name—but they were tellers just the same, naturally so.

"At Greenup, the county seat, men sat around the courthouse, whittled, chewed tobacco, and told stories. And as a child, I was fascinated with both their knives and yarns. At Munn's Barber Shop in South Shore, Speers Grocery, and Paul Davis's Gas Station—they gathered there too and the stories just flew. There was Blue Atkins, a fox hunter and water witch who was skilled equally at both, and Jim Osborn, hunchbacked, with a face like a bull sheep, who went house to house cutting wood for his keep, and John Lozier, the only man I ever knew who could play a harmonica with his nose. They all told stories."

As a child, Lee helped his father farm. "I took the hoe at eight, the plow at nine, and the 'lead row' at eighteen." But as he worked, he heard the tales—especially the exaggerated ones, the tall tales, like the story about the blacksnake that stole eggs from the family chicken house.

"That old snake would crawl up into the henhouse and wiggle his way from nest to nest, swallowing all of the eggs. Then, he'd crawl back to the edge of the woods, where he'd wrap himself around a tree and squeeze himself until all the eggs were broken up inside, and then he'd have himself a good meal.

"My father decided to stop that old snake from stealing eggs. We got a bushel basket of white doorknobs from a neighbor, and he replaced all of the eggs in the nests with white doorknobs. Soon, the snake crawled into the henhouse, up into the nests, and commenced to swallowing the doorknobs, one by one. He could just barely crawl out to the edge of the woods, where he wrapped himself around a tree again, trying to crush those doorknobs. He tore the bark off of so many trees that he ruined forty acres of good timberland."

Though not eager to pursue an education, Lee went to the same one-room schoolhouse his mother and father had attended years earlier, and he carved his initials near theirs on the weatherbeaten boards. There, in that tiny, one-teacher schoolroom, Lee taught his first class —for a teacher who spent all of her time making hooked rugs. "I taught first grade, three students. I passed two students to the second grade and double-promoted one to the third."

Lee planned at sixteen to quit school and tend the family's hillside farm. But one day, Lee's sister—who taught him in the sixth grade in that same one-room school—said to him, "Lee, someday you'll go to college." He just laughed. "My father and mother hadn't gone to high school. None of my brothers had finished high school. And no one in my family line—and it can be traced back to the year 1132 in England —had ever graduated from college. Besides, I liked farming. It seemed easier than going to school.

"But during the seventh grade, I first met Robert M. Waddell, my teacher. I was curious about the moon, the stars, the rains that watered the crops, the strange little imprints I found on the stones in the fields. Mr. Waddell didn't have all the answers, but he knew where to go looking for them, and he convinced me—at least in part—that this was what school was all about. And after the seventh grade, I just knew that I *would* go to college. I didn't know how. We were poor hillside farmers. But someday, somehow, I knew I would.

"I attended McKell High School at South Shore, and there I met two other great teachers—Jesse Stuart, my principal, and Lena Nevison, my English teacher. Both encouraged me to write. I wrote themes for Mrs. Nevison, and she read them all, and she even asked for more. And Mr. Stuart—himself a respected writer—helped me get a job writing for local newspapers, reporting the school news and sports. I played center on the football team, and while coming home on the bus after the game, I would write an article for the next week's newspaper. The newspaper paid me $3 for each game. I made more money writing than I did raising strawberries, so I decided to be a writer instead of a farmer."

With the assistance of Jesse Stuart, Lee was accepted into Berea College in Berea, Kentucky, and in 1962, he graduated with a B.A. degree in English—the first in his family line to earn a college degree. While attending Berea, Lee pursued writing—reporting for the college newspaper, serving as head of the college's news bureau, and writing publicity articles for the Council of Southern Mountains. And it was there he met Tennessee-born Joy Stout, his "greatest critic and editor," and during their last semester, they were married.

Later, after a stint as teachers at Newburgh Free Academy in New York, Lee and Joy both earned master's degrees in English at the University of Iowa in Iowa City. And within a year, they returned home—to the Southern Appalachian Mountains—to teach at Southeast Community College in Cumberland, Kentucky.

"We had seen and heard everywhere—on television and radio, in newspapers and magazines—that Appalachia had the worst schools, the worst students, the worst of everything in America. We didn't believe it. Instead, we felt that education is about life, and Appalachian students—these young men and women we were now teaching—had lived life deeper than any other students in America."

At Southeast Community College, Lee offered the students new opportunities—classes in writing, creative expression, even poetry—pulling out of them their experiences of living, and working, in Appalachia. In four years, his students had published four collections of their literary works, and in addition, they had published over one thousand pieces of creative writing in more than thirty magazines and anthologies.

But *Tomorrow's People*, their fourth collection, created a furor in this tiny college town. Objecting to the poetry as expressions of protest against the way of life in Harlan County, the citizens rose up in anger. Fearing for their lives, Lee and Joy left Harlan County under the cover of darkness, armed and escorted by guard cars.

Since 1967, Lee and Joy have taught at Jefferson Community College in Louisville. And throughout his life, Lee was emerging as a writer. "I've been writing for as long as I can remember. In fact, I can't ever remember when I didn't write." But as he wrote, he was soaking in life—the stories that eddied around him.

"My father, Andy, was a 225-pound man with big, knotty hands and a heart as big as a pumpkin, and my mother, Mary Ellen, was a 90-pound woman, delicate but strong, who was mother to eleven of us. They both loved to hear stories, and they loved to tell them.

"Though my sister Sue is now one of the most generous people I know, she had a reputation as a child of being stingy. She hoarded her toys—carried them around in a cardboard box to keep the rest of us from touching them. At the dinner table, she'd always reach for the largest biscuit or hunk of cornbread.

"One day, when Sue reached out to pick up the biggest biscuit, my mother stopped her. 'I want to tell you a story, Sue.' And she did— about a poor little girl who went to the bakery every day to get a loaf of bread, and how she'd stand back while everyone else pushed and shoved to get the largest loaves.

"'The baker watched her, day after day, and took note of her actions. One day, he took the smallest loaf he had and put a lump of gold inside. Again, the people pushed and shoved and took every loaf except the smallest one. When the little girl picked up the last loaf, the baker smiled.'

"And with that story, my sister placed the large biscuit back onto the plate and took a smaller one. Mother assured her that there was no lump of gold in the small biscuit. But Sue said, 'I know, but someday you can put a lump of gold in one—just for me.'

"And my dad reveled in telling a story about two boys going out one morning to pick blackberries. The father of one of the boys called him aside and said, 'Now, son, when you come to a blackberry bush, stick with it until you have picked every berry. Don't try to run from bush to bush just getting the big berries.' The son acknowledged his father's advice and left.

"That day the two boys worked differently. One boy ran from bush to bush and just picked the large berries. The other took his father's advice and stuck to his bush until the brier was clean, and then he'd go on to another bush. At the end of the day, one boy had his bucket only half filled. The other, the one who stuck to his bush, had his bucket full.

"In 1963, while I was teaching at Newburgh Free Academy in New York, I received a telephone call from my brother Paul.

"'Dad is dying,' Paul told me. 'If you want to see him, you'd better come home. He won't last long.'

"I said, 'Paul, I can't. I'm in charge of a debate tournament here. It's the largest in New York. This sounds hard, but I can't leave. I feel responsible. If Dad dies, of course I'll come. Tell Dad I love him.'

"Later, Paul called me back.

"'I talked with Dad, and I told him your situation. He sends you this message: 'Tell Lee to stick to his bush.'

"I knew exactly what he meant."

The old stories and legends survive, century after century, and for Lee, they suggest that there "is a continuity in life—a connection to the past and a link with the future. We all have a longing for something immortal, and this longing manifests itself in our stories. They are there, still with us, and they are forever a part of us all."

James T. and Aunt Lina both died while Lee was away at college. Their house was left standing but empty and lonely. Once when Lee was home from school, he drove by the old house, stopped, and went in. He was looking for one thing, and he found it—back on the cupboard shelf. And to this day, Lee still has it: a two-headed snake preserved in alcohol, the pride of James T.

The Calico Coffin

When Lee's Grandma Laura Lawson was a young girl, a friend came to spend the night with her. In the wee hours of the morning, the bed they were sharing began to rise off the floor and the walls commenced to knocking.

"If you don't hush up," Grandma Laura's father yelled from his bedroom, "I'm going to give you both a good whippin'."

But the sounds kept coming, and when he came into their bedroom all set to give them a good licking, he was stopped dead in his tracks. He stood in amazement. The two girls were in bed, and it was hovering a foot off of the floor.

Word got around that Grandma Laura had the powers to move furniture. One day a man in the community, a disbeliever, came over to her house, climbed upon a table, and said, "Make it walk." Grandma Laura did. And as the table—with the man on top—moved slowly toward the fireplace, he jumped off, ran out of the house, and they never saw him again.

When Grandma Laura Lawson was in her seventies, Lee asked her about the walking table.

"Yes, I could make a table walk," she told Lee, "but that was the Devil in me. After I got up a little older and joined the church, the powers left me."

There probably isn't anyone who has not shared ghost stories and other strange tales among friends, around a campfire or under the bedcovers into the night. Today, Lee tells the chilling story of "The Calico Coffin," a tale he heard, told as the truth, as a young man growing up in the Southern Appalachian Mountains. This version is based on "The Sound of Wood," a short story written by Lee.

A LONG time ago, there was a beautiful girl with long, willowy hair that looked like sunlight on ripened grain. Her skin was as white as the underside of a dove. Her cheeks always had a red flush, but she used nothing for color—except now and then when she pinched her cheeks just a little before going to a square dance.

One morning in May, the young girl took ill. Her skin lost its glow and turned gray, and the rosy red color left her cheeks. Her mother nursed her—gathered herbs she knew, boiled tea, and gave it to her daughter. But the girl became sicker and sicker, and by morning, when the pale sun slipped over the green hilltop and the lifting fog, she was dead. Her spirit left her quietly while her mother slept.

165

When the mother arose, the girl lay still under the bright, many-colored quilt. The mother rubbed her eyes to chase away the sleep, to try to see the breathing, but the bed was quiet. She touched her daughter, but there was a chill as cold and gray and damp as the stillness of the room. She walked to the window and stood there, watching the sun rise and the fog spin off in little patterns. Then the tears came, and she could no longer see the sun or the fog.

Later in the day, the father and the couple's son waded through sedge grass, carrying mattocks and shovels, and near a little brownish-green cedar and seven vertical stones—all homemade and with names and dates chiseled into them—they dug the grave.

When they returned to the house, the mother, her eyes pained with grief, was standing on the porch.

"We can use the cedar box—the one made for me," she said. "I can wait." She said nothing else, but she turned and went into the house.

The father and son went to the barn and climbed into the loft. They found the cedar coffin—long and narrow, completely lined in cotton calico, top to bottom—and together, they lowered the box to the ground. They carried it, the father in front, the son behind, to the house.

"She's ready," said the mother. And there she lay, silently upon the bed, and dressed in a white gown. "She's wearing my wedding dress. She's just the size I was then."

They placed her body into the calico coffin, carried it to the cemetery, and lowered it into the ground. And by the time the sun had pulled every trace of light from the hill, the father threw the last shovelful of fresh dirt upon the mound, and they returned home.

The son was exhausted, so he climbed the stairs to his bedroom and fell upon the bed, soon asleep. As he slept, he was awakened by a scream—a horrible scream. He raised full up in bed and stared around the upstairs room and then out the window, but there was no moon and he could see nothing.

There was another scream, full and shattering, coming from downstairs. So he quickly dressed, hurried down the stairway into their bedroom, and found his father standing beside his mother, and he was trying to comfort her.

The mother screamed again, and the young boy felt chills shudder throughout his body.

"I know she's alive! I know she's alive! I hear her calling! You must go to her!"

The father looked at his son, standing by his mother's bed—his eyes full of fright. They stayed with her throughout the night, but when morning came, she was still screaming, pleading, begging.

"Please! You must go dig her up! She's alive! I hear her calling!" Her screams felt like ice in the morning. "Please! Please! Go get her!"

The father turned to his son and whispered, "We must do it. We must show her, prove to her, or she will never recover from this agony."

So the three of them slipped into the morning to the graveyard, and the father and son dug the grave as the mother stood over them, watching and weeping. The wind swept through her long graying hair, making a shadow on the freshly turned earth.

Finally, the shovels touched the box. They worked ropes under it and eased it upward and out of the grave. And with the point of the shovel, the father pried open the coffin lid—the lid he had nailed down only the day before.

The father looked at the mother, then the son, then slowly lifted the lid. Horror-stricken, the father dropped his shovel and fell back. The mother sank her head into her hands, and the tears came even heavier. The son fell upon his knees in the fresh dirt.

The young girl lay in the calico coffin. Her dress was torn at the neck, and her face, no longer beautiful, was contorted and twisted in pain. Her fingernails were gone, and her fingers and hands were covered with blood. The coffin's calico lining was shredded, and there were fingernail marks deeply carved in the wood underneath the lid.

Stories of Our American Traditions

Mary Carter Smith

*. . . I have come to believe even more in my work, my
duty, and I have committed myself
anew to truth, freedom, justice, and peace for all peoples,
black or white, young or old, free or in bondage.
My stories are my message.*

* * *

MARY CARTER SMITH is an urban American *griot*—a story-teller in the African tradition—who tells the stories and sings the songs of black America, a heritage with roots deep in Mother Africa. Through these tales of African lore, Mary strives to break down the barriers between people separated by race and nationality, age and religion. Since 1973, when she ended her thirty-one-year career as a teacher and librarian in the inner-city schools of Baltimore, she has performed her stories and songs—her messages of justice and humanity—in schools, libraries, hospitals, and prisons in Baltimore and throughout America and the world.

Mary was born in Birmingham, Alabama, in 1919. And today, it is easy for Mary to imagine the dismay and grief her family must have experienced when it was learned that her mother, then unmarried, was expecting a child. It was a shame and a scandal in those days for a child to be born out of wedlock. But when Mary was born, her family loved her at first sight, and as she grew up, she was always loved, and loved deeply. In one faded letter Mary cherishes, her mother described her as "the sunshine of my life."

"Though I was surrounded by those who loved me, my life was not without hurt and pain—even as a very young child. My mother's first husband had died, and she remarried and moved north to New York City to find work. Mother wanted to take me with her, but I stayed with my grandmother until they were settled. One day, my grandmother called me to her side and quietly told me my mother was dead, murdered by the man she had married. Only through old letters the police had found did they discover she had a family, and they sent her body home for burial.

"I recall someone lifting me up over her casket, and how I looked down upon my mother's body. And I remembered her well—tall, dark, and beautiful, with a kind smile. I remembered her warm lap. And looking back, I realize now that my very first remembrance of storytelling and singing was a very vivid image of my mother, rocking me to sleep, singing to me."

After her mother died, Mary continued living with her grandmother—the woman she called Mama—and together, they shared homes with

Mary's uncles and aunts, living in communities in Ohio, West Virginia, and Kentucky.

"Those were happy years. I recited stories and sang old Negro songs at the Mount Zion Baptist Church, and my grandmother would read to me from the Bible. And when I learned to read—I learned very early—I discovered the public library, and I read a book every day. I can remember how my grandmother would call, 'Mary Rogers, it's time to go to bed.' I'd go to bed, right enough, but I would take the flashlight and read under the covers until I had finished the whole book. Often I'd sit at my window and read by the light as it shone through.

"Sometimes I'd gather my young friends around me, and we'd build playhouses, and cook real food that my grandmother would give me, and roll down the grassy slopes, and roller-skate for miles. And I would tell them stories, usually the stories I'd read."

One day, Mary—who had known only love and warmth and devotion within her family—encountered the painful realities of being black in a white world, and it began to stir in her the very hatred she tries to help eradicate today. "We had observed Columbus Day in our second-grade class, and a little Italian boy named Albert came up to me. He put his thumbs under his arms and proudly announced, 'Me, an Italian, discovered America. All your folks ever did was pick cotton.'" Mary was shocked and hurt. Though she didn't realize it then, Albert's image of the black race had been *taught* to him. He knew or understood nothing else. And looking back, Mary realized even as a black child that that image—of slaves, picking cotton—was all *she* had ever been taught until she met a teacher she remembers as Miss Showalter.

"Miss Showalter was a substitute teacher—white and short, fat and balding. But to me, she was beautiful. For the first time, I heard about George Washington Carver and Booker T. Washington—blacks who had accomplished in a white world, who had done something worthwhile. And from that moment on, I became conscious of our black heritage and began reading about my culture, my past, and about black America.

"But as I learned more of my heritage, I began to recognize—even as a child—the injustice, the hate, and the prejudices that have plagued my people for generations. You see, I was the only black child in my third-grade class. At Christmas, all of the students decided to give our teacher a present. My grandmother gave me a dollar to go shopping, and I bought a white handkerchief with pink edging, wrapped it in tissue, and took it to school.

"We lined up to give the teacher our presents, and when each little white child in front of me handed her his present, she opened it, smiled, and said, 'Thank you.' But when I gave her my present, she turned red, took the gift between her thumb and forefinger, and dropped it into the garbage can. And then, she quickly looked over me to the little white girl behind me and smiled.

"When school was dismissed, I ran home crying. I asked my Mama, 'Why did she do that to me?' And by the stove in the kitchen, my grandmother took me upon her lap and said, 'Dear child, you're colored. And to some people, that makes a difference.' I never forgot that ugly display of intolerance and prejudice, and though I was still a young child, I struggled to cope with the hate I was experiencing."

In 1931, Mary's grandmother longed to return to the "old home place" in Birmingham. She wanted to spend the rest of her life there. So Mary and her grandmother returned to live in the familiar little house behind Groveland Baptist Church—the house with the wide porch, covered with roses and honeysuckle. How Mary loved that house! But Mary's grandmother became ill, and they moved to Aunt Booby's house in Edwight, West Virginia, where her grandmother died in 1932. Mary was only thirteen.

Mary continued to live with Aunt Booby—first in Edwight, and later in Ida May, West Virginia. It was in Ida May that Aunt Booby was stricken with blindness. Upon the advice of her doctors, Aunt Booby moved to Baltimore where she was treated—and cured—of her illness at Johns Hopkins Hospital. While in Baltimore, Mary graduated from Coppin Teachers College in 1942 and began her career as an elementary school teacher and librarian in the inner-city schools.

"By choice, I lived and taught in the inner city. I didn't want to live or work anywhere else. I felt that I knew and understood black children, their problems and their needs. I wanted them to overcome their mistrust and hatred of the white world, to share my love and appreciation for the richness of our black heritage, to learn to be black and live black—without hating."

During her thirty-one years of teaching, Mary told and read stories, sang songs, and wrote and recited poetry—all centered on her African heritage. Then one night she saw a performance of Joanna Featherstone, a black actress, reading and reciting poetry at Morgan State University in Baltimore. Mary was overwhelmed and inspired, and she wanted to share her own stories and songs with others—to tear down walls and build bridges of understanding beyond the classroom.

"I wrote Miss Featherstone's agent, suggesting that he represent me, but his return letter was chilly and disappointing. 'If I ever need you,' he told me, 'I'll call.' But not long afterward, he did call me. He was frantic. Miss Featherstone was unable to perform at Paine College in Augusta, Georgia, and he asked me to fill the engagement. I accepted, and it was a thrilling experience for me. Many of those who heard me at Paine College asked me to perform at their schools and colleges, and following that chance performance, I began to appear frequently—telling the stories and singing the songs that I was sharing with the young children I was teaching. And I added others—those for a more mature audience—that carried my messages of love and understanding.

"After a performance in Virginia, I arrived home late one Sunday night, feeling confident that I had built some bridges with my stories and songs. But when I turned on the television, I was confronted suddenly with a newscast of a riot, and as never before, the violence touched and troubled me. I saw the hatred, the misunderstanding, the frustration etched on the people's faces, and I didn't sleep that night. I felt God's call to be His messenger of peace and justice, and the next morning, I requested sabbatical leave from my position with the Baltimore schools so I could devote full time to my mission—to tell the stories and sing the songs I'd heard and performed all of my life."

Within three years, Mary had quit her teaching job and was telling her stories of justice and humanity and understanding to ever-widening audiences. While she told her tales, she also devoted herself to discovering more about her heritge, returning repeatedly to Mother Africa to experience her native African culture—to learn the stories and songs of her ancestral people.

But in 1978, Mary's own faith and strength were shaken at their very foundation, tested by one senseless, violent act that for a while darkened her whole world. It was a Saturday morning in January, and Mary was barbecuing chicken for a Bible class meeting that evening. As she placed the chicken into the oven, the telephone rang. When Mary answered, it was her uncle, and his voice was tense, urgent. "Ricky is dead." Ricky was Mary's only child. She was stunned beyond words.

"Two friends came for me, and we went down to the police headquarters to a room below ground level, marked 'Homicide.' A body lay on a long table, and it was covered with a white blanket figured in red roses. When someone pulled back the cover, I saw my son's face. The sounds that came out of me were like an animal screeching in agony.

"I later learned that he had stopped at a bar on his way to his girl friend's house, and a woman—a woman he didn't even know—had stabbed him. And on that bitterly cold January morning, I could have killed her for killing my son. When they arrested the woman and placed her in custody, I confess that I wanted to see her reap an equal portion of the hurt she had sown. In June, she was found guilty of manslaughter and sentenced to ten years in prison.

"Ricky was so kind and gentle. 'Why?' I asked. Twenty-nine years earlier, my husband and I wanted him so very much. He was a beautiful baby, and he won our hearts at once. But now he was dead—the last of my immediate family. His father had died thirteen years earlier, and his stepfather—a man I married in 1960—died only two years after our marriage. I was now alone."

So in the months and years following Ricky's death, Mary had to struggle against the very despair from which she had labored to rescue others. Mary believed always in our common humanity—and the power of her stories. During those troubled times, she continued her travels, performing the stories and songs she used to console, comfort, and strengthen—not only those to whom she spoke but also herself, in her own dark moments. Yet no story could have prepared Mary for what she encountered on Mother's Day seven years after Ricky's death.

"I was scheduled to tell stories to a group of young women in a Baltimore prison, and before I left home, I called the prison director to confirm the engagement. She said, 'I think I should tell you that the young woman who killed your son is here.'

"The news rocked me, but I went as promised to fulfill the obligation. Though I didn't see my son's murderess among those who gathered for the program, before I left, she asked for me. For over a half hour, we talked. What I saw was not the arrogant person I remembered from her trial, but instead, a troubled human being—a person who had been suffering in her way as I had in mine, a person who needed love, who was calling out for help. She asked me to forgive her. And I did.

"For through Ricky's death, I have come to believe even more in my work, my duty, and I have committed myself anew to truth, freedom, justice, and peace for all peoples, black or white, young or old, free or in bondage. My stories are my message."

Moseatunya

The Zambezi River flows between Zimbabwe and Zambia, and at one point, this mighty river drops thousands of feet—creating a waterfall much higher than America's Niagara. The first white man to see this waterfall was David Livingstone, the British explorer, and he named the falls for Queen Victoria. But for thousands of years, those who lived along the river called this majestic falls Moseatunya—The Smoke That Thunders—for there is always a vast mist around the top of the waterfall and one can hear its roar for miles.

War was common among the African tribes who lived along the river, and courage was held sacred. One must never run from battle, and if anyone did, his fate was to be thrown into Moseatunya—into the boiling, churning water below—never to be seen again. One night many years ago, the chief Zaweisi, along with his tribesmen, gathered to put to death one who had run from battle.

On a train traveling from Paris to Dijon, Mary shared a compartment with two African students. During the journey, one of the students shared several African folktales with her. This is one of them.

THE POWERFUL Zaweisi stood on a rock, gazing down upon the thousands who had gathered there.

"Bring Konkela forward," he thundered. "He is my sister's child and more dear to me than my own would have been. But if he has run like a coward, he must die as have other cowards before him."

Konkela had sat quietly, his hands tied behind his back. Another soldier untied him and whispered, "Courage, Konkela." He led Konkela forward.

"I am not afraid to die," Konkela said, his head held high.

"Tell me again, Konkela, what happened in the battle?"

"Uncle," Konkela said, "I have told you again and again. There is nothing new to tell."

His uncle said, "But perhaps I've missed something. It brings me no joy to see you die, for you would have been chief in my stead."

"Uncle," Konkela began, "I was honored to be in charge of all of our troops to fight your enemy, Sigary. We had planned the battle well. Half of us stayed in the bush. The other half—I was leading them as planned—quickly scaled the walls of Sigary's village and set the houses

177

on fire. But his spies had outwitted us, and they knew we were coming, so they had gone from their homes. Every house was empty. There we were with burning houses behind us and the enemy facing us.

"As we climbed the village walls to escape the flames, we were perfect targets for their spears, and many of us died as we fell from the wall. Those of us who were still alive regrouped, and we continued to fight. Oh, Uncle, by the gods of our fathers, we *fought*. I saw my mother's own sons fall dead beside me in battle. And we later found that our men who were in the bush had also been killed."

Konkela continued to plead his defense.

"Uncle, I am sick of war and I look forward to dying. But I do tell you with pleasure that your enemy, Sigary, is dead. With my own spear, I pierced him. But my strong arm felt weary no more, and as I looked at it, blood ran down my arm, over my hand, and drenched the ground. An enemy had almost severed my arm from my body. I could do no more."

Zaweisi asked him in agony, "And so you ran? You should have stayed there and died like a hero and not run like a coward."

Zaweisi looked into Konkela's eyes.

"Look at me, Konkela. Look at my ugly face. Once I was as handsome as you are today, but a leopard and I were each stalking the same prey. I got there first. The leopard leaped upon my back, and he clawed out my right eye and tore the side of my face to shreds. But I put my hands around his throat, and I choked him to death. I wish that I had died so I would not have to see this bitter day when you, my sister's own child, must die like a coward."

Suddenly, a sound was heard—the voice of a woman wailing for the dead.

"Oh, Zaweisi! Oh, Zaweisi!"

The ranks of soldiers parted, and there stood a woman, small and beautiful, carrying a tightly covered basket. She was Konkela's wife. She ran and knelt before Zaweisi.

"Mercy, Uncle. Have mercy. Only eleven months have I been Konkela's wife and now, as all mothers before me, I carry our child under my heart. Would you leave me without a husband? Our unborn child without a father? War? What do I care about war? I despise it as all mothers before me. Have mercy, Uncle! Have mercy!"

The tears ran down her cheeks. Zaweisi hid his face with his hands because his eyes too were wet. But Zaweisi said, "Woman, do not ask me to do this, for I am a just man. I have said that all who run from battle must die. But I promise you that when your child is born—be he manchild, be he womanchild—he will be the next head of our family. This is all I can in honor do."

Then she said, "Perhaps you will take a present I brought for you. It might help to change your mind."

Before anyone could say a word, she leapt to the rock beside him, uncovered the basket she held in her hands, and thrust it down over his head. Then, she jumped from the rock and ran to the waterfall, calling, "Konkela! Konkela! Better that I should die than you!"

When she reached the waterfall, she bent her knees and leapt into Moseatunya—The Smoke That Thunders—never to be seen again.

Zaweisi snatched the basket from his head, and everyone recoiled in horror as they saw the present Konkela's wife had given the old chief. It was a snake, cold and deadly, and it had encircled his head like a turban. He felt it bite him again and again.

But Zaweisi was strong. He grabbed the snake by its tail, pulled it from his head, and still holding the snake by its tail, beat it to death on the rocks. Then, he sat down. The snake's poison was also strong, and Zaweisi knew he had only a few moments to live.

"All of my life I have lived with violence and war. It took the death of this brave woman to show me that there is a courage that goes beyond the hunting grounds, beyond the battlefields. My loyal soldiers, before I die, swear to me that Konkela will be your next chief."

And there amid the burning of the torches, thousands of voices rang out.

"Long live Konkela! Long live Konkela!"

Though this happened many years ago, you can go to Mother Africa today and see Moseatunya—The Smoke That Thunders.

Waddie Mitchell

One night ever' week, I do nothin' but tell stories to my
kids. I'll weave a tale about somethin'
I'll want to teach them, and sometimes I even amaze
myself at how much fun it can be—sittin' there,
tellin' stories. And I'm never more gratified
by an audience than when my own children sit
and listen to me—enjoying the story,
rememberin' it against the day when they too
might want to share it.

WADDIE MITCHELL is a real buckaroo, one of the survivors of that fading breed, the American cowboy. Since he was sixteen years old, he has made his living on the vast Nevada range—riding horses and branding calves and driving cattle. And just for the heck of it, Waddie recites poetry. Not Shakespeare, but homespun yarns in rhythm and rhyme, handed down, cowboy to cowboy, for more than a century. These are story-poems about the cowhand who tried to ride Pegasus, the flying horse, or the drunken cowpokes who tied knots in the Devil's tail. The poems—simple verse that is sometimes humorous, sometimes melancholy—have emerged from the long, lonely days on the range, the solitary times spent on a horse. They speak of the ordinary, simple stuff of cowboy life. And when the mood strikes, Waddie will occasionally pen his own verse—of life he has known as a young buckaroo.

Waddie, one of a bevy of cowboy poets keeping the age-old tradition alive, was born in 1950 near Elko, Nevada, a cowboy town surrounded by vast expanses of open range where cowboying is still a way of life. "My Dad was a cowman. He was always a ranch foreman or manager, and I was born on a ranch and grew up there with the cowhands. They called me Little Waddie—slang for little cowboy. And when I was just a child, I'd sit around the bunkhouse with the old ranch hands, listenin' to 'em tell stories.

"I'll never forget old Booger Red, one of Dad's ranch hands. He was tall and lean and had big round hands and a tough, pitted face. At my tender age, I didn't know a good cowboy from a bad one. But he *looked* like a good cowboy ought to look, and that was all that mattered to me then.

"Booger worked with Dad on the ranch during the week, and on weekends he'd go fishin'. Fishin' to Booger meant goin' down to the local bar in Jiggs, some thirty miles away, and gettin' drunk. But because I was young, maybe seven, I'd always believe that ol' Booger really did fish. Ever'time he'd come back, I'd always ask 'im, 'Did you catch anything?' He never did, but he always told me this story.

I caught no fish and I'll tell you why:
The water was too low, the winds too high;

Too many people, drat those boys,
Too many dogs, too much noise;
Left our glasses, brought wrong bait,
Boots sprung a leak, I started too late;
Flies won't float, lost best hooks,
Owner of the stream gave dirty looks;
I caught no fish and could tell you more,
I could talk two seasons,
Caught no fish, plenty of reasons.

"As I was growin' up, all of the cowboys I knew were rich in storytel-lin', 'cause to make a whole cowboy, you had to be pretty good at entertainin' in the bunkhouse at night. It was just a part of a buckaroo's life. And since I've always wanted to be a good cowboy, tellin' stories has been just as important to me as outfigurin' a cow."

Cowboying was all that Waddie had ever done—riding and working cattle—so at sixteen years old, he quit school and "was hired on as a buckaroo" at the Seven Lazy S Ranch near Deeth, thirty-six miles from Elko. At the ranch, Waddie met Kickie, an old, potbellied ranch hand. Although Kickie must have been a good cowboy in his day, Waddie never knew him when he wasn't always complaining, "kickin' about somethin'." That's how Kickie got his name.

"But Kickie was proud of all the things he did, and one of the things he did best was tell stories. He didn't have a tooth in his head and he had a wart on the end of his tongue, and I could hardly bear watchin' 'im talk. But I was young and away from home and like a whipped pup most of the time, and I was lookin' for friendship. I was drawn to old Kickie.

"As we worked together on the ranch, Kickie recited pieces of poetry—over and over again—about anything that would happen during the day. It tantalized me enough to ask him to tell all of the story, but he never would.

"One night in the bunkhouse the boys were passin' the bottle 'round, and I was sittin' there with 'em, and Kickie told a story that choked me up like I'd never been choked up before. It was probably a sad story—I can't remember—but I do recall being ashamed of myself, thinkin' I shouldn't be cryin'. Then I noticed that ever' cowboy in the bunkhouse had a wet eye too.

"So I asked Kickie, 'Would you write that story down for me so I can have it too?'

"But he said, 'No. No. I don't think I will. I wrote stories down for a feller one time and he just lost 'em. That's a lot of writin', and I hate to write.'

"But I persisted. 'If *I* write it down, will you tell it to me?' And he said he would.

"So I got a pencil and some paper, and he started tellin' the story about as fast as he could talk. Since I couldn't write very fast, he wasn't three lines into the story before I was totally lost. Though I asked him to tell it again, he said, 'No. Maybe some other time.' Two weeks later, Kickie was dead."

After his death, Waddie never really thought anymore about Kickie's stories. He was probably thinking about Catfish Charlie and how he hated to ride that old bucking horse, and how bad he wanted clean bed sheets, and how he was looking forward to going to town. But he did begin listening closely to other old cowhands telling stories, thinking about how the stories evolved, how they were structured, what they meant. During those long, hard days in the saddle, Waddie would try to learn the stories he had heard. And the stories he learned comforted, consoled, and amused him.

"Several years later when I had hired on at the Circle A Ranch, Brian Morris was my cow boss. He was as much a real cowboy as had ever come around, and he was a storyteller and could tell stories about horses, and cowpunchin', and pain, and cold, better than anybody I ever knew. He could tell stories all night long, and the more whiskey he drank, the more he could tell.

"I remember well a cold day in February when Brian was leadin' me and the three other buckaroos as we moved cattle from the main ranch at Grayson way out to Owyhee Desert. We had driven cows day after day, sixty miles out to the desert and sixty miles back. It was cold and the wind was blowin', and up came a nasty rain and sleet storm. We were drivin' our cows right square into the wind. We were freezin' up, didn't have enough help, and it'd been a long time since we'd been to town, or had a hot meal, or gotten mail.

"The four of us cowboys ridin' together hadn't said a word for hours —just sittin' there, doin' our job in misery, and each thinkin' seriously of quittin'. But Brian came back to us and, without sayin' a word, rode along right into the cold, bitter wind beside us—his handlebar moustache frozen in ice, hangin' with icicles.

"And then he turned to us and said:

> Red-breasted robin,
> Sittin' on a pole;

Wiggle, waggle went his tail.
Pfft went his hole.

"When makin' the sound *pfft*, he spewed through his lips, and those icicles hangin' from his moustache cracked and fell off, and the four of us looked at each other and started grinnin'. Though we were tired and miserable, Brian's verse struck us funny, and we laughed until I thought we were goin' to fall off our horses.

"Brian didn't say, 'Toughen up, boys,' or, 'Ain't it miserable.' We were tough, and we knew it was miserable. We didn't need anybody to tell us that. But he always was comin' up with appropriate verse, and we perked up for the rest of the day. For me, stories have made the unbearable bearable.

"When I was workin' on the Seven S Ranch, we had a cook who called 'imself Wild Bill. He wore black pants, a black shirt, and a black hat, and he always had a pistol and a bowie knife strapped to his leg. But during the Fourth of July holiday when the men were celebratin' in town, he quit—leavin' us without a cook.

"I was the youngest hand, so I got first turn at the nasty jobs—I went to cookin'. After a couple of days, I asked when it was time to trade off and have some other cowhand do the job. And Shorty Daniels told me a story.

"'Back in the days when I was cookin', the man who complained about the food automatically became the cook. I'd been cookin' for three days and nobody was complainin'. So one mornin', I was fixin' some biscuits and I salted 'em down real good. I salted them biscuits so much they'd make your eyes water just to smell 'em bake.

"'When I served 'em, one old cowboy grabbed 'imself a biscuit, opened it up, poured it full of gravy, took a big bite, and before he could catch 'imself, he yelled, "Holy good heavens, this sure is a salty biscuit." But then he looked up and saw the wide grin on my face, and real quick like, added, "But that's just the way I like 'em."'

"Shorty laughed as he told me that tale. He was an old man, tiny and drawn up, but he was a real cowboy, and as far as I know, he's still ridin' for a livin'. He's wore out more saddles than any man I've ever known."

Since quitting school to buckaroo, Waddie has never been "hired on" to do anything else—even during his two-year stint in the United States Army. While on his way to Vietnam, Waddie stopped for a few days at Fort Carson in Colorado, and there, for an unknown reason, his orders for Vietnam were mysteriously dropped. He lingered longer.

"I was sittin' in a bar one night, and I was wearin' my old ranch clothes, and a feller, wearin' his ranch garb, came up to me.

"He asked, 'Where are you workin'?'

"'I'm not,' I told 'im. 'I'm in the army.'

"He said, 'So am I. I work on a ranch for the army.'

"I was shocked. This feller was spendin' his time in the army on a ranch in Colorado? I asked about the army's ranch, and sure enough, they needed a horseshoer, and I was assigned to the duty. Two months later, I was runnin' the ranch. I became a certified farrier, met my wife, Tootie, and married her in a horseback weddin'. And that's where I started tellin' my stories for the first time—to the other hands on the ranch.

"We got to sittin' around at night tellin' windies, and I was always able to come up with the biggest one. The other ranchers were just young boys like me, but before joinin' the army, they'd never been on a ranch a day in their lives. They knew nothin' of the cowboy life and the traditions I'd experienced, so they would tape my stories and send them home to their parents and wives.

"As I told stories, I began to develop the confidence that I needed to give the story power, and then I realized that what really made the difference was not just the words but how the story was told. I learned that I had to be as involved in the story as much the hundredth time I'd tell it as I was the first time I'd ever heard it. You've got to enjoy the story, say it as though it's comin' out of your mouth brand new."

After being discharged from the army, Waddie buckarooed in Colorado. But soon, he returned home to Nevada and began managing ranches—first the Bar Slash Bar Ranch and later the TM Ranch, both more than 180 miles from Elko in the isolated Nevada range.

"We lived on a dirt road, had no electricity, had no telephone within thirty-five miles. Despite the hardship, our family life was special. Tootie and I were dependent upon each other, and we appreciated everything 'cause nothin' came easy. We just couldn't come in and flip on a light switch. We lit the lamp and kept the lamps clean, and the wicks trimmed, and the bowls filled with kerosene. Our days were full from the time we got up to the time we went to bed. There was very little time for anything except each other. And since we were so far away from town, we couldn't even tune in to a good radio station. So during our family time, we entertained ourselves, and I remember very few times that storytelling didn't occur."

Since schools were so far away, Waddie and his wife taught their children at home, but they became concerned that they would not be able to give them the education they needed. Less than three years ago, Waddie and his family left the isolated Nevada ranches and moved closer to Elko, where Waddie now manages the Stake Ranch near Jiggs.

"Though I'm only thirty-eight years old, I've seen some tough times, but the toughest job I ever faced in the cow business was leaving the life we loved so much. We miss the seclusion, the freedom from life's complexities, and the times we cherished together as a family. But one thing hasn't changed. One night ever' week, I do nothin' but tell stories to my kids. I'll weave a tale about somethin' I'll want to teach 'em, and sometimes I even amaze myself at how much fun it can be—sittin' there, tellin' stories. And I'm never more gratified by an audience than when my own children sit and listen to me—enjoyin' the story, rememberin' it against the day when they too might want to share it."

For it was as a child that Waddie first heard stories, listening to the old cowhands as they sat in the bunkhouse or around the campfire. As Waddie heard the old tales, he absorbed them, and throughout his life, they have wrapped around him like a warm blanket on a cold winter night. "And from my earliest recollections, I can't ever remember a time that stories weren't a part of my life."

Tying the Knots in the Devil's Tail

When Waddie was growing up, a cowboy nicknamed One-Eyed Bill lived on his father's ranch. He was old, but he would do some of the ranch chores, and Waddie's family took care of him. He lived in the ranch house, upstairs with the other cowboys. "One night soon after I'd gotten the privilege of sleepin' upstairs with the cowhands, One-Eyed Bill came home drunk, singin' songs and tellin' stories. He told me how he'd roped the Devil, dehorned and branded 'im, and left 'im with knots tied in his tail. I sure loved that story, and I always thought he wrote it. He used to tell me he did." But years later, Waddie learned that the story One-Eyed Bill told that night was a classic old cowboy poem—verse written long years ago by Gail Gardner. It remains today one of Waddie's favorites.

Away up high in the Sierry Petes,[1]
Where the yeller pines grow tall,
Ole Sandy Bob and Buster Jig
Had a rodeer[2] camp last fall.

Oh, they taken their hosses and runnin' irons
And maybe a dog or two,
An' they 'lowed they'd brand all the long-yered calves
That come within their view.

And any old dogie that flapped long yeres,
An' didn't bush up[3] by day,
Got his long yeres whittled an' his old hide scorched
In a most artistic way.

Now one fine day ole Sandy Bob
He throwed his seago[4] down;
"I'm sick of the smell of burnin' hair
And I 'lows I'm a-goin' to town."

[1] The Sierra Prieta mountain range in Arizona.
[2] A roundup on the range.
[3] To hide in the bushes.
[4] To loose hemp rope.

So they saddles up an' hits 'em a lope,
Fer it warn't no sight of a ride,
And them was the days when a Buckeroo
Could ile up his inside.

Oh, they starts her in at the Kaintucky Bar
At the head of Whisky Row,
And they winds up down by the Depot House
Some forty drinks below.

They then sets up and turns around,
And goes her the other way,
An' to tell you the Gawd-forsaken truth,
Them boys got stewed that day.

As they was a-ridin' back to camp,
A-packin' a pretty good load,
Who should they meet but the Devil himself,
A-prancin' down the road.

Sez he, "You ornery cowboy skunks,
You'd better hunt your holes,
Fer I've come up from Hell's Rim Rock
To gather in yer souls."

Sez Sandy Bob, "Old Devil be damned,
We boys is kinda tight,
But you ain't a-goin' to gather no cowboy souls
'Thout you has some kind of a fight."

So Sandy Bob punched a hole in his rope,
And he swang her straight and true,
He lapped it on to the Devil's horns,
An' he taken his dallies[5] too.

Now Buster Jig was a riata[6] man,
With his gut-line coiled up neat,
So he shaken her out an' he built him a loop,
An' he lassed the Devil's hind feet.

[5]Looping rope loosely around the saddle horn.
[6]Rope.

Oh, they stretched him out an' they tailed him down
While the irons was a-gettin' hot,
They cropped and swaller-forked[7] his yeres,
Then they branded him up a lot.

They pruned him up with a de-hornin' saw,
An' they knotted his tail fer a joke,
They then rid off and left him there,
Necked to a Black-Jack oak.

If you're ever up high in the Sierry Petes,
An' you hear one hell of a wail,
You'll know it's that Devil a-bellerin' around,
About them knots in his tail.

[7]To make an identifying notch in the ear of cattle.

Christmas at the Cross

When Waddie was a young buckaroo, the cowboys would spend the spring, summer, and fall on the range. But during the winter, when the weather was bad, they camped at the Cross Ranch—a remote site where cowboys for years had crossed the Humbolt River. One winter, Waddie was there—his first Christmas away from home. "Though I enjoy tellin' the classic cowboy poems, I have become more aware of the stories in my own life. I realize that I'm the only livin' person who has my stories, and I've decided to share them with others." One of his favorites is "Christmas at the Cross," a story he wrote and now tells.

We were camped at the Cross,
    Where the buckaroos stayed
    In winter, kinda out of the way
Of the rosin-jaws' sight
    With their wagons and teams
    In the days when men forked all the hay.

We were ridin' the feed grounds
    And doctorin' a few,
    But shacklin' up when the weather got strong.
There were six of us there,
    Varyin' greatly in age,
    And by and large, all the crew got along.

The holiday season
    Was on us again
    With festivities startin' around,
And the bunkhouse was busy
    With five buckaroos
    Sprucin' up for the big dance in town.

All but Charley was goin'
    And I didn't understand,
    So I look over at Jim and I say,

"What's wrong with Ol' Charley?
  He ain't' comin' agin;
  I think he's Scroogin' this holiday."

"I've noticed that too,"
  Was Jim's quick reply.
  "He's been about as much fun as a bone.
And lately, durin' our
  Bull sessions at night,
  He's been locked in his room all alone."

"I've seen it too,
  He's been actin' some strange"—
  We were both interrupted by Ron.
"I got up in the night
  Sometime last week
  And the light in his room was still on."

"Let him brew in 'imself
  And just leave 'im be,"
  Harold said with a jig in his gait.
"It's time we was headin'
  In town to the dance,
  To show the girls how we all celebrate."

"These guys are all callin' you
  Scrooge, Charley boy.
  Better come dancin' and prove 'em all wrong."
"Thanks, Gary, but no,"
  Was Charley's reply.
  "You boys had best be gettin' along."

It was long in the mornin'
  'Fore we made it back home
  On that Christmas Day long ago,
With our blistered feet
  And our heads in a fog
  And a new six inches of snow.

Charley met us with a smile
  And a spring in his step
  That he made sure none of us missed.

"Good mornin' fellas,
  I'll tend to the chores;
  Oh, by the way, Merry Christmas."

"He's rubbin' it in,"
  I said to myself,
  As I went down the hall to my room.
All I could think of
  Was the day off in bed
  To help me get over this gloom.

I flopped on my tarp,
  Not botherin' to
  Even rid myself of my coat.
My stomach's a mess
  And my head's throbbin' now
  And there's a blowtorch lit up in my throat.

In addition to the discomfort
  I already felt,
  I laid on something that made my face hurt.
So I push myself up,
  Try to focus my eyes,
  To see a brand new rawhide quirt.

It was of curious workmanship,
  Shot-loaded to boot
  And balanced just right for my hand.
My name was on a tag
  That was tied to the lash,
  Signed "Santa, the jolly ol' man."

In a dumbfounded stupor
  I went to the hall,
  To see Jim lookin' dumb as a bell.
He was holdin' a real nice
  Mane-hair McCarty
  With slobber straps tooled up real well.

Then out came Harold,
  Then Gary, then Ron,
  All holdin' gifts from Ol' Saint Nick.

Every piece was handcrafted
  Especially for him,
  And each man thought his was the pick.

"So this is what he's
  Been doin' of late,"
  Harold said. "We should all be ashamed.
He's give of his talents,
  Effort and time,
  And then didn't even sign his own name."

"And here we all thought
  He's been actin' like Scrooge
  'Cause some dancin' and parties he's missed,
While all of the goodwill
  We've all shown combined,"
  Gary moaned, "wouldn't even start a small list."

Well, about that time
  Charley comes through the door,
  Havin' done all the chores for the day,
And there in the hall
  Stood five hungover punchers,
  Gulpin' hard to find somethin' to say.

"I'll shoe your string for ya."
  "I'll oil your rig."
  "I'll wrangle your turn for six weeks."
"Now hold on there, boys,
  I didn't do this for that;
  You've just all got a case of the meeks.

"If you'll give me a minute
  And open your ears,
  And stop feelin' you should do somethin' for me,
I'll tell you my motives,
  They're selfish as hell,
  And if you try it someday, you'll see.

"As you know, I never married
  Nor had me no kids
  'Twas a saddle I chose for my life,

But I'm older now
   And some ideas I've changed,
   And I regret never takin' a wife.

"But be as that may,
   I've learned to live
   With the situation I've bought,
And in the last few years
   I've come to realize
   That you're the only family I've got.

"Now the Lord, you see,
   He give up his life
   So that mankind wouldn't perish,
And durin' Christmas it's a tribute
   To give of ourselves
   To the folks that we most cherish.

"So a few years ago
   For the first time in my life
   I gave of myself just a bit,
And the reward I got
   From the good feelin's inside
   Was more than I dreamed I would get.

"So now I look forward
   Each year to the time
   When I get to be Santa's elf,
And do a little somethin'
   For the folks I hold dear
   Thus assurin' rewards for myself."

That was the last Christmas
   I spent around Charley
   And I'm sure I will never forget it,
For that was the year five buckaroos
   Learned a little something about
   True Christmas spirit.

The Mail-Order Bride

When Waddie was twelve years old, he met an old cowboy named Tom
O'Dell. "I remember old Tom. He never got married. He just wandered
through the West, workin' for different ranches—whoever'd put 'im to work.
My daddy introduced 'im to me as the last of the saddle tramps. Though I've
heard this tale a hundred times, I remember hearing it first from old Tom."
And today, Waddie enjoys telling "The Mail-Order Bride" as a "true" family
anecdote.

MY GRANDFATHER settled as far west as you could get in those days.
He started his own cattle ranch, and he didn't have the time to court.
So he ordered a wife—a city girl—from back east. On her trip west,
she traveled by stagecoach to the nearest settlement, and then she rode
horseback for two days to get to my grandfather's ranch. And then she
had never ridden a horse until then.

When she took up housekeepin' on the range, my grandmother was
scared of everything. For days, my grandfather couldn't leave the house
because she was afraid of bein' alone. But he knew that he couldn't
spend all of his time in the house with her, so he decided to hang a bell
high in a tree near the house. If anything important happened, she was
to ring the bell and he would be able to hear it anywhere on the ranch.

On the first day, my grandfather was workin' a few miles away from
home. He heard the bell ringin'. He climbed on his horse, galloped to
the house, and when he rode up, his wife was screamin'. She had seen
the old garden snake that my grandfather kept around the ranch house
to keep the rattlesnakes away.

"For heck sakes, woman. That's just my old garden snake. I've lost a
day's work, and I've nearly killed my best horse. Don't be ringin' that
bell 'less it's somethin' important."

A few days later, my grandfather was buildin' a rock fence, and he
was loadin' rocks into his buckboard a few miles from home. He heard
the bell ringin'. My grandfather—with a buckboard filled with rocks—
trotted his horses as fast as they could go back to the house, and when
he pulled up, he found his wife standin' on the porch, tremblin'. She
had seen a pack of wolves.

"They're just wolves." He reached for his gun hangin' over the door.

195

"Just shoot my gun at those wolves, and if you kill the leader, you'll have no trouble."

She reached for his gun, raised it to her shoulders, and shot the leader, and sure enough, all of the others tucked their tails between their legs and ran off.

"For heck sakes, woman. I've lost a day's work, and I've nearly killed a good team of horses. So don't be ringin' that bell 'less it's somethin' important."

About a week later, my grandfather found three wild cows and two calves on the range, and he was tryin' to tame 'em by keepin' the cattle away from water for three days. He was into the second day when he heard the bell ringin'. He assumed it wasn't important, so he continued to work—and the bell finally stopped ringin'.

But my grandfather's conscience got the best of him, and he left the wild cattle and galloped home. When he arrived, he found that his house and barn were burned to the ground, his horses and cattle were all dead, and his wife was lyin' on the ground, face down.

He leapt from his horse, bent down, and picked up his wife. She slowly opened her eyes. "Now, woman," he tells her, "that's more like it."

Gayle Ross

To me, our stories aren't frozen in time, nor do they
simply belong to the past. They reflect
what life used to be, the way it is, and the way it will
always be. And though we can step back into time
through our stories, the tales we tell are really as up
to date as today's news.

T SALI TRUDGED slowly and silently down a winding mountain road through the dense green forestland of the Great Smoky Mountains in the heart of Southern Appalachia. His wife, a brother, his three sons, and their families were by his side— each being escorted by American soldiers, armed with rifles. Tsali's wife, unable to walk as fast as the others, was prodded with sharpened bayonets to quicken her steps. Known as Charley, Tsali was a Cherokee Indian, and he and his family were being forced from their homes into stockades—awaiting removal to the west.

It was a scene from the tragic Trail of Tears, the relocation of thousands of Cherokee Indians from the Southern mountains to the Western plains. American soldiers, under the command of General Winfield Scott, had been ordered to search out every cabin in the Great Smoky Mountains, take their Cherokee occupants as captives, and march them to stockades to prepare for the journey westward. Most of the Cherokees went peacefully, while some—including Charley—did not.

Angered by the treatment of his wife, Charley began scheming— talking secretly among his family in their native language. Suddenly, Charley and his brother and sons leapt upon the soldiers and began to wrest their rifles from them. A gunshot rang out, and one of the soldiers fell dead. Perhaps frightened by the attack, the soldiers retreated, and Charley and his family fled into the mountains, joining others who had escaped the roundup. And there, they lived in a cave, eating roots and berries, awaiting the end of the hunt.

General Scott could not lure the small band from their secret hiding places in the mountains, so in compromise, he sent William H. Thomas, a trusted friend of the Cherokees, with a message. Thomas journeyed alone to the cave where Charley and his family were hiding, and standing between the armed Indian guards and the mouth of the cave, he delivered General Scott's message. It was simple. If Charley would surrender, the general would allow the others to remain in the mountains, to live in peace. The old man listened and thought.

"I will come," he answered.

Charley surrendered to General Scott, and upon the general's orders, the old man, his brother, and two older sons were shot to death by a small detachment of Cherokee prisoners—an act to give witness to the Cherokees' helplessness during this tragic period in American history.

The Cherokees, once seized from their homes and herded into stockades, began the journey westward—a trip plagued by sickness, starvation, and a wilting of the spirit of a people who had known only the freedom and nourishment of the mountains. Thousands died. But due to Charley's sacrifice, those Cherokees who took refuge in the mountains remained, and they became the eastern band of the Cherokees.

Today, Gayle Ross—the great-great-great-granddaughter of John Ross, chief of the Cherokees during the infamous Trail of Tears— honors her Cherokee legacy by remembering and telling the history and legends of her heritage. And as she tells the stories of the Cherokees, she speaks often of the atrocities suffered by the Cherokee Nation.

"But I'm not an authority on Cherokee history," Gayle is quick to add. "I'm a storyteller."

One of four children, Gayle was born in 1951 and grew up in a rambling house on a tiny Texas farm near Lewisville. From her earliest recollections, Gayle loved the outdoors, and she was always happiest when she was roaming the countryside, riding horses, swimming in Grapevine Lake, bird hunting with her father, and playing games in the woods that surrounded her home. She grew to love the land and all the life it supported, and she was drawn to the ways of her ancestry.

But it was Gayle's love of storytelling that led to her discovery of her Native American heritage as her Cherokee grandmother, Ann Ross Piburn, whiled away the evenings with Indian stories and songs. Though she died when Gayle was quite young, she remembers her grandmother. And before she died, she told Gayle the stories of the Cherokees— especially stories of John Ross and the Trail of Tears.

"I was drawn to stories, and more important, I was drawn to telling them—even at an early age. I began by repeating epic poetry in elementary school. I remember one night when my family and I were driving home from Dallas, and my younger sisters were fussy and fidgety. So I began to recite 'The Cremation of Sam McGee' by Robert W. Service. My brother, who was sitting in the front seat, complained: 'Mom, Gayle's got the flashlight and she's reading.' But my sisters came to my defense. 'No, she's not. She doesn't even have the book.' I didn't know I had memorized it, but I had recited the entire poem.

"From there, I learned more poetry, and eventually, I began rummaging through those belongings of my grandmother's which we had saved. Among them was a collection of stories she had learned as a child, those she had written down as they had been told. Through my grandmother's stories, I became fascinated with our Native American heritage—the legends, folklore, and traditions of the Cherokees."

But Gayle's love for this culture—and its stories—were briefly set aside when she began studying radio and television at the University of Texas at Arlington. When she landed a job at a Dallas radio station, she quit college to pursue a career in the news media. Soon Gayle was working for radio and television stations in Dallas and Austin.

"After a few years in broadcasting, I became disillusioned. I wanted a life's work rather than a job. So I quit radio and television and began traveling with a husband-and-wife singing duo to care for their child as they performed, giving myself time to determine my future. It was then that a friend—Elizabeth Ellis, a storyteller at the Dallas Public Library—asked me to attend the National Storytelling Festival with her.

"The trip changed my life. On our return home, Elizabeth asked me to join her in forming a duo—to become professional storytellers and travel throughout the country telling stories. I was overwhelmed, even frightened. But at the festival, I had heard others share the stories they held so dear, and I knew at that moment that I wanted to be a storyteller—to tell the stories I had heard as a child and to honor the legacy of a proud people, the Cherokees."

Gayle and Elizabeth quit their jobs and began performing as The Twelve Moons Storytellers at schools, libraries, festivals, and other events throughout the United States. While Gayle tells a rich and varied repertoire of stories, it's the legends of her Native American heritage and the history of the Cherokees that she recounts to audiences throughout America.

"Through my retelling of the ancient Indian myths and legends, I seek to face the greatest challenge of my people and other peoples throughout the world: to bridge the cultural, religious, and national chasms and to promote understanding. Always understanding. For the stories of our Native Americans have a teaching quality that is inherent in the legends. They are given life by the storyteller's breath, and the power that stories work in the world comes from the essence of the stories themselves. As a storyteller, I want to be a vehicle for what stories have to teach. I don't want anyone to feel guilty about the Trail of Tears. Instead, I want us to learn from this tragic experience."

"Through storytelling, I want to give my listeners a sense of the Native American point of view of our world and the love that the Indians have for our land. Our very existence on our planet is endangered because of the way our American society lives out of harmony with the land, and through stories, I want to convey an understanding of what we all must do to live successfully on our planet. This is the Native American's legacy for our world.

"To me, our stories aren't frozen in time, nor do they simply belong to the past. They reflect what life used to be, the way it is, and the way it will always be. And though we can step back into time through our stories, the tales we tell are really as up to date as today's news.

"While our histories may be founded upon fact and our legends upon fantasy, from a Native American point of view, they are equally important. As one old Sioux storyteller once said, 'All stories are true, even if they never happened.' There is truth found in all good stories, fact or fantasy, and even if a story is legend, it teaches great truths.

"As a child, I was surrounded by a family—an Indian father, my old Indian grandmother, even by a lovely Southern-belle, Alabama-born mother—who took great pride in our Cherokee legacy. They were proud of being Indian, and they reinforced that in me. Many people who have more Indian blood than I have—those even closer to the native tradition—find their Indian heritage no more than a casual, conversational curiosity. But for me, being Cherokee is a true identification—a very real part of who I am.

"While the stories I tell today come from extensive research into the history and legends of the Cherokees and other Native American cultures, my feeling of cultural identification with the Native Americans and my desire to tell our stories come from those I heard as a child, sitting at my grandmother's knee. And though my memories of my grandmother are dim, I feel that she was motivated in her work in large measure by what motivates me—a desire for an understanding of the Native American people among *all* of the peoples of our American culture. To me, you can't understand the people unless you know and understand their history—and their stories.

"In our world of instant history, the assassination of John F. Kennedy is history, yet it happened only twenty-five years ago. But we are products of so much more—time and history and heritage. In the stories I tell, I want to give my listeners an emotional blow so powerful that it will make them stop and think about *their* heritage. And through their stories, I hope to instill pride and inspire an appreciation in them of their roots, of what has gone on before. An identification with your people and your culture is an important aspect of our survival. Through our history and legends, we gain a sense of continuance. I know where I came from, so I'm better able to fashion a sense of where I'm going."

Strawberries

Several years after Gayle had become a professional storyteller, she and her husband were traveling southward from Chicago to their home in Texas—returning from a storytelling tour—and they stopped at The Murrell Home, the Ross Family museum located at Park Hill, Oklahoma. Gayle had remembered when she was a child visiting her great aunt who lived at the old home, and she was excited about her return visit. She had planned to spend three hours. She stayed three days.

Gayle was greeted by Bruce Ross, her cousin and curator of the museum, and while they were together, the duo rummaged through reams of old Ross documents stored in the attic. During their visit, Bruce gave Gayle a copy of James Mooney's Myths of the Cherokees and Sacred Formulas of the Cherokees—a volume consolidating Mooney's two important collections of Cherokee legends and lore.

"As I was growing up, I saw only remnants of Mooney's research, but now I had found a treasure-house of stories. Mooney's collections placed all of the stories I had heard and learned as a child into a larger context, giving me an opportunity to view the whole spectrum—the full mosaic—of Cherokee myths and legends. Knowing them all brings to me a greater depth of understanding of the individual stories I tell."

Gayle first began telling the animal stories, the humorous tales, the stories she could tell to children. They were the stories that first leapt off the page. But then, as she grew to understand the Cherokee traditions more and more, she began to favor the sacred myths, the creation stories—the more complex Indian legends, deep and rich with meaning. She began to study them, learn them, breathe life into them, and today, one of Gayle's favorite stories is "Strawberries," a Cherokee legend she discovered in Mooney's research.

LONG AGO, in the very first days of the world, there lived the first man and the first woman. They lived together as husband and wife, and they loved one another dearly.

But one day, they quarreled. Although neither later could remember what the quarrel was about, the pain grew stronger with every word that was spoken, until finally, in anger and in grief, the woman left their home and began walking away—to the east, toward the rising sun.

The man sat alone in his house. But as time went by, he grew lonelier and lonelier. The anger left him and all that remained was a terrible grief and despair, and he began to cry.

A spirit heard the man crying and took pity on him. The spirit said, "Man, why do you cry?"

The man said, "My wife has left me."

The spirit said, "Why did your woman leave?"

The man just hung his head and said nothing.

The spirit asked, "You quarreled with her?"

And the man nodded.

"Would you quarrel with her again?" asked the spirit.

The man said, "No." He wanted only to live with his wife as they had lived before—in peace, in happiness, and in love.

"I have seen your woman," the spirit said. "She is walking to the east toward the rising sun."

The man followed his wife, but he could not overtake her. Everyone knows an angry woman walks fast.

Finally, the spirit said, "I'll go ahead and see if I can make her slow her steps." So the spirit found the woman walking, her footsteps fast and angry and her gaze fixed straight ahead. There was pain in her heart.

The spirit saw some huckleberry bushes growing along the trail, so with a wave of his hand, he made the bushes burst into bloom and ripen into fruit. But the woman's gaze remained fixed. She looked neither to the right nor the left, and she didn't see the berries. Her footsteps didn't slow.

Again, the spirit waved his hand, and one by one, *all* of the berries growing along the trail burst into bloom and ripened into fruit. But still, the woman's gaze remained fixed. She saw nothing but her anger and pain, and her footsteps didn't slow.

And again, the spirit waved his hand, and, one by one, the trees of the forest—the peach, the pear, the apple, the wild cherry—burst into bloom and ripened into fruit. But still, the woman's eyes remained fixed, and even still, she saw nothing but her anger and pain. And her footsteps didn't slow.

Then finally, the spirit thought, "I will create an entirely new fruit—one that grows very, very close to the ground so the woman must forget her anger and bend her head for a moment." So the spirit waved his hand, and a thick green carpet began to grow along the trail. Then the carpet become starred with tiny white flowers, and each flower gradually ripened into a berry that was the color and shape of the human heart.

As the woman walked, she crushed the tiny berries, and the delicious aroma came up through her nose. She stopped and looked down, and she saw the berries. She picked one and ate it, and she discovered its taste was as sweet as love itself. So she began walking slowly, picking berries as she went, and as she leaned down to pick a berry, she saw her husband coming behind her.

The anger had gone from her heart, and all that remained was the love she had always known. So she stopped for him, and together, they picked and ate the berries. Finally, they returned to their home where they lived out their days in peace, happiness, and love.

And that's how the world's very first strawberries brought peace between men and women in the world, and why to this day they are called the berries of love.

Stories
of Family
and
Friends

Donald Davis

When I was a child, there wasn't a time
set aside as storytime. Stories were always told, and
there was no real separation of story
from the total fabric of conversation. So I didn't
learn stories, I just absorbed them.

F OR EVERY famous literary work, there are thousands of unwritten, unrecorded stories of family, community, and true-life experiences—the sometimes simple, sometimes well-embroidered accounts of commonplace events that add to life's magic and enchantment. And it's not tales of the fantastic that keep us around the dinner table long after the dishes have been cleared and washed; it's these stories of the people and places we know—the experiences we share—that keep us listening for hours.

Donald Davis, a professional storyteller and full-time Methodist minister, grew up in the Southern Appalachians hearing stories. For Donald, storytelling was the language of day-to-day communication. "When I was a child, there wasn't a time set aside as *storytime*. Stories were always told, and there was no real separation of story from the total fabric of conversation. So I didn't *learn* stories, I just absorbed them." And the stories Donald tells come out of his family, out of his oral experiences while growing up.

"I first heard stories from my Grandmother Walker who lived along Fines Creek in Haywood County, North Carolina, where I was born forty-four years ago. She lived in a two-story log house with a wonderful cold spring just outside the back door. There were giant rocks above the house, which backed up against a mountain, and from the front porch a view that stretched across a field to the ridge on the other side of Rush Fork Gap.

"Sometimes in the late afternoon, Grandmother Walker would take me and Aunt Bonnie, my mother's youngest sister, and sometimes my cousins, Andy and Kay, and head up the mountain. We would carry along a black frying pan and some of Grandmother Walker's sausage and eggs.

"We would walk way up into the steep pasture and pick out a big boulder. Then we kids would hunt all around for firewood while Grandmother Walker and Bonnie used what we had already gathered to build a fire in the hollow of a rock. And after the fire was going good, we would fry sausage, break it up into little pieces, and then scramble eggs and sausage together to make a one-dish supper. Gradually, it would grow dark, and we would walk home and go to sleep in Grandmother Walker's big, deep featherbeds.

"On days like this, storytelling was happening, and the stories I heard from Grandmother Walker—fairy tales, often quiet and gentle—were both fascinating and entertaining. But more than that, they provided a safe, vicarious world of adventure into which I could enter and *try* life."

Through stories, Donald discovered a world upon which life could be modeled—a safe world where things worked out as they should, where one could dream any dream, wish any wish, hope any hope. And for Donald, the oral tradition served a strong life-centering function.

Though he now often recalls ancient folktales heard from Grandmother Walker, it was Donald's Uncle Frank, a man "who talked in stories," who taught him that storytelling is more than simply story repetition. "Uncle Frank was the most creative person I've ever known. Storytelling was so interwoven into his life that he could turn any event, any experience, into a story." Through Uncle Frank, Donald came to know the power and excitement of story *creation*.

"During my years of growing up in the mountains, much of my time was spent with my uncle. He was my father's youngest brother, and he lived at Iron Duff on the farm where he and my father grew up. On weekends, we would visit Uncle Frank. And he *talked* in stories.

"Uncle Frank was a civic leader, politician, farmer, husband, Democrat, Methodist—and a fox hunter. For him to have been impoverished would have meant to be without a foxhound. And when anyone asked him a question about a dog, that very question became license for the birth of a story.

"If you were to go there now and visit the house where Uncle Frank lived and stand out in the front yard and look way up on the top of the ridge above the Jolly Cove, you would be able to see what's left of a little white shack. It was a tiny structure, built of cast-off lumber and stretched with worn-out white canvas. You could uncover one side of it if it was hot, or if it was cold, you could close it down and build a fire in a half of a barrel to keep warm.

"It's an unlikely place to call a building, but in truth, that building, right there on top of the ridge overlooking Jolly Cove, was for many years the world headquarters for the Greater Iron Duff Fox Hunters Association. My Uncle Frank was one of the organizers, charter members, perpetual officers, and longtime supporters of that organization.

"When I was a little boy, we would go out there on the mountain and spend hours in that shack listening to the dogs singing and Uncle Frank telling stories. While my Grandmother Walker passed on stories she had heard, my sense of Uncle Frank is that he *created* stories. Even if he was using material that he learned traditionally, when he told a story it was a new story.

"Uncle Frank's was an important place for me, a place where we went squirrel hunting and camping, and Uncle Frank was always there—telling stories. And though everyone talked about Uncle Frank's stories and how someone should write them down, I never thought then that I ever would."

Instead, Donald enrolled at Davidson College in Davidson, North Carolina, and he slowly began to lose his connection to the rich storytelling tradition that had surrounded him as a child. "Sure, I remember telling the stories my Uncle Frank told me. But my sense was not that *I* was telling them. Instead, I was just recounting Uncle Frank's tales— sharing with my friends his exploits, those that intrigued and amused me as a child." And even after graduation from Davidson in 1966, and from Duke University in 1969 with a master of divinity degree, it was Uncle Frank's stories that Donald told at civic club meetings when, as a minister, he was asked to speak.

Not until Donald was teaching a folk dancing course at John C. Campbell Folk School at Brevard, North Carolina, did he quite by accident begin to realize that he wasn't simply telling *about* Uncle Frank—he was telling stories, family stories, that he was creating, embellishing, each time they were told.

"We gathered together in the evening, and before going in to dance, we sang. Then the person in charge would call out to someone and ask, 'How about telling about...' And some of the stories I heard then reminded me of the stories Uncle Frank told me. One day, someone asked me to tell about Uncle Frank's foxhound. And I did. That was the first time I had ever recounted a story in public, simply telling it for its own sake. I was *telling* the story, and the experience was wonderful. In fact, as I told the story, I told more than I ever thought I would, and it became a creative process for me."

From that moment on, Donald began to seriously create and tell stories, calling upon the rich storytelling tradition he knew and experienced as a child. From Grandmother Walker he had inherited a love of the old way the story was told, and from Uncle Frank, a freedom to combine themes and plot segments in different ways from telling to telling. Though most of the stories Donald tells now are much more his own creation than anything he ever heard from Grandmother Walker or Uncle Frank, the spirit of his stories is clearly theirs.

"I create and tell stories that are based on human experiences—those that evoke memories of special people and places in the lives of those who hear them. They are stories of heroes and heroines—not those who had single, great accomplishments but people who helped me get through certain places in my life. Unnamed people, unremembered people. To remember them is nourishing.

"For me, storytelling acts as an interpreter of life's experiences. I don't simply tell stories about life. Instead, I tell stories that get their power, their meaning, their reason for being told, *through* life. When I tell stories in this way, I'm more than just the teller. I'm the creator, the embodiment of the story.

"We live our lives each day through experiences, and every experience that we have we evaluate in some way—either as a unique experience or as a common one. And as we go along day to day, we often think of our negative experiences as being unique. We think this has never happened to anyone else, that it's not happening to anyone else right now, and that no one else would ever understand it.

"Much of the power of storytelling comes from its helping us to see the commonness of human experience, the commonness of our painful experiences, and the commonness of our good experiences. And while I want my stories to be entertaining, beyond that, I want them to pull the listener inside so he can identify with the common experiences. Through this process, the story will remain with him personally—and forever."

Though storytelling is now the focus of his preaching, there was a time when Donald told stories, and preached, but he never brought the two together. And that was something he began to question.

"When I went to seminary training, preaching was taught as being highly conceptual, highly structural, and oriented toward manuscript. Teachers weren't taught to teach, they were taught to write lectures. Preachers weren't taught to preach, they were taught to write sermons. I was trained to write a manuscript every week.

"Through a deliberate process, I rebuilt my understanding of preaching by approaching it as an oral experience—moving away from concepts into images, away from ideas into experiences, away from theory into concreteness. I evolved toward a story-centered method of preaching where sermons are carried by a series of stories, bridged and connected."

Consequently, storytelling is Donald's life—in the pulpit, as he travels through the United States as a professional storyteller, as he lives. "People often ask me when I'm going to become a *full-time* storyteller. I guess I've been a full-time storyteller all my life, but I just can't see myself making storytelling the end of what I do rather than the means by which I am who I am. Storytelling is not what I do for a living, but instead, it is how I do all I do while I am living.

"My storytelling interprets and nourishes who I am, but after a while, I need to hush up and *do something* to nourish my storytelling. For me, storytelling grows out of life and often carries it along, but it isn't life itself. I could never keep from telling stories unless maybe I couldn't do anything else, but then, I don't think I'd be able to tell a story either."

The Crack of Dawn
A Portrait of Aunt Laura

━━━━━━━━━━━━━━━━━━━━━━━━━━━━━━━━━
▲ ▲ ▲ ▲ ▲ ▲ ▲ ▲ ▲ ▲ ▲ ▲ ▲ ▲ ▲

When Donald Davis was a child, Aunt Laura came to live with his family. In this touching portrait, Donald introduces his listeners to her—and through her, to all of the Aunt Lauras in our lives. By telling her story, Donald wants to keep his aunt alive "so the lessons she taught me will live with all of us for generations to come."

AT THE time I was born, my Aunt Laura lived with us. She was actually my father's Aunt Laura, my Great-aunt Laura Moody. She lived with my grandmother until my grandmother died the same year that I arrived. And then, she became what my dad called a "floater."

Aunt Laura would live at our house for three or four months, and then one Sunday afternoon, we would take her for a ride. When we would get back home, she would be at Aunt Esther's house. Three or four months later, Aunt Esther would take her for a ride and she would go to Aunt Mary's house, then out to Aunt Kathleen's house, and then back to us.

I loved it when Aunt Laura lived at our house. She was the first person in my life to love me no matter what. And she was the oldest living thing I had ever seen. She had worked out in the sun all of her life, and her skin was so wrinkled and brown that she looked as if she was made out of wadded-up brown paper bags.

Aunt Laura would get up earlier in the morning than anybody I ever knew. It didn't make any difference how early we got up—just didn't matter at all—I would get up as early as I could and rush to the kitchen and she was always up, had a fire in the stove, and would already be fixing breakfast.

I'd say, "Aunt Laura, how do you get up so early?"

And she'd say, "Well, son, I hear the crack of dawn."

I was only four years old and I said, "Can you really *hear* the crack of dawn?"

"Why, yes, I can hear it and it wakes me up. And once I hear it, nobody else can and they just have to get up the best way they can. But one of these days when I'm dead and gone, I'll leave that to you, and then you'll be able to hear the crack of dawn."

At our house, Aunt Laura washed the dishes. It wasn't a job we gave her; it was a job she took because, she said, my mother didn't do it right. We had remodeled our kitchen, which meant that we had taken down the sink that was just bolted to the wall and replaced it with a contraption that had a sink in the middle, drains on each side, white enameled drawers with shelves underneath, and a stopper that worked. It spoiled my mother. She could wash dishes in the sink, pull the stopper, and the water would run down the drain. But Aunt Laura would say, "That's a waste of water." She believed you're supposed to wash dishes in a dishpan so you can take the water out and pour it on the flower bed. So we let her wash dishes.

She would wash the dishes in the dishpan while standing on a Coca-Cola crate—she was a tiny, short woman—and when she was finished, she would put the dishes on the drainboard and rinse them off with boiling water. Then she would go over and open the back door, prop it open with the yellow flint rock she used as a doorstop, come back to the sink, pick up the dishpan, step down off the Coca-Cola crate, back up, and run for the door.

She would go through the door, down a little step, and across the back porch until she hit the porch rail. It would stop her, but the water would keep going—out of the dishpan, over the edge of the porch, and down onto the flower garden.

One night, she went out the door carrying her dishpan of water and never came back. I looked out, and I saw nothing but darkness. I called my daddy, but by the time he had gotten there, Aunt Laura was coming back through the kitchen door. The porch rail hadn't held, and she had fallen off the porch and into the yard—dishpan, water, and all.

When Aunt Laura returned to the kitchen, I became excited. You see, Aunt Laura wore thick, rimless glasses that turned into mirrors when she looked at you. For all of my life, I had never seen Aunt Laura's eyes. When she came through the door, she was wearing her glasses but one lens was missing. I thought I was finally going to see one of her eyes. But as luck would have it, that was the side that hit the ground and that eye was swollen shut.

Every night after supper, Aunt Laura would take me into the cow pasture behind the house and teach me about the stars. We would stretch out on the ground, and in the wintertime she would say, "Put your feet toward the Burgins' house." That was north. And in the summertime she would say, "Put your feet toward the McHaffie house." That was southwest.

We would begin with the Big Dipper and work our way across the sky—learning about the stars. In the wintertime, my favorite was Orion, looking down from the southern sky, watching what we were doing on Plot Creek. And in the summertime, from the whole parade of constellations across the southern sky, my favorite was the Scorpion, with his long arms outstretched and his red-beaded heart pulsing away in the sky.

Aunt Laura would always say, "Someday, son, you're going to grow up and travel throughout the world, and you'll get homesick and won't know where you are. But just remember that everybody lives under the same sky. So just wait until it gets dark and go outside and look up at the sky, and those stars will take you home."

Aunt Laura never got married. It was not really because she had never met any men, but it was because she had never met a man she thought she would like as much as she loved Dental Scotch Snuff. And she wasn't going to stop dipping snuff for anybody.

She dipped it twenty-four hours a day. You could smell her coming before you saw her. You could tell whether she was breathing in or breathing out. I finally decided that she was brown not from working in the sun all her life but because that snuff for years and years had just been absorbed into her whole system and was working its way out through her skin. She had snuff complexion.

One day when nobody was home, I decided I'd try Aunt Laura's snuff. It had to be good. It looked like chocolate. Nobody was in the house, so I looked into Aunt Laura's room. She always kept a big brown box of snuff on the dresser in her bedroom in front of the mirror. She kept the whole corner cut off the box. She'd say, "You can't get snuff out through one of these little spouts. Snuff dippers don't make these boxes." And she'd cut the whole corner off so it would come out easily.

She always loaded in front of the mirror. I'd watched her so many times I knew exactly how she did it. So I got the box—a nice full box—pulled my lip out, and got the box up there just like I had seen her do it. And nothing happened. I shook it a little and tried again. Nothing happened still. I must not have had it just right. I made one more try. I pulled my lip way out, tapped the box lightly, and when that snuff started sliding, it didn't stop, and the whole box full—every bit of it—came out like a truck dumping sand, and it came right down all through my mouth and my nose. It was such a shock, I let out my breath. And that was the wrong thing to do. A box of snuff will cover a good-sized room.

Aunt Laura was the first person to get back to the house, and she saved my life. She helped me clean it up. But she said, "Let me give you a hint. If you ever have to clean up a lot of snuff, don't use water. If there is anything worse than snuff dust, it's snuff mud."

Not many days after that, my daddy came into my bedroom in the middle of the night when I was asleep. He woke me up and said, "Get up and go with me to milk." Well, I loved to milk with Daddy. So, while it was still dark, I got out of bed and slipped on my clothes, and we started out the back door of the house for the barn. When he flipped the switch to the light hanging on the front of the barn, we both saw that there had been a heavy ice storm during the night. The whole world seemed glazed in ice, and the light from the barn created a shimmering pathway across the backyard. Daddy got the milk bucket in one hand and took my hand with the other, and without ever picking up our feet, we scooted across the ice to the barn.

Daddy milked by lantern light. He never spoke a word, but as we stepped over the old log threshold of the barn door to leave, my daddy turned to me and without any warning said, "Aunt Laura died. But if anybody says anything about it, just say that she passed away."

I knew that everything that got old enough died, and Aunt Laura was the oldest living thing I had ever seen. That didn't upset me. But I didn't know what "passing away" was. I didn't know whether Aunt Laura was dead or alive, whether she was going to be there when we got back or not, or if I was ever going to see her again.

But as we made our way toward the house, we passed my favorite tree—a giant walnut with a split trunk that we, as boys, climbed in the winter. It was covered with ice. Suddenly, that ice became so heavy that this huge walnut tree went *craacck* and split from top to bottom. And as we looked over our shoulders toward the old tree, we saw the edge of the sun creeping up over the hill. It was the crack of dawn. I had heard it, and that answered all of my questions. I knew Aunt Laura was really dead, but most important of all, I knew she would never, ever be gone from me.

Miss Daisy

While growing up in the mountains of western North Carolina, Donald Davis attended the Hazelwood Elementary School in Haywood County. It was there that he met Miss Daisy Boyd, his fourth-grade teacher. In Donald's poignant tribute to Miss Daisy, he is honoring teachers everywhere who have "poured all of their lives into that important mission, that calling."

I HAVE discovered that schools today are different from the way they were when I was growing up. They have something today that we didn't have: young teachers.

Though I don't really know what they did with young teachers in Haywood County when I was growing up, I always suspected that they sent them off somewhere to ripen for a while. But now I believe the teachers retirement system may be partly to blame because, you see, back then, teachers couldn't retire. They just kept coming to school until, one day, they finally couldn't come any more.

That gave them a real advantage. They had been around long enough to have some important experiences—like having taught the principal, having taught most of the members of the school board, and being about ten years beyond being afraid of the Supreme Court.

My favorite teacher was Miss Daisy Boyd. She was my teacher at Hazelwood School in the forty-second year of her teaching the fourth grade. She knew what she was doing. And during the year I had Miss Daisy as a teacher, she taught the A's through the Gr's. There were no high groups, no low groups, no carefully balanced groups—just purely alphabetical ones.

We went into her room on the first day of school, an old room that had been there as long as she had, and there she was in front of us, a little, worn-out-looking wisp of a woman, and we began to wonder if this tiny person could really handle thirty fourth-graders.

After we had all been seated at our desks, the door from the room into the hallway was still standing open, and out of the hall and into the room—trying to find a safe place after living in an empty school all summer—came a mouse. Poor thing: it hadn't invited all those little boys and girls to come to school, but there we were, and there it was, running around, trying to get away from us. The mouse came through Miss Daisy's door and ran along the base of the blackboard behind her.

By the time that mouse got to the corner, Miss Daisy had turned and seen it, but she didn't make a sound. She just eased open the top drawer of her desk, took out two brown paper towels, slipped over to the corner, squatted down and surrounded that mouse, caught it in those paper towels, walked back over to the front of the room, held the mouse up, wrung its neck, and dropped it into the trash can. Do you think we were going to mess with her after that? No way.

My whole year in the fourth grade was built around Miss Daisy's imaginary trip around the world—a trip that began with a train ride to New Orleans aboard the Southern Crescent. Then, we boarded a ship and sailed to South America.

While we went along every day in our imaginary travels, we made long lists of all of the places we passed through, all the things we saw, and all the people who had ever lived there who had ever done any-thing important, and throughout the whole year, we never figured out that we were making our own list of spelling words that were harder than the words in the spelling books.

And all year long, when we figured out how far we had traveled each day, how much it took to buy train tickets and boat tickets, and, even later, how to change money from one country to another, she didn't tell us we were working math problems that were more complicated than the problems in the math books.

Miss Daisy had never been out of Haywood County in her life, except for four years, forty-two years before that, when she had gone to Ashe-ville Teachers College to learn how to teach the fourth grade. But dur-ing all those years, she had ordered by mail thousands of picture postcards. It wasn't possible for us to go anywhere, from the smallest little town in Mississippi to a temple garden in Japan, without Miss Daisy being able to dig through her boxes and finally come up with a ragged-edge postcard to show us what that place looked like.

On the third day of our voyage, a little boy named Lucious Moody Grassty came scooting through the door. He had a wool knit hat pulled way down over his ears, and he wouldn't take it off. He went past his desk, stood right in the corner of the room, and wouldn't come out. Miss Daisy came in, took one glance at him, and said, "Now, boys and girls, today is the day we cross the equator. And when we cross the equator for the first time, we have a big party for Neptune, King of the Deep."

She went into the coat room and began bringing out things the kids had left there at the end of school for forty-two years. Old raincoats. Broken umbrellas. Old galoshes. She began dressing everybody for our big party for Neptune, King of the Deep. She pulled out the window shades to show us how they used the sails on the boats to catch rain-water and make bathtubs, and she told us how some of the sailors had their clothes run up the masts. Why, for this party, some of them even shaved their heads. And she pulled off Lucious's wool knit hat, and his head was shaved. We were all jealous. How did he get picked to be the one?

It was a long time later before I learned that the day before, when Lucious had gone home from school, his mother had found lice in his hair, shaved his head, and washed it with kerosene. But Miss Daisy, without pausing for a moment, had taken this little boy with a blistered head and transformed him into the hero of the crossing of the equator.

Within a few days, we had arrived in South America and begun our journey up the Amazon River. Miss Daisy said, "Now, children, the Amazon is the longest river in the Americas. There are butterflies there so big we could ride on them."

"But, Miss Daisy, what if you take the Mississippi and Missouri rivers and put them together? Wouldn't that be the longest river? That should have been one river anyway."

But Miss Daisy always answered, "No, no, no. That's two rivers. Two names, two rivers. The Amazon is the longest river."

And it didn't make any difference to me where we went from there —down through South America, across to the tip of Africa, up the Congo, or down the Nile—the Amazon was always my favorite place, because my art project for the year was making a butterfly so big you could ride on it.

A few years before, my Uncle Frank had tried to invent a way to fly. He made a machine, something like a primitive hang-glider, except it had a piano hinge down the middle so the wings could flap. He made a frame out of copper tubing and pieces of orange crate, glued about two million chicken feathers all over it, and put the harness from a pack frame on the bottom so you could strap it on your back. And he was ready to fly.

He got on top of the front porch and was going to take a short flight to a maple tree. He told us later a downdraft got him. Lucky for Uncle Frank, it didn't kill him. Lucky for me, it didn't tear up the wings.

On Friday afternoon, I begged my daddy until he took me to Uncle Frank's house, and then I begged Uncle Frank until he hunted up those old wings and gave them to me. I took them back home and went to work. I took off the harness, built a body out of big mailing tubes with the ends stopped up, made antennae out of two coat hangers, painted those wings orange, green, purple, yellow, and red in swirls of patterns, and by Sunday afternoon I had a butterfly so big you could ride on it.

I knew I couldn't ride the school bus with my butterfly on Monday morning, so my daddy took me to school. He drove his old Plymouth with the window rolled down, holding the butterfly outside and trying to go slow enough to keep it from blowing away.

He wasn't in a very good mood by the time we got to school. But Miss Daisy loved my butterfly, and she took a big coat hanger, hooked it into the butterfly's back, and hung it up over the middle of the room. For the rest of the year, it floated there over the top of all of us.

During the next several weeks, we traveled throughout the Mediterranean, across Eastern Europe, into Central Asia, China, and Japan, across the Pacific, and during the last two months of the year, we took a long imaginary train ride across North America, from Canada to Mexico. And finally, on the last day of May, there we were in Hazelwood School where we had been all the time.

The school year ended, and I soon finished grade school, then high school, and I began college. I was home one summer, working as a busboy at the Mount Valley Inn in Maggie Valley. And one afternoon, just before opening, I was outside sweeping off the front steps, getting ready for the first customers to arrive, when a big green Roadmaster Buick came roaring up. I knew who it was—there was only one of those cars in all of Haywood County. It was Meg Clayton, one of Miss Daisy's sisters. She got out of the car and came around to the other side. The other door opened and out stepped Miss Bessie, another one of Miss Daisy's sisters. Together, they opened the back door, took something out of the backseat, and started coming toward the restaurant. I ran down to meet them. As I got closer, I saw what they had. Between them, hanging on to their arms, they had what was left of Miss Daisy. She was just a ..iy little woman, nothing but skin and bones—a wisp of a person, with her head drooped down, her toes barely touching the ground as they carried her along, bringing her out to supper.

Miss Bessie knew me and she spoke, and then she turned to Miss Daisy and said, "Look, Daisy, look! It's one of your old boys. It's one of your old boys, grown up." Miss Daisy raised her head and looked at me, but her eyes were white, colorless, and dead.

Her head dropped down and Miss Bessie said in a loud voice, "Daisy's had a stroke."

I didn't know what to say.

"When did she have it?"

"About six years ago, just after she retired."

And they took her inside to feed her supper.

I passed by their table occasionally, trying not to look, trying to do what I had to do without watching. But finally I had to go to the table one last time to clear off their dishes and to see if they wanted dessert.

I rolled my cart up to their table and started slipping off the dishes, and all of a sudden, I could feel somebody looking at me. I looked up and it was Miss Daisy, her eyes as clear and as blue and as alive as they had ever been. And from way down inside of her came a tiny little voice. "The Amazon is the longest river. There are butterflies there so big we could ride on them."

Her eyes went blank and her head dropped down, and I went to the kitchen as fast as I could go. Mr. Gibson, the cook, was looking out the door, watching, and he kept muttering to himself. "Oh, isn't it sad about poor Miss Daisy. Oh, isn't it sad."

And I thought, no, it isn't sad. I thought it was until a moment ago, but now, I know it's not. For I'd remembered how when we were in the fourth grade, we'd ask, "Miss Daisy, why do we have to learn all of this? Why?"

And she always said, "Because—because one of these days you're going to be able to go anywhere you want to go and you must know where you're going."

No, it isn't sad about Miss Daisy. I have seen that she is now in a world in which she can go anywhere she wants to go and she knows where she's going. She can even ride the butterflies.

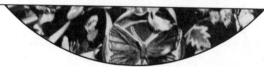

Brother Blue

Ever' time I tell a story, I risk all on
that deep feelin'—tryin' to do somethin' real, from the
middle of me, movin' in the spirit, trustin'
completely with my life. For my work is like that of an old
jazz musician: blowin' an old song
but blowin' it ever new.

FOR MORE than forty years, Brother Blue—barefoot and adorned in a colorful disarray of ribbons, bows, balloons, and butterflies —has told stories. Enhanced by the music and rhythm of his voice, he chants a concoction of poetry, story, and song to those who gather, gawk-eyed, to witness the spectacle. His body swirls and stomps, his fingers snap in a poetic cadence, his toes brush the cold asphalt. And while some scoff, there are others, often those standing in the miserable cold of a New England winter, who hang on every word and become immersed in Brother Blue's messages built on image and mood.

Brother Blue is actually Dr. Hugh Morgan Hill, a man who has dedicated his life to telling stories for social change, for world peace with justice, and for love, in settings as diverse as the stories themselves— from prisons to nurseries, hospitals to libraries, seminars to Sunday schools, and often in the streets. And while Blue feels that he must sometimes appear like a "living Christmas tree," the carnival, the birthday party—both flamboyant and colorful—to get and hold the attention of people in the streets and subways, he wants his listeners to see beyond the mask, the costume, and soak in the stories, their words and meaning.

Brother Blue was born in poverty in Ohio to parents who each had only a third-grade education. "I was the only black kid in a white school, you know, and I kinda had the feelin' that ever'body was different from me. The only black button in a field of snow, you know. The Ugly Ducklin'. And I could hardly talk. I stammered terribly.

"But somebody said if I could recite poetry or sing, my stammerin' would stop. So one of my teachers gave me a poem to recite. And, you see, I was a small guy. A kinda rough-lookin' kid. A tough little boy. But they had me recitin' poetry for the whole school. I would do that stuff, and the other kids would love it—and mother loved it too. And sure enough, I overcame my stammerin'. And whenever they had storytellin' time, I just loved to recite poetry or tell stories."

Though his parents could barely read or write, Blue's world was filled with tales—of his mother picking cotton in Mississippi, or of his father, son of a slave. Blue remembers how his father, a huge man, the first and most powerful storyteller in his life, stood over his bed at night, casting a long shadow against the wall, pacing back and forth, reading aloud from the Bible. For Blue, it was as if he was singing.

"My father was a bricklayer, a man whose heart and soul were in the church. And I came out of that trustin' tradition, out of the wide-open, rockin' black church, out of the rhythm and blues, out of the shouts and hollers. We'd walk five miles to church every Sunday to hear that preacher man rock, and he'd get up there and *show* you God scoopin' out the valleys and puttin' up the mountains."

Despite his obstacles as a child, Brother Blue attended Harvard College and Yale Drama School, earning degrees from both. One day, in a class on American church history, Blue told his professor, "You've taught through 1890 and you haven't discussed slavery at all." But the next morning, the professor came into the class and dropped a paper bag on the table. Inside were chains.

"'Yes, Blue, they're slave chains from a slave market in Richmond, Virginia. My great-grandfather got them when he was going through Virginia with the Union army.'

"I grabbed the chains, and I tried to break them, and I found I couldn't. And then I knew... the chains have not been broken... the visible chains, the invisible chains... chains of suffering, chains of hunger, chains of disease... and I decided at that moment that I wanted to spend my life breaking them. I thought about people like my daddy who could barely read and write but was so noble, and I wondered how I could bring to him the beauty I was finding. What I wanted to do was take what I knew and break it down for those who didn't have the literary teeth to chew it, so they could at least gum it. The poor, the sick, the lonely."

Blue studied drama, theology, and the oral tradition, and in 1968, he performed "O Martin, O King"—a play, a requiem, a happening—a homage to the recently slain civil rights leader, and a spontaneous theater form of storytelling was born. Blue became a singer and a poet, a dancer and a chanter, an actor and a storyteller. Friends urged him to pursue and develop his newly discovered storytelling style, and in 1972, the ideas and the acts crystalized into Brother Blue's Soul Theater. Through this self-made forum, storytelling has become for Blue the perfect vehicle for speaking to people of all ages, backgrounds, and levels of understanding—seeking to effect a transformation in their hearts and souls.

"I've given my life to storytelling; it's sacred to me. We can touch human hearts forever. It's my whole life and being. I want to change the world—to ease the burden of those who suffer, to feed the hungry, to lighten the struggle.

"My kind of theater can be presented anywhere, in any setting, with nothin' but a place to stand—and imagination. I can take it to the poorest people. I can take it to one person or many. I can take it any-place. It's in my body, in my soul. I've told my stories by candlelight, at high noon beside the sea, in convents, in hospitals, in college classrooms and graduate seminars, in Sunday schools, in public schools, in nursery schools, in theaters, in halls, in prisons—I like to work in prisons.

"I tell stories wherever people are—even in the streets. And when you're there in the streets, you meet the street people. The people who are suffering, dying, lost, some going mad, some drunk. 'Tell the drunk a story, Blue.' You know, you can sober up a man with a story. Stories are healing. But people are in a hurry in the streets. You've got to make things concise. Boom! You can talk all you want, but how does the recipe taste in your mouth and your belly? Did you give them somethin' they can use?"

And wherever there are those who gather to listen, there is always that incessant question: "Why, Blue? Why do you do it, Blue?"

"Once I was invited by a friend to a party at the home of a million-aire. The millionaire watched me all evening, and about two o'clock in the mornin' when ever'body had gone, the man said, 'Blue, tell me your story. Are you jivin' me or somethin'? Why do you tell stories?'

"As I talked with the man and saw his skepticism, I thought of the death of my brother, Tommy, who was mentally retarded. I looked the millionaire straight in the eye, and for the first time since Tommy's death, I told the story of my brother.

I had a brother once. He died on me. He could have been you, peekin' through your eyes of blue. He couldn't read or write, but he could read and write music in the air. He lived for love.

I taught him how to say my name, and that became our game. And one night, he said, "Brother Blue." I jumped over the moon with the cow and the spoon. And that's when I began to wear rainbow colors on my clothes.

I tried to teach him how to write his name. He tried, he tried. He couldn't. He didn't want to hurt the pencil. I tried to teach him how to read. He tried. He couldn't. He was scared of the fire in the dragon's eye.

One night when I was far away, they put Tommy someplace. They locked him behind one door, then two, three,
and four. He cried. He upped and died on me so fast. If I had
been there, would he have flew? It's a true story, true inside
of true.

And now, if I see someone on the street—or if you do—
who's confused and unhappy, that's my brother. And I'm
goin' to love 'im. How about you?

"When I had finished tellin' my story, the millionaire didn't ask me
any more questions. He just looked at me. He understood.

"Several years later, I was asked to tell stories at a school in Canada
for the so-called mentally retarded. I stood in the middle of a large
gymnasium, and I was surrounded by a group of young children. I saw a
boy who looked like my brother. I went over to him and began to tell
'im a story. He couldn't talk. He began to cry.

"I said, 'Child, you're so beautiful. I love you.'

"And he cried all the more.

"'I had a little brother like you. He was my best friend. And you
know something? He could fly like a butterfly, up into the sky. And so
can you.'

"As I turned to leave the gymnasium, the little boy ran up to me, put
his head on my chest, and then backed off and spread his arms as if he
were flyin'.

"You want to know why *I* tell stories? If I never get another response
from anyone—no one ever again tells me that they like my stories—
I've got that memory. And whenever I see someone tryin' to get out of
the cocoon of loneliness, sadness, trouble, I always think of my brother.
There is always a beautiful soul, a butterfly, within.

"For, you see, storytellin' has become a sacred mission. Ever' time I
tell a story, I risk all on that deep feelin'—tryin' to do somethin' real,
from the middle of me, movin' in the spirit, trustin' completely with my
life. For my work is like that of an old jazz musician: blowin' an old song
but blowin' it ever new."

Miss Wunderlich

When Brother Blue was attending graduate school, he was offered an internship at Harvard Graduate School of Education to teach in an alternative school for children with special problems. The professors asked him, "What do you think about teaching? What's your philosophy of education? Your theories? Just tell us." And Blue told them a story. "I'm goin' to tell ya about a teacher. Miss Wunderlich. She had blue eyes and skin like snow. But next to my mama and my wife, she is the love of my life. I want to be like her."

HEY, EVER'BODY. I'm Brother Blue, a street cat callin' you. Come close. Let me touch your pretty nose. Can I tickle your toes? This story is about rainbows. I wear them on my clothes and a butterfly in my hand—for a teacher. Did you ever fall in love with your teacher? It happened to Blue.

It was like this, you see. I was eight years old, and I hated school. The kids were cruel to Blue. I was one black button in a field of snow. You know how it goes. They called me ever'thing but Blue. And I cried. I liked to died. My name was D in everything. D in readin'. D in writin'. D in 'rithmetic. D incarnate, you might say. All I'd do is cry 'cause I wanted somebody to look past my eyes and see somethin' in me pretty.

Hey, people. You wanna hear a secret? In the middle of you and in the middle of Blue, there's some kind of magic. It's there for love. If someone don't love you, you can cry. You could even die. I almost did, but she come along. Like a rainbow song. Her skin was like snow, you know, but inside was her bright soul. She had magic eyes. She could look through muddy water when children cry and see the beautiful butterfly. Well, in school I was cryin' all the time.

I come home cryin' and Mama say, "What's the matter, Blue?"

And I say, "Mama, let's play peek-a-boo."

She say, "Come on. You're no baby."

I say, "Mama, kiss me once, kiss me twice. It'd be nice." You know how mamas do. When they kiss ya, they mostly miss ya. Talkin' 'bout "blow your nose" and "don't tear your clothes."

Daddy seemed seven feet tall. Like a brick wall. A bricklayer when he could get work. Didn't wear no gloves on his hands, you understand. He had a trick, squarin' off my face. Gonna turn it into a brick and put it in a wall someplace. And I cried, and that's when she come along. When I was dyin'.

Miss Wunderlich. Like an angel. A magical angel. On my first test in arithmetic, I got D minus. I cried. I almost died. She said, "Come on, Blue, give me that paper. Let's play peek-a-boo like children do."

She's lookin' inside of me. She's sayin', "Blue, I love you. In you, I see a butterfly. Come on. Don't die, don't cry." She took my paper, and she put somethin' on there like a kiss.

Oh! Something happened in my heart. I heard music. I fell in love with the woman. I did numbers in my sleep. One plus one is two. I love you. Two times two is four. I won't be late no more.

Next test, guess what I got, folks? A plus. That's what happened to Blue. If they only knew what love can do. It can change you. I fell in love with school—with the ceiling, the floor, the window, and the door—'cause she was in there. I fell in love with the sky 'cause it was blue like her eye. It can happen to you. All you have to do is fall in love with someone who can look through your eye and see the butterfly in you, in your soul, and you become what that person sees in you.

Well, I went through all the schools, and I went to war. I traveled across the sea. I saw so much dyin'. I heard cryin'. One night a man came to me and said, "Blue, I can't read or write."

I say, "That's all right. Let's play peek-a-boo. I know a lady with eyes of blue. She taught me a trick. Come on, I'll give it to you. I believe in you. I see a butterfly in you. Don't cry. Just try. And I love you, brother, to my soul."

I taught that man to read and write, and when I come home again, I thought I was cool. I went to the school to say, "Thank you, Miss Wunderlich." But guess what. There were tears in my eye. I didn't want that woman to see me cry, and I walked away without tellin' her I loved her. What a fool was I. She died in the snow, you know. I loved her, but I never told her so.

Miss Wunderlich, I'm Brother Blue. I love you. I'm playin' peek-a-boo in the streets, in the jailhouses, in the hospitals, in the subways as I travel around the world in my bare feet—and look in the eyes of the people I meet. I pray someday before I die, before I blow away, that I'll save one life, maybe two, like you saved Blue.

Good night, Miss Wunderlich. Good mornin' too. I'm Brother Blue. I love you in this life, in the next one too. I'm a storyteller travelin' through the world. All I do is play peek-a-boo, lookin' for the butterfly in all people. I believe in love. And that's you.

Maggi Peirce

When I'm telling my stories, I'm not
there — on that stage. I'm not doing something I was
trained to do. But instead, I'm part
and parcel of the tale, and I'm just telling things as I
remember them — watching a film that's
rolling in front of my eyes — and I'm living the story at
that moment. For through storytelling,
I can see my country. I can hear my people.

* * *

MAGGI PEIRCE'S childhood was fraught with hurt feelings and sobs under the blanket at night, for she was an overly sensitive child, and her life was plagued with disappointments and unfulfilled hopes and dreams. Yet somehow, there was something very special about those years growing up in Belfast, Ireland, and she found comfort in the tales from her childhood that she still holds dear.

"The stories and rhymes and chants flowed around me—at home, in the streets, on the playgrounds—and they enchanted and wove a spell about me that I've never quite been able to shake off. It seems only yesterday that I was running down Irwin Avenue on the east side, my bobbed hair bouncing wildly, mouthing wee rhymes as I went."

Maggi was born in Belfast in 1931. Her father was Scottish, of the clan Kerr, and he loved the music hall and singing around the piano. Her mother's family, the Walkers, favored the old hymn singing, and recitations, and children's songs and stories. Woven into Maggi's childhood was this twin inheritance of both story and song.

"When Mammy was working—plucking a hen or cleaning her copper pots—my sister, Dorothy, and I hung on to her apron as she sang a hymn or told a story. We often asked, 'Mammy, where did you get that story?'

"'Oh, that's not a story, loves. That's just a lot of nonsense.'

"But it was *always* a story—a charming old fairy tale, perhaps—and we hung on every word.

"While Mammy never actually set aside a special time for stories, my daddy—he was a great storyteller—would often lay down his book, gather us around him, and devote himself solely to telling us tales, over and over again. When he'd launch into an old, much-too-familiar story, Dorothy and I would always moan, 'Oh, Daddy, you're not going to tell that old chestnut again?'

"He'd laugh, throw up his leg, and say, 'Oh, have I told you this one before?'

"We'd scream with delight and throw cushions at him, for he certainly knew, and knew well, he'd told us that story before—many, many times."

During these years of growing up, Maggi remembered and collected the sayings, songs, and stories of her native Ireland. And as she grew older, Maggi and Dorothy traveled throughout Europe, collecting bits of folklore wherever they went. In 1957, Maggi settled in Edinburgh, Scotland. And it was there, two years later, at a gathering of the Edinburgh University Folksong Society, that Maggi first sang in public—a song from her Ulster heritage, one true to her tradition, one which she performed unaccompanied. After her first performance, Maggi, over the next few years, grew to become a respected folksinger in her adopted home of Edinburgh.

"But in 1964, I married an American and moved to Massachusetts, and during those early days living in the United States, I was unhappy and longed for Ireland and home. I didn't have a blanket to hug, so I hugged my memories. As I stood in my kitchen washing dishes, I was no longer in Fairhaven, Massachusetts. Instead, I was walking up the tracks to Bloody Bridge or shopping at Rob's in downtown Belfast or playing hopscotch on one of the small streets just off Irwin Avenue. My memories fed me like a child who had turned to her mother's breast, hungry for the nourishment of home.

"Our house in Belfast had often been filled with a multitude of cousins who were as close to me as my sister, Dorothy, and a bevy of aunts and uncles who were like second mothers and fathers. And in looking back, there's something quite comforting about remembering my beginnings—when love was only an arm's length away in the kitchen, and life was small and cozy, and all of my relatives were endearing or funny, or both.

"I would think back to my Irish childhood, and the times we nippers would play, and sing, and the special times—at Christmas, especially, when my mother's friends would send me a book as a present. And while today we would be swamped with books, then, oh, we waited with bated breath for that single book. One of my fondest memories is of Christmas and the story we always tell of my dear old Uncle Nelson.

"At every Christmas, for as far back as I can remember, my mother, May, gave Uncle Nelson a toilet roll. Every year, there was always secrecy, and whispering, and excitement. For my mother, this was a gift of love. And for Uncle Nelson, the ritual represented a moment when love just swirled around him.

"You see, my Uncle Nelson was well-to-do. In a house where everyone wore tweed jackets, he wore three-piece suits. And since he worked in a cigar and cigarette shop in the middle of Belfast, his boast was always about what lord or lady or judge he had spoken with that day as they shopped for cigars, cheroots, and cigarettes.

"Every year, Uncle Nelson and Auntie Vie would invite us for tea on

Christmas Day. Late in the afternoon, we would walk a mile and a half up Old Park Road to their house, and every year my mother would carry a large, neatly wrapped package.

"For much of the afternoon, the menfolk—Uncle Nelson included—would stay in the sitting room playing with the toy railway. But soon the womenfolk would come to the door, demand entrance, and with them, they always carried my mother's package, which they slipped in front of Uncle Nelson. The ritual would begin.

"Auntie Vie would say, 'Oh, Nelson, we must have missed this Christmas box this morning.'

"Wearing his three-piece suit as usual, Uncle Nelson would turn around, surprised. 'I never noticed that. Who do you think brought it?'

"Then he would ask us children, 'Did any of you wee nippers bring this?'

"And we all would say, 'Oh, no, Uncle Nelson. We didn't bring it. We never saw anybody bring it either.'

"'Well, it's addressed to me. I best open it.'

"He would bring out his knife—not an ordinary knife like our fathers would have, but a dapper little penknife that went with his three-piece suit, you know. He would meticulously cut off the card and then the paper, and as the wrapping fell away, there would be yet another box. It would go on and on, layer after layer and box after box.

"With each layer of paper and each new box, Uncle Nelson would say, 'My dears, somebody must be thinking well of me to have given me this kind of gift. Now, I wonder who it could be?'

"And Auntie Vie would say, 'Maybe it's that blonde that you're always winking at down at church.'

"'Do you think so, Vie? Well, I don't know. I don't think I'm on that sort of friendly terms with her.' Then he would appear to be deep in thought. 'Maybe it was Her Ladyship herself.'

"And we would all exclaim, 'Maybe it was, Uncle Nelson. Now open the next box.'

"On he would go, and each time he came to an unopened box, he would stop and say, 'I don't know, but I think there's a bit of a woman's touch about this. Just look at how it's wrapped.'

"Finally, in the last box, Uncle Nelson would find a huge mess of tissue paper and newspaper and brown wrapping, and nestled in the very center, he would find a toilet roll.

"Uncle Nelson, looking so dapper and sounding so polite in his Belfast accent, would lift out the gift and say, 'A toilet roll! Why, that's just what I'm needing!'

"We would all shriek with laughter, and Uncle Nelson would turn to us wee children and say, 'Did you know that that was what would be in the middle of all of this?'

"And we would all answer, 'Oh, no, Uncle Nelson. We didn't know. We never knew at all.'

"Then Uncle Nelson would pick up the card and read it. 'From May. With much love.'

"And he would look at Mother and say, 'May, how did you know that I was needing a toilet roll? I can't thank you enough. All I can say is that this shows the sympathy and good nature that you hold for me as a sister-in-law.'

"During his speech, Uncle Nelson's face would remain wooden. But my mother—she was a giggly sort of woman—would laugh uproariously. 'Well, Nelson, I always know that that's what you *really* prefer for Christmas more than anything else.'

"So every year—as constant as Christmas itself—my mother would wrap Uncle Nelson a toilet roll. It was as much a part of the celebration as the holiday goose or my Christmas box. And until the day she died, my Auntie Vie and I often recalled that tale, and we would laugh and laugh.

"Though I'm a person who lives in the present, I still look back and remember my roots, my earliest beginnings. When I'm driving on a long trip or working at home alone, I enjoy playing with my memories—pushing them as far back as they can go to search for special times and places and people—to experience them, to savor them, over and over again."

As Maggi recalled her early days in Ireland, she remembered the love and stories and songs that eddied around her. Her reputation as a folksinger in Edinburgh had followed her to America, and a few years after her arrival, Maggi began receiving invitations to perform—to sing the songs of her native land, the ballads her father and mother had sung to her as a child. And in 1972, quite by accident, Maggi discovered she was also a storyteller.

"I was singing and conducting workshops on ballads at a local folk festival when Ken Goldstein, a friend and well-known American folklorist, rushed up to me.

"'My God, Maggi! We're in a dreadful hole! We're conducting a storytelling workshop, and one of our presenters isn't going to arrive in time to perform. Could you take his place? Do you know anything about ghosts?'

"I had never heard of a storytelling workshop, but I said, 'I suppose I could tell some family stories—about ghosts.'

"So I joined two other storytellers in conducting the workshop, and I told stories—personal remembrances—of growing up in Ireland. After my performance, I turned to leave the stage and I heard Ken call for me.

"'Maggi! Come back! Come back! Why didn't you tell me you told stories?'

"I just looked at him with a newfound air of confidence and said, 'Nobody ever asked me.' He rolled his eyes skyward and walked away.

"One year later, I was asked to perform at the Folklife Festival at the Smithsonian Institution, and for the first time, I was billed as both a singer and a storyteller."

Pushing herself beyond her current capabilities, Maggi—who had quit school at fourteen to begin working—passed her high school equivalency test, and in 1976, at forty-five years of age, she entered Southeastern Massachusetts University in North Dartmouth. While there, she began to recall more of the stories of her Ulster past and write them, preserve them.

"Dr. Norman Rehg—one of my professors, meticulous in dress and manner—asked us to write a story. We all groaned. We were horrified.

"He said, 'Oh, come, come. It's not as bad as all that. All you have to do is write a story—you know, an anecdote.'

"And I thought, oh, an anecdote. I'll have no trouble writing an anecdote.

"So I thought of my childhood—those memories of home, of my Ulster family, those that had nourished me as a child. Then I thought of my father, who during World War II spent most of his days, and often-times his nights, guarding the entrance to the Belfast harbor. It was a serious job, but to my sister and me it was a source of stories of adventure and humor that our daddy shared with us nightly.

"Some of our favorite stories were about a man with whom Daddy worked—William Dynes—known throughout our childhood simply as Stinker. We would wheedle our father into telling us of Stinker's latest escapades—stories that if told without benefit of Mr. Dyne's favorite adjective would have seemed only ordinary, or perhaps downright dull.

"But Daddy would tell about Stinker Dynes, using the man's own words, over and over again. I can hear them still. 'Isn't it one stinkin' col' day, and am I stinkin' well starvin' from standin' all the lifelong day until my stinkin' feet are stinkin' well frozen to the stinkin' puddles on the stinkin' pavement, and just as I was thinkin' of nippin' 'round the stinkin' corner...' And they went on and on, and such spiels would make my sister and me curl up and roll with glee on the carpet. Daddy would just beam, well pleased at amusing his wee daughters so easily.

"Years passed, and when I was nineteen, my daddy died. As is usual in Ireland, the remains were laid out in the back bedroom, and my sister and I were kept busy answering the doorbells, pouring strong tea, and serving small, round ham sandwiches. The house was full of grieving relatives and friends, recalling my father's life. And once again, the doorbell rang.

"I hurried to answer. Standing on the cement step, wearing a raincoat much too long for him, and turning a stained gray paddy hat between his nervous red hands, was a little man with white hair and a devout face. I bowed slightly to him, and he edged forward.

"'You won't have heard of me, Miss Kerr, but I used to work with your father during the war. My name's Dynes. William Dynes.'

"I had an overwhelming desire to shriek, 'Welcome, Stinker Dynes, welcome and a thousand times welcome!'

"But instead, I placed my young hand into his old one and said, 'We are most pleased that you had the time to visit us on this sad occasion. Would you care to view the remains?' And sedately, Stinker Dynes and I climbed the stairs.

"I wrote about my father, and Stinker Dynes, and this most lovely little remembrance from my childhood, and it was the first time I ever wrote a story about my family, and it was the only story that my professor read to the whole class.

"But you know, I've been writing and telling stories ever since: the folktales my mammy and daddy told me and stories of my childhood, of my growing up in Ireland. Oh, my, you can get through to people with the singing of a good ballad. But for me, I feel stories *personally*, and I can make better connections with people through storytelling—touching them in ever so many ways.

"When I'm telling my stories, I'm not there—on that stage. I'm not doing something I was trained to do. But instead, I'm part and parcel of the tale and I'm just telling things as I remember them—watching a film that's rolling in front of my eyes—and I'm living the story at that moment. For through storytelling, I can see my country. I can hear my people. I can walk the tracks to Bloody Bridge and shop in Rob's in downtown Belfast and play hopscotch on one of the small streets just off Irwin Avenue. And my listeners can go with me, anywhere a story lovingly told can take us—out of ourselves, and back home again."

The Large Stuffed Rabbit

Maggi's mother was very stern, a strict disciplinarian. Yet there was another side to her mother—one that bathed Maggi in love, understanding, and complete devotion. In "The Large Stuffed Rabbit," a poignant story of a child's disappointment, there is a special kinship between Maggi and her mother, for "the little girl in my mother saw—and understood—the little girl's suffering in me."

MONEY WAS scarce as hen's teeth when I was a child growing up in Belfast, but tradition dies hard. So the year I turned an "adorable six," my mother—blessed be her memory—resolutely put away sixpence a week so that Margaret, her baby as she called me, could have a studio photograph taken.

On the morning of the big event, I was put through my paces like a year-old colt. My hair was transfixed with curling irons into tight, biddable curls and then brushed until my scalp tingled. My patent-leather shoes, button-hooked across my instep with agonizing correctitude, were wiped with olive oil to make them glisten. My eyebrows, forever unruly, were licked into shape by a well-aimed flick of my mother's spittle-smothered pinky. And over my liberty bodice, white petticoat, and hand-knitted knickers, my skinny body was engulfed by a party dress of apple-green organdy, with frills below the waist and colorful flowers bunched at intervals above my belly button.

In order to keep this pristine and glorious picture unruffled by wind, splatter, or downpour, my mother spent her money on a tramfare to Mountpottinger—a journey of only two miles and usually made on foot —to the Hollywood Studio, renowned in the neighborhood as the place to have your likeness taken.

Off I skipped with my mother—my shoes squeaking on the pavement, my hair bobbing madly and still smelling slightly of scorched ends. And finally, agog with excitement, I found myself climbing the narrow stairs—every prancing step smothering my shoes in old dust puffs—until we eventually reached the studio. Mr. Heggarty met us at the door, ushered us into the room, sat me upon a raised platform, and then kept disappearing behind his camera and a welter of black cloth. I was fascinated. I was nervous.

236

When I'm nervous, I eat my fingernails. So I ate my nails. Mammy admonished me loudly. I felt irritated with my mother, so I hung my legs over the edge of the box—like dead turkeys in the butcher's window. Mr. Heggarty appeared from behind the black cloth and cautioned me. "Now, now, pet. You must cross your ankles neatly. No nice little girl hangs her feet like that."

I scowled into the unwinking lens. Again, the photographer's head appeared. This time he had had a thought. "Margaret," he said, "come with me into the next room and let me show you what I have for you."

Obediently, I slipped off the hard bench and followed his stooping figure. There in the corner of the room was the largest stuffed rabbit I had ever seen. He was as tall as I. His pale gray body had a bib of white, and he had the sweetest, pinkest nose in all creation—a nose from which had sprouted bristling white whiskers.

I was enraptured, entranced, and had to be led back to my pose, while Mr. Heggarty promised, "Now, if you are a good wee lassie, I'll give you this bunny to take home with you." Well, I was so good, I couldn't do enough for Mr. Heggarty. I smiled brightly toward his shrouded form, crossed my ankles precisely, with the tiniest of squeaks from my oiled shoes, and pointed my fingers just so on each side of my frilled skirt. The flashbulbs popped three times, and on each occasion, I showed my sharp, little teeth in the most charming of smiles and held my pose like the little girl I wasn't.

"Wonderful! Wonderful!" Mr. Heggarty said to my mother. "What a grand, wee darling you have there. Do you want the picture framed? Three shillings and sixpence. Call for it next Wednesday." And with these words, he hustled us down the stairs and into the street, thronged with home-going workers.

"But he forgot to give me my rabbit, Mammy. I'll run back and get it."

There was an embarrassed cough from my mother. "Darling," she said, "he didn't mean it."

"But, Mammy," I said, "you know that no one should ever break a promise."

Again, there was an uncomfortable pause.

"He only promised you the rabbit so that you would sit still and stop fussing. It was just a ruse, honeybun, to get what he wanted from you."

I gazed at my mother unbelievingly. A grownup did not mean what he said? A promise is not really a promise? Even an ice-cream cone smothered with raspberry cordials didn't cheer me up. You see, the adult world had been found wanting. In my heart, there was an empty space that should have been filled by a large gray-and-white stuffed rabbit with the handsomest of whiskers.

Slowly I trudged homeward, tears coursing down my face and salting my ice-cream cone. Gone were my glistening shoes, now dust-smeared. Gone was my curling hair, now slowly unwinding in the damp night air. Panic-stricken, even as young as I was, I realized that the outside world was filled with peril, promises not kept, and principles not upheld. But for once my mother, normally short-tempered about my crying in public, held my hand tightly. And she cautioned, "Ah, my wee birdie, always remember this:

> "Love many, trust few;
> Always paddle your own canoe."

It wasn't until many years after this, however, that I came to fully understand what she meant.

Cousin Norman

When Maggi was a young girl, it was seldom that an older cousin would give attention to the younger children. So it came as a wonderful, glorious surprise when Maggi's cousin Norman—a handsome, uniform-clad soldier on leave from Her Majesty's Navy during World War II—asked her and a friend to join him on a shopping spree. Though he's been dead almost fifty years, he still lives in Maggi's heart—for "giving me a Christmas present that, even today, I remember lovingly." In "Cousin Norman," Maggi pays tribute to this older relative who "made two little girls feel very special."

THERE WAS once a time I had nothing to do at Christmas except be there. I didn't have to pluck a turkey, stir the Christmas pudding, or bake solidly for five days beforehand. Neither did I weep copiously because something had fallen flat that should have risen or something had risen that should have remained flat.

No, these were the days I shared with my friend Eileen Kelly. She and I would shop in Belfast with our mothers, pressing our noses to the windows of the shops downtown and talking about all of the lovely things we would like for Christmas—knowing well that none were for us.

Eileen's father had been an invalid for all of the nine years I had known him, and my father was a policeman, earning a princely sum of $14 a week. But such facts didn't stop their small daughters from dreaming.

One day just before Christmas in 1941, my handsome cousin—Norman Cruthers, a petty officer in Her Majesty's Navy—came to visit. He asked Eileen and me, "Would you like to go shopping in the city—in Belfast?"

And with only these words, our minds sprang to the unbelievable hope that perhaps, just perhaps, he would buy us something. Unfortunately, I shared this thought with my mother before we left, and she was horrified.

"Sure," she told us, "young Norman has the money just to squander on you two wee hussies. But remember, if he does offer you something, be careful to think of his pocketbook."

We took the train downtown, and Eileen and I sat on each side of

Norman, not knowing what to say. Eileen had dimples, so she dimpled prettily. I didn't, so I just hung my brown wool stockings over the edge of the seat and hoped he'd offer to buy me a book. I loved books, and nobody ever bought me a book, except for the Greys of Dunmurry who sent me one every Christmas. But wouldn't it be marvelous if Norman allowed me to choose?

As my friend Eileen twinkled up at him, I sat solemnly, wishing that I weren't of two halves. One side of me was saying, "Just think, I could pick out a wonderful adventure book with ghosts and murderers and the like." But the other half cautioned me about what my mother had said. "I shouldn't accept anything, but if I do, it must be cheap."

When we finally reached the city, he asked us to help him choose something nice for his girl friend, Maureen. From department to department, we shopped, and we became so caught up in the spree that we forgot about ourselves. We were dazzled by the jewelry and soft pretty clothes. Together, we chose a lovely Christmas gift for Maureen.

As we turned to the escalator, Norman said to us, "Seeing you were such a couple of bricks helping me buy Maureen's present for Christmas, let's go upstairs to the toy department."

Well, you could have knocked us over with a feather. Eileen and I stole little glances of greed and delight at each other. Our dreams were going to come true after all. But as we entered the portals of toyland, my guardian angel hissed in my ear in a most unladylike fashion. "Not expensive! Remember what Mother said."

Norman took us over to the counter covered with pretty little dolls. And oh, Eileen and I loved dolls—soft, cuddly, and sweet. We loved dolls that blinked, said "Mama" in a weird, bleating tone, had eyes that opened and closed or even stared straight ahead. We just plain loved dolls.

One year earlier, I had received for Christmas my pride and joy: a dollhouse with a front that swiveled off its hinges to disclose five tiny rooms, sparsely furnished. When I saw the dollhouse on the counter that day, I realized that my furniture was utility in comparison to the plush-cushioned chairs, the metal standard lamps, the graceful chaise longue, and the darling sewing basket with petite scissors displayed there.

While I was gazing at this marvelous collection, I felt Norman's eyes upon me. Quickly, I seized a box of terrible, gimcrack furniture in brittle poor wood, and croaked, "Oh, this is lovely, Norman. I like this."

But Norman took the box out of my hand and gently laid it down. "No, dear. Eileen chose the doll she wanted, so you must take this one." He picked up my first choice.

"No! No!" I squeaked.

I had noted that it cost nine shillings and sixpence. Why, that amount could buy three books. Oh, that was a sinful amount. But when I looked up into Norman's eyes and then back at the box in his hand, my eyes filled with happy tears, and I nodded speechlessly.

Norman handed the two gifts to the clerk and said, "Kindly erase the prices, please." I breathed a big sigh of relief, and my heart filled with thankfulness.

"I'll tell your mum that it cost five shillings." He and I smiled like conspirators.

Eileen hugged her doll, while I swung my package, tied with a red ribbon. The three of us marched down the stairs, spurning the clanking escalator. We felt like rich stars in a movie. I longed to do some fancy tap dance like Shirley Temple, but we all just jumped the last two steps.

After the Christmas holidays, Norman returned to duty and in one of the battles of the Mediterranean, he was killed, presumed drowned in the sea.

Though I never really knew Norman well, *something* just told him that he wanted to buy the best for two little girls who'd never had the best before. We who had been taught to make do with what we were offered had our first taste of walking into the largest toy department in Belfast and walking out with *exactly* what we longed for. Believe me, it was a glorious feeling.

The Lucky Package

Maggi's father was a kindly man, a quiet man, and there was always a gentle warmth that permeated the days with her father. While her mother was forever trying to moralize, to teach, "my daddy just accepted me for who I was." In "The Lucky Package," a youthful Maggi is consoled and comforted by an understanding, loving father.

THE FORMAT was invariably the same. On the Fridays that Daddy was free from his police work, he, Mammy, my sister Dorothy, and I would journey into town and see the latest movie. Daddy was patience itself, and he always allowed our mother to choose. Therefore, my childhood was filled with weepy films, as Mammy was of the sort who never believed she had enjoyed herself unless a handkerchief was wrung to a sodden, tattered ribbon by the end of the performance.

On one such Friday afternoon, my parents met us at the gates of North Road School to find me dancing with excitement. Somehow that day I had won Miss Moore's weekly Lucky Package, a gift conferred only upon the good, the brilliant, or, I often surmised darkly, the offspring of one of Miss Moore's cronies. I was none of these, but that day I stood proudly, waving a pink paper bag, sealed at the top and loudly proclaiming "Lucky Package—A Bundle of Surprises."

I knew there would be conversation lozenges with such titillations as "Kiss me quick" or "You are a perfect peach" stamped in red on their chalky surfaces, but what thrilled me more than anything was that lying in the bottom of the bag was the unknown prize. Being the type who always eats her marzipan last off the Christmas cake, I carefully carried my reward unopened and unexamined into the tram, and just as painstakingly, climbed down that vehicle and to the Imperial Picture House, gleefully hugging myself in anticipation.

Unfortunately, my mother, who was of the old brigade and believed that not only should children not be heard but neither should they rustle paper while the movie was in progress, directed a loud *"Ssshhhh"* when I tried to rip the package open. We arrived just as the big picture commenced, and Mammy quickly lit up a cigarette and puffed enjoyably as the strains of sobbing violins heralded *The Barretts of Wimpole Street.*

As was normal with these weekly cinematic jaunts, the story was far above my six-year-old head. I watched a woman lying on a sofa having a fit of the vapors, a father thundering demands, and a poetic young man, whom I presumed to be the hero, promising undying devotion—all with total delight and complete incomprehension. Daddy, who was sitting on one side of me, slipped me a chocolate bar and I munched happily, still fingering the mystery prize in my lucky package.

This object seemed to be quite long and slim, and I wondered if it might be a little pen. Nobody had a fountain pen in my class. Actually, we hadn't learned to write in ink yet, and I rather coveted the tawny brown one of my father's. On the other hand, maybe it might be a funny little game, or better still, a tiny flag which would burst into a million colors when swirled above the head. I squirmed in happy expectation.

The screen was flickering slightly, mottled by black dots reminiscent of the pepper on my potatoes which Daddy always insisted on giving me. He swore that pepper cleared the head. Somewhere along the row a woman sobbed brokenly. I peered through the gloom, but could only decipher that it was neither my mother nor sister, so I sat back feeling relieved and surveyed my woolen stockings. As usual, they were wrinkled across the knee like an elephant's behind, and I surreptitiously hitched them flat by pulling them up through the pockets of my coat. My mother gave me such a poke in the ribs I nearly lit on the floor.

"Be at peace, can't ye," she hissed. "Don't annoy the devil out of the folks around ye."

I pouted and lay on the seat, so that my head leaned crookedly on the lower portion of the back, while my licorice-legs spiraled forward, where they suddenly hit the docile pair of shoes sitting in front of me. The owner turned around and tut-tutted at me, and I was hauled up by a mighty heave of my mother's irate arm. Cowed, I sat and stared at the scene in front of me.

The story had hit its peak of pathos. The daughter was leaving her father's house forever, but he didn't know this, and with a manly tear bejeweling his eye, he was lecturing his invalid daughter. There was not a dry eye in the house.

It was at this juncture that I finally succeeded in wiggling the prize from my pink package. Squinting at it in the darkness, I could dimly make out the shape of a cigar. I turned toward my father, who was delicately holding his Player's cigarette poised in his right hand. I swiveled toward my mother, whose cigarette—a Gallagher's Blue, as both parents were loyal to their own particular brand—was glowing like a tiny beacon. I slowly lifted the toy cigar to my lips.

I sucked. Nothing happened. I blew in the other direction. A noise, halfway between the gasp of a dying cow and the wail of a sick banshee, raspberried throughout the Imperial Picture House. For one moment there was an electrified silence as people tried to associate the sound with the soul-inspiring speech issuing from the silver screen. The next instant my father, habitually the soul of discretion, slapped his thigh and, with an enormous guffaw of laughter, kicked his heels in the air. All up and down the packed rows of the Imperial, people who a moment before had been weeping copiously roared with laughter until their tears of merriment far outweighed their celluloid-induced grief.

Fortunately for me, the film was almost at its end, and as it was such a dark picture, nobody could quite ascertain where the squeaking honk had originated, so I was able to creep from the cinema, head hung in shame and tears tripping me. Nothing that either Daddy or Mammy said could quite calm me. Dad chuckled and even Mammy saw the joke, without the usual social implications pertaining to bad manners. But it didn't matter. I sobbed brokenly all the way to Castle Junction where we caught our tram, because somehow or other my feelings had been hurt. I felt that the whole cinema, nay, the whole world of Belfast, had laughed at me, and I had made a fool of myself. I scuffed my toes in the gutter and moped my way up the twanging-metal stairs of the homebound tram.

For once Daddy did not sit beside Dorothy, his favorite, but jostled me in by the window, and I snuggled in the arched safety of his arm as the conductor came upstairs and rang the tickets.

Daddy squeezed my shoulder and said, "You know, chickabiddy, that today reminded me of the time I sat on the minister's hat."

Immediately, I sat up. "What," I giggled, "you really sat on a minister's hat?"

"Yes," said Daddy. "And to make it worse, he was praying on his knees in the middle of the kitchen at the time. Everybody in the house laughed, including dear Pastor Willoughby, God rest his soul, but you know, I thought they were laughing at me, and do you know, daughter of mine"—he paused and opened his eyes wide and gazed down at me in astonishment—"even though I was a boy, I almost cried. I definitely remember a big lump in my throat. My family, you see, was only laughing at the situation, the way the folk in the cinema did today. Both your cigar tooting and my hat squashing were accidents. Do you understand what I'm gettin' at, honeybun?"

Dumbly I nodded. Now it was I who had the lump in my throat, but I definitely did feel more cheerful by the time our tram finally reached

Irwin Avenue. I curled my hand into Daddy's, and jauntily we strolled along. Mammy and Dorothy hurried on before us, so that the fire could be roused and the sausages frying before the man of the house arrived home.

Daddy and I took our glorious time. We looked at one another and smiled. Taking my cigar from my pocket, I placed it to my lips and blew several penetrating blasts. A flock of pigeons pecking by the bread man's horse rose with a great flapping of wings, and Daddy and I stood and watched them in the waning light, rising and wheeling in the air above, and then we turned and looked at each other again and laughed and laughed and laughed.

Stories of People from Truth and Fantasy

Jay O'Callahan

When I began telling stories . . . it was as if the
students were challenging me to hold their interest when
nothing else would. Then, as the story emerged,
I could see on their faces a sense of wonder, for they were
shaping images in their own minds, and it was
better, far better, than any novel I had ever written.
And after struggling as a writer for five years,
I found that my future—the dream of being
an artist—lay in storytelling.

*   *   *

J AY O'CALLAHAN stands alone on a stage. He's tall and lean, red-haired and balding, with a salt-and-pepper beard. The stage is bare. There are no props, no scenery, and Jay wears no makeup, costumes, or masks. Yet through the art of storytelling, he peoples his bare stage with sages and simpletons, poets and plain folks, heroes and villains—an entire cast in one man. And they're not just characters. They're people, each with flaws and fears and dreams, and Jay becomes all of them.

Jay calls himself a storyteller, but he's more. He's both the storyteller and the story *maker*, and he stands astraddle the two worlds of literature and theater. Through the stories he creates and tells, Jay gives us a model for molding tales from real-life experiences, proving that there are stories all around us just waiting to be told.

Jay was born in 1938 in Cambridge, Massachusetts, but grew up in nearby Brookline. For Jay, storytelling began in childhood, one that was rooted in mystery and delight.

"As a boy, I loved the wonder of King Arthur and the marvels of imagination. I'd run home from school and climb a great tree in the woods behind my house and feel the presence of the tree and imagine I was just another branch. I'd explore the tree, its rough heights, and I'd thrill at being far out on a bouncing limb.

"The house where I grew up was a dramatic one—a vast house with thirty-two rooms on five floors and a cellar and attic that stretched on forever. Near the house was a cave, a beautiful cave, and I just *knew* there was a secret door, behind which all manner of passageways were just waiting to be explored. All I had to do was find the lever or button that opened them.

"When my parents had parties, drama filled every nook and cranny of our house—the drama of laughter, of singing, of conversation punctuated with debate and occasional outbursts of shouting. And as I grew up, I came to love any book or play or movie that touched on the drama that was all around me.

"When I was fourteen, to lull my younger brother and sister to sleep, I began telling them stories—wonderful stories about Tiny Tim, a detective the size of my thumbnail who solved complicated mysteries with

250

their help. And soon, I was tellling hand stories—using any mark on a child's hand to trigger the imagination. Anything on the hand was a doorway, a secret passage, the beginning of a story."

For Jay, there was a sense of fascination and wonder with the world around him—a stirring of his imagination—and as he grew into manhood and faced the realities of life, he remained true to this imaginative self: the part of him that climbed trees and explored caves and searched for hidden passageways. And as a student of English literature at Holy Cross College in Worcester, Massachusetts, his appreciation of words and books and poetry and drama he had experienced as a child was sharpened. "I learned that if you used words right, they came alive."

Upon graduation from college, Jay entered the United States Navy and it was then—as an officer aboard a naval oiler often stationed off the Japanese coast—that he began observing life even more closely.

"I remember most vividly a fellow named Jones—a nice, likable young sailor who was on the deck force. He had had a lot of problems, and he didn't have the toughness to ward off people who were laughing at him—even the ordinary jokes—and he started to deteriorate.

"This nice, happy young man went ashore to Japanese bars and came back to the ship, drunk. Something was wrong. This was not his type of adventure.

"Late one night when I was the officer on duty, Jones pulled himself up the gangplank and staggered on board. He was drunk, and I ordered him taken below.

"But Jones said, 'Request permission to go ashore, sir.'

"I said, 'No, Jones, you can't go ashore.'

"Later he snuck to the bow of the ship and began to climb down a line that stretched from the ship to the pier. About halfway, he lost his grip and fell into the sea. It was winter in Japan, terribly cold, and Jones would have died had it not been for a sailor who jumped into the sea and rescued him. We wrapped Jones in blankets, and he lay there, close to death. And though he survived, he continually found himself in trouble and he was thrown out of the navy—marked for life.

"I never forgot Jones, and I never forgot the struggles, the hardships, the agony I saw as a young naval officer. But when I came home from the navy—from tragedies like Jones's—I still found myself telling the simple hand stories I'd learned to create as a child. I was living, almost soaking up, the reality of life but at the same time falling back, recapturing the world of imagination, a world that for me was deeply rooted in my past."

Even then, it was the story in Jay that longed to leap forward, to be caught up, molded, and shaped, and Jay wanted to be an artist—a writer—to portray the mysteries and tragedies of life. And though he was serving as a dean of his parents' secretarial and finishing school in Boston, Jay devoted his summers to writing.

"During my first summer home from the navy, I drove into Vermont looking for a place to live and write. I was sufficiently impractical that I didn't look at newspaper ads. I just assumed a place would appear.

"On my trip, after much futile looking, I finally stopped at a rectory and knocked on the door, and a priest, barefooted, appeared. I said, 'I'm exhausted. I've been driving through the countryside for hours, looking for a place to live during the summer. Do you know of something?'

"He looked down at his bare feet, and as if he couldn't talk without his shoes, said, 'Oh, let me get my shoes.' Then, returning to the door, he told me, 'There's a little ski lodge not used in the summer. You might be interested.' It was perfect. And there I was, writing in the Green Mountains of Vermont. And I wrote every day, morning to night.

"But occasionally, in the evenings, my landlord's young children would come to the lodge and I would tell them stories—stories of my imagination, tales I created as I spoke. Though I didn't realize it then, the stories that were really coming to life were the stories I was making up, not those I was writing, laboring over during the day, sticking with in a very disciplined way."

Though Jay had unknowingly discovered the power of the *told* story, he persisted in his writing with unswerving commitment. In 1970, Jay quit his job as dean, moved his wife and two children to Marshfield, Massachusetts, and began writing full-time. Within five years, Jay had written two novels, neither of which would be published. But as he wrote, he *told* tales—first to his two children and later to patrons at the tiny Clift Rogers Library in Marshfield.

"One day, a friend said to me, 'You tell wonderful stories. Why don't you tell them all of the time?' It was a compliment, but I was infuriated. I wanted to be an artist, a writer. Who tells stories? Nobody tells stories! Yet I was also intrigued. So in the late afternoons, early evenings, I would go down to the marshes that stretched eastward from our cottage and practice telling stories—acting them out, trying my voices, moving my body. And there on the saltwater marshes, it became clear that there was something in me that must not only make stories, but also tell them.

"Then came the day when my urge toward storytelling collided with the casual prompting of a person I didn't even know. I was in the cottage, and not knowing what direction my life was going to take, I was feeling very depressed. An announcer on the radio said something absurd, like, 'If you're feeling sorry for yourself, get up and *do* something.' It seemed so bizarre, but what he said struck a note of truth. So I went to the telephone and called Leo Dauwer, a very likable, very kindly principal in Marshfield—a man who was not afraid of experimentation—and I said, 'You've heard me tell stories before. Well, *now* I'm a professional storyteller.'

"He said, 'What's the difference?'

"And I replied, 'Now you *pay* me.'

"'Oh, I see,' he said, 'I understand the difference. Come by and we'll talk about it.'

"Leo Dauwer, one of those angels you need just at the right moment, agreed to pay me $150 for three days of telling stories. I was a *storyteller*. I thought I was king of the world.

"When I began telling stories at Leo's school, it was as if the students were challenging me to hold their interest when nothing else would. Then, as a story emerged, I could see on their faces a sense of wonder, for they were shaping images in their own minds, and it was better, far better, than any novel I had ever written. And after struggling as a writer for five years, I found that my future—the dream of being an artist—lay in storytelling."

Jay began telling stories at other schools throughout the area, and the stories he told he created. Little was needed to spark a story in his mind, for now the details of life that he had savored and stored—as far back as childhood—were waiting, insisting on being shaped and molded into tales to be told.

"One day when I was in the barn near our cottage, I noticed a scratch on the wall—one that appeared to have been made by someone drawing his hand heavily down across the boards. It was noon, and I needed to create a story to tell at two o'clock. I thought about the scratch. If you scratch something on the wall, you curve your fingers just so. You give them strength. And I wondered. Who would do this? And why?

"Then I had an image of a man whose whole body was curved, and he was almost like a rat. And the name came to me. Vargo. His name is John Vargo. He's a sailor, and he's been hurt. And in the little town of Canton, they laugh at him and cross the street when they see him coming. They laugh and say, 'Hey, Vargo, you look like a rat.' Their jokes get out of hand, and Vargo, living like a rat, is on the edge of insanity.

"As I thought and wondered, I developed a story from a tiny scratch on the barn wall, and I think that Jones—that tragic sailor I knew in the Navy—was underneath it all. Jones was a man like Vargo who was overcome by his own plight. And at two o'clock at the Clift Rogers Library in Marshfield, I told the story of John Vargo."

Since beginning his career as a storyteller, Jay has created and told hundreds of stories—drawn from a measured blend of truth and fantasy, trusting always in the boundlessness of imagination. "I love to create stories. It's so refreshing, often breathtaking, to have a chance, especially as an adult, to use my imagination in creating, shaping, painting scenes, feeling deeply. My mind is constantly, furiously, making stories." For Jay, there's a haunting voice—something in the stories that must be heard and something in him that must make them, tell them.

The Herring Shed

In 1979, Jay and his wife and children were vacationing in Nova Scotia. While there, they met a man named Charlie Robertson—eighty-nine, old and weathered, but kind, who had a blind housekeeper, Maggie Thomas. Maggie was seventy, frail and bent, just skin and bones, but very sharp and alert. She could remember everything.

"I recall how I was really drawn to Charlie and Maggie. They both loved to talk, and more, loved to have people listen. I sat and listened to them for hours. One day, Maggie began, 'I remember when I was fourteen, working in the herring shed.'

"I told her, 'I don't know about the herring shed. What was it like, Maggie?'

" 'It was cold, very cold, and I hated it.'

" 'What did you do in the herring shed?'

" 'We picked up a rod, and we put eighteen herring on it.'

" 'But Maggie, how did you do it?'

" 'We put our thumb in the gill, we opened the mouth, and we slipped in the rod.'

" 'Then what did you do, Maggie?'

" 'We put it on the drying rack.'

" 'What's that, a drying rack?'

" 'Well, Corner Murdock would take those rods of herring to the drying shed.'

"And we talked on and on, for hours, about intimate details of Maggie's life, her struggles as a child, her cold and tiring days of working in the herring shed. A story was being born.

"Maggie was talking about her life. But she didn't say, 'I remember that life was hard.' Instead, she talked about objects, something specific. And as she rambled on, detail after detail, my imagination leapt out and grabbed even the slightest one.

"As I searched to mold the details of Maggie's life into shape—to create the images—the rhythm of Maggie's work moved in my body.

Thumb in the gill, open the mouth, slip it on the rod in the herring shed.

255

Thumb in the gill, open the mouth, slip it on the rod in the herring shed.

As Jay tells "The Herring Shed," he becomes all the characters, giving us an immediate sense of their words, the movement of their bodies, and the rhythm of their lives.

NOVA SCOTIA. World War II. This is Cape Tormentine. That's the Northumberland Strait down there and way beyond it is Prince Edward Island. It's six in the morning, spring here. All these people in the farmhouses around are up, and tonight they'll be turning on the radio to listen to the news about the war. We've all got people over there.

That's Maggie Thomas who just came out on the porch. She's fifteen. She worked in the herring shed last year, and the season's beginning again this morning—one hour from now, seven o'clock. She's the one to tell you about the herring shed.

I'm Maggie Thomas. I couldn't sleep last night. I was thinking all night about last season at the herring shed. I'll tell you and you'll know why I couldn't sleep. I got to be down there in one hour. Oh, before I tell you, that's Papa's boat. See, out in the strait with the brown-and-white sail. The best thing about the war is there's no gasoline so you make your own sail. I helped Papa.

Well, let me tell you about last season. As a girl of fourteen, I was very, very keen to take on the work in the herring shed. In years before, my brother Harry had worked there, but he was in the war fighting over there, so I got the job in the herring shed. At seven in the morning, I stepped into the shed—Peg to my right, Mrs. Fraser across. Peg is fifteen and she has long black braids and merry eyes, and Mrs. Fraser has the longest nose I ever saw and the nicest smile. She's my boss, a widow, Mama's age.

"Maggie?"

"Yes, Mrs. Fraser."

"Now, Maggie, I know your brother Harry worked here, but just let me explain everything. Now the great big barrel outside—that's the pickle barrel—and the herring come right down on the slides. See? They're coming down now right onto the zinc table. You get on the rubber apron. That's it. You don't want to be wet because then you'll be cold. All right. Now what you want to do is put eighteen of the herring onto the rod—it's called stringing it—and you put the rod on the rack there, and Corner Murdock will come and bring it to the drying shed. You know Corner?"

"Yes. He leaves his cows in the corner."

"That's right. Now all day he's sipping at a vanilla bottle. Gets kind of silly. Pay no attention."

"I won't."

"Fine. Now, you pick up the rod like this, put your thumb in the gill, open it up, and slip the herring right onto the rod. Now wait a minute. There's a rhythm. Thumb in the gill, open the mouth, slip it on the rod in the herring shed. Thumb in the gill, open the mouth, slip it on the rod in the herring shed. All right?"

"Yes. I can do it." I gave them a nod and I picked up a rod and began the work in the herring shed. "Thumb in the gill, open the mouth, slip it on the floor . . . I'm sorry."

"Slow, Maggie. Slow. Slow."

"Yes. I will. Thumb in the gill, open the mouth. There, I got it on. Don't look at me. Thumb in the gill, open the mouth, slip it on. I've got it. I'm all right, Peg." Thumb in the gill, open the mouth, slip it on the rod in the herring shed. Thumb in the gill, open the mouth, I was doing the work in the herring shed. Eighteen on a rod, put the rod on the rack, pick up a rod without any slack, and go on with the work in the herring shed. Thumb in the gill, open the mouth, the hours passed by in the herring shed.

"Peg, I know we've got to do a lot for forty-five cents, but how much?"

"What you do, Maggie, is a hundred rods. That's called a bundle, and that's about forty-five cents."

"A hundred rods? That's eighteen hundred fish. It'll take me all summer."

"No it won't. You'll do a bundle in a week or so. You're fast."

"I better get a lot faster." Thumb in the gill, open the mouth, slip it on the rod in the herring shed. Thumb in the gill, open the mouth, it was getting so cold in the herring shed. The floor was dirt, the sea to our backs, and the door was opened, so Corner Murdock could pick up the racks and bring them across to the drying shed.

"Peg, I don't want to complain my first day. I can't feel my feet, my knees. Honest!"

"Well, it's almost lunch. Just dance or something. Go ahead."

"Well, I will." Thumb in the gill, open the mouth, I can't get it on the rod this way. Slip it on the rod in the herring shed. Thumb in the gill, open the mouth, oh, at last, it was noon in the herring shed.

We got outside and the sun was warm. We had a lunch of potato and a herring without its head. We talked of the war and the farms around and then went back to the cold, cold ground of the herring shed.

Thumb in the gill, open the mouth, slip it on the rod in the herring
shed. I finished the day, my very first day, in the herring shed.

"Thank you, Peg. Thanks, Mrs. Fraser. A quarter. Oh, thank you.
I'm faster than Harry."

I ran on home, straight by the sea, glad to be free of the cold of the
herring shed. Charlie Robertson's wheat was tiny and green in the evening light, a sight to be seen.

"Hello, Charlie."

Charlie Robertson is the most wonderful old farmer. He's eighty-nine,
but he looks thirteen, except for the white hair. He's the kindest man.
You've got to say his name right—Charlie Robertson. He's a Scotsman
and proud of it.

"Charlie, you didn't have to come over."

"Well, of course I did, Maggie. You finished the day. You did a bundle."

"Oh, I didn't do a bundle, Charlie, but I did more than half a bundle.
I'm faster than Harry."

"Oh, of course you're faster than Harry. No question about that."

"I was looking at your wheat. It looks good."

"Well, you know, I told you. There are wet seasons and dry seasons
and good seasons. It's going to be a good season."

"I think it will. I'm going to show my mother the quarter. I'll see you
later."

"Well, I hope so, Maggie."

I ran home, up the porch steps, but I didn't go in. I turned around,
and I looked at the herring shed. It was my herring shed now. Not just
Harry's and Mama's and everybody's. It was mine. I was going to run in
and say, "Look, Mama." It's silly, but we all do it. Mama's gone blind,
the way her mama did and her mama before her. They say someday I
might go blind. Anyway, I knew just where Mama would be. She'd be
sitting on the couch, right by the fire, kneading the bread. I opened the
door very quietly. I don't know what it was. Maybe it was making the
quarter. Mama's pretty and she's young, but she looks so frail.

"Mama! Open your hand."

"Maggie! You finished the day, dear. Come over. I'm so proud of you,
Maggie. I know it's cold. And aren't they wonderful, Mrs. Fraser and
Peg. And I suppose Corner Murdock's got his vanilla bottle. Don't tell
your father. He doesn't think that's funny. All right? You can have my
hand. A quarter! You're faster than your brother Harry. You take it.
You're wonderful. Oh, I hear your father, Maggie. You show it to him."

Well, Papa came in and he was stringing the herring net across the room. It divided the room. He did it to mend the net. Papa doesn't frown and he doesn't smile, but I knew he was proud of me.

"Look, Papa, a quarter. I'm faster than Harry, I'm faster. No, I want you to take it, Papa. I want you to take it. I'm helping like everybody."

Well, Papa took it, and that night for a change, I did all the talking at supper. I told them about everything—about Mrs. Fraser and Peg, and Corner Murdock and his vanilla bottle. Papa didn't think that was so funny. I was eating my chicken to the rhythm. Thumb in the gill, open the mouth, slip it on the rod in the herring shed. I must have sung it fifty times for Papa. Thumb in the gill, open the mouth, slip it on the rod in the herring shed.

"Thanks, Maggie, very much. I've got hold of it now."

"You're welcome, Papa."

After supper, we did the dishes and Papa went over and snapped the radio on, and they were talking about Dunkirk, and there were so many people killed there. Papa went over and snapped it right off because that's where we thought Harry was.

I've never gone to sleep so fast in my life. I dreamed of Harry and he was far from dead. I could see him with that wild red hair, laughing at the cold in the herring shed.

At seven in the morning, I was back in the shed—Peg to my right, Mrs. Fraser across. I gave them a nod and I picked up a rod and went on with the work in the herring shed. Thumb in the gill, open the mouth, slip it on the rod in the herring shed. Eighteen on a rod, put the rod on a rack, pick up a rod without any slack, and a week went by in the herring shed.

I was going fast one day and Peg shouted, "You can do a bundle today, Maggie! Keep it up!"

"I will! I will!"

Thumb in the gill, open the mouth, slip it on the rod in the herring shed. Thumb in the gill, open the mouth . . . I did it! I did a bundle in the herring shed!

"Thank you, Mrs. Fraser. Forty-five cents. Thanks, Peg. See you later."

I was so happy and proud. And I'm glad it happened because the next day was terrible in the herring shed.

We were working away. Thumb in the gill, open the mouth, and the rector came in in his odd, shy way to the herring shed. The rector's got the worst job. He's twenty-six and never been a rector before. Whenever anyone dies in the war, the station agent gives the telegram to the rector, and it's got so no one wants to see the rector coming up the path. Well, he's sandy-haired and he leaned forward. "Maggie, could you come outside?"

And I knew my brother Harry was dead. For a moment, I couldn't move. I saw the telegram outside the shed. It was at Dunkirk.

"Thank you, Rector."

"I'm sorry, Maggie. I'm going to take you home."

"No . . . please. I don't want to go home. I'm sorry, Rector. I won't be any good to Mama like this. Let me get my feet on the ground. I would be very glad if you'd come tonight, Rector, with everybody."

And I went on with the work in the herring shed. Thumb in the gill, open the mouth, I went on with the work in the herring shed.

That night at home, the neighbors came around. Mrs. Fraser brought pie, Peg brought bread.

"Thanks, Mrs. Fraser. Come on, everybody. Sit down."

We must have had thirty people sitting in the kitchen. We just had the one kerosene lantern. People were telling funny stories and sad ones about Harry, and we were laughing and crying. All of a sudden the door opened, just about six inches.

"Mama! It's all right, Mama. It's Harry! It's Harry!"

I threw the door open and threw my arms around him. "Harry!"

"It's me, Corner Murdock, Maggie! It's Corner Murdock!"

"Oh, I'm sorry, Corner. I'm so sorry. Come on in."

Oh, I was so embarrassed. I wanted to run out into the night. Well, Mrs. Fraser took care of me, and Papa took care of Corner. Papa even gave Corner a whole bottle of vanilla. He never did that before.

I couldn't tell anyone why I did it. . . . Well, I did it because of the way Corner opened the door. Ever since my brother Harry was about eight, he opened the door six inches until everybody looked, and then he threw the door open and came in. That's what Corner had done.

I was so glad to be alone when everybody left. I went up to my room and looked out at the stars.

"Why did you take him, God? Do you need him up there?"

And for hours, I looked out into the blackness. I was looking at the strait, and I was trying to find the burning ship. For a hundred years, they say there has been a burning ship out there. They say the people won't give up until they find a port.

Charlie Robertson saw it. Mama saw it before she went blind. And Harry saw it on his birthday. Well, it wasn't there.

At seven in the morning, I was back in the shed—Peg to my right, Mrs. Fraser across. Peg held my hand and Mrs. Fraser gave me a big hug. The strange thing was that I felt so numb I just wanted to eat and sleep and work. And I went on with the work. Thumb in the gill, open the mouth, slip it on the rod in the herring shed. He lay in the ground, in the cold, cold ground, and the ground that was cold as the herring shed. Thumb in the gill, open the mouth, slip it on the rod in the herring shed. Thumb in the gill, open the mouth, the weeks went by in the herring shed. Thumb in the gill, open the mouth... I didn't realize it, but I was so fast one day, Peg shouted, "You can do two bundles, Maggie!"

"I will! I will!"

Thumb in the gill, open the mouth, slip it on the rod in the herring shed. Eighteen on a rod, a hundred to a bundle, forty-five cents. I did it. I did *two* bundles in the herring shed!

"Oh, thank you so much. Ninety cents, Mrs. Fraser. We'll buy a whole herd of cows. I'll see you later."

I ran on home, straight by the sea, glad to be free of the cold of the herring shed. Charlie Robertson's wheat was tall and green in the evening light, a sight to be seen.

"Hello, Charlie."

"Hello, Maggie. You were looking pretty far down there for a while. Good to see you."

"Oh, we're better. We're much better. Honest. We still wake up crying, and Mama says we'll do that for a year. Oh, Charlie, thank you for everything you and Margaret sent—all the meat and vegetables."

"Oh, listen, would've gone to rot at my place."

"They wouldn't have gone to rot, Charlie. You're wonderful. We talk about you all the time. Charlie, can I ask you something?"

"Well, I hope so Maggie. What is it?"

"Were you ever lonely when you were my age?"

"Oh, I was lonely all right, you know. I don't remember so much being fourteen and fifteen, but I was lonely. When I was nine, ten, eleven, I had nobody to play with. I used to go outside. Who was I going to play with? Jimmy Davis's boy? Little brat. I wouldn't play with him. I made up an imaginary friend. Nobody could see him but me. Jimmy Scotsman. He was enormous, big shoulders. I'd come out and I'd say, 'Jimmy Scotsman, take my hand.' As soon as he took my hand, I was nineteen, enormous."

"I want to meet someone like that, but someone real."

"Oh, you will, Maggie."

"I don't think so. Papa doesn't approve of dances. He says I can never go to a dance."

"There are other ways of meeting someone."

"Do you think I'm pretty?"

"I think you're pretty, Maggie. I think you're pretty wonderful."

"Thank you. I'll see you later."

"Well, I hope so, Maggie."

Thumb in the gill, open the mouth, slip it on the rod in the herring shed. The weeks passed by in the herring shed. Thumb in the gill, open the mouth, slip it on the rod in the herring shed.

One day, I must have had a good sleep or something because I was flyin'. By ten-thirty, I had done a bundle and Peg shouted at me:

"Maggie, you can do three bundles today. You might never do it again, but you can do three today."

"I will! I will!"

Thumb in the gill, open the mouth, slip it on the rod in the herring shed.

"Peg, I'm not going to have lunch. Get a potato and stick it in my mouth."

Thumb in the gill, open the mouth, slip it on the rod in the herring shed. By two o'clock I could barely move, but I was going to do three bundles today. I kept at it. Thumb in the gill, open the mouth, slip it on the rod in the herring shed. Thumb in the gill, open the mouth . . . I did it! I did three bundles in the herring shed.

"Oh, I'm so proud, Mrs. Fraser. I never thought I'd do it. A dollar thirty-five. We can buy a new farmhouse. Oh, thank you. I'll see you later."

Well, it was a wonderful day. I felt so good. But the next morning when I got there, I was so stiff I could barely pick the rod up. I picked it up and I felt awful giddy, so I started laughing and pretending I couldn't even get the fish on. I pretended to groan. Thumb in the gill, open the mouth . . . Well, Peg started laughing, and the two of us were laughing, pretending we couldn't get it on. Thumb in the gill, open the mouth . . . We looked at Mrs. Fraser and we were trying to make her laugh, but nothing breaks her concentration. Her hands are like fairies gone mad. Thumb in the gill, open the mouth, slip it on the rod in the herring shed. Thumb in the gill, open the mouth, slip it on the rod in the herring shed.

The two of us bent over calling, "Mrs. Fraser." We said it slow as molasses. Thumb in the gill, open the mouth . . . We saw the littlest bit of a smile, and we knew we had her. Peg picked up her black braids and pretended she was an opera star. Thumb in the gill, open the mouth . . . And I bent over with my rod. "Mrs. Fraser." Thumb in the gill, open the mouth . . . She couldn't resist us. She dropped the rod and she bent back and started laughing and clapping. And we danced around.

Thumb in the gill, open the mouth, slip it on the rod in the herring shed.

We were dancing around and Corner Murdock came in. He looked like an elephant's trunk, and he bent over and picked up the drying rack, and all of a sudden, Peg got one arm, and I got the other. Thumb in the gill, open the mouth, and we danced around with him. I was dancing with a man though it was Corner. Thumb in the gill, open the mouth, slip it on the rod in the herring shed.

"All right now," corner said wildly. "Thank you very much. That's enough."

We wouldn't let him go, and he stared at Mrs. Fraser. She picked up the rod and pretended she was conducting. Thumb in the gill, open the mouth... Well, poor Corner Murdock dropped the rack and ran outside, and with all watching, he opened his vanilla bottle and he drank it down. Oh, and we laughed and danced and sang, and Mrs. Fraser told stories about her grandmother. And we worked too. I made six cents that day. It was the most wonderful day of the whole summer, and it was good it was, because the next two days were the worst.

We were back to normal the next day. We were working away at ten o'clock. Thumb in the gill, open the mouth, and the rector came into the herring shed. He leaned forward in that shy way. "Mrs. Fraser, will you come outside?" She came right around the zinc table. She wasn't going out.

"It's one of my sons, isn't it? Dead?"

"I'm sorry. It's Jack."

"Oh, God!"

She wept right in front of us, and then she straightened up and she cried, "Well, please God, if it has to be one, it should be Jack. Gannett's got a wife and a son. You know that!"

"I've got the car outside. I'll take you home."

"I'm not going home, Rector. Thank you. There's no one at home. I'll finish the way Maggie did. But I'll be very glad if you come tonight with everybody."

And she went on with the work in the herring shed. Thumb in the gill, open the mouth, the war came home to the herring shed.

I ran on home, straight by the sea, glad to be free of the cold of the herring shed.

"Hello, Charlie."

"I'm sorry, Maggie. Sad day. Is she all right?"

"She's a strong woman, Charlie. She kept working to the end. We'll see you there tonight. We'll bring the chicken."

"We'll bring the scalloped potatoes."

"See you later, Charlie."

"Well, I hope so, Maggie."

At seven in the morning, we were back in the shed—Peg to my right, Mrs. Fraser across. She came to work despite her loss, and we went on with the work in the herring shed. Thumb in the gill, open the mouth . . . The Rector came in at ten o'clock, and Mrs. Fraser came right around.

"Rector, very kind of you, but I'll be all right now. I've got Peg and Maggie here and at least Gannett's alive."

And the rector was still.

"Gannett's alive, isn't he?" Then she cried out, "Gannett's alive?"

"No, he's dead."

"God! Oh, God!"

And she fell to the floor in the herring shed. She was taken on home and put to bed, and we went on with the work. Thumb in the gill, open the mouth, slip it on the rod in the herring shed. We went on with the work in the herring shed. I ran on home, straight by the sea, glad to be free of the cold of the herring shed, and I swore I would *never* go back to the herring shed. It was too cold, and it was too sad. I'd make money, but some other way.

"Hello, Charlie. Don't want to talk, Charlie. I'll see you there to-night."

We paid Mrs. Fraser another evening call and brought food. Then we went home, and Papa turned on the radio. Mr. Churchill was speaking, and he sounded so strong. His words were old and simple and bold. "We shall never give up. We shall never give in. We shall fight on the beaches. We shall fight in the fields. We shall fight in the streets. We shall never surrender. We'll go on to the end." We sat at the table and our eyes were wet, and I looked at Papa and his fists were set. Papa stood up and then he smashed the table with his fist and cried, "Damn it, Maggie! We'll go on to the end!"

At seven in the morning, I was back in the shed—Peg to my right, and Mrs. Fraser came in. She looked so old and so thin. But she gave us a nod and she picked up the rod and went on with the work. Thumb in the gill, open the mouth, slip it on the rod in the herring shed. The herring that are dried are put on the ships and sent to England for hungry lips. We went on with the work in the herring shed. Oh, we went on, yes, we went on, dear God, we went on with the work in the herring shed. We went on with the work in the herring shed.

Well, the season finally ended, and I was so glad. I stood outside until Corner Murdock snapped the lock, and it was done.

It was harvest season. Everyone had to help, even Mrs. Fraser. You couldn't be too sad. And finally the winter came, and I'll never forget. It snowed all day and all night, and Mama said we'd find the laughter underneath the snow. She was right. Sometimes there would be six or seven people sitting around the kitchen at night telling stories. It was fun outside, too. I built a snowman one day.

"Charlie! Charlie! Who do you think the snowman is?"

"I don't know, Maggie."

"It's you."

"Well, I thought so."

"You did not."

"Well, listen. Your father doing the cutting?"

"Well, he's cutting all right. Four cords of wood for you on Friday."

"What about the grain?"

"He's going to bring the grain over as soon as the ice is hard. Let's have a snowball fight."

"I think I'll pass it up, Maggie."

"I'll see you later."

"Well, I hope so, Maggie."

I wanted the winter to go on forever. But it's over. You can smell the air this morning. It's spring. Oh. It must be seven o'clock. I'm going to have to hurry. That's Peg going into the herring shed. Mrs. Fraser's already there. Well, you know why I couldn't sleep. But before I go, that's Papa's boat you see down there. I told you the best thing about the war is there's no gasoline. You make your own sails. I helped Papa make those. Well, I've got to go. I'll see you later.

Thumb in the gill, open the mouth, slip it on the rod in the herring shed. Eighteen in a row, a hundred in a bundle, forty-five cents. We'll go on with the work in the herring shed.

"Hello, Mrs. Fraser. Nice to see you. Hello, Peg. Your braids look so nice. Mrs. Fraser, you'll have to tell stories again this year. Oh, I'll never be as fast as you."

The herring that are dried are put on the ships and sent to England for hungry lips. We'll go on with the work in the herring shed. Thumb in the gill, open the mouth, slip it on the rod in the herring shed. Thumb in the gill, open the mouth, that is my tale of the herring shed.

Edna Robinson

Jay was once commissioned to create and tell a story commemorating the three hundred and fiftieth birthday of Harvard, Massachusetts. To begin his research, he sat down with some of the older citizens of the town, and they talked about their memories of living in Harvard.

Mario Barba, a former selectman, said, "I remember Edna Robinson."

"Well, what about Edna Robinson?" Jay asked.

Mario thought for a moment.

"Edna was the clerk in the store. She was a beautiful woman."

Jay listened carefully.

"I remember her selling us candy when we were kids."

There's nothing special about that, Jay thought.

"I'll never forget that she walked two and a half miles into town every day. Nothing stopped her. She always got to work."

It would have been easy to say, "I'll not tell about Edna Robinson. She's not important. She's just the clerk." But as Jay listened, she began to haunt him.

On a later visit, Mario told Jay about Blueberry Jack, the hobo, immaculately dressed, who picked and sold blueberries every summer; and Bicycle Kelly who lived in a cave, sold rags, and chanted the rosary as he pushed his bicycle about town; and Fillebrown—now he was full of life—an eccentric old plumber who lived in his plumbing shop and cooked steaks with his blowtorch.

Jay listened carefully. And he trusted. He looked for images, listened to the rhythms, sought out the details—and shaped the story from the people and places of everyday life.

EDNA ROBINSON. September 21, 1921. The town of Harvard, Massachusetts.

Everybody's getting up and getting to work. There are clouds everywhere, but the sun is peeking through and falling in pools of light. One of the pools is falling in the Shaker Village—that's part of the town—one of the pools of light is falling on the apple orchards, and one of the pools of light is falling right in town, on Fillebrown's Plumbing Shop.

Rubin Lambert Fillebrown. That's his name. Everybody calls him

Fillebrown. They love the sound of his last name: Fillebrown. Fille-brown is an older man; he lives in the plumbing shop alone, and he's just getting out of bed. Fillebrown's got his long johns on. He's got to make it to the sink to wash up, but that's not so easy because he's got plumbing supplies all over the place. He's got them on the table, on the bed, on the chairs, and he's got copper pipes all over the floor. Those copper pipes can be cold to the toe. Fillebrown has never quite got his own sink hooked up. He uses bottles of water to wash up, and he starts washing. "Oooh, that's the wrong one. That's the white gasoline. Wakes you up anyway."

Fillebrown is getting up, and two and a half miles away, Edna Robin-son is marching into town. Edna Robinson is thirty-two, and straight, and red-haired, and nothing stops Edna Robinson. She's the clerk of the general store—the store of Kerely, Reed, and Bryant—and she always gets to work. Her elbows bruise the air and she's marching into town.

"Morning, Dr. Royal. Nice to see you in the carriage. Oh, nothing like September."

There's old Elvira. "Morning, Elvira." She's a botanist. She's pulling a flower out of the earth and studying the root. She'll be there four hours from now looking at the root. "Nice root, Elvira."

Edna slows up for something she loves; it's the mist. Secretly she thinks of herself not as a clerk but as a poet, and she knows what makes the mist: the struggle between the new, cold air and the warm earth. And she marches through the struggle.

Then she *stops* for something she loves. It's the wagons coming—three wagons filled with empty wooden barrels, but tonight those wooden barrels will be filled with apples from the town of Harvard. Those apples will wind up in London and Paris. She loves that. "Ned, I hope the picking's good for you."

"Oh, yeah, Edna. Nice morning."

Edna gets to town and stands with her back to the general store—the store of Kerely, Reed, and Bryant. It's the only big building in the town. Before going into the store to work, she likes to know what's going on in the town. Over on the Big Common is Spout Brown; he's the janitor in the school and he's got a tongue like no one in the town. A bird just dropped a present on his head. "Come on down there, birdie, I'm goin' to take the wings off ya." The rest of what he said brought color to Edna's cheeks.

She started into the store, but she didn't get in—the school barge was going by. It's like a covered wagon. The school barge—the kids were inside, and it was driven by Miss Mary Jane McLaughlin. Single

whip and a single horse. Miss Mary Jane McLaughlin is a tall, mascu-
line-looking woman. Her nickname is "Yer out." She loves to be the
umpire, and she always says, "Yer out." You could hear one of the kids
fooling: "Jaaanie's got a waaart, she's a spoil spooort." Miss Mary Jane
pulled up. "Mario Barba, you stop teasing her. You sit beside me. Any
more fooling around, I'll hold your hand." *Nothing* was worse than that.

Edna smiled. She went into the store and she took her time smelling
the mixture of coffee, kerosene, and cheese. There was one of the
owners, Big Bill Kerely. Big Bill Kerely was shaped like a bell—small at
the top, then he sloped out. Bong! "Morning, Edna. If you'll excuse me,
I'm pulling up a barrel of pickles." There was little Reubin Reed. He
always had his pencil ready to take your order. "Morning, Reubin."

"Excuse me, Edna. I've got to turn the cheese." He ran downstairs.
Edna turned and went into the cage. That's what they called it—Edna's
cage—because of the wire mesh walls. That's where she kept the books.
She took out her account book; the figures were so neat they danced in
front of her. In ten years, Edna Robinson made two errors and caught
them in five minutes. Edna Robinson didn't make mistakes. She got her
pen and her bill and started entering the information: the people that
paid and the people that owed.

At seven that night, she was still working, and she was exhausted.
Oh, she needed the September night air. But she didn't get out of the
store. Two kids wanted penny candy. "No, it's all right. Come on in.
You got two pennies each? Come on." She went behind the glass case.
"All right, make up your mind. You got two pennies? What do you
want?"

It was little Carrie Blue and Mario Barba, both ten years old—Carrie
from one of the few black families in town, Mario, the only Italian
family. "All right. Make up your mind. What do you want? The pepper-
mints? The candy kisses? There you go." The kids waited. You see,
Kerely, Reed, and Bryant always gave you one extra candy. Edna never
did. "Two candies, two pennies. That's fair. 'Night."

The kids left so Edna left, and she started marching right down the
middle of the dark road. She loved that. Marching right down the
middle. Going fast until her elbows bruised the air again. And just
then, a leaf struck her in the face. It startled her—it was like being hit
by an insect. In the early darkness, she saw it was a reddish-yellow leaf,
just fallen. She let it go and she knew it was a mistake. She wanted the
leaf. There was no one to look at her, so she took a chance. She got
down and crawled around in the darkness, looking for the leaf. She
didn't find it. Then she got up and did something she rarely did. She

went over and she hid on the edge of the road. She was going to cry, and it upset her. Edna Robinson didn't cry. "Oh, my gosh . . . it's Daddy —he died a year ago today. I remember thinking there was nobody between me and eternity. Oh, I miss him. At least, I know what it is."

Then she took hold of a tree and held it. She admitted to herself it wasn't her father's death that upset her; her father's death saddened her, but it didn't terrify her. She was terrified. She held onto another tree and a friend of hers, Doc Royal, pulled right up in his carriage. "Edna? Edna? You all right? You wanna ride?"

"I'm fine. Thanks, Dr. Royal. I love to walk. You know that. 'Night."

She wasn't fine at all. She didn't know what was wrong, but somehow she made the walk of two and a half miles to her house. She didn't go in—there was nobody in there, there was nobody ever in her house. And then she heard someone coming. Nobody was going to see her cry. She hid behind a tree and waited. And then she realized what it was. It was the three wagons coming, and the wooden barrels were filled with apples. Those apples were going to wind up in London and Paris. That was important to her, and she was pulled in the wake of those three wagons all the way back into town. But she didn't know what she was doing. Edna Robinson walked all over that town, everybody knew that, but she always knew where she was going. Not tonight. She got in the center of the town—there was the store—and suddenly she knew she was headed to Fillebrown's Plumbing Shop. Fillebrown was like a father since her real father died.

Edna went around to the Little Common. She was about to knock on the door of the plumbing shop. She didn't quite have the courage, and she stood there smelling the grapes. Then she froze. She heard voices in the shop, and she didn't recognize them. So she listened.

"Now, Orlando, there was two of them."

"I saw them. Ebinezer, did you see them?"

"Yes, I saw them. There was two of them."

She didn't know those voices. But she didn't care if it was a meeting. She had to see Fillebrown. She stepped into the plumbing shop. There was nobody there. "Fillebrown, I thought you had a meeting."

"Oh, no, no. Just voices I make up to keep myself company. Well, Edna, how are you?"

"I'm fine, thanks . . . I'm not fine at all. Something happened tonight and I am scared to death. I don't know what to do, Fillebrown."

"Here. Sit down. Let me get the pipes off the chair. What is it?"

"I don't know if I can tell you . . . A leaf struck me in the face tonight, and I realized I'm just like the leaf. I'm going to blow away one of these days and no one's going to notice I was here. It scares me to death, Fillebrown."

"Edna, you're the clerk of the store. The store is the heart of the town."

"Fillebrown, I'm going to be thirty-three years old on Saturday. I just want *someone* to love me or at least to care whether I live or die. Is that too much to ask?"

"Edna, you're a beautiful woman. You're a smart woman."

"I'm not a beauitful woman. I'm a plain, ordinary woman."

"You're going to be mad with me, but you should go to the dances every Friday night."

"Nobody's asked me in five years...Oh, telling you all that was so hard. I feel much better. At least, I know what my tombstone's going to look like. I've figured that out. It's going to say 'Edna Robinson,' and it's going to have two columns of figures that balance just right. That's all I've ever done."

"Now, Edna..."

"I'm fine. Honest. I was standing outside your shop in the dark, scared to knock. I was smelling the grapes. You know what else I figured out? Clerks are always grape juice, and poets are always wine. I'm going to ferment, Fillebrown. I mean it. In a month or two, I'm leaving the town and I'm going... well, I might go to Paris to live. Momma said it's the City of Light."

"Ah! City of Light! There's light all over the town of Harvard. I see it every morning. Edna, would you do me a favor? Would you stay for supper? I got a steak around here somewhere if I can find it. That would be nice if you would wash up. Wash the plate under that chair there, and there's a fork sticking out of that chair. Don't use that bottle. That's white gasoline. I know. Edna, here's the steak. It was under the newspaper. I had this thing two weeks. Kinda ripe. I'm only foolin', Edna. I got it an hour ago. It's safe, Edna. What are you looking for? A stove? I'm an old man, I don't need a stove. I just take a knife, Edna, and put a hole in the steak. Now you see this pipe hanging at a right angle? I hang the steak on it, get my blowtorch, and cook her up."

Edna was amazed. And the steak was delicious.

"Now, Edna, you're lookin' like yourself. Tell me the truth. I want the truth. What do you think of my place?"

"The truth, Fillebrown? I think it's disgusting."

"Atmosphere! Atmosphere! Do me one more favor, come on down to the train station. I got supplies comin' in. Then I'll take you home. The air will do you good."

He convinced her, and the two of them went two and a half miles down Depot Road. They were almost at the train station, and Fillebrown pulled up. "Shhhhh. Edna, I'll show you something interesting. Can't see in the dark, but sitting on the station bench is a hobo, a real hobo. He comes in the summer, picks the blueberries, and then disappears in the fall. Blueberry Jack—the riffraff love him. They talk to him. You ask the hobo anything about his background, and that's the end of the conversation. Nobody knows nothing about him, but they love him. They do. Oh, watch what he does when the train comes." The train whistled and roared closer. "See? He's running. He goes hiding every time the train comes. He doesn't want someone from Boston to see him. He's hiding something. But he's a nice fellow. Come on."

They got down to the train station and Fillebrown had supplies coming in. He was busy, so Edna paced back and forth looking for the hobo. She wondered where he was hiding, and she wanted to know what he looked like. He had disappeared, and she finally went over and sat on the station bench. "Oh my gosh, you startled me."

There was a man standing in the doorway of the station, but *he* was clearly a cultured man. Intelligent face—she thought he was a lawyer —black hair, forty or forty-five years old, but he did have a scar. He had a scar from his right eye back. Immaculate blue shirt and trousers. "You startled me," Edna said.

"I'm very sorry."

"I don't mean it was your fault. I was so busy looking for the hobo. We saw him go hiding when the train came. I imagine that he looks like a circus clown."

"I'm sorry to disappoint you. I'm the hobo."

"I'm sorry. You look like a lawyer."

"When I was a lawyer, they said I looked like a hobo."

"Please sit down. I'm Edna Robinson."

"I'm Blueberry Jack."

"What's your last name?"

"Jack."

"Yes . . ."

Fillebrown came out. "Well, I see you've met Jack. That's good. Listen, Jack. We got to go. It was good to see you. Come on, Edna."

"Wait a minute, both of you. Edna, Fillebrown, I wonder if you'd like to come to my place for supper tomorrow night? The abandoned house right up the hill there. Tomorrow night, seven o'clock, Sunday. I'll do the cooking."

"All right, Jack," Fillebrown wheezed delightfully. "The abandoned house. That all right, Edna? Good! Tomorrow night, seven o'clock, Jack. Come on, Edna. What do you know, Edna? I told you he makes friends with mostly the riffraff. Well, I guess he took a sudden likin' to me." But Fillebrown knew who he'd taken a liking to.

All Sunday—the next day—Edna walked all over the town of Harvard, and she saw with brand-new eyes because she was leaving for good in a month or two. She spent the morning in the Shaker part of town; she knew lots of them, worked with them during the war. She had lunch at Still River all by herself, the way she always did. And during the afternoon, Edna picked apples—she was having a wonderful time, she loved apples—and she ate three or four and got a stomachache. Then she realized it wasn't from the apples. She was going to supper tonight in an abandoned house with a hobo. She was leaving in a month or two, but still if the word got out, the talk could really hurt. She just hoped Fillebrown would forget about it. She was scared.

At seven that night, she was in her kitchen looking for Fillebrown, but he hadn't come to get her. At seven-fifteen, he still hadn't come, and she relaxed. At seven-thirty, Fillebrown wasn't there. "Oh, he forgot. He forgets everything." Edna went over and sliced the tomatoes in the kitchen. Fillebrown wasn't coming. She was laughing. Twenty years ago, just once, he forgot his trousers. The town never forgot that.

The door opened, and Fillebrown came in. He did a little dance, saying, "I forgot! I remembered! Let's go!"

She couldn't say no. They rode two and a half miles down Depot Road over the tracks and up the steep hill to the abandoned house. Fillebrown knocked and Jack opened the door.

"Well, I was disappointed. I thought you'd stood me up. Come on in."

"No. We didn't stand you up. I forgot, Jack. I'm an old man. Let's see your place. Come on. Come on. Let's see your place. Oh, it's a nice place. Where's your furniture? You got three orange crates. Ha! What's upstairs?"

Jack took them upstairs, and there was nothing upstairs but a single blanket and a leather-bound book. "Let's see what you're reading. Oh, Catullus. I read that, that's good."

"Oh, no, that's Catullus He's a Roman poet."

"Yeah, I read that one too. Where we eating?"

"We're eating outside, Fillebrown. Will you get the orange crates— bring them into the backyard?"

The three of them went outside. The yard was wild with grass but Jack just made a circle, a circle with rocks, and that's where he did the cooking. Maybe that was it. Maybe it was the night air and the stars, because the nervousness disappeared. By ten o'clock, they were like children. Fillebrown was delighted.

"Jack, you're a good cook. Now, I'm gonna pay you back with one of my famous imitations. You're a lucky man. Now, I'm imitating someone in the center of the town. You never come into the center, Jack; you won't guess. But, Edna—you'll guess. The whole imitation is in the feet. All right, here we go. Ooo...oh...oh...ooo. Come on, Edna, guess. I can't keep this up. Oh...oh....ooo. Oh, Edna. It's Joe Dixon breaking in shoes for Henry Dale. Oh, oooh. Come on the two of ya, get up. Stop sitting down. I've got a little dance. Take hands, take hands. Little dance now. I gotta song about everybody. Jack, here's a good one:

> "Royal, Dr. Royal, he delivered us all;
> Royal, Dr. Royal, he's a man six feet tall;
> He's got the magic lotion,
> A wonderful, blue potion;
> Royal, Dr. Royal, he delivered us all."

It was twelve-thirty when they broke up. You'd think they'd been drinking wine all night. But there was no wine—they didn't need it. They had a wonderful time and decided to do it again Monday night.

All day Monday, Edna was in the cage, and she was excited and frightened because she was going to supper again, in an abandoned house, with a hobo. And Fillebrown didn't forget. He picked her up, he brought his blowtorch, and he did the cooking. They stayed until one-thirty in the morning, and they decided to do it again Tuesday.

All day Tuesday, Edna was excited, frightened, but she went. She did the cooking. Ten o'clock Tuesday night, Fillebrown got up in the wagon. "Jack, I'm very tired. I'm an old man. I'm not used to these nights. I know you're going Saturday morning on the ten o'clock train, but, Jack, I'll have to see you during the day—no more nights for me. Thanks a lot, though. Come on, Edna."

"No, Fillebrown, I'm going to walk home. I know it's five miles. I'm a good walker, you know that. Good night and thank you, Fillebrown. Thank you, Jack. 'Night."

Fillebrown was off, and Edna started down the steep hill. Jack called after her.

"Edna! Edna! Could I walk you home?"

"Well, sure, Jack. That'd be nice."

The two of them walked, laughing together. "Oh, Jack. I love September. It's my month, you know. The frost is coming. You watch the leaves tomorrow; they'll change. I always know. What's your favorite month?"

They walked over the railroad tracks and started up Depot Road, and they saw someone coming. "Jack, I can't be seen with you this late at night. It's not worth the talk. I've got to hide. I'm sorry."

She hid, and Jack waited to see who was coming down Depot Road. It looked like a camel was coming. The camel had a big hump, and a lantern in the front, and the camel was kind of clanking, and now he could hear the camel sort of chanting, "Hail Mary full of grace the lord is with thee blessed art thou amongst women and blessed is the fruit of thy womb, Jesus..." It was Bicycle Kelly, the rag man. He never rode that bike. All day long he pushed it, and he'd pile up rags and old clothes on the seat until he had a huge hump. And all night long as he pushed it, he chanted the rosary. He lived in a cave. "Is that you, Jack, up there? Jack, is that you?"

"Kelly, that's me."

"Well, that's me too, Jack. That's me too. I've been looking for you, Jack. Here, let me lean the bike against the tree. Now, Jack, I know you're going Saturday morning on the ten o'clock train. Up on top of the hump is a coat—a bargain."

"I don't want the coat. I've got a coat. But, Kelly, I like the hat on the handlebar."

"It's not *just* a hat... This hat belonged to an actress in Paris. She paid sixty-five dollars; I got it for twenty-five. It's yours for ten, not a penny less."

"I'll give you a dime."

"Sold to the man! I'll see you in the morning—I wanna talk to you. Please, don't be late. We'll see you at the cave...."

When Kelly was long gone, Edna finally came out. "So that's Bicycle Kelly. I've heard about him. Is he crazy?"

"Edna, let me try the hat on you. Just move, just a bit. I think the hat *is* from Paris. It's beautiful. Turn to the moon, turn to the moon. Let me see you in the moonlight. Wait 'til you see that hat on you, Edna. It's wonderful and you look wonderful in it.... No, he's not crazy. He's a lonely man. A nice man. Come on, I gotta get you home. The frost is coming and it's cold."

The two of them laughed as they walked two and a half miles into the center of town. They stood in the wet grass in the Big Common, looking at the stars together, and all of a sudden, Jack coughed violently. He almost fell backward onto the grass. He coughed so violently that he fell onto the bench, and it was a minute before he could control himself. Edna sat down. "Oh my gosh, Jack, what's wrong with you? That's a terrible cough. Doc Royal lives over there. He's a friend. See him in the morning."

"No, it's fine. It's just a catch. What's the big building?"

"Jack, you never come into the center. It's the heart of the town: the store of Kerely, Reed, and Bryant. I work there, keep the books. I'm leaving the town in a month. I'm going to miss that store. I might go to Paris to live. I'll tell you something. There are some people in the town that haven't paid their bill for two years. They don't have any money. Nobody's ever been turned away in the store. That's the truth—I know the secrets.

"Jack, I haven't laughed this way since I was a little girl. But that's a terrible cough. You go home now. I'm safe. I'll walk the rest of the way myself. Good night. And thanks."

"Wait a minute, Edna. All right, I'll let you walk home by yourself, but tomorrow I'll see you at my place at eight o'clock. I'll do the cooking."

"Jack, I can't. Without a chaperone—can you imagine the talk? It's a small town. 'Night."

"Wait . . . please, Edna. I'm leaving Saturday on the ten o'clock train. I'm never going to get back again. Please."

"You don't understand a small town, Jack. . . . Let me put it this way . . . I'll come. I'd love to." Edna started off and turned. "I love the hat, Jack. I love the hat." She turned and walked into the darkness and Jack watched her. He hesitated, then called out, "I love the wearer of the hat . . . I love the wearer of the hat."

Wednesday morning, Edna Robinson marched to work and she felt wonderful. "I love the wearer of the hat, I love the wearer of the hat." She was marching through the fire of the fall because all of the leaves had changed that night. "Morning, Dr. Royal. Nice to see you. Oh, yes, thanks. It *is* a nice hat." Her elbows bruised the air as she went marching in. "Morning, Elvira . . . oh, it's your best root ever."

Edna went into the cage, and she was having a wonderful time keeping the books that day—whistling, humming. She made so much noise keeping the books that big Bill Kerely and little Reubin Reed crept over to the cage. They peered in, and there was Edna Robinson with a beautiful hat, keeping the books. She looked up and winked at them, and the two of them turned red and crept away. Everyone around her had a wonderful time that day.

That night, she made the walk two and a half miles to see Jack. They had a wonderful time. They didn't have wine, they didn't need it. Wednesday was *magnificent*.

Thursday was just the opposite. On Thursday, there was a bitter cold rain like the winter, but she made the two and a half miles. When she got into the cage, she was shivering and wet, but she kept working until ten o'clock in the morning. Finally, she took a break. She went over to the stove, and she was sorry she did. The rain was rushing down, rushing into the gutter. "Just like my life, rushing away. Jack's going Saturday morning, ten o'clock train, and I'm going somewhere in a month. I don't even know where." She shook it off. She wasn't going to feel sorry for herself. But things kept going wrong.

Hour after hour, things were busting and falling around in the store. At two o'clock, the shelving broke in the cellar. Big Bill Kerely and Little Reubin Reed ran down into the cellar, and Edna was left with fourteen customers. She was rushing back and forth, and things were falling apart. Everybody was understanding except Miss Mary Jane McLaughlin, and she was getting an inch taller every second. "Edna," Mary Jane commanded, "I've been waiting a half an hour. Get two men and load the sack of flour."

"Mary Jane," Edna said at the end of her patience, "you have to take your turn like everyone else."

It was just then that Edna, standing behind the counter, felt something sticky and looked down. The molasses barrel had sprung a leak: she was stuck to the floor. And then Fillebrown came into the store out of the rain. "Everybody, listen. I just made a bet with the minister. It's a secret, so I'm only telling you. Edna . . ."

"Fillebrown, I don't want to hear. I'm stuck to the floor."

"I know what you mean."

"You have no idea what I mean."

"Well, I've got to tell someone. Everybody . . . I made a five-dollar bet with the minister. I told him you can get whatever you want in the store. He says you can't. Here's the test case. Big Bill Kerely, are you down in the cellar?"

"I'm down in the cellar! What do you want, Fillebrown?"

"Do you happen to have a secondhand pulpit down there?"

"I don't know! Reubin, we got a secondhand pulpit?"

"Yeah, there's one in the far corner!"

"I win *five dollars!*"

Everybody was amused except Miss Mary Jane. And now her head was touching the ceiling. "Edna, I've been waiting an hour. Get two men and load the sack of flour."

"Mary Jane!" Edna exploded. "Load it yourself and it's yours for nothing."

Mary Jane wasn't passing that up. She stooped. "Thank you." Mary Jane left with the sack on her shoulder, and she took the air in the store with her.

"I'm glad she didn't drive *my* school bus," Fillebrown laughed.

Fillebrown helped Edna clean up the molasses. Things kept going wrong. Edna stayed an hour later to talk to Bill Kerely, and at eight o'clock, she made the walk two and a half miles to Jack's. The two of them brought the orange crates right by the fire. At eleven o'clock, she was dizzy. She was so tired she realized she could faint. But she wasn't going to let herself faint. She reached over and took Jack's hand. "Jack, what a day I had. I was stuck to the floor. I mean it. I never had a day in my life like this. You know what I've done though? I've decided to stay. I love the town. I'm going to take my chances here, and I want you to stay too. Please, Jack, stay for me—at least the winter. Will you?"

"Edna, I'm in love with you. I've never been in love before in my life. But I can't stay. Let me tell you why, but promise you'll listen to the whole story. I'm married, and that's one . . . wait, wait, wait . . . you said you'd listen. I've been married more than half of my life, Edna. I come from an old family, a Boston family with money. When I was a little boy, I loved to play with what my mother called the roughnecks, the ruffians, the wild kids. I loved them. I was *alive* with those kids. But I wasn't allowed to be with them. One day when I was twelve, my mother came by the Boston Common and I was wrestling with one of the ruffians. She was furious. She brought me home and gave me a lecture about my responsibility to my family name. And I took it very seriously. No more ruffians.

"The day after I graduated from college, Edna, I married the woman my mother picked out. My wife was nineteen, I was twenty-one. We were like children; we grew up in two years. And we didn't like each other. We discovered it, but you don't get divorced in an old family. You stick it out. We lived in the same house, but we went our separate ways. I became a lawyer—you made a good guess—but you didn't guess this. I had money, Edna, and I used it. I kept life at bay, but I watched everything, and then I realized my life was getting away. I got into the war to do something with my life, and I was hit, right here, Edna, and almost lost my eye. I was hit twice in the chest. I fell. When I woke up, I couldn't move, and I knew what I wanted out of life. I wanted to die. I don't mean because of the pain. I lay there, Edna, and there was poison gas all over the place, and you could hear the horses shrieking—that was the worst sound. I was in pain, but I wanted to die because I knew there was nothing to live for.

"I lay there, and my right eye was shut—I couldn't see anything with it—and with my left eye I was staring right at a blueberry. So I looked at the blueberry, Edna. I mean I *looked* at the blueberry. I'll never forget it—right in the center, that blueberry was red, Edna. And that red slowly became blue. It was like waves, and the blue slowly became black, and I looked at the crown. The blueberry was cut away from everything on earth and I looked right back at the red, and I kept looking at the blueberry until I wanted to live. I swear that blueberry pulled me through.

"They told me in the hospital I had three years to live because of the poison gas. I settled everything with my wife, and three summers ago, I came here, Edna, and picked the blueberries, and tried to find out what to do with my life. Three years. Well, I started talking with the ruffians —Bicycle Kelly, the rest of them. Just like when I was a kid. Edna, I never liked the way the twentieth century was going—nobody listens to anybody, not with their toes. But I listen to Kelly with my toes, and I swear, Kelly talks to me the way he's talked to nobody in his life. I'm good at it; it's the only thing I'm good at. And during my best moments, I think I'm going to reinvent the twentieth century. I love you. I love you. I would like to stay, but I'm going to do what I can do best. Saturday morning at ten o'clock, I'm going to get on the train. You know what I do? I'll go to a city, get off, take a rock, heave it through a window. I'll be arrested, thrown into jail, and I'll start talking with the ruffians. Crazy?"

"No, Jack. But I've never heard anything like it. I'm not giving up. I'm going to be here tomorrow morning at eight o'clock with a carriage. I'm going to take you all through this town. You'll fall in love with it, and you'll stay. Eight o'clock tomorrow morning. I'm serious. Be ready."

At eight o'clock the next morning, Edna Robinson rode up the steep hill to the abandoned house. She had borrowed a carriage from Doc Royal, and she was biting her fingernails. She knew the whole town was going to see him in the carriage and the whole town was going to say, "That's Edna riding with the hobo. She's running after him." Edna laughed. "It's true. I am."

She pulled up at the abandoned house. "Come on, Jack. I've got the carriage."

The door opened and a woman stood there dressed all in pink. Pink hat, pink veil, pink dress, and pink gloves. Edna began to leave. The woman ran down the stairs. "Edna! Edna!"

She stopped and turned. The woman lifted the veil, and there was Blueberry Jack. "Hello, Edna."

"What are . . . what are you doing in a dress?"

"Sixty-seven cents from Bicycle Kelly," he said, turning around to show off the dress.

"What are you doing in a dress?"

"I don't want the whole town thinking you're running after a hobo. So you just tell them this is your deaf old Aunt Catullus. I won't say a word."

"All right, Aunt Catullus. Get in and keep your mouth shut."

The two of them rode all through the town. They went to the Shaker part of town, and then they had lunch at Still River. And all afternoon they picked the apples together, and once in a while Edna lifted up the veil and gave Jack a bit of apple. Then she'd drop the veil and there was Aunt Catullus. They had a wonderful time laughing together. That evening they headed home in the carriage, and they were going by little Carrie Blue's place and little Carrie waved. "Hello, Miss Robinson."

Edna pulled up. Carrie had no idea what was happening, but in the bull pen, the bull had suddenly begun to attack Carrie's father. Her father nearly made it out, but not quite. He was hit. The bull was going to attack a second time, but Aunt Catullus jumped out of that carriage, climbed into the pen, and pulled Carrie's father to safety.

"Is my father all right?"

Aunt Catullus lifted the veil and winked.

"There's a man under the veil."

Aunt Catullus hitched up her skirts and was away. They got back to the abandoned house, and Jack got into his ordinary clothes. He put the Aunt Catullus dress right down in front of them by the fireplace. The two of them danced and laughed and kept telling the same stories about their day. It was well after midnight when they finally ate. They had wine that night.

"Jack," Edna said, taking his hand and pausing, "you look great in a dress. . . I know you have to go tomorrow morning on the ten o'clock train. I want you to take the apples with you, and I want you to invent a wonderful century."

"I love you, Edna. I've never been in love before in my life." And they parted.

Saturday was the longest day in Edna Robinson's life. She said she'd be at work, and she was at work all right. But there was no keeping the books. There were customers all over that store, and Edna was busy with all those customers. She forgot what time it was. "You want the strawberry jam, two of them? Oh sure." The clock read ten o'clock. She turned, reached up, and got the jam, and heard the train whistle and she stood motionless. Jack was leaving on the train. She could almost see Jack's face in the train window. Edna finally turned around. "Strawberry jam? What else do you want?"

At ten-thirty, Fillebrown came into the crowded store. "Edna, I know you're busy. I'll be right out of your way. Listen, we all saw Jack off— me, Kelly, everybody was there. And Jack wanted you to have the poems from Catullus." He gave her the book.

"Thank you. I am busy, Fillebrown. I'll have to see you later."

At seven o'clock that night, the store had cleared out and Edna was in the cage. She took her time putting on the hat. She picked up the poems by Catullus and opened to the flyleaf. It said, "I love the wearer of the hat. Jack." She just needed the September night air. She'd be all right.

But she didn't get out of the store—two of the kids wanted penny candy. "No, it's all right. You have two pennies each? Come on." She went behind the glass case. "What do you want? Make up your mind. You got two pennies."

It was Carrie Blue and Mario Barba. "Carrie, tell your father to be careful of that bull. He's dangerous."

Suddenly, Edna took two bags and put about seventy candies in each of the bags. "Keep your pennies. Happy birthday to you."

"It's not our birthday."

"Well, it's my birthday, then. 'Night."

The kids left, so Edna left. She marched down the middle of the dark road, and she made a promise to herself. Nothing was going to budge her tonight. Nothing at all. She went fast 'til her elbows bruised the air. She saw the wagons in the shadows. They were filled with apples from the town.

"Well, it's my town. I love it. I'm going to stay here, take my chances. I'll go to London and Paris, but I'll live here. It's a welcoming town. Not just the Royals are here. The Barbas are here. And the Blues." The train whistle sounded in the distance, and it pulled the tears right down the middle of her cheeks. "It welcomes the lonely people too. Mary Jane McLaughlin. Bill Kerely. Me. And the different people, they're here. The Shakers. Even the hobos, like Jack."

It was just then that Doc Royal pulled right up beside her. "Evening, Edna." He saw the tears and had enough sense to move along. Then she saw something coming down the middle of the road toward her. She stopped and waited. It was Fillebrown.

"Edna, I've been looking for you. I was hoping you'd be out here. I've got another steak. I want you to come to supper."

"I couldn't tonight, Fillebrown," she said, the tears coming freely. "I just couldn't tonight. Maybe tomorrow night."

"Oh, tomorrow night will be good. I'll clean the place up."

"Don't do that. You'll ruin the atmosphere."

"Happy birthday, Edna."

"Thanks, Fillebrown. That was very nice of you. 'Night."

She straightened her hat. "You're a wonderful woman, Edna Robinson. You didn't just fall in love, you fell in love with a man who's going to reinvent the twentieth century. You're a wonderful woman, Edna Robinson." And her elbows brushed the air and she walked on home.

Stories

of

Contemporary

Life

Spalding Gray

*When someone asks me, "What happened to you
today?" I don't have to think about my response. There's
always a story there—a story I want to tell—
and I will tell it with the most energy, the most precision,
that I can muster. But there are people who do
this every day. They're not actors or professional
storytellers; they're people, like all of us, who are
storytellers just the same.*

285

*   *   *

S PALDING GRAY is an actor, and since 1979, he has performed his own brand of theater to critical acclaim throughout Europe, Australia, and America. Call it storytelling, if you will, for Spalding Gray speaks through just one character, himself, as he weaves tales chronicling true-life events. "I appreciate people who can create from their imaginations, but I'm more interested in poetic journalism: the stories that exist *outside* of me, the stories that demand to be soaked up."

Sitting at a small, bare table on a vast stage, Spalding, in a voice both conversational and energetic all at once, recounts his life. His stories—always long but never rambling—are reincarnations of the Homeric epics that move freely through truth and experience, both present and past. They expose those hidden things in all of us—our fears and phobias, our vulnerabilities, our doubts and despair. "I'm talking the common American language to emphasize life—speaking to people as simply as possible, but at the same time, communicating what our feelings and ideas really are."

To Spalding, the fabric of our lives is sewn with stories. And during his career, he has created in theater a forum for the tales he tells—a dozen or more monologues which report actual, though sometimes slightly embellished, events.

Spalding was born in 1941 in Barrington, Rhode Island. As a child, he disliked school. His teachers thought he was slow; in reality, he was dyslectic, which no one understood at the time. Everyone expected Spalding to become a dropout. Instead, he became deeply involved in drama in high school, and upon graduation, he began to pursue a career in theater—first as a student at Emerson College in Boston and later as an actor in experimental theater in New York.

As he studied theater, the stories that filled him up and pressed all around him nagged to be told. "While studying at Emerson, I worked at night at the Katharine Gibbs School. And as I washed dishes or collected garbage, I told the story of my day to my first audiences—a handful of ex-merchant marines, Irish cooks, and Emerson students who, lucky for me, were good listeners." Spalding's impulse toward storytelling stayed with him even after he moved to New York. He recalls the first few months—living on $32 a week of unemployment,

286

sleeping on the floor in a friend's apartment, and experiencing New York for the first time. "I can remember going back to the apartment each day, overloaded, and I would have stories to tell—stories that *demanded* that I tell them.

"Once in a theater workshop in New York, we were asked to stand up and relate a quick, simple story of our everyday life. If we became nervous or needed time to think, we were to jam—like a jazz musician— to repeat the last few words over and over again until we were able to proceed with the story. As I began to tell, a series of rather mundane, insignificant events of the past week flowed freely—like a memory film with images, frame by frame—and I edited them as I spoke, and I told my story without jamming. When I finished, the teacher hurried over and asked me, 'Who wrote that monologue?' She thought I had read and memorized the story. Instead, it was *my* story, and I had told it, and the internal film within me was playing it."

But Spalding didn't consider himself a storyteller. Instead, he viewed himself as an actor—the conduit, not the root, of creativity. Yet it was while working in experimental theater—where normally words are few and the narrative form is given little chance to flourish—that Spalding Gray began to discover himself, both the storyteller and his stories.

"I became deeply involved in experimental theater, and it was there, with the Performance Group, that director Richard Schechner told me to be myself first *before* I ever thought of acting a role or taking on a character—something no director had ever said to me. In one play, Richard asked me to drop the character I was playing—just to stand there, neutral—and I began to feel the character peel off of me like the skin of an onion, and suddenly, I experienced the presence of me, Spalding Gray, in that space.

"But it was only after I joined Elizabeth LeCompte and others to form The Wooster Group a few years later that I stepped completely out of a character to actually *become* Spalding Gray. In *Rumstick Road,* one of our productions, there were times when I walked directly forward, down to the audience, downstage, and stood there, quite neutral, and said, 'I'm Spalding Gray...' And I think that was the first breakout: the first direct experience of a vignette of storytelling, for I was saying who I was in the first person and giving a small description of an incident.

"The monologue form I was gradually developing found a fuller expression in *Nyatt School,* when I again stepped forward as Spalding Gray. Sitting at a long table, I delivered a monologue, my first, with The Wooster Group cheering me on, saying how much they loved my stories, laughing enormously each time I told them.

"Several years later, when we were performing *Point Judith,* we had returned to acting, to playing the characters. But every night when I walked offstage, I passed through a series of spotlights, waving goodbye like Jimmy Durante. And I knew in some profound way that that wave was actual. It was *my* wave."

After *Point Judith*, Spalding felt that he had come to the end of the group collaboration he had found so challenging and exciting, and he decided to go out on his own. In both panic and despair, Spalding left New York and took a long bus ride across the United States to Santa Cruz, California, to teach a workshop in performance. While there, he sat in on Amelie Rorty's Philosophies of Emotions class, and after the class, Spalding told Amelie his dilemma.

"I've been working in experimental theater for ten years, but I'm tired of being cooped up in a windowless art house. I'm curious about people and what's going on in the outside world. But I don't know what to do. I feel my world is about to come to an end, and I don't know what to do in the face of that."

"And Amelie told me, 'Well, Spalding, during the collapse of Rome, the last artists were the chroniclers.' And at that moment, it occurred to me that I should chronicle my life."

Spalding returned to New York to the Performance Group and tried to remember everything that had ever happened to him when he was growing up—in the simplest way, without writing it down—and he called his first monologue "Sex and Death to the Age 14." He performed it before sixteen people while sitting at a small table, working from a notebook containing an outline of all he could remember about sex and death until he was fourteen years old.

"The first night I performed it, the monologue ran for forty minutes. Then on subsequent nights, it grew to fifty, then sixty, then an hour and five minutes. And though I didn't realize it at the time, my memory was acting like a muscle, and it was growing, expanding, with use. It wasn't as though I was having new memories; instead, I was having memories I hadn't had in ages. As I performed, I no longer struggled with the discovery of the material and how the audience was reacting to it; I began to color in the details, making the piece richer, finer. And as I told my stories, Spalding Gray—the quiet, contemplative, shy young boy just looking at life from the outside—met Spalding Gray the actor, and it was like a good marriage. I was now performing the material and being both the source and the conduit of the story."

As Spalding performs, he works not from a memory of a rehearsed performance, but from his recollection of real occurrences. The stories are true, their presentations spontaneous. "I'm reporting actual events, a memory of a memory. But I don't *memorize* my stories. In fact, I'm not a good memorizer. Instead, I see images. And when I sit down to tell my story, I know that I'm never going to go blank as long as I know the topic and focus on it, because I'm describing an inner film running through my mind as I go through the story.

"Memory is metaphysical. I lie down at night assuming that I'm going to go to sleep, but there's no way I can force that sleep. I sit down at a table onstage assuming that I'll remember the story, but there's no way I can force the telling of the story. It just happens. I trust it. The re-remembering of the story each time it's told makes my listeners feel that I'm telling it for the first time, because it doesn't appear rehearsed. There's a spontaneous tension. All stories are at their best when seren-dipitous.

"Through the process of poetic journalism, I'm free to be the exper-iencer. I can get involved in anything that comes along—trusting the observer in me—not taking notes, but instead, allowing the memory to give random events structure. As I see stories coming at me, it becomes a simple matter of editing my life and my memories.

"When the story is told, the listeners form a visualization of their own—a film in their own minds—and that often rekindles a personal story in them. And through remembering, they begin to clarify the details of their own lives and come in touch again with how these simple things can be very wonderful if recalled and examined. The pro-cess is therapeutic.

"When I become confessional in my stories, I say things that are on my mind; I talk about my fears, phobias, idiosyncrasies. As I look into the faces of my audience, I often see a wonderful recognition where they say, 'Yes, I have them too.'

"I was staying at a health farm recently, and two women and I were sitting at a table, eating. One of the women asked me if I had walked around the woods yet.

"I said, 'You know, I tried it but I was afraid.'

"She said, 'What? You afraid?'

"And I said, 'I don't know, but I think it might be bears. I'm afraid of bears, and I was uncomfortable in the woods alone.'

"During the next morning, the three of us were again seated at the same table, eating, and the second woman who had said nothing the day before smiled widely and said, 'I wanted to take a walk this morn-ing, but I was afraid. I don't know what I was afraid of. Maybe a hunter.' And I saw the pleasure in her eyes, because now she was more comfort-able about expressing her fears.

"When I'm feeling under the gun of reality, I begin to recycle my negative experiences by retelling them as a story. I begin to master the event that's gotten me in its clutches. Though riding on a wave of reality, I step back from it as I make my way through the story.

"When someone asks me, 'What happened to you today?' I don't have to think about my response. There's always a story there—a story I want to tell—and I will tell it with the most energy, the most precision, that I can muster. But there are people who do this every day. They're not actors or professional storytellers; they're people, like all of us, who are *storytellers* just the same."

Terrors of Pleasure: The House

Several years ago, Spalding Gray and his girl friend, Renée Schafransky, rented a tiny cabin in the Catskill Mountains in New York. But having grown up in Rhode Island near the shore, Spalding longed to live near water. Gradually, he was drawn to the nearby town of Phoenicia because of the Esopus River—a beautiful, clear trout stream that flowed into the Ashokan Reservoir.

"So, like the old pioneer, I guess, I began to be obsessed with the idea of buying my own house there. I had never dreamed that I would ever buy a house. But I was living in a loft in New York City where there were no rooms at all, and I was beginning to long for rooms. I grew up in a house with rooms, and I was beginning to have dreams of rooms—houses with rooms."

Finally, after two years, Spalding and Renée discovered a tiny, Adirondack-style cabin in the Catskills—a house owned by Carlo Carbone, a Brooklyn florist. One cold January day, Carlo showed Spalding the cabin—a hodgepodge of tiny rooms, floored in brick-patterned linoleum, with a big fireplace built of stones from the Esopus River, and a ceiling of unhewn wooden beams. Spalding loved the wooden beams. It was here, he knew, that he could write the Great American Novel.

As Spalding looked through the house, he tried to act as though he knew something about house buying.

"Why is that beam slanted?" Spalding asked.

"It's not slanted," Carlo responded.

Spalding believed him. He didn't want it to be slanted.

"You know, the fireplace," questioned Spalding, "it looks like it's sinking."

"Oh, no," answered Carlo, "that's not sinking. That's settled."

"Well, look over there," Spalding said, pointing. "The floor looks a little slanted. How come this door doesn't close properly?"

Then Spalding noticed the foundation. There wasn't one. "It was only the thought of one, it was kind of conceptual—cinder block, but caved in."

Still, Spalding didn't want to ask. He wanted to see the view. After all, Renée had reminded him again and again, "You can change the house, but you can't change the location."

In snow up to his knees, Spalding walked over to a huge sycamore tree near a rushing trout stream, and Carlo, panting and gasping for breath, followed him.

"I haven't been in deep snow since I had my heart attack," choked Carlo. "My doctor told me never to walk in deep snow again."

They looked over a wide, panoramic view of the Catskills.

"Isn't it beautiful?" Carlo asked. "Wasn't I right when I told you that you had to buy this house because of the view? Look at it."

Then Spalding turned to Carlo, looked at him standing there, panting, his eyes watery. How could this guy sell me a bad house? Spalding thought to himself.

A few weeks later, Spalding closed the deal—signing the papers "while Carlo and his attorney sat around trying to convince me how lucky I was to get a house in the heart of trout-fishing country."

In excerpts from his epic monologue, "Terrors of Pleasure: The House," Spalding tells about his disastrous yet comic experience refurbishing his newly acquired cabin in the Catskills. Anyone who has ever purchased a "dream home," only to discover that dream is much more an illusion, will appreciate this chronicle of woe.

ON MY first night at the cabin, it rained, and I discovered my first leak. Rain is leaking onto the big log ceiling and I think, my God, if this keeps up those beautiful beams are going to rot. At that point, I realized that I needed a handyman, an honest fellow who could come up and do some maintenance whenever I needed him.

The next morning at breakfast, I asked around and found Coot Dunbar. He gave me his card, which had a picture of him at eight years old, sawing a board with the saw upside down on the edge of a Hires Root Beer crate. His head is completely shaved, like he had ringworm or something. The card read, "Coot Dunbar, Entrepreneur." He was an ex-hippie from Tennessee, living off the money he made from odd jobs. He didn't want any hassle at all. He didn't even want to make a lot of money from me. He just wanted, he said, to turn me on to life.

I brought him up to the house and said, "I think the leak is coming from the chimney."

He said, "Yeah, I can grok that." He rushed up onto the roof with some tar and slapped it on the chimney. (I didn't realize it was next to impossible to stop a leak if it's coming from the chimney.) He charged me $20 for that, and then he fixed my porch screens for another $100. That was very important because I was spending a lot of time out on that porch. It was the only place I felt at ease. I was cooking meals out there.

When I could sleep, I was sleeping with my big knife by the bed, because of the silence. Every morning I'd wake up with this incredible anxiety about what to do next. And part of the way I would alleviate this anxiety was to call various service people, using a responsible voice. You have to act normal on the telephone if you want them to come up and fix stuff.

The first service person I called was a refrigerator man, Starky Jakes. I said, "Hello, Mr. Jakes. This is Mr. Gray, the new home owner up on the hill."

"Oh, yes, we know all about the houses up there. We can come up. We've been there many times before."

"I need you to check my refrigerator. I think it has a little freon leak."

So I hang up and I'm kind of pacing around barefoot on that cool brick linoleum when there's a knock at the screen door. I peer out to see what looks to be my first visitors—maybe the neighbors have come to welcome me. They're not bearing cakes or pies, but there are two women and a little boy with a string tie tight around his neck standing there.

One of the women calls out, "Have you heard about the Great Crowd yet?"

"Nope, not yet."

"The Great Crowd is everyone born after 1914 who has joined the Jehovah's Witness. They're going to live forever."

"I've never heard about that, that's incredible. Isn't it going to get a little crowded?"

She goes on, "We will all sit in his glorious throne, and the Lord will divide the sheep from the goats."

She opens up her Bible and quotes from Matthew 25:30, something about the gnashing of teeth. Then she says, "When you call on your neighbors with the Kingdom's message, you may find some who display a goatlike disposition. This they do by showing indifference or rudeness or by outright opposition."

By now I'm trying to be sheeplike and open and listen to her, and she continues, "Isn't it a lovely thought that we're going to live forever? And it's just around the corner. Adam and Eve didn't have children before they sinned, and until you understand that, all of your prayers will be useless. It will be like putting paint on a house that is falling down."

I thought, she's got my number. She must have chosen this text when she first saw the house from the road. She sold me a book called *Let Your Kingdom Come,* and that got rid of them for the time being. I read the entire book while waiting for the refrigerator man to come.

Shortly, Starky Jones arrived, with "Speed Queen" written on the side door of his pickup. He jumped out with a young boy trailing behind him and strolled right into the house as though he owned the place. He told the boy to stand in the corner and stay there. He said, "By Jeezum crow, I hope you didn't buy this house, did you? If you did, I hope you didn't pay more than $26 for it." He had one of those horrible thin wrap-around beards, with no moustache. I noticed that he looked a little bit like a goat.

"I'll tell you why I know about this house. I helped build it. And you know who I worked under? Old Diefenbach. Old Boss Diefenbach. I bet you don't know about him, do you? He owned all the property up here, was what you'd call an Adirondack-style developer. Well, he's dead now. He died of a stomach ulcer, but he used to come up on this big hill, fold his arms, and say, 'By Jesus, there's a sucker born every minute.'

During this diatribe, the boy, who I took to be his son—I was never introduced—began to wander around in a naturally curious way. Jakes yelled to him, "You watch it or I'll bash you like you've never been bashed before. You stay where you're put." Then he smiled at me and asked, "Whatcha got for a problem here?"

I said, "Well, actually . . . before you look at the refrigerator, could you take a look at the chimney?"

"Oh, the chimney. It's sinking. This house is built on clay. We didn't put no proper footings under there, you know. There's no footing under the chimney and there's no footing under the house. Of course, it's gonna drop."

And I walked over, and sure enough you could see that it had sunk a little, but I figured that it had stopped years ago. Now I wasn't so sure. I said, "While you're at it, what are those little holes up there? You see the holes in my ceiling beams?"

He said, "Those little pinholes? Oh, them. Them's powder-post bee-tles. Boy, they do a job. Well, they've been eating in there since 1957. We call that cancer of the house. But aren't those beams lovely? In fact, that's how Old Diefenbach figured we'd sell these houses to city slickers. They'd come up and that's the first thing they'd look at. They'd buy it every time."

So I said, "Why don't you try pumping up the refrigerator with the freon, see if it holds." And he does and says, "Looks like it's not hold-ing." He charged me $30, grabbed his son, and left.

I was spending a lot of time now just drinking out on the porch, taking it "one day at a time," as Alcoholics Anonymous says, just sitting outside and cooking on my hibachi.

I decided to call a chimney sweep because I really wanted a fire in the fireplace. That was a big part of the reason why I bought the house. I called Jiminy Sweep, and he comes over wearing one of those black chimney-sweep hats and gives it a careful examination.

"Don't light a fire in that chimney. That thing is pulling away from the house. If it's not stopped, the chimney will pull the whole house down with it."

And I said, "Can't you put a metal sleeve in it for the time being? Just so I can make a little fire?"

"Oh, nooooo," he says, "you can't do anything until you right the house. Don't you know it's the foundation, not the location, that counts? Until you get a proper foundation, nothin's gonna be right. The doors won't close, the windows won't fit, and you can't rebuild the chimney until you do something about that foundation."

So now I'm thinking only about foundations. I see them everywhere I go. So I called two young locals to come up; a neighbor gave me their number. They were both about thirty years old. One talked and smoked a lot. The other, a stonemason, was dark and dour. He hardly ever spoke but seemed certain he could rebuild the chimney and his price was right. They said the reason the cinder blocks were cracked and pushed in under the house was because there wasn't proper drainage for the rainwater. The water collected and then froze around the blocks. They told me it was a badly constructed house. I told them I was beginning to realize that.

For $2,500, give or take a little, they were going to jack up the house, remove the cinder blocks, and then dig down four feet by hand, which would put the blocks below the frost level. Then they could put in a whole new drainage system. The only problem was that they still couldn't guarantee that the earth wouldn't freeze and shift again because the house was built on clay. That's why everything including the chimney—and the old family barbecue in the yard, which was now at a very disturbing angle—was that way. Essentially, the house was sitting on a big mound of wet clay moving toward the trout steam on the other side of the road. Nature was taking its own course. The thought of the house in perpetual motion was too much. I wanted a house that would stand still for years. The only way to ensure that was to have the house jacked up and a full concrete foundation poured under it. They didn't have the equipment to do that, but they gave me the number of a guy who did—Franz Klinger.

I didn't waste any time. I called Franz from my front porch during cocktail hour that night, and he said he'd be up in the morning. I didn't know where I was going to get the money, but I figured I could pay in installments.

As soon as I saw Franz, I knew he was the right guy for the job. He was very Germanic, stood with his arms folded like an ancient plowman, and said, "I can do the job for you for $8,000, but the porch has to go. There's no way I can get underneath to do my digging."

Now I'm thinking, if there's a sucker born every minute, I should be able to sell this house. I drop in on Micky Micadella, a local real estate agent, and Micky looks more like a spider than a goat. He gets me into this web and says, "I would never . . . never . . . never buy a house unless it was through an agent. If you go through a private owner, you have no protection. And besides, what's a guy with a name like Spalding Gray doing up here on that back road? With a name like that, you should be governor of the State of New York." So now I was beginning to think of changing my name. Maybe that was why people were charging so much.

When I woke up the next day, Sunday, all I could hear in my head was Harry Belafonte singing, "House built on weak foundation, will not stand, oh no, oh no." Over and over again. I went outside to get into my van to go downtown for breakfast and my van wouldn't start.

So I call up the service station and no one can come up, but they happen to know a mechanic who's at the coffee shop. So I call him there and he comes right up. He charges me $35 just to cross two wires because it's Sunday. While he was getting the van started, I talked to the plumber who had ridden up with him. He asked, "This house winterized?"

So I get real proud, because it's the last good feature of the house left. Maybe I couldn't have a fire in the fireplace, but at least I could turn on the heat. I said, "Yes it is. As a matter of fact, I've got a furnace in the attic."

"You gotta be kiddin' me. Don't you know heat rises. You got an oil burner up there? That's totally against regulations. You can't have liquid fuel in an attic. If the stuff leaks through and this house burns down, you couldn't even collect the insurance."

I called Renée in New York. She didn't help. "If you just wanted to throw your money away," she told me, "you could have bought me a bulletproof chinchilla coat."

Everyone Has a Story to Tell

The Storytellers Talk About Their Craft

* * *

I T WAS HOT, and I was tired. We were in the midst of the fifteenth
annual National Storytelling Festival, and, as director, I was over-
seeing the details of this three-day event. Eager for a moment of
quiet, I eased into one of the performance tents and took a seat.
Storyteller Jay O'Callahan was alone on stage, performing *Village
Heroes*, a one-man show he had created several years earlier. I was in a
hurry, and I meant to stay only briefly. But I lingered to listen, and as I
listened, I met a character named Edna Robinson.

Within moments of meeting Edna, I admired her. She is thirty-two
years old, and she works at the general store in the center of Harvard,
Massachusetts. Sitting in the audience, listening, I could see Edna at
work in her cage of mesh wire, selling penny candy to the children.

Yet there was no one on stage but the storyteller. There was no general store, no wire-mesh cage, no children buying candy. Jay, as the
storyteller, was weaving language into our imaginations and creating the
story with us—a visual, palpable experience whose only props were the
images inside our minds.

Almost an hour later, I slipped away—refreshed, invigorated, and
realizing anew that storytelling recalls to us in this modern age one of
the special aspects of being human: the ability to shape and create, both
in the real world and the infinite one we call imagination. We don't
need actors. Or scenery. Or props. Or music. Just by listening, we can
see real people, doing real things, and they're going more places than
we could ever replicate on stage or screen.

The art of storytelling is a co-creative process, requiring both the
teller and the listener, working together, to weave the whole fabric of
the tale, the warp and weft of it. While the teller tells the story, allowing it to unfold, the listener creates an image of what's happening—
conjuring up mind pictures—and the story comes alive.

As the tale is told, a special bond is forged between the teller and the
listener, and within the safety of that bond, each listener visualizes the
storyteller's words in his own way. For inside the world of story, our
minds run free—to do what children do when they are drawing—to
color beyond the lines, all over the pages. We are free to choose the

scenery, provide the props, design the costumes, and give life to the characters in a way that is just right for us.

Once after storyteller Laura Simms told stories, a man approached her and asked, "Aren't you the one who told the story about the boy who...?" and then described a story she didn't recognize.

"I don't remember telling that story," Laura said. "You must have heard it from another storyteller."

"Oh, no," he insisted. "It was you."

Then Laura named four or five storytellers who resemble her, and again he said, "Oh, no. It was you, and I remember your telling this story at..." And Laura had been there, she knew, telling stories.

"Tell me more," she suggested.

And then as he elaborated, Laura began to recognize the story. "Oh," she cried, "you mean *that* story."

Yes, it was Laura's story. She had told it. But through the magic of storytelling, he saw different images, and what he saw became *his* version of the story Laura told.

Laura could have been telling a personal story of what happened to her as she walked down Broadway in New York City one evening, or a family tale about her great-grandfather, a rabbi, on his way to the synagogue, or the ancient myth of Persephone as she was walking among the hills and suddenly stopped to pick a narcissus growing along the path. Regardless of what Laura was telling, as the storyteller, she was engaging her listeners in life—resensitizing and heightening their senses, their minds, and their imaginations all at once.

Several years ago, storyteller Kathryn Windham shared her stories in the cancer ward of a Wisconsin hospital. The patients were sick, terminally ill, and death was there among them, right at their elbows.

Kathryn thought to herself, "I want to give them some pleasure, allowing them to forget for just a little while that death is soon to come calling." So she told them stories. They listened, and they laughed, and they were amazed. For a little while, they forgot.

"Upon my return home from that Wisconsin visit," adds Kathryn, "I received a letter from the hospital director. She said after I had left the cancer ward that the patients stayed in the day room, and for the first time, they talked to each other about the things that mattered to them. They talked about dying, about their fears, about their faith, and about how they wanted to be remembered. Storytelling had broken down the walls that divided them, and for once they were free, open, and honest with each other so they might share fully the deep feelings they each had."

Later, as Kathryn was preparing to tell stories in a nearby nursing home, the nurses brought into the common room a woman in a wheelchair, and then left her, alone, in the corner of the room.

"I don't know why they bother to bring her here," Kathryn remembers someone saying. "She doesn't even know what's going on. She's never said a word."

But Kathryn began telling stories, her father's animal tales, and then she sang a song.

> Prettiest little girl I ever did know,
> Prettiest little girl in the county-o.

The woman in the wheelchair began to sing. It was the first evidence in months that she was aware of what was happening around her. And after Kathryn told a tale about a rabbit, she went over to the woman.

"Did you like the tale?" Kathryn asked.

"My father told me that tale in Finnish," she replied.

The woman began to talk again. She emerged from the cocoon she had wrapped around herself, and it was the story that had pulled her out.

"Whether it's in a hospital cancer ward or a nursing home," says Kathryn, "storytelling, for me, is simply giving my listeners pleasure. After a good story is told, we—both storyteller and listener—become one, and for a little while we are all caught up together, and while the mental pictures we have drawn are different, the story has touched us all deeply in the same way."

And as we listen to the storytellers, we are often reminded of *our* stories, for to listen to another's story is often to hear one's own.

When Spalding Gray performs, he sits alone at a table on a bare stage and recounts his life. After one of his performances, a man from the audience quietly approached him. "When I first came in and saw that table," the man explained, "I was puzzled. Is he going to just sit there all night and talk to us? But when you started to tell your story, I listened and I began to *see* what you were saying. As I heard you tell about the pets you owned as a child, I remembered my own pets—and I hadn't thought about them in years."

The man stopped to take a deep breath.

"Do you know," he continued, "I had a parakeet once. And my father..." And he shared his own story with Spalding. "People tell me that my stories are important to them because of the details," explains

Spalding. "How we've lost touch with the details in our own lives and how wonderful simple things are if examined, looked at closely."

Stories often nudge us, causing us to remember, to visit old experiences, and in so doing, they allow us to deal more effectively with moments in our own lives—even those seemingly unimportant ones—that we have pushed far back into our memory.

When Maggi Peirce was six years old, some neighborhood ruffians snatched her favorite doll from her hands, almost ripped its head from its tiny body, and tossed it about. Maggie was horrified. It was a childhood experience she would never forget. And today, she tells the story of "The Most Beautiful Doll in the World."

"It's a painful story—a painful story to create, a painful story to tell—because it focused on a childhood memory of violent cruelty to a doll I adored. When I first wrote about it, I literally sobbed. When I first told it, I wept. The experience had festered in me. Though it had happened when I was only six, its memory had been agony for me for years. But creating and telling the story was a cleansing experience.

"I remember first telling the story in a church in Duxbury, Massachusetts. After I had finished the telling, a young woman—perhaps in her twenties—came up to me. She was crying. She said, 'I wanted to tell you that I had the same experience when I was only six. For me, it was a teddy bear.'

"I listened intently.

"'Your story not only reminded me of my hurt,' the woman continued, 'but for the first time since I was a little girl, I was able to bring my teddy bear out of my subconscious where I'm now weeping for it and the little girl that I was. This is the first time in twenty years I've felt at peace.'

"We're taught not to weep, not to show our feelings, and in so many cases, these incidents can become gnawing wounds. But through creating and telling our stories, we allow ourselves to dive down deep into the depths of our souls and bring up huge hurts we once had—hurts that had never healed."

Kathryn Windham remembers telling stories in a prison for juvenile offenders, being in the center of a large gymnasium surrounded by young prisoners—some sitting, some lying. Armed guards stood all around.

"As I faced them," recalls Kathryn, "I knew what they were thinking: 'Who wants to listen to this white-haired old woman with a thick Southern accent?' But as I began to tell ghost stories, and some of the tales my daddy told me, they began to listen. The more I told, the more attentive they became. And soon, they were caught up into storytelling, and they wanted more and more.

"After I told my last story, several of the young prisoners came to me and said, 'You know, lady, *nobody* ever told me a story.' And, oh, how sad. For as children, they had had no lap time—no time for their parents to sing them a song, to tell them a story. And you wonder what a difference it might have made if they had had that sense of well-being, that feeling of security that comes with the love of a story."

While we can all quickly recognize the power of a well-told story, many of us would be horrified if we were asked to tell a story ourselves —perhaps to close friends or a class of small children. Many of us lack the confidence to tell stories publicly.

Sure, there are those, like Maggi Peirce, for whom stories just seem to flow, one after another, delighting every listener. Ever since Maggi was a young girl she has told stories—long before she realized she was a *story-teller*. For her, it just came naturally.

"When we were wee children," recalls Maggi, "and someone would ask, 'Well, tell us what happened,' any one of the boys would begin telling the story. Invariably, one of the others in the crowd would always say, 'Oh, hush up! Let Maggi tell it!' And I would tell the tale. You see, I have always been gifted with story, and I could always, even as a child, tell stories people enjoyed hearing. And today, years later, when I'm telling stories, I'm telling them naturally, just being me."

Yet within us all is the power of the told story—no matter to what measure—and we should search for it, pull it out, give it a chance. And those to whom storytelling doesn't seem to come naturally can, with practice, overcome their fears and inhibitions.

"Two years ago," remembers Jay O'Callahan, "I taught a course on the storytelling art and its uses in education to twenty-three adults. Most of them were teachers working on a master's degree. As a require-ment of the course, I insisted that everyone tell a story before the entire group. One of the teachers, however, was so anxious about the require-ment that it was ruining the course for her.

"But on the fifth day of the class, she stood before the group and recounted a tale with such warmth and beauty that it moved and charmed us all. It was shaped around a memory of an uncle who took her on magical trips to the local dump. And gradually, all the members of the class—one by one—told their stories. They did wonderfully, and they were all surprised by their success."

Everyone has a story to tell. And while we could spend a lifetime learning the art and technique of storytelling—perfecting our style and performance—for most of us, it is the simple telling of a tale that's important. Something as ordinary as the events of the day, an old joke, or a traditional story we heard as a child. Storytelling comes from the heart, not the head, and nothing should keep us from the exhilaration and sheer pleasure of telling a story.

Discovering Your Story

When I was a young child, preparing me for bedtime was a torturous task for my mother. I squirmed and wiggled, fussed and fretted, until one day, we entered the world of make-believe. Preparing for bedtime became a time of wonder and delight.

"We pick up Little Mary riiiiight here," my mother would announce as her washcloth, stretched across the tip of her finger, was poked into one of my ears. I would squeal with pleasure. The washcloth was an imaginary school bus, and we were on a make-believe trip.

Over my forehead my mother would scrub until she came to the other ear. "And we pick up Little Billy riiiiight here," she would exclaim as she twisted the washcloth into my other ear. I was overjoyed.

Sliding the cloth down the side of my face to the end of my chin, my mother would rub furiously. "And riiiiight here," she would cry, "we pick up Little Sally." I couldn't have been more oblivious to the fact that I was getting clean, preparing for bed.

Then, in a dramatic dip downward, my mother would slide the cloth across my neck, scrub frantically, and say, "And riiiiight here in this hollow, we pick up Little Johnny, Little Tommy"—and she would pause —"and Little Patty too."

On and on we would travel—not a facial feature overlooked—and our bus would soon be filled with children, everyone I had known or imagined in my little world.

"But . . . but . . . Mama," I pleaded, "where do I get on the bus?"

Without my mother uttering a single word, her washcloth would circle my mouth, again and again, and in a moment of anticipation—as though it had *never* happened before—I would wait while she pinched the end of my nose and said, "And riiiiight here on the very top of this mountain, we pick up Little Jimmy." I would giggle wildly, and I was ready for bed.

My mother created this snippet of a story for me in a moment of parental frustration, providing for both of us an escape from the drudgery of this simple childhood routine. But there were other tales too— the ancient folktales, fairy tales, and legends I heard and read as a child, the family stories, those forged from the stuff of life, and the stories that unfolded around me daily.

Stories are everywhere. They abound in endless supply. But finding a story to tell, the *right* one, is the storyteller's first task.

In communities throughout America, library shelves are lined with books, many of them story collections. In them, you can discover a treasury of tales just waiting to be read—and told. "But I rarely go in search of a story," notes Laura Simms. "It's almost like we meet each other—like you find a friend."

One night Laura was working late in a library in Oneonta, New York. She was going to leave early the next morning to return to New York City, but before she left she was looking through the books. Laura stumbled upon a collection of old Scottish tales, and as she thumbed through its pages, she discovered the story of the Seal Maiden.

Laura read the story quickly. It was late, so she slipped the book onto the shelf and quietly left the library. The next morning, she awoke early, caught a bus to New York City, and as the bus wound its way through the countryside, she slept. As she slept, she dreamed.

When Laura awoke, she discovered a man sitting beside her. He was not feeling well, and to comfort him, she told him a story—the ancient Scottish tale of the Seal Maiden she had found the evening before in the Oneonta library. As she began to tell the story, her memory of it failed her, and she began to mix the tale with her dreams. She knew it was very different from the story she had read, but she didn't care. The story soothed him, and it comforted her. And at that moment, Laura added "The Seal Maiden" to her repertoire.

Stories often come mysteriously. They just appear, cling to us, excite us. Barbara Freeman and Connie Regan-Blake were once performing in Birmingham, Alabama. During their stay, they joined their hostess for lunch.

"I had a dream last night," she told them. They listened attentively.

"I dreamed that the two of you were telling a story," their hostess continued. "The telling was so powerful and strong that this morning I went to the bookstore and bought the book for you."

It was *Come Again in the Spring,* a children's book by Richard Kennedy. Before Barbara and Connie left Birmingham, they had read the book—and enjoyed it.

In a curious twist of fate, when Barbara and Connie returned home, they discovered a box of books on their doorstep. A note from the publisher was attached: "We've heard you tell stories, and here are some books containing stories you might tell."

The two women rummaged through the box, and tucked snugly among a pile of books they discovered *Oliver Hyde's Dishcloth Concert*—another children's book by Richard Kennedy. Connie quickly scanned its pages, and she became intrigued with the story. So in the ensuing weeks, while Barbara was being drawn to *Come Again in the Spring*, Connie was feeling a closeness to *Oliver Hyde's Dishcloth Concert*. They have been telling both ever since.

"I really believe," says Maggi Peirce, "that there's *something* out there that wants a story told. For, you see, I don't always find a story. Sometimes a story finds me.

"Once I was thumbing through a collection of stories, and finding nothing that interested me, I quickly closed the book and tried to return it to the shelf. Instead, the book fell, and as I reached to catch it, the book opened to a story about a mermaid. And Lord love a duck, I know sooooo many mermaid stories—they're typical of Ireland, my homeland.

"But I was drawn to the story, so I glanced over it. Then, I began to read it. And as I read, I discovered that this story was very different from the mermaid stories I had known and read as a child. I found the story interesting, intriguing, and it began to tickle my mind. And even today, I tell 'The Kerry Mermaid.'"

But not all stories will come to you mysteriously, arrive unannounced on your doorstep, leap from the library shelves. Finding a story to tell often requires hard work, hours of research, and thoughtful and careful selection. For Jackie Torrence, finding a story is like selecting a dress.

"If I'm going to a formal dinner and I need a new dress," says Jackie, "I wouldn't go into a department store, walk up to the clerk, and say, 'I need a new dress. Would you select one for me and try it on to see if I like it?' No, I wouldn't do that. It's impossible.

"Instead, I would walk into the store, find the racks of formal dresses, and begin looking at them, one by one, until I find one that appeals to me. Then I'd pull it off the rack and look at it closely.

"'Maybe I can wear this,' I would probably mumble to myself. 'Let me try it on,' I'd likely tell the clerk.

"Once I have it on, I know it's lovely, but I discover it's too big in the shoulders. 'I like the dress,' I'd probably say to myself, 'so I'll make a few tucks here and there.'

"Then I'd look at the length. 'Well, it's a bit too long,' I might think, 'but I'll hem it.'

"In storytelling, we follow the same process to find a story. If I'm looking for a tale to tell, I wouldn't go into the library and say to the librarian, 'I want to tell a story. Would you browse through the books and find a story I can tell?' You can't ask someone to find a story for you to tell anymore than someone else could find a dress for you to wear.

"So instead, I would go to the library, sit down in front of the shelves, and pull out the story collections, one by one, looking, searching, for the story that appeals to me. Just as I tried on the dress, I would read the story. If the story needs 'tucking' or 'hemming,' I would make the changes in the story that seem to fit me just right."

No matter how stories come to you—by accident or by careful, thoughtful selection—the choice is always a personal one. Finding a story to tell happens in the heart, not the mind.

"As a storyteller," explains Diane Wolkstein, "I can't tell a story year after year unless it nourishes me each time I tell it. Whether the story is about contemporary life or is thousands of years old, a good story—a really good story—will talk to the inside of all of us, about invisible things, about reflections, about things we don't often know or understand."

While America's community libraries are storehouses for a generous supply of good stories, a vast treasury of tales can also be found through story collecting—mining our family and community heritage, finding stories, refining them, retelling them, making them our own.

Jackie Torrence was once driving over the mountains into North Carolina from Tennessee. On a whim, she began to follow a narrow, winding road to look for antique and junk shops. Soon she saw a dilapidated shack filled to overflowing with odds and ends. Several old men sat on the front porch. Jackie stopped, went inside, and browsed for an hour. As she left, one of the old men stopped her.

"Is that your car?" he asked.

"Yes, it is," Jackie replied.

He glanced at her license plate. It read STORY LADY.

"What's a story lady?" he asked.

"I'm a professional storyteller," she answered.

"What's that?"

"I tell stories."

"Tell us one."

So Jackie told them a joke, and they all laughed.

"You're pretty good," one of the old men told her. "But now, did you ever hear the one about..."

That was at ten o'clock in the morning. At three-thirty, Jackie left the shop, but they had told her Jack tales and tall tales and yarns she had never heard. And today, she tells many of the stories she encountered along that narrow, winding Tennessee road.

Kathryn Windham recalls a time when she was leaning against a rusty post watching a domino game in a little Mississippi town she was simply passing through. That was the afternoon she heard one of the finest ghost tales she had ever encountered—a story about a conjure man and a black cat. The tale was laced with folklore, superstition, and humor, but it was based on fact.

Another good ghost story came to her during a radio talk show, an improbable tale about the ghost of a man who fell to a fiery death in a blast furnace in Birmingham a century ago.

"Only his heart was saved," the caller told her.

Kathryn had serious doubts, but a visit to the Birmingham library verified the story. On a microfilm of an old newspaper, she read of the accident and how fellow workers rigged up a long shovel and retrieved the man's heart.

Then, there was the dreary day at a craft show in Alabama when an attractive middle-aged lady came up to Kathryn and said, "If you have the time, I need to tell you about a ghost who visited my grandmother and me nightly for five years. I've got to talk to somebody about that experience." Of course, Kathryn had the time to listen.

As Kathryn began collecting ghost stories, she quickly discovered that they exist in *every* Southern town—stories just waiting to be listened to, researched, and told. For her, the supply was endless, and she never knew when she would come upon a truly great tale of the supernatural.

One method Kathryn discovered early in her career is that to collect stories, one must tell them. A good story, one that reaches into the listener's own memories and emotions, often elicits the recollections of the stories in other people's lives.

"In my research," says Kathryn, "I've discovered that if I say, 'Please tell me a ghost story,' the reply will almost always be, 'I don't know any.' But if I tell one first, my listeners relax and suddenly they will begin to recall tales they've heard before. It rarely fails.

"As a result, some of the best ghost stories that I've collected were told to me after a public storytelling event, when someone lingered to say, 'I don't know whether you have time to hear this or not, but I remember a story Grandpa used to tell.' I always have time to listen to a good story. All collectors do. But listening takes time—and patience.

"I've heard innumerable versions of the four most often-told stories of the supernatural—about the phantom hitchhiker, the ghost that wanders around with a lantern looking for his head, the ghostly baby whose cries drift from a lonesome creek or hollow, and strange markings that suddenly appear on certain tombstones. If I listen patiently without blurting out, 'I've heard that too many times,' I'm often rewarded with an exciting story that's new to me. Hearing one really fine ghost story is worth enduring a hundred rehashings of these worn-out tales.

"But people won't share any story at all unless they know that it will be genuinely appreciated—nobody wants to be laughed at, ridiculed, or accused of lying. So it's important to establish a feeling of confidence and trust. When I talk freely about the antics of Jeffrey, the ghost that 'inhabits' my house, it encourages listeners to share similar stories without embarrassment. Having Jeffrey to talk about is a definite advantage.

"While the teller, usually a stranger, is relating a story, I give him or her my full attention. I don't interrupt, no matter how many questions are running through my head. When the story has ended, we talk about it. If it interests me, if it has promise of developing into a story worthy of being preserved, I ask questions. Exactly where did the occurrences take place? When? What were the names of the people involved? Who can provide other details? I ask the kinds of questions I asked as a newspaper reporter. For me, the questions just come naturally.

"Only after I gain the confidence of the teller do I take notes. Taking notes while a story is being told is not only rude, it's distracting. For the same reasons, I don't use a tape recorder. Nothing—no mechanical device, no note pad, no pen—should intrude on the telling of a story. The initial focus should always be on the listening. There's plenty of time to take notes after the story has been told and talked about.

"After the story has been listened to and after the basic facts have been gathered, I visit the location where the event happened—to get the feel of the place and even to imagine the characters at the scene. I look especially hard for distinctive features in the landscape and buildings. I take pictures. I talk to the neighbors to find out what they know about the story. If the characters involved are buried nearby, I visit their graves, not only to verify names and dates but to build another bond with persons who will live again, however fleetingly, in my stories.

"And then I visit the local library. Librarians are invaluable in helping with research, filling the gaps. They provide old newspaper clippings, genealogies, and regional histories, and they often put me in touch with local historians who can help.

"The story grows, becomes fleshed out with details and images, and I soon have a tale to tell and enjoy. And as I collect background information on one ghost story, I likely hear others—stories worthy of investigation and preservation, just waiting to be heard and researched and retold."

No, there's no trick or gimmick to collecting stories—whether they are ghost stories or other tales and legends. All it takes is time, patience, a fondness for people, and curiosity. Always curiosity. But in collecting stories, much of what we hear is often only snippets of stories, bits and pieces of life. Yet if we listen to them, are willing to let them grow in our imaginations, then a story can often emerge.

David Holt has been collecting the stories and songs of the Southern Appalachian Mountains since he was in college. He remembers A. P. Bell, a man who lived in the mountains of western North Carolina. He had never been married. A.P. had worked thirty-five years at a local factory, raised cats, and entertained himself by playing the banjo and doing unusual things like growing blue and red corn, making colored cornbread, and serving it at the church dinners. One day, A. P. told David about his neighbor—a man everyone called Uncle Ike—who had invented his own telephone from groundhog hide and wire.

Then David met Dellie Norton, who, at eighty-seven years of age, still lives in Sodom Laurel, probably the most remote community in North Carolina. Dellie has been a moonshiner, herb doctor, and ginseng collector, and though she has only a third-grade education, she is a masterful old-time musician and balladeer.

One day, Dellie told David about a man who, long years ago, built a log cabin—without a door hanging hinged in the framed opening. Every night, a big black bear would try to wander into the cabin, so the man would sit on the front porch, a shotgun astraddle his lap, to keep the bear from entering his mountain home and killing his wife and newborn baby.

"This is all rather incredible," David thought to himself. "There *must* be a story there somewhere."

So David combined the two true-life stories he had heard and created a tale he calls "Uncle Ike and the Hog-o-phone"—a story about a man who strung wire from the groundhog hide stretched in one of his windowpanes to the hide stretched in the window of Granny Beecher's cabin, just down the hollow. Granny and Ike would talk to each other on the Hog-o-phone line, and when there was time, Granny would play her radio on Uncle Ike's new invention.

> One morning, Granny heard the growl of a bear on the other end of the Hog-o-phone line, and she turned up her radio as loud as it would go, and then she struck out for Uncle Ike's house.
>
> "Granny," Uncle Ike said, "you saved my life. When you turned up the radio that old bear did the finest little buck dance you ever saw. And instead of grabbin' for my neck, he grabbed my banjo and went a-runnin' right outa here."
>
> Well, Uncle Ike was never bothered by that bear again. But sometimes late at night, when ever'thing is still, one can hear that old bear tryin' to pick out a tune on Uncle Ike's old banjo.

We are all surrounded by people and places, and there's a story in each of them. As David journeys through the Southern Appalachians, he watches and listens and sees the importance in seemingly insignificant things. From them, a story is often born. But while we can easily reach out for the stories in other people's lives, we should strive to discover the story within our own.

"I tell family and community stories," explains Elizabeth Ellis, "because I want people to realize that we are *all* important, our stories are important, and we should go back, return to our past, and reacquaint ourselves with the stories—and value—of our own lives. As I'm telling stories about *my* life, I'm holding up a mirror to my listeners—trying to jog their memories, getting them to look at their stories, the tales that lace their lives."

Donald Davis collects, creates, and tells stories of his experiences growing up—tales of human existence that evoke memories of special people and places in the lives of those who hear them. One of his most endearing stories is a tale about Miss Daisy Boyd, Donald's fourth-grade teacher at Hazelwood Elementary School.

"I loved and admired her," began Donald. "And after I grew up, I realized that each of us can probably remember our own Miss Daisy— teachers who poured their hearts, and their lives, into their mission. I wanted us to remember them, so I created and now tell a story I simply call 'Miss Daisy'—a year-long adventure of my days in Miss Daisy's class.

"But when I'm collecting and creating my stories," Donald says, "I don't try to remember the things that happened in my life. Instead, I first try to mentally re-create the place, to return to it, walk around in it, feel it, smell it, describe it in my mind in the minutest detail. As I wander around in that place, I think about the people who are there with me, and soon, I begin to remember what happened. But I don't see stories. Instead, I see fragments of stories. From a fragment, a story will grow.

"As I developed the story about Miss Daisy, I discovered that I remembered a lot about being in Miss Daisy's class, and as I began telling the story, I remembered more. But even now, I simply don't remember it all. While the basic plot of 'Miss Daisy' is true—we *did* take an imaginary trip around the world—much of the story is re-created and reconstructed.

"In creating stories from true-life experiences, it is important to remember that the truth doesn't necessarily rest in what really happened, but instead, depends on the story rekindling in the listener a memory in *his* life. For we often have the idea that what happened *actually* happened, and if we don't tell it 'right,' we're not being true to the events. But what actually happened, we don't know. No one does. Everyone has separately stored an interpretation of what occurred, and each is different. So in story creation, our task is to be true to *life,* true to the *characters,* true to *place.*

"The real difference between telling what happened and telling a *story* about what happened is that instead of being a victim of our past, we become master of it. We move from being abused by the events to having learned enough from them that we can share them with other people. We can't change our past, but we can change where we stand as we look at it.

"In my stories, I want to prompt my listeners to visualize—to go places with me, back to places *they* know, places *they* have been. And if I can get them laughing at their own memories, laughing at things in their own lives, then they are protected, and they'll go anywhere and see anything with me."

Whenever Donald Davis tells his stories of family experiences, people often come up to him after his performance and say, "I really enjoyed your story. Can I tell it?" Donald always replies, "Whenever I tell a story, it's yours. Do with it whatever you wish." On the other hand, there's a part of Donald which wants to say, "Wait! You can't do that! You can't tell *my* stories. Not because I won't allow you, but because it can't be done. You can't tell my stories because they are so much a part of me. Instead, my stories should bring out, and uncover, the stories in *you.*" And if the stories you hear remind you of a story in your own life, recapture it, create it, write it down, and tell it—from your own experiences. *Then* the story is your story.

When Doc McConnell was a young boy growing up in the tiny Tennessee farm community of Tucker's Knob, his life was rich with traditional mountain experiences—those he calls upon to add a measured dose of reality to the tall tales and yarns he enjoys weaving. Doc remembers when he was six, maybe seven, years old, and every evening, just before dark, he would go out to the corn crib and shuck a washtub full of corn.

"Me and Mama would sit around the stove of our old fireplace and shell corn," recalls Doc. "And when we got done, Mama would throw the cobs into the wood box, so we'd have 'em for buildin' a fire, and dump the corn into a white, freshly washed flour sack. The next day when I would get home from school, I would go get the old mare—if they weren't workin' her—and lead her to the house. Mama would tie the loose end of that flour sack, and it full of corn, and lay that bag across the front shoulders of the old horse. I would ride that horse a mile or more down the holler to John Mauk's old mill. John would dump the corn into his hopper, pull some levers, and I would hear water runnin' down the mill trough and over the wheel, and the timbers in that old mill would commence to groanin'. Soon, out came beautiful, white, warm cornmeal, and I'd take it home to Mama."

The water that turned John Mauk's mill came down the trough from his mill pond, and it was in that pond that Doc and his brothers, Steamer and Tom, went fishing as young boys. It was there that young Doc caught a "walkin' catfish" in a traditional tall tale that Doc has made his own—given life through his own personal experiences.

For Doc, stories begin with remembrances of his childhood, his growing up in the Southern mountains. Though most of the stories Doc tells are traditional tales he has mined from his Southern Appalachian heritage, he laces these old stories with bits and pieces of true-life experiences.

"Though I may tell a traditional story or a series of anecdotes tied together, I am able to tell them in such a way that they *appear* to be stories that actually happened—or *could* have happened—to me in my past experiences. Since I've lived the life my stories portray, the story seems real. I can actually experience the story as I tell it, because I've been there where that story might likely have happened.

"When I tell 'The Snake-Bit Hoe Handle,' the story and its every detail become real to me. I can see myself hoein' corn in that hillside cornfield, or runnin' up the bank to the house to confess to Daddy, or loadin' up those logs on our old truck and takin' 'em to the sawmill at Surgoinsville, or buildin' that new chicken house out there in our meadow. I see it all as if it actually happened to me."

Within us all lies the power to create, and during our lifetime, we have all invented stories—childish, fanciful tales—to entertain ourselves or perhaps others. The stories we create may be true or imagined and peopled with those we know or an assortment of characters as wild or wily, mean or mad, as our imaginations will dictate.

Once at bedtime, after Jay O'Callahan had tucked his son, Teddy, under the covers, the child was restless. So Jay began to think, searching for a tale to tell, and he began to recall the days when he was also a child, no bigger than Teddy, and visited his grandmother in Cambridge. He remembered the darkened hallways, the strange smells, the mystery that seemed to fill every pore of the house. Then he remembered one afternoon when he penciled tiny marks on the walls throughout his grandmother's house, and she discovered his scribblings.

"But I'm a businessman, Grandma," young Jay argued, "and business-men write things." His grandmother wasn't impressed. She scolded Jay, and he cried.

From this single, seemingly insignificant moment, colored by the power of Jay's imagination, a story—a gentle tale about a little boy and his visit with his grandmother—began to flow. Teddy soon fell asleep, and the story became "Orange Cheeks"—one of Jay's most poignant and powerful stories.

Tales are created from the world around us, given life by everything we know and understand, taken in through our senses, and gleaned from our memories. All we must do is pay close attention and when the image comes that promises a *story*, be willing to follow wherever it might lead.

"When Teddy was four," continues Jay, "he banged his shin outside our cottage and was weeping. 'I broke my leg,' he cried.

"'Nooooo,' I said. 'It's just a little bump.'

"'Little bump,' he wailed. 'If it was you, it would be a big bump . . . with me, it's nothing.'

"'All right,' I said. 'I'll put you in a nice warm bath and you'll be fine.'

"I drew the bath, put him in, and he shouted, 'My leg's floating away!'

"'No, Teddy, that's refraction.'

"'What?'

"'Never mind. Here's a funny story to make you laugh.'

"'Go,' he sobbed.

"'Once upon a time, there was a sad farmer. Everything went wrong in his life.'

"'That's a funny story?' Teddy grumped.

"'Will you let me finish? Everything went wrong until one day the farmer found some wonderful raspberries and he ate one and sprang up singing, "Rassssssspberrieeeeees."'"

From this insignificant event, a story called "Raspberries" emerged. At first it was short. Jay wrote it down and put it away for a year. Then one day at the Pierce School in Brookline, Massachusetts, he decided to tell it to the fifth-graders. They loved it, and through each telling, it grew and grew.

"For me," explains Jay, "story creation—whether it's an imaginary story or a true-life event—begins with an object, a strawberry or the scribblings in my grandmother's house. Any object can give birth to a story.

"I'm an organic gardener, and for me, story creation follows the same principles. The hull of the grapefruit I eat every morning for breakfast goes into a heap of grass clippings and leaves, and over the months, they will lie there and build heat and gradually become humus.

"When I create a story, I get those leaves, and those leaves are the details. And when pulled together, a heat is created and the details begin to shape themselves into something—very much in the way compost turns into earth."

Whether our stories are created from true-life events or the world of imagination—or a blend of both—they often pull us along, lead us through the language of the story to feelings we have ignored but which, when discovered and told, reveal to us things we wouldn't have seen otherwise. Created stories are often rich with meaning, speaking to us on many levels, and through them, we can begin to *feel* our own lives.

"In a story-creation workshop that I was once conducting," says Jay, "I asked my students to close their eyes and become an object. Any object. One woman in the workshop said to the others, 'I'm a piano and I'm not being played. I'm never played, and that's unfortunate because I like to make music.'

"Only later did I learn that the woman was married to a very busy man, a minister who had expectations of her playing the role of the minister's wife and staying home. I don't think the woman would have consciously admitted to us that she was unhappy because she was not doing what she wanted to do. But she clearly was. And that object, the piano, told her story—and told it powerfully.

"If we can find that object that releases our story, that story will talk in the language of imagery, not the language of logic. It will carry more truth, more deeply, and help us to see the truth in a way that we've never dared to see it before.

"When I was young, I went to school with a lot of tough kids. I wore glasses and had big ears, so behind my back, these tough kids were saying, 'He has big ears and four eyes.' I soon came to realize what they were saying about me. I couldn't do anything about my big ears, but I could do something about my glasses. So each day, I would slip my glasses into my back pocket, and often during recess, I would sit down and break them. Each time, I would have to go home and tell my father.

"'Twelve dollars!' my father would always say. 'Twelve dollars!'

"'I won't do it again,' I told him. But in the second grade alone, I broke my glasses seven times.

"I really got into a horrible pickle when I broke my glasses on the morning of my uncle's wedding. I couldn't dare tell my parents. It would ruin the grand wedding. So like a spy, I crept up the stairway to the third floor and borrowed my grandmother's glasses.

"But before the wedding, I was playing in the cellar and lost my grandmother's glasses in the coal pile. Now, my glasses were broken and hers were lost. Unfortunately, my grandmother soon discovered that her glasses were missing, and she told my father. He looked at me, saw I wasn't wearing my glasses, and asked me if I had taken my grandmother's glasses.

"'I didn't take them,' I assured him. 'I borrowed them.'

"There was an intense search, and fortunately, we found her glasses. But while this incident seems insignificant, it loomed large in my young world, and today, I share this tiny vignette of my childhood—a story called 'Glasses.'

"When I first created the tale, it was a lighthearted story about a little boy, and his glasses, and an uncle who comes home from World War II. But at a friend's suggestion, I began to think more about the war. And just as the little boy began *seeing* the world differently through glasses, I began to see things I had never seen before.

"As I thought about the story, I began to *see* my Aunt Ann, a person I hadn't seen for twenty-five years or more. She was of Japanese-Canadian descent, and during the war against Japan, people would whisper about her, point at her, even spit upon her. In desperation, she retreated to her apartment and never came out. As I continued to create the story, I thought about my aunt. I remembered her pain, the hurt that filled her life, and she became a part of 'Glasses.'

"You see, we are all filled with memories, and it's often a simple object, like glasses, that releases the story. It's exciting to see beyond the objects—to ask questions, to allow our imaginations to see, to feel, to smell, to take in life. And yes, a story will soon emerge."

But no matter how stories come—whether they're discovered, collected, or created—storytellers must love the stories they tell and believe in them.

"I tell stories hundreds of times each year to thousands of children and adults," explains Jackie Torrence, "and I love my stories. All of them. I love the sounds of them. I love the feel of them. And I want everyone to enjoy them as much as I do. If I'm telling the story of a gigantic turnip, one so big that sheep could climb inside and spend the winter, I've got to believe there really *is* a turnip that big. I can't expect my listeners to believe it, to love and enjoy the story, unless I do."

Learning, Shaping, and Telling
Your Story

During all of my sixteen years of school, I was never *told* a story, but my fondest memories are of the times my teachers *read* to us. The stories they read charmed and enchanted me.

I remember Sarah Keys, my eighth-grade teacher. Once each week she would read to the class, and the stories I recall most vividly came from *Miss Minerva and William Green Hill*, a turn-of-the-century book by Frances Boyd Calhoun. This small volume was about an orphan who, after having lived with slaves, came to live with his unmarried aunt, Miss Minerva, "a sober, proper, dignified, religious old maid unused to children." As a child, Mrs. Keys had adored the book, and she shared the story with zeal and enthusiasm.

I sat near the rear of the room, and as Mrs. Keys read, I would scoot my desk into the aisle, so I could watch her read. Her eyes sparkled, her head, as if attached to a spring, bounced in timely cadence with the tale, and she told with infinite energy. As I watched her read, I soaked up every word.

One day, Mrs. Keys sent a message home to my mother. "Mrs. Smith, when I read to my students, Jimmy always pulls his desk into the aisle and watches me read. I'm afraid he's having trouble with his hearing."

Alarmed, my mother immediately took me to a hearing clinic for tests, but my hearing was perfect. What Mrs. Keys didn't know was that I was enthralled by her reading. I was caught up by her energy, her loving commitment to the tale, its every word.

Thirty years later, in an antique shop in Orlando, Florida, I discovered a worn, ragged copy of *Miss Minerva and William Green Hill*. Even today, I often thumb through its pages, read and relive its humor and warmth, and realize that *how* Mrs. Keys read, how she shared the tale, was as important to me as *what* she read. For how one tells a story is the mark of the storyteller.

Anyone can tell a story. There are no secrets, no mysterious potions, no magic wands to become a storyteller. All of the abilities are within us, just waiting to be called upon. But storytelling is a personal art, and how we tell a story is a very personal affair. There are as many ways of telling a story as there are stories—and storytellers—and you must find your own way, your own individual storytelling style.

While there is no specific set of rules on how to tell stories, there are techniques that aspiring storytellers must watch for and heed—just as a writer should follow the rules of grammar, spelling, and construction. With some effort and direction, everyone can discover his or her own way, and with practice, a style will develop, and confidence will grow.

Learning Your Story

Several years ago, Jay O'Callahan and Donald Davis were telling stories in Westport, Maine, to an audience with few experiences in hearing stories. Actor Jason Robards was the host, and in his introduction, he tried to give the audience a better understanding of the storytelling art.

"When I'm playing a Eugene O'Neill character," explained Robards, "I'm playing the character best when Jason Robards disappears. It's exactly the opposite in storytelling. Storytelling is at its best when the story can't be separated from the teller."

For the teller is more than just the teller, he or she is the creator, the embodiment of the story. And we should search for that powerful point when the teller and the tale become one—when we learn a story so completely that it actually becomes a part of us. The teller tries it on, soaks it in, makes it his or her own. There is, however, no formula for this process. In any learning experience, you develop your own style—the way that works best for you—and the same is true for learning a story.

"When I learn a story in printed form," says Connie Regan-Blake of The Folktellers, "I read it over and over, think about it, live with it—trying to take it in as a whole. I usually read the story just before I go to bed—to put it into my dreamworld, because that's where all stories begin. If I put it back into the dreamworld, I'm much more inside the story, and soon, the story becomes mine."

Laura Simms researches a story. "I outline it and study it. And through this process, I can better understand the story and more easily examine its power and meaning. I often map the story. I make maps of landscapes, and sometimes, I turn my living room into a story, and I walk through it—actually getting 'inside' the tale."

"I sit down and quietly think about the story," states Elizabeth Ellis, "creating a set of very vivid mind pictures, trying to see them as clearly as possible, allowing the story to come into my heart. When I tell the story, I describe each picture, each frame. The more vividly I can visualize the story, experience being within the tale, the more vividly I can recount that experience to my listeners."

Barbara Freeman, also of The Folktellers, learns a story the way most people learn a joke. "When I hear a joke," explains Barbara, "I won't remember it unless I turn around and quickly tell it to someone else. I learn stories in the same way. If I'm reading a storybook and discover a story I want to tell, I'll tell it right away. I'll tell it again and again, and soon, I learn the story and it becomes mine forever."

"When I learn a story," adds Donald Davis, "I just soak it in. By hearing the same story over and over again in slightly different ways, I absorb not one version of the story but, instead, the underlying *picture* of it. It's the difference between making a cake from a recipe or making a cake after you've helped your mother make hundreds of cakes for twenty years."

And when you learn a story, you needn't worry that the first time you tell the tale, it may only be the "bare bones." In time, as the story is told again and again, you will become more comfortable with the telling and embellish the tale, giving flesh to those bones.

"I have told stories in Central Park in New York City for more than twenty years," Diane Wolkstein explains, "and most of the stories I told in my early years as a storyteller were short. But when a violinist plays a piece for ten minutes and masters it, he wants to play a violin piece for fifteen minutes. And then, thirty minutes. And then, even longer and longer. Similarly, after telling stories for years, I wanted to tell longer stories—more difficult, more challenging ones. When I first told 'Elsie Piddock Skips in Her Sleep' in Central Park, it was twelve minutes long. Now, it's a forty-minute story. Consequently, learning a story is often an ongoing process."

For seven years, Jay O'Callahan has told the story of Edna Robinson as one of a half-dozen stories of *Village Heroes*, Jay's one-man show. In its opening run in Boston, Jay performed "Edna Robinson" eighty nights in a row.

"That sounds laborious," Jay begins, "but it wasn't. To me, it was an opportunity to be with the story—with friends—every night for eighty nights. I enjoyed seeing Edna Robinson and Blueberry Jack and Fillebrown—again and again. I enjoyed Edna's courage. I was thrilled with the mystery of Blueberry Jack. I admired Fillebrown's sassiness. And each night, I got to know the story and my characters a little better.

"But you see, there are still mysteries in Edna and Blueberry Jack and

Fillebrown that I couldn't unravel if I performed the story three hundred nights in a row. There are still things that I haven't yet grasped that are alive in them. But I'm going to tell the story over and over again, and I'm going to try to learn more, to get closer to it, to understand it better."

Regardless of how a story is learned, we want the tale to become a part of us gradually. "We want to internalize the story," explains Brother Blue, "like a musician who has played 'My Funny Valentine' a zillion times. And when the story is internalized, we're on automatic. Now we're free to give the story power—to give ourselves over to the tale and the tellin'."

Changing and Adapting Your Story

Elizabeth Ellis often tells a delightful folktale about a tailor who is unable to sleep each night because someone—or something—pulls the covers off his bed. While consulting the Wise Woman, he learns that a Hudgin has come to stay with him. To rid the tailor of the Hudgin's nightly playfulness, she advises him to make the Hudgin his own bed.

Every night, the tailor tries a new bed—first a high oak bed, then a bed of fern and feathers, and then a cupboard, a hammock, and a cradle—but nothing pleases the Hudgin. And still the tailor cannot sleep. How he finally satisfies his difficult guest makes a charming story, a tale retold as *The Bed Just So* by Jeanne B. Hardendorff.

"When I first told this story to a roomful of young children," began Elizabeth, "they just sat and looked at me in total bewilderment. They were dazed. They didn't understand my telling of this wonderful story. So when I told the story again, the high oak bed became a king-size bed, the bed of fern and feathers became a bunk bed, the cupboard became a waterbed. Now when I retell the tale, it's popular with everyone who hears it.

"Why allow a good story to die on the vine for want of a child's understanding of a few simple words, phrases, or concepts? I changed the story ever so slightly to make it more compatible with the experiences of my audience, without destroying the value of the tale or its telling."

When Elizabeth told the story recently to a group of young children, one of the youngsters jumped up. "What's he goin' to do with all those beds?" he asked.

She paused, looked him in the eye, and said confidently, "Why, he's going to have a garage sale." And Elizabeth has since added that line to the telling of the story—again, making it more believable, more understandable, to her young audiences.

By its very nature, storytelling is an improvisational art. As you learn and tell your story, you will gradually begin to shape the tale—to change and adapt it—to fit yourself and your listeners. Changing and adapting stories can be fun and entertaining for both the teller and the listener, but often the story simply cannot be told unless it is modified to fit the telling.

"When someone told a story a hundred years ago," Laura Simms points out, "a word or phrase might have had very different implications than it does today. And consequently, I'm often not telling a story to people who are informed by that same knowledge. So I must investigate what the images and words mean, and then tell the story in such a way that its meaning can be understood in today's world."

Gayle Ross considers it a responsibility of the modern-day storyteller to adapt stories—to make them more relevant to today's world. "Storytellers have been passing down stories since the dawn of time," adds Gayle, "and all of them have made contributions to the tales—reflecting in their telling the time and place and society in which they live. I believe it's my duty as a storyteller to take the essence of the story and put my creative powers to work to see if I can make that story just as relevant, just as important today as it was centuries ago."

In changing and adapting stories, however, extreme care should be exercised. Stories should not be changed arbitrarily. Connie Regan-Blake and Barbara Freeman of The Folktellers often tell "The Bet," a delightful tale from the Southern Appalachians. "When we first began telling the story," says Barbara, "we told it in its traditional form. But the more we told the story, the more our personalities began to seep into its telling. We didn't try to stop this process. Instead, we let it flow, and we grew to love the story more and more. But we don't launch into a tale by changing it. Instead, we tell the story, and the changes just come." For as we modify stories, we discover the possibilities—and limits.

Modifications and modern adaptations are generally acceptable if, warns Laura Simms, the changes "protect the intrinsic value of the story." But most storytellers agree that some stories should *never* be changed: sacred, ritual stories in reverence for the culture and its tradition, and literary tales out of respect for the author's literary process, labor, and love.

Using Your Voice

One of Jay O'Callahan's most popular stories is "The Herring Shed," a story about Maggie Thomas, who, when fourteen years old, begins stringing fish in a herring shed. Every day, she picks up a rod in one hand, a herring in the other, and as she opens the herring's mouth with her thumb, she slips the fish on the rod. Each rod holds eighteen fish, a hundred rods is a bundle, and one day, Maggie strings three bundles. Her work is long, cold, and frightfully routine.

When Jay tells this powerful and poignant story, he *becomes* Maggie Thomas. But he is not concerned about *sounding* like Maggie Thomas. He is not a mimic. Instead, Jay tries to capture the tone of the story— its emotional voice.

As a listener, one sees Maggie on her first day—learning the work that she would do for much of her life. She feels clumsy and awkward, and when she picks up her first fish to slip it on the rod, she drops it.

"Thumb in the gill, open the mouth, slip it on the floor . . . I'm sorry."
"Slow, Maggie. Slow. Slow."
"Yes. I will. Thumb in the gill, open the mouth. There, I got it on. Don't look at me. Thumb in the gill, open the mouth, slip it on. I've got it."

"I don't want to imitate Maggie," begins Jay. "Instead, I want to stay within the ranges of my natural voice and capture Maggie's freshness, her eagerness and willingness to learn, and when she has learned her work, I want a sense of a fourteen-year-old girl's triumph."

The voice is the instrument of the storyteller, and you can use your voice effectively to enhance the telling of your tale—enlivening your performance, helping to make the story more real, more believable, and heightening your listeners' involvement. While your voice may be soft and gentle, even calming, boisterous or dramatic, perhaps mysterious, or simply ordinary, use it naturally, genuinely, and as you grow in your skill and technique, you will gradually learn more about its power and possibilities.

Jackie Torrence awoke early one morning in a hotel in Wilmington, North Carolina, and began preparing for a full day of storytelling performances. As she was showering, she practiced her telling of Sir

Arthur Conan Doyle's "The Hound of the Baskervilles." She was barking and howling, trying to perfect the sound of the ferocious hound.
When she stepped from the shower, she heard someone knocking at her
door.

"Who is it?" she asked.

"I'm the desk clerk," came the reply. "Our guests in the rooms next to
you have reported that you have a dog in your room, and our rules
strictly prohibit you from having pets in our hotel. If you have a dog, we
have a kennel."

"You must have the wrong room," Jackie countered. "I don't have a
pet."

"But ma'am," the desk clerk argued, "we *know* you have a pet in your
room. Our guests have heard the dog barking."

Jackie was amused.

"I'll have to search your room," he demanded.

Jackie quickly dressed and opened the door. The desk clerk leapt into
the room and began looking for the dog—opening doors, looking under
the bed, even pulling open the drawers. He found nothing.

Then he turned to Jackie, pointed his finger at her, and said, "If our
guests are disturbed again by a barking dog, we must ask you to leave."

The desk clerk walked out of her room and slammed the door behind
him, and as he stepped away, Jackie softly said, "*Wofff. Wofff.
Woooooofffff.*" He *never* found the dog, but Jackie knew at that moment
that she had developed an effective bark. She was pleased, for Jackie
skillfully uses her voice—especially through sound effects—to enliven
her tales.

One day, Jackie was performing at a high school in New Orleans, and
she was in the midst of telling W. W. Jacobs's "The Monkey's Paw," a
gripping story about a man and woman who lose their son in a sawmill
accident. They hope to bring him back to life through the magic spell of
a monkey's paw. They are sitting alone, waiting for his return.

"On the other side of midnight, the candles had burned low and the
fire had gone out. The old woman heard the screen door opening"—
and Jackie groaned and moaned and creaked like a squeaky door—"and
she saw the doorknob turning. She said to the old man, 'That's my son!
He's come back! I shall open the door.'"

But before the old man could utter a word, one of the young men in
the audience yelled out, "No! No! Don't open the door!"

"He was lost in the story," explains Jackie. "The sound of the squeaky
screen door—a sound we've all heard—allowed the story to come alive
for him, to be real and believable. And while words are often all that's

necessary—the scenes they create in the listeners' minds—sound effects, if chosen carefully and performed naturally, can enhance the telling of the tale and even deepen its meaning."

In Jay O'Callahan's "Edna Robinson," Edna, the clerk at the general store, falls in love for the first time—with a mysterious hobo named Blueberry Jack. But one Saturday morning, while Edna is at work at the store, Jack boards the train—leaving Edna behind, forever.

"I turn my back to the audience," explains Jay, "and I'm Edna, and I'm pulling two jars of jam from the shelf. Just then, I re-create the sound of a train whistle, long and lonesome. When the whistle stops, I, as Edna, turn around to continue Edna's work as if nothing had ever happened.

"For Edna, life goes on—despite her loss. But for the listener, there's a special sadness. The sound of a train whistle is haunting, and for all of us, it brings to the surface all manner of feelings of loneliness. In 'Edna Robinson,' it's a sound that touches my listeners' emotions more deeply than any words I could utter. Consequently, maybe there's a point in storytelling when words fail but sounds—and even silence—can touch people's emotions more deeply than words."

Using Effective Timing and Pauses

Storyteller Ed Stivender attended the National Storytelling Festival in 1976. He was eager to see other storytellers, watch them perform, learn from them. He was looking for clues, for rules, and he found Doc McConnell. Doc was having a great time, telling stories, talking to people—that combination of lying and laughter that Doc seems to do so well—and Ed watched him closely.

"What I discovered," Ed says, "was that Doc was only doing part of the work. His pipe was doing the rest. Doc was saying funny things but only half the time, and the other half of the time the audience was laughing, waiting for Doc's next wave of humor. What he was doing was keeping them relaxed—drawing on his pipe, doing something obviously very normal and human—while he was preparing for his next lines.

"I came back home to Philadelphia, and though I may have tried the pipe, it wasn't too long afterward that I was playing the harmonica. I had learned the harmonica growing up, playing 'Oh, Susannah,' performing for my family on Sunday afternoons. And now for me, the harmonica distracts the audience while I'm creating the story, working on my lines, in my mind."

Pausing is an effective tool for Doc McConnell. "To enhance the stories I tell, I often stop for a moment—to puff on my pipe, to give a twinkle of the eye, a slight smile, an expression of disbelief that helps reinforce and make more powerful the statements I've just made. And during those pauses, I'm thinking ahead, to my next words, and my listeners are given time to think, to contemplate, to build the mental images of the story." And as Doc pauses, his listeners can *see* themselves with him—hoeing corn in a hillside cornfield, fishing in the old mill pond, or sharing brother Steamer's excitement as he discovers mule eggs in John Mauk's General Store at Tucker's Knob.

"In music," maintains Jay O'Callahan, "the sounds between the notes are often as important as the notes themselves. In storytelling, we also play with the sounds between words. And when we hear a pause, that too plays with our imagination."

In Jay's "The Herring Shed," young Maggie Thomas is working in the shed, stringing fish, when the rector, in his odd, shy way, comes into the shed.

> The rector's got the worst job. He's twenty-six and never been a rector before. Whenever anyone dies in the war, the station agent gives the telegram to the rector, and it's got so no one wants to see the rector coming up the path.
>
> "Maggie," the rector said as he leaned forward, "could you come outside?"
>
> And I knew my brother Harry was dead. For a moment, I couldn't move. I saw the telegram outside the shed. It was at Dunkirk.

"It's a terrible moment for Maggie," explains Jay, "and I want to pause for her, to allow her silence. I want Maggie to be able to absorb the tragic news, and I want my listeners to be able to take the time to feel more deeply—for Maggie and her hurt.

"If a storyteller tells a story enough times, he knows the story so well that there's a natural tendency for him to race through its telling. But most of our listeners probably haven't heard the story, and they need time to see the images, feel the emotions, get to know the characters. So, I try not to rush, and I try to be brave enough to be silent. The most effective moment in a story may be that pause, that moment of silence."

Using Gestures

When Jay O'Callahan tells "The Herring Shed," his right hand picks up an imaginary rod. The thumb of his left hand carefully goes into the gill of an imaginary fish and opens it up as the thumb comes back, and the left hand goes down as the fish slides onto the rod. For Jay, this simple gesture falls into a rhythm.

> Thumb in the gill, open the mouth, slip it on the rod in the herring shed.
> Thumb in the gill, open the mouth, slip it on the rod in the herring shed.

"I feel the gesture is important," explains Jay. "It places me—and my listeners—firmly in the herring shed, with Maggie, and gives us all a sense of her constant, cold work. As Maggie gets faster—first one bundle, then two, then three bundles—the gesture becomes faster.

"Gesturing, for me, helps make the images more intense and, therefore, clearer to my listeners. But in using gestures, I try to be natural. I make them as succinct, as simple, as possible, and every gesture becomes useful to the story and its telling. I use gestures only if it deepens my listeners' understanding of the characters or the time and place."

The gesture may be ever so slight. In Doc McConnell's telling of "The Snake-Bit Hoe Handle," a hoe handle, bitten by a poisonous snake, begins to swell until it becomes so large that Doc and his father saw enough lumber from it to build a chicken house. But after they paint the house, it begins "creakin' and moanin' and groanin'... and shakin' and movin' around."

> You see, I had mixed some turpentine in that paint, and that turpentine... was such good medicine that it started takin' the swellin' outa that lumber. And that chicken house went to shrinkin' and shrinkin' and shrinkin'. And when it got done shrinkin', it was no bigger than a shoe box.

"And when I'm telling that tale," explains Doc, "I bring my two hands together, palm to palm—showing the dimensions of a small shoe box—and that simple gesture alone reinforces my telling and my listeners' understanding of just how small that chicken house finally became."

For Jackie Torrence, it's difficult to tell a story without gesturing, using her hands, making facial expressions. "It's something I've done all of my life, since I was a child, and it's a part of me and who I am."

In Jackie's rendition of "How Brer Rabbit Outsmarts the Frogs," Brer Coon, his sack in his hand, goes down to the river each day to catch frogs for his supper. But the frogs get wise, station the old bullfrog to watch for Brer Coon, and when Brer Coon gets near the pond, the frogs all jump into the water. Brer Coon can't swim, but his wily old friend Brer Rabbit thinks up a plan to outsmart the frogs.

> "This here's your plan," said Brer Rabbit. "Go down to the river. When you git to the river, fall dead."
> Brer Coon said, "But I don't want to die."
> Brer Rabbit said, "Sssshhhhhhh. I don't mean die. I mean play dead."
> So, he picked up his ol' sack and headed toward the river, and when he got to within a half a mile of the river, he heard it. "Here he comes. Here he comes. Here he comes." And he commenced to dyin'.... He fell on his back and kicked his legs up in the air.

"For the next two minutes," adds Jackie, "Brer Coon twitches, quivers, and shakes, and there's no doubt, no doubt at all, that those frogs—and my listeners—are convinced that Brer Coon is *dead*, just plain dead. But during those two minutes, I don't have to say a word. The gestures tell the story for me."

While gestures are important to many storytellers, there are still others who choose not to use them—preferring to depend, instead, upon the power of te story, its words and images.

"I remember my kindergarten teacher," says Jackie, "a kind, lovely woman named Helen Woods. She read to us every day, and when she read, she would always stick her hands into her dress pockets. When it was time to turn the page, she would slip her hand quietly but quickly out of her pocket, flip the page, and then, just as quickly, slip it back into her pocket. She *never* used a gesture, but we were lost in the story."

Practicing and Polishing

One day, Elizabeth Ellis was telling stories to a group of small children. Suddenly, one of the children jumped up and said, "Do you memorize those stories?"

Before she could answer, the little boy next to him poked him in the ribs and said, "No, stupid! She knows them by heart."

"I chuckled inside," says Elizabeth, "but I was struck by the truth of the child's statement. No, my stories aren't memorized. I *do* know them by heart. For if the story isn't told through the heart, the story has little power. The stories that really move us are those that we learn, take in, and tell through the heart—not the head."

Once you have learned and told your story, only practice and repeated tellings will allow you to polish your performance. For through telling the story over and over again, you take it inside, deeply and completely. And according to Jay O'Callahan, the best way for a new storyteller to practice and polish his or her storytelling is by using mirrors: real mirrors, human mirrors, and recorded mirrors.

By using a real mirror, you can see yourself as others see you. Consequently, you can more easily detect and correct obvious defects in your performance—your use of facial expressions, gestures, and movements. And without fear of a live audience, you can experiment with new techniques.

Through the use of a human mirror—a friend or relative—you can get another kind of reflection, of what your friends and relatives hear and observe. Such a "mirror" can give you the benefit of a more objective evaluation. They can say, "You told that story awfully fast." Or, "It was wonderful, but I didn't get all of the names straight." Or, "I wish you had paused a moment before you began."

By listening to or viewing a mechanical mirror—an audio or video recording of your performance—you can sit down, make notes, and even ponder over your telling of the story. You can see for yourself if the gestures seem unnatural, the voice is strained, or if there's a need for more pauses and silences.

To Ed Stivender, however, storytelling is like dancing: he needs a partner. "Though I can practice in front of a mirror or in front of friends, I *need* an audience—and their responses—to shape and mold my stories and strengthen my telling." With the audience's help, Ed can find the pauses, the gestures and movements, the climaxes, and consequently his stories develop themselves and become richer and more refined.

Whether you're telling a story before a large audience or simply telling a joke to friends, your listeners give you clues, send you messages, that will help polish your telling and strengthen your story.

As a young child, Donald Davis heard his Uncle Frank tell stories. When Donald began repeating Uncle Frank's tales, they were told very simply, but the stories he now tells are greatly developed and elaborated upon. "As I tell a story," says Donald, "my listeners help me mold it. They respond to some parts of the story, and they don't respond to other parts. Those parts they respond to gradually grow, and the parts they don't respond to are edited out."

Spalding Gray, sitting alone at a table on a bare stage, talks to his audience, telling them stories of personal experience. "My listeners are my editors," he adds. "I can see a line coming that really didn't work the last time I performed—it either didn't get a laugh or the audience was inattentive—and when I get to that line, I drop it. So the audience helps me edit my stories."

Even Ray Hicks, sitting on his porch on Beech Mountain in western North Carolina, uses his listeners to help shape his tales. "I can never tell a tale the same way each time I tell it," says Ray. "It's jist the mood I'm in or how the people a-listenin' to it are a-takin' it. If you see the people's interest, that gives you an influence. You tell it and they tell you, and you can put more into it and think of more words and make it funnier. You can make it fit 'em better."

Choosing the Right Story

Barbara Freeman of The Folktellers had been working as a reference librarian at the Chattanooga Public Library in Tennessee for only a few months when the library director offered her a job as head of the children's and young adult divisions. Barbara was startled. She knew she loved children—she had even taught in junior high school—but she didn't know if she could be effective with preschoolers.

"Think about it," the director told her.

"I'll give you my answer within a month," Barbara replied.

Barbara went to the children's room, held out her arms, and asked the librarians to load them up with the best children's books in the library. They gave her thirty books, and during the coming month, Barbara read each one. As she read, she began to love the literature for the young child, and she accepted the job.

Eager to be effective in her new role, Barbara built a ten-foot plywood castle—a perfect haven for storytelling, she thought. On the first day she told stories, she faced twelve young listeners—mostly preschoolers —sitting quietly in the castle.

Barbara sat down before her young audience and began telling *Thidwick, the Big-Hearted Moose*, a story by Dr. Seuss about a moose whose horns were weighted down with animal friends who had come to live with him and who was simply too kindhearted to ask them to leave.

"As I told about Thidwick," Barbara recalls, "I placed a cutout of the moose on the flannel board. Then I added Bingle Bug and Tree-Spider and Zinn-a-zu Bird and all of the other little characters that came to live on Thidwick's horns, and by the eleventh character, my little pre-schoolers were bored to tears. One by one, they slowly rose from their seats and left the room.

"I began pleading to their backs as they left. 'Wait! Wait! You'll never believe what happens next.'

"But it was too late. I had chosen the wrong story for the age group. I knew right then I had to make better choices, and I did. During story-time the next week, the children returned, and I was prepared. I told *Where the Wild Things Are* by Maurice Sendak, and they loved it."

When you are ready to perform, you must select the right story to tell. In order to be effective, you must choose stories that are compati-ble with your listeners—their ages, backgrounds, and ethnicities—and play upon their experiences.

Jackie Torrence was once telling stories to a group of kindergarten children in a school in Florence, South Carolina. The children were gathered around her. She had just completed telling a Brer Rabbit tale when one of the young children popped up and said, "Are you goin' to tell us a scary story now?"

Jackie took a deep breath. Then, she began to tell "Tilly," a story about a little girl, alone in her bedroom at night, who began to hear strange noises. Someone ... or something ... was creeping slowly up the stairs to her room.

> She waited, and then she listened, and then she heard the
> door of her room opening... Tillllly... Tillllly... Tillllly
> ... I'm... coming... in... your... room... to...

In the midst of the story, one of the youngsters, frozen with fear, yelled, "Get the axe!"

The teachers and parents, listening to Jackie's performance, began to chuckle, then laugh. But the young children didn't budge—they re-mained transfixed, lost in the telling of the tale. Jackie had chosen the *right* story. Every child in the audience became Tilly, for they each had the same fears every night—fear of what's in the closet, what's going to crawl out from underneath the bed. They were living the story.

"It's obvious," says Doc McConnell. "The stories I tell to a group of senior citizens would not be the same stories I would tell to elementary school students or preschoolers. And *if* the stories are the same, I will often change the words, modify the phrases, so that the story becomes more understandable to my listeners without damaging the telling or its enjoyment."

While it is important to choose stories for the right age groups, care must also be exercised in telling stories to listeners of diverse backgrounds, cultures, and ethnicities. What may be understandable to one listener may be incomprehensible to another.

"When I'm telling stories," adds Doc, "I try to be conscious of my audience—its education, its culture, its geographic location. Some of my stories might have terms and phrases in them that many of my listeners wouldn't understand. So I often try to explain those elements of my story that may present some difficulties to my listeners—giving them a better foundation for understanding and enjoying the stories I tell."

In 1980, Jay O'Callahan told stories at the Winter Olympics in Lake Placid, New York. During his stay there, Jay was asked to tell stories in a large cafeteria, crowded with a thousand hungry athletes from throughout the world. Many of them couldn't speak nor understand English.

As Jay stood near a table of English wrestlers, he began to tell "Owl" —a Haitian story collected by Diane Wolkstein—about an owl who has no self-confidence. As he told, he acted out the tale, singing boisterously, dancing around the room.

> Dong ga da, Dong ga da, Dong ga da, Dong.
> Dong ga da, Dong. Eh-ee-oh.

All the athletes in the room laid down their forks and knives, turned toward Jay, and began listening to the story, watching him as he told it.

"As I was ending my story," remembers Jay, "I could see two Japanese athletes sitting in the back of the room. Though they couldn't understand a word of English, they sat wide-eyed, their mouths hanging open, a look of total amazement and wonder filling their faces. It was obvious: I had made the right choice. I selected a tale that was highly dramatic, delightfully musical, and *everyone* could become involved in the story and its telling, and enjoy it. The experience was clearly the highlight of my Olympics performances."

Creating the Proper Place

One day, Jay O'Callahan was to tell stories at a dentists' convention. He arrived early, eager and willing. But the hall was vast and filled with round tables that stretched far to the back of the room. He was awed by the space and disturbed by the height of the stage that loomed ten or twelve feet above the floor. The space was wrong, he knew.

Jay had agreed to sit at the head table, and for two hours, he nibbled on his food and made dismal conversation—and worried. He was finally introduced, and he climbed onto the stage. Jay was overwhelmed by the lighting, and the sound, reputedly good for music, was terrible for the speaking voice.

Despite the obstacles, he began his story—a long tale of Magellan's search for the strait—and soon both Magellan and Jay were "alone on the high seas." The dentists clanged their cutlery, rattled their china, and fiddled with their desserts. As Jay sailed on, the back tables began emptying. The performance ended in disaster.

Jay left the convention and went to a tiny bar. It was deserted. The lone voice came from the television. But he was glad to be there—for a moment of solitude, of quiet—to think through what went wrong.

Stories can be told anywhere—at home, school, community library, club meeting, community festival, or wherever people are gathered. But whether it's a public performance before a large audience or a quiet evening at home with friends, successful storytelling depends significantly upon the quality of the performance space—that strategic but subtle blend of acoustics, lighting, staging, audience arrangement, and other elements that contribute to the mood surrounding a performance.

"As I sat in that lonely bar after my performance," remembers Jay, "the problems began to come clear to me. The tables were deadly, especially since there were a great many of them. People sitting at tables tend to whisper and be more interested in eating and drinking and talking than listening. And the stage? It was Mount Olympus. Built for Zeus. I needed to be on the same level as my audience or at least only modestly separated.

"The acoustics were bad. Words bounced about the room, and many were completely lost. Keeping the thread of a story with fourteen characters was too difficult. The lighting didn't help. It was too general, too bright, focused on the entire platform, and I became a tiny, wild figure on a vast stage.

"Rather than sitting at the head table and making idle conversation and picking at my food, I should have taken the time to warm up my voice and my body. The time and freedom to practice would have helped me to ground myself, begin to feel the situation, and respond to its needs. I could have selected tales that would have been more effective—shorter stories, no doubt."

After suffering through this performance, Jay learned to inquire about the setting. Is it intimate? Or can it be made to "feel" intimate? Are the acoustics effective? Is there proper lighting? Can the listeners sit close to the teller? Though not every situation is a perfect setting for a story performance, a storyteller, by knowing what he's facing when he arrives, can request minor modifications in the performance space and adjust his own performance to become more compatible with the setting. And for Jay, and many others as well, it's important to be alone before a performance, to be quiet, to warm up the voice and body, to think about the flow of the event, and to choose stories carefully and effectively.

"Later," adds Jay, "I performed at a college in Ohio, and the woman who scheduled my performance thought carefully about the space. She chose a hall, a large hall, but we arranged it so the audience could sit in a great semicircle and feel a part of the whole. We even dragged out large mats for the children. We spent hours on the lighting, and the result was warm and had the spirit of a cozy fire of old. The sound was perfect. And I spent a long time thinking about the tales I would tell. The evening was sparkling and fun, and after my performance, I was so excited I couldn't sleep all night. I flew home exhausted but delighted."

Whether you are telling stories to your child at home or to a large group of children or adults, it's important for you to take responsibility for creating the proper setting for storytelling to occur—to ensure quiet and protection for both yourself and your listener. But once the best possible scene has been set, you must step forward, begin your tale, and forget about the surroundings. If a helicopter flies over or if someone with a loud transistor radio walks by, don't panic. While interruptions should be minimized, they are simply a part of the storytelling process. No matter what you can do to prepare the performance space, things can—and often will—go wrong.

"I can remember telling a story in a school near Brookline," says Jay, "and the loudspeaker began to blare: 'Will the person who owns the 1974 Chevrolet, license number 86523, please move your car?'

"I paused, and the whole class waited until the announcement was over. The audience remained suspended in the story. Then I continued. Moments later, the loudspeaker blared again.

"'Will the person who owns the 1974 Chevrolet, license number 86523, please move your car? At once!'

"I paused, and once again, the whole class waited until the announcement was over. The flow of the story was broken. But I went on, and soon the story was told.

"Then there was the time when I was telling 'The Golden Drum' to a classroom of young children," laughs Jay, "and I realized that the zipper on my pants was broken and was sliding down inch by inch. When I made the discovery, I turned around, my back to the children, thinking frantically, What will I do?

"Almost at once, I leapt into a chair, bent over, and, changing the viewpoint of the story, I told the tale as an old man. When it was over, I fled the classroom as quickly as I could."

Elizabeth Ellis was once telling stories to an audience, half children and half adults. Some of the children sitting in the front row held balloons in their hands, so one of the parents, concerned for the storyteller, took several of the balloons away from the children and placed them under her chair.

In the middle of Elizabeth's telling of a poignant family story from the Kentucky mountains, one of the balloons exploded. It sounded like a cannon, but Elizabeth continued telling her story. She didn't respond.

"My listeners," explains Elizabeth, "are much more likely to react to an interruption if I, as the teller, react to it. Consequently, if I just act as if it didn't happen, the listeners will settle down faster, remain calmer, and I'll regain their attention quicker than if I react to the disruption."

But in any storytelling occasion, there is always an unspoken trust between the storyteller and the listener, and it is a trust—regardless of the circumstances—that should never be broken.

"During a recent Halloween concert," recalls Laura Simms, "I was telling ghost stories to a group of three hundred children. When I came to the scary part of the story, one of the children screamed, 'Ma'am, don't tell the rest of that story! Don't finish it!' There were other children in the audience, and it was dark. So I said, 'I must finish the story, but *you* can put your hands over your ears. I'll tell the story to everyone else but you.'

"In this unexpected situation, I stopped telling the story and addressed the child so she knew I was actually aware of her and her needs. She was frightened, and I knew it, and I gave her immediate attention. But just as important, I let everyone *else* know that I was aware of the child and her needs. If I had ignored the child's screams, there would have been a disruption of our trust—between the audience and me. For that trust is the very bond that is vital to the successful, mutual creation of the story, a trust that no storyteller who wants to connect with her audience can ignore."

Approaching Your Listeners

When Jackie Torrence was growing up, she remembers her grandmother faithfully watching *The Ed Sullivan Show* every Sunday night. When Ed was on sage—introducing an act, even waving goodbye at the close of the show—he always looked directly into the camera. Throughout Ed's program, Jackie's grandmother, thinking Ed was talking only to her, always talked to him—chatting with him, responding to his comments, waving goodbye as he closed each show.

There were millions of us watching *The Ed Sullivan Show,* and really, I suppose, we all thought he was talking only to us. For even through the medium of television, Ed Sullivan was making that all-important contact with his audience—bringing us to him, creating a vital one-on-one connection between us. As the storyteller, your contact with your listeners is just as critical to effective storytelling—whether you are telling your story to an audience of five or five hundred.

In some cultures, the eyes of the storyteller and the listeners never meet. It is considered rude and improper, so the storyteller tells stories gazing outward or looking at the ground. But in most American cultures, developing eye contact between the teller and the listeners is the first step toward connecting with your audience—reaching out to them, meeting them halfway.

When your audience is small, it is easy to look everyone in the eye as you tell—recounting the tale as if it were being told directly to each listener. Several techniques are used, and you, as the storyteller, can choose what works best for you.

Elizabeth Ellis often breaks her story down into phrases, and as she tells each phrase, she tells it to a different person in the audience. "There was once an old king... who had three daughters... and one by one... he called them to him..." And with each phrase, she spans the audience and looks into the eyes of each person in the room, one at a time. Unfortunately, this is only possible with a small audience.

"When I'm telling a story to a large audience," explains Maggi Peirce, "I always tell the story to the people in the first four rows. And when I see those who are reacting, enjoying the tale, I tell the story to their wonderful faces. Though I will occasionally span the entire audience, I will always come back to them for succor.

"And I don't worry if I look into a listener's eyes," counsels Maggi, "and he doesn't seem to be responding—sitting there like a wooden Indian. He's listening. When the performance is over, he is the very one who will always come up to me, wring my hand, and tell me how wonderful my telling was."

While eye contact is critical, a simple but effective story introduction is another vital building block in creating that special connection between you and your listeners.

Waddie Mitchell remembers One-Eyed Bill. He was an old cowboy who was too feeble to work, so he just lingered on the ranch where Waddie grew up and did what chores he could to pay his room and board. One night, One-Eyed Bill came home drunk, singing songs and telling stories, and Waddie, sleeping with the old cowhands, heard about the time that One-Eyed Bill roped the Devil, dehorned and branded him, and left that old Devil with knots tied in his tail. Waddie was enchanted and amused, and although he was only a young child, he never forgot One-Eyed Bill. Today, Waddie retells "Tying the Knots in the Devil's Tail," a classic cowboy poem penned years ago by Gail Gardner.

"Storytelling is personal," says Waddie. "And though I've heard a lot of stories, I only tell the ones that are important to me, those that touch me personally. And when I tell a story—like the tale old One-Eyed Bill told us years ago—I want my listeners to know how special that story is to me. And if I share that with them, it's like givin' them an extra gift."

Through the few simple words of an introduction, you can share with your listeners why you are telling your story, why the story is important to you, and how it became a part of your repertoire. And in some cases, your stories will need introductions to create a setting, introduce the characters, explain any obscure words or phrases, and give whatever background is necessary for the listeners to better understand and enjoy the tale and your telling.

"But introductions shouldn't interpret the story," warns Donald Davis. "When I tell a story, I never want to tell my listeners what *I* think the story means. I'm not even going to tell them what the story means to *me*. There are always those who hear much more than I tell, and I never want to close the door to any possibilities a story offers."

While Mary Carter Smith seldom uses introductions, there is always an exception. For her, it came one February—Black History Month—when Mary was invited to tell stories at a large high school. When she arrived, the students were in the gymnasium, singing, and she saw immediately that they were undisciplined, unruly, and the principal was afraid of them.

"Children," he began, "this is Mary Carter Smith." Then he turned and walked away, leaving Mary onstage, alone.

"I could see the students were seething, raging inside, ready to rise up," explains Mary. "I could see it, feel it. I paused briefly and looked into their eyes, and I saw Ricky—my son—in all of them. Ricky was important to me, and I wanted these young people to know how important *they* were.

"So I told about Ricky and his brutal death—a stabbing in a Baltimore bar—and the agony and pain I suffered then and seven years later when I met his murderess in a Baltimore prison. Once they had heard the story of Ricky's death, they listened. After the performance, those young people came to me—each telling me what my stories had meant to them—and that was my reward. But I had to touch them in a special way, a meaningful way, before they could listen, accept, and understand my stories."

Sometimes, the contact between you as the teller and your listeners becomes stronger when your listeners participate actively in your story. Being involved in the performance allows your audience to be there with you, inside the story, part and parcel of the tale and its telling.

One of The Folktellers' favorite stories is *Where the Wild Things Are*, a storytelling classic by Maurice Sendak and the first story Connie Regan-Blake and Barbara Freeman ever told in tandem. Every time they tell this delightful children's tale, they ask their audience to "stand up, open your closet door, take out your wolf suit, and try out your wolf's roar."

Whether they are children or adults, all the listeners rise to their feet and, following Barbara and Connie's cues, don their imaginary wolf suits, growling all the while. The listeners return to their seats, and The Folktellers launch into the tale—swapping lines, chorusing others.

"And that night Max wore *his* wolf suit," begins Barbara.

". . . and made mischief of one kind . . ." adds Connie.

". . . and another," continues Barbara.

And as the story is told, the listeners become involved, ever so wrapped up, in the telling. They are inside the story, watching it unfold, and between the tellers and their listeners, a bond is being forged that strengthens the telling and heightens the story's power and effectiveness.

Expanding Your Opportunities

▲▲▲▲▲▲▲▲▲▲▲▲

When Donald Davis was growing up in the mountains of western North Carolina, he heard about Jack from his Grandmother Walker. While Jack was best known for cutting down the beanstalk, this imaginary Appalachian farm boy encountered all manner of adventure—from giants and dragons to seeking life's fortunes.

"From Grandmother Walker's stories of Jack," explains Donald, "I thought that Jack was either a little boy who lived just around the mountain or a boy, long since grown up and gone, who had lived a long, long time ago in another time and place. But after I had grown up, I began to realize that *I* was Jack. And yes, he was also the little boy around the mountain *and* the boy from long ago. For you see, we are *all* Jack—if we have ever dreamed a dream, wished a wish, hoped to find our fortune, or found ourselves in trouble over our head."

Within us all is the magic of stories—and the yearning to tell them. And if this brief exploration of storytelling has awakened the "Jack" within you, perhaps you will want to begin your own personal discovery of storytelling—finding tales, learning and shaping them, sharing them with others. If so, you may want to expand your opportunities to learn more about the storytelling art.

- Read and study a variety of books about storytelling and stories from a growing selection of materials now available through your local bookstore, community library, or by mail through the *National Catalog of Storytelling*—a publication of the National Association for the Preservation and Perpetuation of Storytelling. Through these valuable materials, you can become more deeply acquainted with the art and technique of storytelling.
- Browse through your local bookstore, community library, or the NAPPS-produced catalog for albums and audio- and video-cassettes of storytelling performances by some of America's foremost storytellers. And if possible, see and hear storytellers firsthand by attending the National Storytelling Festival or any of the storytelling festivals, conferences, and events that dot the United States. Through seeing and hearing storytelling, you can learn more about the stories, the styles, the techniques.

- Enroll in one or more of the ever-expanding number of story-telling classes, conferences, workshops, and residencies being offered by NAPPS or by colleges, universities, storytelling centers and organizations, and other agencies throughout the United States. Through them, you will be able to hear story-tellers and storytelling scholars discuss their art, and you can participate in one-on-one learning experiences about storytelling and its performance.

- And finally, tell stories—for telling tales is the best way to learn about storytelling. Share your stories with your family and friends, at the community library or neighborhood school, at civic club meetings or church socials, or wherever people are gathered. And as you tell, you will grow in knowledge and understanding, develop a style, improve your technique, and build a repertoire of stories to tell.

While you share your stories, you may be reminded of a tale, often told by Elizabeth Ellis, about an old peddler who, though seemingly foolish, gives away his merchandise to the young children until it appears that he has nothing left to sell. But then, in a dream, he is guided to a chest of gold coins hidden in his own backyard.

"As a storyteller," says Elizabeth, "I often tell stories all day long. Sure, it's easy to think that I'll dry up and not have anything left to tell—to give to my listeners. But fortunately, I'm always replenished and, just like the peddler, I *never* seem to run out of anything to give. My stories are always there—to be shared."

And so it will be with you.

A Quick Review

- Discover the right story to tell—a story you love and believe in.
  - Find a story at your local library.
  - Collect a story from your family and community heritage.
  - Create a story from the world around you.
- Learn the story in a way that works best for you.
- Change and adapt the story to fit yourself, your needs, and the needs of your listeners.
- Use your natural voice.
- Use sound effects naturally, cautiously.
- Be brave enough to be silent.
- Use gestures succinctly, simply, naturally.
- Polish your telling by practicing—telling your story again and again.
- Choose the right story to tell, one compatible with your listeners' ages, educational level, and background.
- Prepare a proper place for stories to be told.
  - See that the room is comfortable and intimate.
  - Provide effective lighting and acoustics.
  - Assure quiet, protection, and freedom from interruptions.
- Develop a direct, one-on-one contact with your listeners.
  - Tell your story into your listeners' eyes.
  - Introduce your story.
  - Involve your listeners in your story and its telling.
- Expand your opportunities to learn more about storytelling.
  - Read and study how-to books and materials.
  - Listen to others tell.
  - Enroll in a class, workshop, or residency.
- But most important of all, tell whenever and wherever you can.

Resources

The Storytellers as Resources

![decorative divider with triangles]

The twenty-one storytellers featured in this volume are valuable resources to anyone wanting to know more about the storytelling art. They perform at festivals and other storytelling events, conduct workshops on the art, and offer a wide variety of books, albums, and audio- and videocassettes. For more information, contact the National Association for the Preservation and Perpetuation of Storytelling, your local bookstore or community library, or, perhaps, the individual storytellers.

BROTHER BLUE
30 Fernald Drive
Cambridge, MA 02138

He is really Dr. Hugh Morgan Hill, but he is known throughout the United States and the world as Brother Blue—a storyteller who integrates song, dance, and poetry to tell stories of understanding and love. A graduate of Harvard College and the Yale Drama School, Brother Blue—adorned with ribbons, bows, butterflies, and balloons—performs, teaches, lectures, and conducts workshops for audiences here and around the world. For five years, he told stories on two Boston radio stations, and he was a regular guest on the highly acclaimed Boston-based television program *Playmates/Schoolmates*. In 1981, he played Merlin in the movie *Knightriders*. Brother Blue has been the recipient of many honors, including a special citation for outstanding solo performance from the Corporation for Public Broadcasting for his telling of "Miss Wunderlich." He has also produced a videocassette of the same story. In 1987, Brother Blue was named the official storyteller of Cambridge, Massachusetts, where he lives with his wife, Ruth, and still performs regularly in Harvard Square.

Videos
Miss Wunderlich. American Storytelling Series, Volume Six. Story-Tel Enterprises and H. W. Wilson Co. 1986.

DONALD DAVIS
1306 North Rotary Drive
High Point, NC 27262

Donald Davis grew up in the mountains of western North Carolina listening to stories told by his Welsh and Scottish forebears. As a child, he heard the

345

traditional stories of the Southern Appalachians, and though Donald still tells
the old mountain tales, he is best known for portraits of human experience
created from his childhood memories. While Donald is a professional storyteller, performing and conducting workshops throughout the United States, he
is also a full-time Methodist minister—now pastoring the Christ United Methodist Church in High Point, North Carolina, where storytelling is the focus of
his preaching. As a proponent of the storytelling art and a leader in America's
storytelling revival, Donald has served as a member of the Board of Directors of
the National Association for the Preservation and Perpetuation of Storytelling
and, since 1986, has acted as its chairperson. He has produced numerous
albums and audio- and videocassettes. Donald lives in High Point with his
wife, Beth, and sons Douglas, Kelly, and Jonathan.

Recordings

Cats and Catfish. Cassette. 1983.
Christmas Memories. Cassette. 1987.
Favorites from Uncle Frank. Cassette. 1983
The Lighter Side of Jack. Cassette. 1983.
Live and Learn. Cassette and album. Weston Woods. 1984.
Meet the Jollies. Cassette. 1983.
Miss Daisy and Miss Annie. Cassette. 1986.
More Than a Beanstalk. Cassette and album. Weston Woods. 1985.
My Lucky Day. Cassette. 1983.
Mystery and Magic. Cassette. 1983.
Old Testament Stories: To Hear, To Tell. Cassette. Graded Press. 1984.
Traditional Tales for Children. Cassette. 1983.
Two Jack Tales. Cassette. 1983.

Books

My Lucky Day: Stories from a Southern Appalachian Storyteller. Johnson
    Publishing Company. 1984.

Videos

The Crack of Dawn. American Storytelling Series, Volume Eight. Story-
    Tel Enterprises and H. W. Wilson Co. 1986.

ELIZABETH ELLIS
P.O. Box 64882
Dallas, TX 75206

As a child, Elizabeth Ellis was surrounded by stories—both those she heard,
growing up in the Southern Appalachians, and those she read, gleaned from
the world of literature. It was not surprising that in 1967 she graduated from
Milligan College in Tennessee with a degree in education, and four years later,
she earned a degree in library science at East Tennessee State University in

nearby Johnson City, Tennessee. Upon graduation, Elizabeth began a career as a library storyteller at the Dallas, Texas, public library. But in 1978, after attending the National Storytelling Festival and hearing storytellers from throughout the United States, Elizabeth realized that storytelling was truly at the center of her life. She returned home to Dallas, quit her library job, and began telling stories professionally—both alone and in tandem with Texas storyteller Gayle Ross as the Twelve Moons Storytellers. Today, Elizabeth performs and conducts workshops on the storytelling art throughout the United States, and in addition, has produced two audiocassettes and a videocassette. She continues to live in Dallas.

Recordings
Like Meat Loves Salt. Cassette. 1985.
Stories Imagine That. Cassette. 1986.

Videos
The Peddler's Dream. American Storytelling Series, Volume Seven. Story-Tel Enterprises and H. W. Wilson Co. 1986.

THE FOLKTELLERS
Connie Regan-Blake
Barbara Freeman
P.O. Box 2898
Asheville, NC 28802

Connie Regan-Blake and Barbara Freeman are The Folktellers, and since 1975, they have traveled throughout the United States telling stories—forging the way for America's storytelling renaissance. Both former librarians, they attended the first National Storytelling Festival in 1973 where each told a story, and two years later, they became charter members of the Board of Directors of the National Association for the Preservation and Perpetuation of Storytelling. As chairwoman from 1983 to 1985, Connie helped to galvanize the role of NAPPS as America's foremost organization devoted to the practice, uses, and applications of storytelling in the modern world. During their storytelling careers, Connie and Barbara have produced three award-winning albums and companion audiocassettes and a videocassette. Though their repertoire is diverse, many of the stories The Folktellers perform come from the richness of the Southern Appalachian tradition. And in 1986, Connie and Barbara expanded the perimeters of storytelling by drawing upon these mountain tales they tell to create and perform *Mountain Sweet Talk*—an original two-act play that celebrates life in the Southern Appalachians. This heartwarming drama is performed annually to critical acclaim during the summer and fall at the Folk Arts Center Theater on the Blue Ridge Parkway in their hometown of Asheville, North Carolina.

Recordings

Chillers. Cassette and album. Mama-T Artists. 1983.

The Folktellers: Tales to Grow On. Cassette and album. Weston Woods. 1981.

The Folktellers: White Horses and Whippoorwills. Cassette and album. Mama-T Artists. 1981.

Mountain Sweet Talk: The Play. Double cassette. Mama-T Artists. 1988.

Videos

No News. American Storytelling Series, Volume Five. Story-Tel Enterprises and H. W. Wilson Co. 1986.

SPALDING GRAY
International Creative Management
40 West 57th Street
Sixth Floor
New York, NY 10012

After more than a decade in experimental theater in New York City, Spalding Gray, in 1979, created and performed "Sex and Death to the Age 14." It was the first of a dozen autobiographical monologues he has created and performed to critical acclaim in theaters throughout the United States—including the Goodman Theater in Chicago, the Mark Taper Forum in Los Angeles, and Lincoln Center in New York. In addition, he has performed in Canada, Europe, and Australia. Spalding's appearance in *The Killing Fields*, his first motion picture, was the basis for his monologue, "Swimming to Cambodia," which was published as a book in 1985. His second book, *Sex and Death to the Age 14*, was published in 1986, and during the same year, he appeared in David Byrne's movie, *True Stories*. In 1987, Jonathan Demme—whose directorial credits include *Melvin and Howard* and *Stop Making Sense*, the Talking Heads' live-concert film—directed Spalding in *Swimming to Cambodia*, a feature-length film version of his most successful monologue. His "Terrors of Pleasure: The House" has appeared on HBO cable television. Spalding lives in New York City, where he continues to write and perform.

Books

Sex and Death to the Age 14. Random House. 1986.
Swimming to Cambodia. Theatre Communications Group. 1985.

Videos

Swimming to Cambodia. Cinecom. 1987.

RAY HICKS
Route 3, Box 546
Banner Elk, NC 28604

Ray Hicks, a western North Carolina farmer, is considered the patriarch of traditional storytelling in America. Though well known for his telling of the Jack tales he learned while perched on his grandfather's knee, Ray has seldom performed in public. Yet his relatively obscure storytelling talents have gained national recognition, largely through his annual appearances at the National Storytelling Festival. Ray performed at the first festival in 1973, and he has been invited to perform at every one since—an honor bestowed upon no other storyteller in the event's fifteen-year history. In 1983, the National Endowment for the Arts presented Ray with the coveted National Heritage Fellowship, special recognition given to a select few of America's traditional artists and craftspeople who have preserved and promoted the richness of America's cultural heritage. Ray, his storytelling talents, and his striking Southern Appalachian dialect were recently recognized in the highly acclaimed *Story of English* and its companion Public Broadcasting System television version. He and his wife, Rosa, still farm and gather herbs on Beech Mountain near Banner Elk, North Carolina.

Recordings
Ray Hicks. Album. Folk Legacy Records. 1963.

DAVID HOLT
Route 6, Box 572
Fairview, NC 28730

While he is recognized as an accomplished collector and performer of old-time mountain music, David Holt is equally known as a storyteller. And since 1981, he has pursued a full-time career singing the songs and telling the stories of the Southern Appalachian Mountains. He now performs throughout the United States, including frequent appearances in the long-running country music and comedy show, *Hee Haw*, and the Nashville-based Grand Ole Opry. David has also toured India, Thailand, Bolivia, Colombia, and Africa for the United States government, introducing world audiences to the traditional music, dance, and tales of the Southern Appalachians. He has produced two storytelling albums with companion cassettes, and he is the performing host of the *American Storytelling Series*, videocassettes of storytelling performances. David also performs *From Here to Kingdom Come*, one man's mountain adventure that retraces the highlights of his eighteen-year search for songs and stories, and *Banjo Reb and the Blue Ghost*, a two-man musical play of the Civil War. As a leader in America's storytelling revival, David has served as a member of the Board of Directors of the National Association for the Preservation and Perpetuation of Storytelling. He lives in Fairview, North Carolina,

near Asheville, with his wife, Ginny, and their two children, Zeb and Sara
Jane.

Recordings

The Hairy Man and Other Wild Stories. Cassette and album. High Windy
    Audio. 1981.
Tailybone and Other Strange Stories. Cassette and album. High Windy
    Audio. 1985.

Videos

Barney McCabe. American Storytelling Series, Volume Five. Story-Tel
    Enterprises and H. W. Wilson Co. 1986.

DOC McCONNELL
Scenic Drive
Rogersville, TN 37857

A native of Tennessee, Doc McConnell grew up in Tucker's Knob listening
to stories in his family's cabin home and around the potbellied stove at John
Mauk's General Store. Today, Doc travels throughout the United States telling
stories—sharing many of the old tales he heard as a child. He also conducts
workshops on the storytelling art, and when asked, will perform his highly
popular Doc McConnell's Old-Time Medicine Show. As an early leader in the
national storytelling revival, Doc was a charter member of the Board of Directors of the National Association for the Preservation and Perpetuation of
Storytelling and has been a prime mover in the development of the organization and its programs. He has produced two audiocassettes. In addition to
performing professionally, Doc also promotes Rogersville, Tennessee, and surrounding Hawkins County—including his much-loved Tucker's Knob—as director of the Hawkins County Chamber of Commerce. Doc and his wife,
Virginia, and daughter, Hannah, also a storyteller, live in Rogersville.

Recordings

Spinning More Magic. Cassette. 1987.
Where's Tucker's Knob? Cassette. 1987.

WADDIE MITCHELL
Lee-Jiggs Waysack
Elko, NE 89801

Waddie Mitchell is a professional cowboy, and since 1985, he has managed
the Stake Ranch, located in an isolated Nevada community just twenty-two
miles from Elko. For as long as he can remember, Waddie has heard, and told,
stories—usually long, narrative story-poems of a cowboy's life on the range.
And in 1979, with his reputation as a storyteller beginning to grow, Waddie

was invited to tell his stories-in-verse at a folk festival in Elko. Since that first public concert, Waddie has performed—both the classic old poems of old and new lines he has penned himself—at festivals and cowboy gatherings throughout the United States. He is probably best known, however, as one of the founders and ardent supporters of the highly respected Cowboy Poetry Gathering, a convention of cowboy poets from throughout the West held annually in Elko. Waddie has also produced a book, a videocassette, and an audiocassette of cowboy poems. Together with his wife, Tootie, and their five children, Waddie makes his home in Jiggs, Nevada.

Recordings
Cowboy Verse. Cassette. 1985.

Books
Waddie Mitchell's Christmas Poems. Peregrine Smith. 1987.

Videos
Cowboy Poetry with Waddie Mitchell. BYU Productions. 1987.

JAY O'CALLAHAN
P.O. Box 1054
Marshfield, MA 02050

Once an aspiring novelist, Jay O'Callahan gave up writing in 1978 to create and tell stories—a decision that launched one of America's foremost storytelling careers. Since then, he has created and told stories for audiences throughout the United States, Canada, Europe, and Africa. Not content with the more traditional forums for storytelling performance, Jay has also directed his talents toward the ever-expanding perimeters of storytelling by producing and performing the critically acclaimed *Village Heroes,* a one-man show that brings to the traditional theater audience man's oldest art. He has also performed his stories with the symphony orchestras of Boston, Detroit, and Indianapolis. During his career as a storyteller, Jay has produced numerous albums, audiocassettes, and videocassettes—including his award-winning *Jay O'Callahan: A Master Class in Storytelling.* As a former member of the Board of Directors of the National Association for the Preservation and Perpetuation of Storytelling, Jay has been a leader in the movement to revive storytelling in America. Jay lives in Marshfield, Massachusetts, with his wife, Linda, and children, Ted and Laura, in a 300-year-old house near the marshes.

Recordings
Earth Stories. Cassette and album. Artana Productions. 1984.
The Golden Drum. Cassette. Artana Productions. 1984.
The Herring Shed. Cassette and album. Artana Productions. 1983.

The Little Dragon and Other Stories. Cassette and album. Weston Woods. 1982.

Little Heroes. Cassette. Artana Productions. 1985.

The Minister of Others Affairs. Cassette. Artana Productions. 1984.

Mostly Scary. Cassette. Artana Productions. 1987.

Petrukian. Cassette. Artana Productions. 1986.

Raspberries. Cassette and album. Artana Productions. 1983.

The Strait of Magellan. Cassette. Artana Productions. 1985.

Village Heroes. Double cassette. Artana Productions. 1986.

Videos

Dodge City. American Storytelling Series, Volume Six. Story-Tel Enterprises and H. W. Wilson Co. 1986.

Herman and Marguerite. Vineyard Video. 1986.

The Little Dragon. Family Circle Storyland Theatre Series, Volume Three. Paperback Video Publishing. 1987.

A Master Class in Storytelling. Vineyard Video. 1984.

New Year's Eve. Family Circle Storyland Theatre Series, Volume Two. Paperback Video Publishing. 1987.

Orange Cheeks. Vineyard Video. 1984.

Six Stories About Little Heroes. Vineyard Video. 1986.

Superbowl Sundae. Family Circle Storyland Theatre Series, Volume Four. Paperback Video Publishing. 1987.

MAGGI PEIRCE
544 Washington Street
Fairhaven, MA 02719

Though she has lived in America since 1964, storyteller Maggi Peirce was born in Belfast, Ireland, and as a child, grew up hearing the old tales and ballads of her homeland. During her early years in the United States, Maggi became well known and respected as a singer of the ballads of her native Ireland. But in 1972, Maggi, quite by accident, rediscovered the wealth of stories in her life, and since that time, she has both sung the songs and told the tales of her Irish homeland for audiences all through the United States. Maggi has produced several audio- and videocassettes and is the author of *Keep the Kettle Boiling*—a collection of reminiscences, songs, and rhymes of her Ulster childhood. She serves as director of the Tryworks Coffeehouse in New Bedford, Massachusetts, and lives in nearby Fairhaven with her husband, Ken.

Recordings

Cream of the Crop. Cassette. Miracle Records. 1985.

Maggie Peirce Live. Cassette. Yellow Moon Press. 1982.

An Ulster Christmas. Cassette. Yellow Moon Press. 1986.

Books

Keep the Kettle Boiling. Appletree Press. 1983.

Videos

Why the Dog Has a Cold, Wet Nose. American Storytelling Series, Volume One. Story-Tel Enterprises and H. W. Wilson Co. 1986.

LEE PENNINGTON
11905 Lilac Way
Middletown, KY 40243

A native of Kentucky, Lee Pennington teaches English and creative writing at Jefferson Community College in Louisville. But during his free time, he is a writer, poet, folksinger—and storyteller. He has authored eleven books, mostly collections of poetry, and has had over one thousand poems, short stories, and articles published in more than two hundred publications. In 1977, Lee was nominated for the Pulitzer Prize for poetry for his book, *I Knew a Woman,* and four years later he was named poet laureate of Kentucky. In 1974, Lee was invited to the second annual National Storytelling Festival to sing the ballads and tell the tales of his Southern mountain homeland, and since, he has become a leader in the national revival of storytelling. He was a charter member of the Board of Directors of the National Association for the Preservation and Perpetuation of Storytelling, and in 1975, he founded the Corn Island Storytelling Festival in Louisville—America's second festival devoted exclusively to the storytelling art. Eight years later, Lee helped organize the Louisville-based International Order of E.A.R.S.—dedicated to promoting the preservation of the storytelling art. Lee lives in Middletown, Kentucky, with his wife, Joy, in a restored 1850s tavern, and devotes much of his time to performing the songs, stories, and poems of Southern Appalachia.

GAYLE ROSS
Route 3, Box 215-B
Fredericksburg, TX 78624

Though she has a rich and varied repertoire of stories from throughout the world, storyteller Gayle Ross is perhaps best known for recounting the history and legends of the Cherokee Indians. Gayle is the direct descendant of John Ross, who for forty years was the principal chief of the Cherokee Indian Nation, and as a child, she grew up with her Cherokee grandmother who often told her stories. From her, Gayle developed an appreciation of the Native American traditions. In 1978, Gayle attended the National Storytelling Festival, and the experience rekindled in her a desire to share the tales she heard as a child. Today, Gayle travels throughout the United States telling stories and conducting workshops—both alone and in tandem with Texas storyteller Elizabeth Ellis as The Twelve Moons Storytellers. She has also produced an audio-

and videocassette. Gayle lives in Fredericksburg, Texas, with her husband, Reid Holt, and their two children.

Recordings

To This Day: Native American Stories. Cassette. 1986.

Videos

Mosquitos. American Storytelling Series, Volume One. Story-Tel Enterprises and H. W. Wilson Co. 1986.

LAURA SIMMS
814 Broadway
Third Floor
New York, NY 10003

Laura Simms, a professional storyteller living in New York City, has been telling stories since 1968. A noted storytelling scholar and teacher, she has performed and conducted workshops throughout the United States, Canada, and the South Pacific. For eight years, she has taught her highly respected Storytelling Residency—a full week of intensive storytelling study held each year in August. Laura is a leader in the revival of storytelling in the United States, and for seven years, served as a member of the Board of Directors of the National Association for the Preservation and Perpetuation of Storytelling. As a board member, she helped to expand the vision and role of NAPPS as America's foremost storytelling organization by serving as an artistic director of the National Storytelling Festival and being an early advocate for the National Storytelling Institute and the National Congress on Storytelling. Laura founded the Storytelling Center of Oneonta at Oneonta, New York, in 1977, and in 1985, she cofounded the New York City Storytelling Center. She has produced numerous albums, audio- and videocassettes, and articles on the storytelling art. Laura lives in New York City where she continues to perform, teach, write, and record.

Recordings

Fairy Tales for Adults. Cassette. Shambhala Music. 1988.
An Incredible Journey. Cassette. A Gentle Wind. 1981.
Just Right for Kids. Cassette and album. Kids' Records. 1984.
Moon on Fire. Cassette. Yellow Moon Press. 1987.
Stories: Old as the World, Fresh as the Rain. Cassette and album. Weston Woods. 1981.
There's a Horse in My Pocket. Cassette. Kids' Records. 1987.

Videos

Donkey and Goose. Family Circle Storyland Theatre Series, Volume One. Paperback Video Publishing. 1987.

The King of Togo Togo. Family Circle Storyland Theatre Series, Volume Two. Paperback Video Publishing. 1987.

The Magic Princess. Family Circle Storyland Theatre Series, Volume Four. Paperback Video Publishing. 1987.

Moon and Otter. Family Circle Storyland Theatre Series, Volume Four. Paperback Video Publishing. 1987.

The Woodcutter. American Storytelling Series, Volume Three. Story-Tel Enterprises and H. W. Wilson Co. 1986.

The Wooden Box. Family Circle Storyland Theatre Series, Volume Three. Paperback Video Publishing. 1987.

MARY CARTER SMITH
P.O. Box 11484
Baltimore, MD 21239

In 1973, Mary Carter Smith ended her thirty-one-year career as a teacher and librarian in the inner-city schools of Baltimore, Maryland, but she didn't retire. Instead, she launched a new career as a professional storyteller—singing the songs and telling the stories of Mother Africa, many she heard as a child. It's a message she lives daily, telling her stories to audiences—from festivals and conferences to hospitals and prisons—throughout America and the world. Long recognized as a humanitarian in her Baltimore community, Mary helped found Big Sisters–Little Sisters, a part of Big Brothers–Big Sisters of Central Maryland, and Big Sisters International, now merged with Big Brothers–Big Sisters of America. She was also a founding member of Baltimore's Arena Players, the longest continuously active black amateur theater group in America. In 1983, Philadelphia storyteller Linda Goss joined Mary in founding the annual National Festival of Black Storytelling, and in the same year, Mayor Donald Schaefer proclaimed Mary the Official Griot of Baltimore. Mary has produced several audio- and videocassettes, has authored three books—including *Heart to Heart,* a collection of her poems—and for the past eleven years, has produced an hour-long weekly program of her stories and songs on WEAA-Radio at Morgan State University in Baltimore, where she continues to live.

Recordings

Mary Carter Smith. Cassette. 1982.

Videos

Cindy Ellie. American Storytelling Series, Volume Five. Story-Tel Enterprises and H. W. Wilson Co. 1986.

Mary Carter Smith. Kartes Video Communications. 1986.

ED STIVENDER
Clancy Agency
5138 Whitehall Drive
Clifton Heights, PA 19018

Since 1976, Ed Stivender has performed his own brand of storytelling to audiences all through the United States—combining story, song, and participatory theater to tell a diverse collection of stories. While Ed is perhaps best known for his renditions of ancient folk and fairy tales—usually fractured and always speckled with bits and pieces of humor and wit—his religious comedy serves up his favorite stories and helps to "break down the barriers that keep people from hearing and understanding more about religion." In addition, he has been host of *The Christophers' Story Laboratory,* a television series produced for children. Ed has been a major force in the national reawakening of interest in storytelling, and through his own unique storytelling style, he has helped to expand the definition and role of storytelling in the modern world. Since 1984, he has been a member of the Board of Directors of the National Association for the Preservation and Perpetuation of Storytelling and has produced several audio- and videocassettes. Ed continues to live in Philadelphia, where he was born and grew up.

Recordings

Ed Stivender Live. Cassette. 1983.
The Juggler of Notre Dame. Cassette. 1986.
Some of My Best Friends Are Kids. Cassette. 1987.
The Sound Track: An Evening with Ed Stivender at Friends General Conference. Cassette. 1987.

Videos

The Christophers' Story Laboratory. The Christophers. 1985.
An Evening with Ed Stivender at Friends General Conference. ECCE Video. 1987.
Hansel and Gretel. American Storytelling Series, Volume Six. Story-Tel Enterprises and H. W. Wilson Co. 1986.

GIOIA TIMPANELLI
Box 217
Village Station
New York, NY 10014

One of America's foremost storytellers, Gioia Timpanelli began her career as a literature teacher. In 1964, however, her life took a creative turn when she began teaching on New York City's educational television station. During her eleven-year broadcasting career, she created, wrote, produced, and presented one program each week, ultimately completing seven different series. During one of the seven, *Stories from My House*, Gioia began to tell tales, and for her early work in the art, she won two Emmy citations—one for the program's "compelling storytelling format." When Gioia concluded her television career in 1975, she devoted all of her energies to storytelling, and today, she is considered a master storyteller—widely respected as both a scholar and teacher of the ageless art. She has performed and taught at universities, museums, art galleries, festivals, and conferences throughout the United States, and she is also known for her storytelling performances in collaboration with respected masters of other art forms—especially in the world of poetry and letters with Robert Bly, James Hillman, Joseph Campbell, Nor Hall, and Gary Snyder. Gioia is credited with establishing storytelling as an ongoing offering at Artpark, a respected cultural arts center located in the Niagara River gorge in New York State, and in 1983, she became one of the cofounders of the New York City Storytelling Center. Most recently, Gioia was honored by the Women's National Book Association as one of seventy women "who have made a difference in bringing books to the public." She is the author of *Tales from the Roof of the World*, a book of Tibetan stories. Gioia lives in the Hudson River Valley where she continues to write, teach, and perform.

Books

Tales from the Roof of the World. Viking. 1984.

JACKIE TORRENCE
Traditional Artists
2518 Southeast 17th Avenue
Portland, OR 97202

While Jackie Torrence was growing up in the sparse farm settlement of Second Creek in North Carolina, she was surrounded by a family who told stories—often the tales of Uncle Remus, stories representing the richness of her black tradition. In 1972, Jackie, then a librarian, accidentally tapped within herself an undiscovered reservoir of storytelling talent, and within four years, she was traveling throughout the United States performing a mixed repertoire of folktales, legends, and yarns. Jackie, affectionately known as The Story Lady, has received international acclaim as one of America's foremost storytellers, and as a leader in the national storytelling revival, she has served on the Board of Directors of the National Association for the Preservation and Perpetuation of Storytelling. Jackie has hosted two television storytelling series and produced numerous albums and audiocassettes. She lives in Granite Quarry, North Carolina, with her daughter, Lori.

Recordings

Brer Rabbit Stories. Cassette and album. Weston Woods. 1984.
Country Characters. Cassette and album. Earwig Music. 1986.

Legends from the Black Tradition. Cassette and album. Weston Woods. 1982.

Mountain Magic I, The Jack Tales, Volume One. Cassette and album. Earwig Music. 1984.

Mountain Magic II, The Jack Tales, Volume Two. Cassette and album. Earwig Music. 1984.

The Story Lady. Cassette and album. Weston Woods. 1982.

Tales for Scary Times. Cassette and album. Earwig Music. 1985.

KATHRYN WINDHAM
2004 Royal Street
Selma, AL 36701

Since *something* she called Jeffrey came to live with her family in their Selma, Alabama, home, Kathryn Windham has been collecting and writing stories of the supernatural. During the past twenty-two years, she has written fourteen books—six of which are collections of ghost tales, including 13 *Alabama Ghosts and Jeffrey,* her first, and volumes of stories about favorite ghosts from Mississippi, Georgia, Tennessee, and all through the South. While she has distinguished herself as an author, Kathryn is known equally as a storyteller who, since 1974, has recounted many of the tales she has collected throughout the United States. An ardent supporter of the revival of storytelling in America, Kathryn was the first member of the National Association for the Preservation and Perpetuation of Storytelling and served as a charter member of its Board of Directors. Kathryn has produced numerous audiocassettes, has often been heard on National Public Radio, and has also helped found the Alabama Tale-Tellin' Festival in her hometown of Selma.

Recordings

Kathryn Windham Tells Ghost Stories, Volume One. Cassette. Title Books. 1977.

Kathryn Windham Tells Ghost Stories, Volume Two. Cassette. Title Books. 1979.

Kathryn Windham Tells Ghost Stories, Volume Three. Cassette. Title Books. 1979.

Kathryn Windham Tells Ghost Stories, Volume Four. Cassette. Title Books. 1979.

Kathryn Windham Tells Ghost Stories, Volume Five. Cassette. Title Books. 1983.

Recollections by Kathryn Tucker Windham. Cassette. WUAL Public Radio. 1986.

Books

Alabama: One Big Front Porch. Jeffrey Enterprises. 1987.

Count Those Buzzards. Stamp Those Gray Mules. Jeffrey Enterprises. 1986.

The Ghost in the Sloss Furnaces. Birmingham Historical Society. 1987.
Jeffrey Introduces 13 More Southern Ghosts. University of Alabama Press.
   1988.
Jeffrey's Latest 13: More Alabama Ghosts. University of Alabama Press.
   1987.
A Serigamy of Stories. University Press of Mississippi. 1988.
13 Alabama Ghosts and Jeffrey. University of Alabama Press. 1987.
13 Georgia Ghosts and Jeffrey. University of Alabama Press. 1987.
13 Mississippi Ghosts and Jeffrey. University of Alabama Press. 1988.
13 Tennessee Ghosts and Jeffrey. University of Alabama Press. 1988.

DIANE WOLKSTEIN
10 Patchin Place
New York, NY 10011

Since 1967, Diane Wolkstein has told stories each summer at the Hans
Christian Andersen statue in New York City's Central Park and, throughout
her twenty-one-year career as a storyteller, has collected and told a wealth of
tales from around the world. A major force in America's reawakening of interest in the storytelling art, Diane performs and conducts workshops throughout
America and the world and has taught the art and technique of storytelling at
the Bank Street College of Education in New York City for eighteen years. In
1977, Diane helped found the National Conference on Storytelling—sponsored annually by the National Association for the Preservation and Perpetuation of Storytelling. She is also a founding member of the New York City
Storytelling Center, and for five years has served as a director. A cofounder of
Cloudstone, a recording company in Montvale, New Jersey, Diane has produced numerous audio- and videocassettes. In addition to performing and
teaching storytelling, Diane is the author of twelve books of stories—including
The Magic Orange Tree and Other Haitian Folktales, which is considered a storytelling classic, and *Inanna, Queen of Heaven and Earth.* Diane lives with her
daughter, Rachel, in a garden apartment in New York City and continues to
teach, perform, write, and record stories.

Recordings
The Banza. Cassette. Listening Library. 1988.
The Cool Ride in the Sky. Album and cassette. Miller-Brody. 1975.
Diane Tells Fairy Tales of Estonia. Cassette. Cloudstone. 1988.
Diane Wolkstein Tells California Fairy Tales. Cassette. Spoken Arts. 1985.
Diane Wolkstein Tells Eskimo Stories. Album and cassette. Spoken Arts.
   1985.
The Epic of Inanna. Cassette. Cloudstone. 1986.
Hans Christian Andersen in Central Park. Cassette and album. Weston
   Woods. 1981.
Hasidic Stories: Tales of the Heart. Cassette. Cloudstone. 1988.

Psyche and Eros. Cassette. Cloudstone. 1984.
Romping. Cassette. Cloudstone. 1986.
The Story of Joseph. Cassette. Cloudstone. 1986.
Tales of the Hopi Indians. Album and cassette. Spoken Arts. 1985.

Books

The Banza. Dial. 1980.
The Cool Ride in the Sky. Knopf. 1973.
8,000 Stones. Doubleday. 1972.
Inanna, Queen of Heaven and Earth. Harper & Row. 1983.
Lazy Stories. Seabury Press. 1976.
The Legend of Sleepy Hollow. Morrow. 1987.
The Magic Orange Tree and Other Haitian Folktales. Schocken Books. 1980.
The Magic Wings. E. P. Dutton. 1983.
The Red Lion. T. Y. Crowell. 1977.
Squirrel's Song. Knopf. 1975.
The Visit. Pantheon. 1974.
White Wave. T. Y. Crowell. 1979.

Videos

INANNA. Cloudstone Productions. 1988.
Stories in the Park. Cloudstone Productions. 1988.
White Wave. American Storytelling Series, Volume Two. Story-Tel Enterprises and H. W. Wilson Co. 1986.

More of America's Favorite Storytellers

Since the first National Storytelling Festival in 1973, over one hundred different storytellers have appeared at the annual gathering. Together, they bring to this national forum a spectrum of America's rich and varied storytelling heritage. An additional sampling of America's favorite storytellers ranges from a Scottish weaver and a blustering stump orator to a storytelling theater, a Celtic harper, and a traveling herbalist. They each have been showcased at the National Storytelling Festival and, as professional storytellers, are available to perform and conduct workshops on the storytelling art.

Augusta Baker

Augusta, coauthor of *Storytelling: Art and Technique,* is a veteran of a half century of storytelling performance and teaching—first as coordinator of children's books and storytelling at the New York Public Library and now as storyteller-in-residence at the University of South Carolina at Columbia. *Augusta Baker, 830 Armour Street, Columbia, SC 29203.*

Patrick Ball

A respected Celtic harper, Patrick blends the power and delicacy of the brass-strung Celtic harp with the wit and enchantment of folktales he has collected throughout Ireland, Scotland, England, and the mountains of Appalachia. *Patrick Ball, P.O. Box 551, Bodega Bay, CA 94923.*

John Basinger

John Basinger and Bernard Bragg, longtime associates of the National Theatre of the Deaf, perform a wealth of artfully prepared stories, fables, and poems—all offered with a special expressiveness and utilizing sign language. *John Basinger, 133 Lincoln Street, Middletown, CT 06457.*

Carol Birch

Carol, a librarian, retells folktales and literary tales from cultures throughout the world—combining facial expressions, speaking rhythm, and voice timbre to create a dramatic, effective style. *Carol Birch, 30 Blueberry Hill Road, Weston, CT 06883.*

Milbre Burch

Milbre combines her background in mime and her love of language to create and tell stories—blending words and movement to perform original monologues, folktales, and stories from around the world. *Milbre Burch, P.O. Box 1763, Monrovia, CA 91016.*

Pleasant deSpain

A former teacher, Pleasant tells folktales, myths, and legends, but he is equally known as the author of *Pleasant Journeys*—two volumes of stories collected and retold from around the world. *Pleasant deSpain, P.O. Box 85785, Seattle, WA 98145.*

Doug Elliott

Doug is a traveling herbalist who tells colorful, humorous stories and nature tales—intertwining his own experiences in the natural world with traditional lore, song, and mythology. *Doug Elliott, Route 1, Box 388, Union Mills, NC 28167.*

Heather Forest

Heather, an accomplished composer and dancer, performs traditional tales and original story-songs—blending music, movement, poetry, and the sung and spoken word in a unique minstrel style. *Heather Forest, P.O. Box 354, Huntington, NY 11743.*

Jackson Gillman

A respected pantomimist, Jackson uses his background in movement to perform stories ranging from the traditional tellings of Rudyard Kipling to irresistibly zany animal tales. *Jackson Gillman, 70 Morning Street, Portland, ME 04101.*

Linda Goss

Linda, a native of Tennessee who heard tales and stories of slave life from her grandfather, tells Afro-American, African, and international folktales. *Linda Goss, 6653 Sprague Street, Philadelphia, PA 19119.*

Ellin Greene

Ellin, coauthor of *Storytelling Art and Technique*, has been a storyteller in the library tradition for more than twenty-five years—telling literary fairy tales and folktales from all over the world. *Ellin Greene, 113 Chatham Lane, Point Pleasant, NJ 08742.*

Mary Hamilton

A former English teacher and children's librarian, Mary tells stories from a variety of world cultures—retelling them in a simple, straightforward style. *Mary Hamilton, P.O. Box 6244, Louisville, KY 40206.*

Henry Hatch

Henry is a traditional storyteller who shares folklore about real people and real events of "awhile ago" with a special emphasis on coastal Maine, his homeland. *Henry Hatch, Turtle Head, Islesboro, ME 04848.*

Joe Hayes

Though born in Pennsylvania, Joe moved with his family to the Southwest where he became charmed by the region's rich storytelling traditions, and today, he retells the Native American legends and Hispanic stories that he has collected there. *Joe Hayes, 626 Paseo De Peralta, Santa Fe, NM 87501.*

Vi Hilbert

Vi, an elder in the Skagit Indian tribe of western Washington, has sought to preserve her Lushootseed language, literature, and traditions, and through her efforts, she has discovered and begun to tell the myths and legends of her native people. *Vi Hilbert, 10832 Des Moines Way South, Seattle, WA 98168.*

Norman Kennedy

A weaver by trade, Norman is a traditional singer and storyteller who tells the stories and sings the songs he learned from his family and neighbors while growing up in his native Scotland. *Norman Kennedy, Kents Corner, Calais, VT 05648.*

Chuck Larkin

Chuck, who resembles a bombastic, blustering stump orator, recounts a lively repertoire of mountain yarns, tall tales, ghost stories, and other tales of the South. *Chuck Larkin, P.O. Box 54573, Atlanta, GA 30308.*

Gwenda LedBetter

A former teacher and librarian, Gwen is a twenty-five-year veteran of storytelling who continues to tell folktales, myths, legends, and literary tales from around the world. *Gwenda LedBetter, 55 Beaverbrook Road, Asheville, NC 28804.*

Syd Lieberman

Syd, a high school English teacher, has spent a lifetime collecting, preserving, and telling the stories of his Jewish tradition and especially the family tales of growing up in Chicago. *Syd Lieberman, 2522 Ashland Avenue, Evanston, IL 60201.*

Doug Lipman

Doug combines singing, folk music, and story games to tell a mixed repertoire of traditional and historical stories—including lively versions of tales he has created himself. *Doug Lipman, P.O. Box 441195, West Somerville, MA 02144.*

Jim May

Born on a dairy farm in rural Illinois, Jim tells the stories of his Midwestern rural background—the tales he has heard and collected at the horse-trading barns and general stores and around the dinner tables in his native McHenry County. *Jim May, P.O. Box 1012, Woodstock, IL 60098.*

Glenn Ohrlin

While he may be best known as a collector and performer of cowboy songs, Glen—a former buckaroo and rodeo circuit rider—is also a master raconteur and tells a passel of tall tales, delivering them in his classic deadpan style. *Glenn Ohrlin, Co-Media, P.O. Box 7690, Little Rock, AR 72217.*

Michael Parent

Michael, a Maine native of French-Canadian descent, is an accomplished storyteller and musician who performs his folk and original tales in both English and French and often with musical accompaniment. *Michael Parent, 709 Park Street, Charlottesville, VA 22901.*

Roadside Theatre

A traveling storytelling troupe, Roadside Theatre develops and produces a series of productions drawn from the stories of the Appalachian Mountains—performed by storytellers and musicians who were born, grew up, and now remain in this colorful region. *Roadside Theatre, P.O. Box 743, Whitesburg, KY 41858.*

Gamble Rogers

Formerly of the Serendipity Singers, Gamble is a professional musician and storyteller who travels throughout the United States performing an assortment of stories and songs—each speckled lavishly with humor. *Gamble Rogers, Blade Agency, P.O. Box 1556, Gainsville, FL 32602.*

Lynn Rubright

Lynn, a former teacher and now a storytelling consultant, is an energetic storyteller who recounts tall tales, fairy tales, myths, and true stories—often involving the audience in singing, chanting, and dancing. *Lynn Rubright, 340 East Jefferson Avenue, Kirkwood, MO 63122.*

Steve Sanfield

Steve, an author and poet, re-creates and tells the Jewish tales and Hasidic legends he first heard as a child from his Lithuanian grandfather—a blend of folk wisdom and sophisticated wit. *Steve Sanfield, 22000 Lost River Road, Nevada City, CA 95959.*

Nancy Schimmel

Nancy, the author of *Just Enough to Make a Story*, tells traditional and original tales from around the world—often using audience participation in songs, stories, or simple folk crafts. *Nancy Schimmel, 1639 Channing Way, Berkeley, CA 94703.*

Peninnah Schram

Peninnah learned the proverbs and folktales of the rich Jewish tradition from her mother, and today, Peninnah recounts these ancient Jewish stories. *Peninnah Schram, 525 West End Avenue, Apartment 8C, New York, NY 10024.*

Jon Spelman

Jon, a former actor, performs American literary stories and original retellings of folktales, epics, and fairy tales, but he is equally known as the creator and performing host of *Three Stories Tall*, a successful children's television storytelling series in Washington, D.C. *Jon Spelman, 1526 Buchanan Street NW, Washington, DC 20011.*

Bibliography

This bibliography offers a sampling of the growing selection of storytelling resources—including both books on storytelling and collections of stories to tell. They can be obtained at your local bookstore or community library or, in some cases, through the *National Catalog of Storytelling*—a publication of the National Association for the Preservation and Perpetuation of Storytelling.

Books on Storytelling and Stories

American Negro Folk Tales. Fawcett, 1956. 378 pp.

An extensive collection of short tales, written as told, for the experienced storyteller, the scholar, or the curious with a special interest in the black folktale.

Arthur, Stephen, and Julia Arthur. *Your Life and Times: How to Put a Life Story on Tape.* Heritage Tree Press, 1986. 50 pp.

A simple and useful handbook for recording one's own family heritage. Includes questions to jog the memory.

Baker, Augusta, and Ellin Greene. *Storytelling: Art and Technique.* Bowker, 1977. 142 pp.

A comprehensive aid for all storytellers—including how to select, prepare, and present stories. Extensive bibliography includes collections and specific stories for various age groups. Complete index.

Barton, Bob. *Tell Me Another: Storytelling and Reading Aloud at Home, at School, and in the Community.* Heinemann, 1986. 158 pp.

An informal approach for the beginning or experienced storyteller—including solid suggestions for choosing and using stories, equally helpful hints on reading aloud, and an assortment of songs, games, and chants. Extensive bibliographies and index.

Bauer, Caroline Feller. *Handbook for Storytellers.* American Library Association, 1977. 381 pp.

A handbook for creating a variety of storytelling programs—using music, film presentations, puppets, and even recipes for passing out eatables. Includes an extensive list of fully annotated stories, arranged by subjects and program objectives.

Bettelheim, Bruno. *The Uses of Enchantment: The Meaning and Importance of Fairy Tales.* Knopf, 1976. 328 pp.
A full discussion of the role of the fairy tale in helping children find meaning in life. Includes a detailed analysis of the symbolic meaning of nine very familiar folktales.

Breneman, Lucille, and Bren Breneman. *Once Upon a Time: A Storytelling Handbook.* Nelson Hall, 1983. 192 pp.
Straightforward advice for the beginning storyteller from a class taught by the authors at the University of Hawaii. A fully annotated bibliography of stories to tell.

Campbell, Joseph. *Myths to Live By.* Viking, 1972. 304 pp.
A discussion of the importance and meaning of myths in our lives.

A Celebration of American Family Folklore, edited by Steven J. Zeitlin, Amy J. Kotkin, and Holly Cutting Baker. Pantheon, 1982. 291 pp.
A volume that truly celebrates family folklore, emphasizing the importance of mining our family heritage. Includes examples of family stories and an in-depth study of five families and their folklore.

Cook, Elizabeth. *The Ordinary and the Fabulous: An Introduction to Myths, Legends, and Fairy Tales for Teachers and Storytellers.* Cambridge University Press, 1969. 152 pp.
Discussions of the importance and value of fairy tales in children's lives, suggestions for a variety of tales for various ages, and advice on story presentation. Includes an extensive, fully annotated list of storytelling sources. Complete index.

Dorson, Richard. *America in Legends.* Pantheon, 1973. 336 pp.
A cultural history of America through folklore—divided into four historical periods. Includes discussions of characteristic folklore of each era, with brief illustrative examples.

Eastman, Mary. *Index to Fairy Tales, Myths, and Legends.* 1926. 610 pp. Supplement I, 1937. 566 pp. Supplement II, 1952. 370 pp.
The pioneer source for finding stories known only by bits and pieces. Stories listed by title with references to similar tales under different titles. Includes index by geography, race, subject, and motif.

Funk and Wagnalls Standard Dictionary of Folklore, Mythology, and Legends, edited by Maria Leach. 1972, 1950, 1949. 1,236 pp.

An encyclopedia of folklore with an extensive index to countries, regions, cultures and culture areas, peoples, tribes, and ethnic groups.

Harrell, John. *The Man on a Dolphin: The Storyteller and His Tales.* York House, 1983. 157 pp.
A discussion of storytelling, the storyteller, and the stories, with tales for illustration. Includes sources.

———. *A Storyteller's Omnibus.* York House, 1985. 80 pp.
A slim volume in two parts—one devoted to a discussion of teaching tales, fables, and parables, with illustrations, and one offering several varied tales well chosen for storytelling.

Iarusso, Marilyn Berg. *Stories: A List of Stories to Tell and to Read Aloud.* New York Public Library, 1977. 64 pp.
An extensive list of stories, alphabetically by title. Includes four separate indexes, making the stories accessible by geographical area, heroes, festivals or holidays, and other special needs.

Livo, Norma, and Sandra A. Rietz. *Storytelling: Process and Practice.* Libraries Unlimited, 1986. 462 pp.
A complete storytelling manual discussing the functions of the art and the dynamics of working with audiences of all ages.

Luthi, Max. *Once Upon a Time: On the Nature of Fairy Tales.* Indiana University Press, 1976. 179 pp.
Eleven lectures by a Jungian folklorist on the meaning and form of the fairy tale.

MacDonald, Margaret Read. *The Storyteller's Sourcebook.* Gale, 1982. 818 pp.
Indexes of 556 folktale collections and 389 picture books by motif, tale title, subject, ethnic group, or geographical region. Very useful in finding that story you only remember bits of. An up-to-date replacement for the Eastman indexes.

———. *Twenty Tellable Tales.* Wilson, 1986. 220 pp.
Abbreviated versions of folktales for the beginning storyteller, including sources and suggestions for telling each tale.

Maguire, Jack. *Creative Storytelling: Choosing, Inventing, and Sharing Tales for Children.* McGraw-Hill, 1985. 187 pp.
A step-by-step guide to sources and types of stories, gearing them to various age groups and interests, and techniques for learning and adapting stories.

Opie, Ione, and Peter Opie. *The Classic Fairy Tales.* Oxford University Press, 1974. 255 pp.
Twenty-four classic tales as they first appeared in English, complete with original illustrations and each prefaced by a discussion of the source. Includes an extensive bibliography and index.

Pellowski, Anne. *The Story Vine: A Source Book of Unusual and Easy-to-Tell Stories from Around the World.* Macmillan, 1984. 116 pp.
String stories, picture drawing and sand stories, tales with dolls or figurines, finger-play stories, riddling stories, and tales using musical instruments—all from around the world. Ample, clear instructions for each activity, a bibliography for each type of tale, and a list of sources.

————. *The World of Storytelling.* Bowker, 1977. 296 pp.
A comprehensive history of the practice of storytelling in all parts of the world, all forms and locations, and all formats. Includes a multilingual dictionary of storytelling terms, notes on sources, and an extensive bibliography and index.

Ross, Ramon Royal. *The Storyteller.* Viking, 1972. 226 pp.
Sound advice on choosing, learning, and presenting stories. Includes annotated bibliographies.

Sawyer, Ruth. *The Way of the Storyteller.* Viking, 1942, 1962. 360 pp.
An inspirational discussion of storytelling techniques by a legendary storyteller. Includes eleven stories from Sawyer's repertoire, all fairly long and more appropriate for the advanced teller.

Schimmel, Nancy. *Just Enough to Make a Story: A Sourcebook for Storytelling.* Sister's Choice Press, 1972, 1982. 55 pp.
Practical basics for the beginner, with an assortment of simple stories, ways to use stories in programs, and a fully annotated list of tales with active heroines. Complete index.

Shedlock, Marie. *The Art of the Story-Teller.* 1915, 1936, Dover, 1951. 291 pp.
A classic book on storytelling that offers solid advice about this changeless art from a legendary, turn-of-the-century teller. Includes eighteen stories from her repertoire.

Trelease, Jim. *The Read-Aloud Handbook.* Penguin, 1982. 217 pp.
Wise advice on introducing children to literature by reading aloud. Includes an excellent annotated list of more than 300 books.

Collections

Abrahams, Roger. *African Folktales*. Pantheon, 1983. 384 pp.
Some 100 traditional stories of Africa.

———. *Afro-American Folktales*. Pantheon, 1985. 327 pp.
Stories from the black traditions of the New World, from earthy comedy to tales of origins. Includes an introduction to each section, extensive notes, and an index by story type.

Afanas'ev, Alexander. *Russian Fairy Tales*. Pantheon, 1945, 1973. 661 pp.
A comprehensive collection of the tales of Afanas'ev, the Russian equivalent of the Grimm brothers. Includes a history of the Russian folktale and a title and subject index.

American Indian Myths and Legends, selected and edited by Richard Erodes and Simon Ortiz. Pantheon, 1984. 527 pp.
One hundred and sixty-six varied legends, each prefaced by information on the tellers and their cultural heritage.

Andersen, Hans Christian. *Eighty Fairy Tales*. Pantheon, 1976. 483 pp.
A solid translation of many of Andersen's tales—both the familiar and the obscure. Includes a commentary and a title index.

Asbjornsen, Peter Christen, and Jorgen Moe. *Norwegian Folktales*. Viking, 1960. 189 pp.
Thirty-five varied tales—some poking fun at human foibles, some magical, some adventurous. Length from short to medium.

Botkin, B. A. *A Treasury of American Folklore*. Crown, 1944. 934 pp.
A complete collection of American folklore. Includes both a title and a subject index.

———. *A Treasury of Southern Folklore*. Crown, 1949. 776 pp.
Some 400 tales mined from Southern folklore. Includes an index by title, place, and subject.

Briggs, Katherine. *British Folktales*. Pantheon, 1970. 315 pp.
A solid introduction to the British folktale—including some seventy-five stories, short to long, ranging from nursery tales to Celtic legends.

Calvino, Italo. *Italian Folktales*. Pantheon, 1956. 763 pp.
Two hundred tales of the Italian tradition. Includes extensive notes, a bibliography, and an introduction to Italian folklore.

Chase, Richard. *American Folk Tales and Songs*. Dover, 1956, 1971. 239 pp.
Stories, ballads, songs, and games from the oral tradition of the Appalachian Mountains and other regions of the country. An adult collection. Includes notes and sources for each selection.

————. *Grandfather Tales*. Houghton Mifflin, 1948. 239 pp.
Twenty-five tales collected in the mountains of North Carolina and Virginia. Stories varied in length, excellent for telling.

————. *Jack Tales*. Houghton Mifflin, 1944. 201 pp.
Eighteen traditional European folktales about Jack collected in the mountains of North Carolina and Virginia. Stories varied in length and eminently tellable.

Cole, Joanna. *Best-Loved Folktales of the World*. Doubleday, 1982. 792 pp.
Two hundred tales chosen from the cream of world folklore, arranged by geographical area and indexed by title, appropriate age of the audience, and broad subject or type categories.

Colum, Padraic. *Orpheus: Myths of the World*. Macmillan, 1930. 327 pp.
A magnificent collection of the world's great myths, culled from the rich mythologies of seventeen cultures. Full index.

Courlander, Howard. *Cow Tail Switch and Other Ethiopian Stories*. Holt, 1947, 143 pp.
Seventeen stories of varied length, some fairly sophisticated, with a strong sense of the African culture. Includes notes and a glossary.

————. *The Crest and the Hide and Other African Stories of Heroes, Chiefs, Bards, Hunters, Sorcerers, and Common People*. Coward McCann, 1982. 144 pp.
Twenty stories, short to medium length, from tribes of central and southern Africa—each emphasizing the values and life of the people. Includes notes on the stories.

————. *Fire on the Mountain and Other Ethiopian Stories*. Holt, Rinehart & Winston, 1950. 141 pp.
Twenty-four short tales from Ethiopia, each with a sophisticated message. Includes a detailed introduction to the country's storytelling traditions, notes on the stories, and pronunciation guide.

————. *Hat Shaking Dance and Other Tales from Ghana.* Harcourt, Brace, 1957. 115 pp.

Twenty-one brief stories from West Africa, mostly describing the tricks and sometimes the comeuppance of Anansi. Excellent for telling. Includes an introduction to the Ashanti people, notes on Anansi stories, and sources of each tale.

————. *The People of the Short Blue Corn: Tales and Legends of the Hopi Indians.* Harcourt Brace Jovanovich, 1970. 189 pp.

Stories of magic, sorcery, trickery, and the origin of all things related by a man known for his respect for the origin and culture of his stories. Includes pronunciation guide, notes, and glossary.

————. *Terrapin's Pot of Sense.* Holt, 1957. 125 pp.

Thirty-one tales gathered from the black tradition in the rural areas of Alabama, New Jersey, and Michigan. Includes notes on sources and variations of the stories.

————. *A Treasury of African Folklore.* Crown, 1976. 618 pp.

A scholarly collection of a large variety of tales arranged by sources, for those who want to compare stories, find origins, or create a story from an original source.

DeSpain, Pleasant. *Pleasant Journeys.* The Writing Works, Inc., Mercer Island, Washington, 1979. 96 pp.

Two volumes, each with twenty-two familiar tales from around the world— all uniformly brief and adapted with deSpain's own imaginative style and twists of imagination.

Dorson, Richard. *Folktales Told Around the World.* University of Chicago Press, 1975. 622 pp.

Some 150 tales collected to illustrate the variety, style, and cultures represented by world folklore. A good source for non-European folktales. Extensive index.

Fillmore, Parker. *The Shepherd's Nosegay.* Harcourt, 1958. 192 pp.

Eighteen stories of humor, courage, kindness, trolls and devils, clever peasants, lads and lasses.

Finger, Charles. *Tales from Silver Lands.* Doubleday, 1924. 225 pp.

Nineteen stories from Latin America, medium to long in length. Includes a few good ghost stories.

Glassie, Henry. *Irish Folktales.* Pantheon, 1985. 376 pp.
One hundred and twenty-two tales of Ireland. Includes sources, bibliography, and an extensive introduction to the Irish folktale tradition.

Graves, Robert. *Greek Gods and Heroes.* Penguin, 1955. 160 pp.
A brief retelling of the stories of Greek mythology by this famed poet and classical scholar.

Grimm, Jacob, and Wilhelm Grimm. *Complete Grimm's Fairy Tales.* Pantheon, 1944, 1972. 863 pp.
More than 200 tales, both the familiar and the obscure, translated by Margaret Hunt. Includes an introduction on the traditions of folklore by Padraic Colum and a commentary on the Grimms by Joseph Campbell.

Hamilton, Edith. *Mythology.* Little, Brown, 1942. 497 pp.
An unequaled source for a literary retelling of most of the Greek and Roman myths. A full index.

Hamilton, Virginia. *The People Could Fly: American Black Folktales.* Knopf, 1985. 178 pp.
Brer Rabbit trickster tales, tall tales, stories of the supernatural, and tales of freedom retold in a rhythmic dialect that fits the mood of the tale without creating problems for the teller. Includes bibliography and notes.

Hyde-Chambers, Frederick, and Audrey Hyde-Chambers. *Tibetan Folktales.* Shambhala, 1981. 186 pp.
Twenty-six tales and legends from origins to modern-day living, reflecting the spiritual and humorous values of an ancient culture.

Jacobs, Joseph. *English Fairy Tales.* Putnam. 261 pp.
Forty-three stories—varied in length, subject matter, and age level—from one of the first collections of English folklore.

Lang, Andrew. *The Blue Fairy Book.* Dover, 1965. 390 pp.
A facsimile edition of the first of Lang's "color books" of fairy tales, first published in 1889. Thirty-seven stories, mostly very familiar.

Leach, Maria. *American Folktales and Legends.* World, 1958. 318 pp.
A large, colorfully illustrated book of tall tales, lore, legends, ghost stories, and other tales—each short and well constructed for telling.

Lester, Julius. *The Knee-High Man and Other Tales.* Dial, 1972. 32 pp.
Six short tales from black American folklore, with notes on each story. A fine collection of black tales for a young audience.

Minard, Rosemary. *Womenfolk and Fairy Tales*. Houghton Mifflin, 1975. 163 pp.
  Eighteen tales from a variety of cultures, unified by a strong female heroine in each. Includes sources.

Phelps, Ethel Johnston. *The Maid of the North: Feminist Folk Tales From Around the World*. Holt, Rinehart, & Winston, 1981. 174 pp.
  Twenty-one tales from the far corners of the earth, each with a spunky heroine. Includes an introduction and notes on sources.

————. *Tatterhood and Other Tales*. Feminist Press, 1978. 164 pp.
  Twenty-five tales—romantic, magical, and adventurous—with a resourceful and responsible female heroine. Includes notes on collecting tales and the discovery of these collected stories.

Randolph, Vance. *Pissing in the Snow and Other Ozark Stories*. University of Illinois Press, 1976. 153 pp.
  A collection of 101 short, bawdy tales collected in the Ozarks, probably the first such unexpurgated collection outside of the scholarly journals. Includes sources and bibliography.

Roberts, Moss. *Chinese Fairy Tales and Fantasies*. Pantheon, 1979. 256 pp.
  Some 100 tales from Confucian and Taoist traditions, ranging from very brief to medium length. Includes sources, notes on the tales, and index of titles.

Russell, William F. *Classics to Read Aloud to Your Children*. Crown, 1984. 312 pp.
  A collection of great stories, poems, and excerpts from novels and plays that spans centuries and styles. Includes introductions and pronunciation and vocabulary guides for each selection. Categorized by age groups.

————. *More Classics to Read Aloud to Your Children*. Crown, 1986. 264 pp.
  More selections from the world's greatest literature, categorized by age groups. Includes introductions and pronunciation and vocabulary guides for each selection.

Schwartz, Alvin. *Scary Stories to Tell in the Dark*. Lippincott, 1981. 111 pp.
  Twenty-nine tales, mostly very brief, ranging from the gruesome to the humorous, the purportedly true to the fantastic, and collected from American folklore. Sources and notes included.

Schwartz, Howard. *Elijah's Violin and Other Jewish Fairy Tales*. Harper, 1983. 302 pp.
A collection of thirty-six medium-length tales from sources all over the world—from the ancient and medieval to the more recent. Includes sources and glossary.

Shah, Idries. *World Tales*. Harcourt Brace Jovanovich, 1979. 258 pp.
Sixty-five stories not usually found in the major classic collections. Includes discussions of origin and parallel tales.

Singer, Isaac Bashevis. *Stories for Children*. Farrar, Straus and Giroux, 1984. 337 pp.
Fourteen stories of fools and tricksters.

————. *When Schlemiel Went to Warsaw and Other Stories*. Farrar, Straus and Giroux, 1968. 116 pp.
Eight tales, including stories of trickery and humor, parables, numbskull tales, and stories of devils and demons.

————. *Zlateh the Goat*. Harper, 1966. 90 pp.
Seven wonderful stories from Middle European Jewish folklore.

Uchida, Yoshiko. *The Dancing Kettle and Other Japanese Folk Tales*. Harcourt Brace, 1949. 174 pp.
Fourteen tales from Japanese folklore. Includes sources and a pronunciation guide.

————. *Magic Listening Cap*. Harcourt Brace, 1955. 146 pp.
Fourteen Japanese tales of courage and kindness with a background of gentle humor. Includes sources and pronunciation guide.

————. *Sea of Gold*. Scribner's, 1965. 136 pp.
Twelve more tales from Japan. Includes sources and pronunciation guide.

Williamson, Duncan. *The Broonie, Silkies and Fairies*. Harmony, 1985. 153 pp.
Twelve stories heard from the Scottish countryfolk. Includes sources, historical notes, and a glossary.

————. *Fireside Tales of the Traveller Children*. Harmony, 1983. 170 pp.
Twelve more Scottish stories told as Williamson heard them as a child. Includes sources, historical notes, and a glossary.

Wolkstein, Diane. *The Magic Orange Tree and Other Haitian Folktales*. Schocken, 1980. 212 pp.

Twenty-seven stories, short to medium length, presented in the style of the Haitian storyteller. Includes introductions to each story.

Yolen, Jane. *Favorite Folktales from Around the World.* Pantheon, 1986. 498 pp.
   One hundred and sixty stories from forty cultures. Arranged by subject. Includes an introduction on storytelling and its renaissance and extensive notes on the sources.

Storytelling Organizations and Centers

From informal story swap groups to fully organized associations, storytelling organizations now dot the United States. They form a web of support for America's storytelling revival and offer opportunities for people throughout the United States to join others who share a love of stories and storytelling. They welcome new members.

To find a local story swap group or an association, contact your community library, college or university, or arts council. Or perhaps you can find an organization near you in this extensive listing developed from the resources of the National Association for the Preservation and Perpetuation of Storytelling.

NATIONAL
Association of Black Storytellers P.O. Box 27456, Philadelphia, PA 19118

International Network of Biblical Storytellers 1810 Harvard Boulevard, Dayton, OH 45406

National Association for the Preservation and Perpetuation of Storytelling P.O. Box 309, Jonesborough, TN 37659

National Story League 3508 Russell #6, St. Louis, MO 63104

ALABAMA
Southern Association for the Preservation and Perpetuation of Storytelling P.O. Box 1154, Fairhope, AL 36532

The Spellbinders P.O. Box 443, Huntsville, AL 35804

ALASKA
Fairbanks Storytellers P.O. Box 1702, Fairbanks, AK 99707

ARIZONA
Tellers of Tales 4432 South Paseo Don Juan, Tucson, AZ 85746

CALIFORNIA
Baybottom Talespinners 1448 Valdez Way, Fremont, CA 94539

The Community Storytellers 19573 Cave Way, Topanga, CA 90290

Pacifica Storytellers 2316 Palmetto, Pacifica, CA 94044

Peninsula Story Guild 1900 Tasso Street, Palo Alto, CA 94301

San Gabriel Valley Storytellers 1130 South Marengo Avenue, Pasadena, CA 91106

Storytellers of San Diego 3406 Elliott Street, San Diego, CA 92106

COLORADO
Rocky Mountain Storyfolk *11960 West 22nd Place, Lakewood, CO 80215*

CONNECTICUT
Connecticut Chapter of the International Network of Biblical Storytellers *15 Dogwood Drive, Prospect, CT 06712*

Connecticut Storytelling Center *Department of Education, Connecticut College, New London, CT 06320*

Southeastern Connecticut Storytelling Support Group *3 Main Street, Noank, CT 06340*

DISTRICT OF COLUMBIA
Voices in the Glen, Ltd. *2631 Kirklyn Street, Falls Church, VA 22043*

FLORIDA
The Dream Spinners, The Storytellers of Sarasota *Selby Public Library, 1001 Boulevard of the Arts, Sarasota, FL 34236*

Sandbar Storytellers Guild *10531 Southwest 53rd Street, Miami, FL 33165*

The Storytelling Center *5247 81st Street N, St. Petersburg, FL 33709*

GEORGIA
Athens Storytellers *160 Hall Street, Athens, GA 30605*

The Southern Chapter of the International Network of Biblical Storytellers *Chandler School of Theology, Emory University, Atlanta, GA 30322*

Southern Order of Storytellers *980 Briarcliff Road NE, Atlanta, GA 30306*

ILLINOIS
Chicago Storytellers' Guild *1372 West Estes #25, Chicago, IL 60626*

Copper Beech Tree Folktellers Guild *Arlington Heights Memorial Library, 500 North Dunton Avenue, Arlington Heights, IL 60004*

Great Lakes Region Chapter of the International Network of Biblical Storytellers *3344 North Broadway, Chicago, IL 60657*

Heartland Story League *Tinley Park Public Library, 17101 South 71st Avenue, Tinley Park, IL 60477*

Illini Storytellers' Guild *208½ East Jefferson Street, Clinton, IL 61727*

Lincoln Story League *Dundee Township Library, 555 East Barrington Avenue, Dundee, IL 60118*

McHenry County Storytelling Guild *1210 Menge Road, Marengo, IL 60152*

North Shore Storytelling Guild *2127 Bennett Avenue, Evanston, IL 60201*

Prairie State Story League *1813 Prairie Avenue, Downers Grove, IL 60515*

Riverwind Storytellers Company *Edwardsville Public Library, 112 South Kansas Street, Edwardsville, IL 62025*

INDIANA

The Northern Indiana Storytelling Guild *1225 East Third Street, Mishawaka, IN 46544*

Northwest Indiana Storytelling Guild *Lake County Public Library, 1919 West 81st Avenue, Merrillville, IN 46410*

IOWA

Fireside Consortium *Iowa City Art Center, 129 Washington Street, Iowa City, IA 52244*

KENTUCKY

Bluegrass Storyweavers *1384 Tanforan Drive, Lexington, KY 40502*

International Order of E.A.R.S. *12019 Donohue Avenue, Louisville, KY 40243*

MAINE

Maine Chapter of the International Network of Biblical Storytellers *12 College Avenue, Gorham, ME 04038*

MARYLAND

Frederick Area Tale Spinners *P.O. Box 254, Middletown, MD 21769*

MASSACHUSETTS

New England Storytelling Center *Lesley College Graduate School, 29 Everett Street, Cambridge, MA 02238*

Western Massachusetts Chapter of the International Network of Biblical Storytellers *Granville Federated Church, Granville, MA 01034*

Western New England Storytellers' Guild *6 Round Hill Road, Northampton, MA 01060*

MICHIGAN

Community Storytellers Club *P.O. Box 521, Oshtemo, MI 49077*

Detroit Story League *2825 Kimberly Street, Ann Arbor, MI 48104*

Great Lakes Storytellers *Suite 186, 1043 Robbins Road, Grand Haven, MI 49417*

Story Spinners of Grand Rapids *East Grand Rapids Public Library, 746 Lakeside Drive SE, East Grand Rapids, MI 49506*

MINNESOTA

Northlands Storytelling Network *P.O. Box 758, Minneapolis, MN 55458*

Storyfront *4825 Wellington Lane, Plymouth, MN 55442*

MISSISSIPPI

Carousel StorySpinners 1505 61st Court, Meridian, MS 39305

OSIMILA (Order of Storytellers in Mississippi and Louisiana) 1505 61st Court, Meridian, MS 39305

MISSOURI

Gateway Storytellers 527 Greeley Avenue, Webster Groves, MO 63119

Jacob's Pillow Coffeehouse 14455 Clayton Road, Ballwin, MO 63011

Midwest Storytelling Theatre 9100 Cherry Street, Kansas City, MO 64131

Missouri Storytelling 636 Elmwood Avenue, St. Louis, MO 63119

NEW HAMPSHIRE

Seacoast Storytellers Portsmouth Public Library, 8 Islington Street, Portsmouth, NH 03801

NEW JERSEY

North Jersey Storytellers 145 Walnut Street, Englewood, NJ 07631

NEW MEXICO

Library Storytellers 1730 Llano Street, Santa Fe, NM 87505

NEW YORK

Genesee Storytellers 203 Whistle Stop, Pittsford, NY 14534

Jewish Storytelling Center 525 West End Avenue, Apt. 8C, New York, NY 10024

New York and New Jersey Chapter of the International Network of Biblical Storytellers 229 West 78th Street, New York, NY 10024

New York City Storytelling Center 10 Patchin Place, New York, NY 10011

Odyssey Story Tellers Finger Lakes Library System, 314 North Cayuga Street, Ithaca, NY 14850

Pearl in the Egg Storytellers' Guild Kirkland Art Center, P.O. Box 213, Clinton, NY 13413

Spin-a-Story Tellers of Western New York 31 St. Paul Mall, Buffalo, NY 14240

Story Circle of the Capitol District 1117 Ardsley Road, Schenectady, NY 12308

Storytelling Center of Oneonta Route 2, Box 206, Delhi, NY 13753

Westchester Storytellers' Guild 60 Southlawn Avenue, Dobbs Ferry, NY 10522

NORTH CAROLINA

Chapel Hill Area Storytellers P.O. Box 8, Bynum, NC 27228

Tarheel Association of Storytellers 740 Cleveland Avenue, Winston-Salem, NC 27101

OHIO
Cleveland Storytelling Guild 5832 *Clearview Drive, Parma Heights,* OH 44130

Miami Valley Storytellers *Dayton and Montgomery County Public Library, 215 East Third Street, Dayton,* OH 45402

Ohio Chapter of the International Network of Biblical Storytellers *1481 East Huffman Avenue, Dayton,* OH 45403

OOPS (Ohio Order for the Preservation of Storytelling) *1985 Velma Avenue, Columbus,* OH 43211

Word Weavers of the Public Library of Columbus & Franklin County *Whitehall Library, 4371 East Broad Street, Columbus,* OH 43213

OKLAHOMA
Territory Tellers *704 North Dryden Circle, Stillwater,* OK 74075

OREGON
Eugene Storytellers Association *1975 Olive Street, Eugene,* OR 97405

PENNSYLVANIA
Hola Kumba Ya *P.O. Box 50173, Philadelphia,* PA 19132

Lancaster Chapter of the International Network of Biblical Storytellers *545 College Avenue, H-302, Lancaster,* PA 17603

Patchwork: A Storytelling Guild *101 West Harvey Street, Philadelphia,* PA 19144

Philadephia Chapter of the International Network of Biblical Storytellers *1043 Nicholson Road, Wynnewood,* PA 19096

Tapestry of Tales *York Area Storytelling Guild, Route 6, Box 253-S, Red Lion,* PA 17356

RHODE ISLAND
The Spellbinders *301 Jacob Street, Seekonk,* MA 02771

SOUTH CAROLINA
South Carolina Storytellers' Guild *101 Verdin Drive, Mauldin,* SC 29662

TENNESSEE
Chatta-Tellers *84 Lake Shore Lane, Chattanooga,* TN 37415

Tennessee Association for the Preservation and Perpetuation of Storytelling *East Tennessee State University, Box 21910A, Johnson City,* TN 37614

Yarnspinners of Memphis *1950 Felix Avenue, Memphis,* TN 38104

TEXAS

Dallas Storytelling Guild *5310 Keller Springs Road #833, Dallas, TX 75248*

Heart of Texas Storytelling Guild *2924 Braemar Street, Waco, TX 76710*

Houston Storytellers' Guild *1525 West Main Street, Houston, TX 77006*

Tarrant Area Guild of Storytellers *P.O. Box 470273, Fort Worth, TX 76147*

Texas Storytellers' Guild *P.O. Box 6901, NT Station, Denton, TX 76203*

Texas Storytelling Association *P.O. Box 441, Krum, TX 76249*

"Voices of Excellence" *Preston Royal Library, 5626 Royal Lane, Dallas, TX 75229*

VIRGINIA

Northern Virginia Storytellers *Route 1, Box 576, Chantilly, VA 22021*

Richmond Story League *920 Clearlake Road, Richmond, VA 23236*

Turning Stone Story Guild *Route 1, Box 147, Barboursville, VA 22923*

WASHINGTON

Seattle Storytellers' Guild *16741 37th Street NE, Seattle, WA 98155*

Storyspinners of the Inland Northwest *East 44 Hawthorne Road, Spokane, WA 99218*

CANADA

Stone Soup Stories *154 Queenston Street, Winnipeg, Manitoba R3N 0W7*

The Storytellers' School of Toronto *412A College Street, Toronto, Ontario M5T 1T3*

T.A.L.E.S. (The Alberta League Encouraging Storytelling) *10523 100 Avenue, Edmonton, Alberta T5J 0A8*

Vancouver Storytelling Circle *4143 W15, Vancouver, British Columbia V6R 3A4*

Festivals, Conferences, and Other Storytelling Events

Since the first National Storytelling Festival in 1973, storytelling festivals, conferences, and other events have sprung up throughout the United States. Each celebrates the ageless art of storytelling through storytelling performances, workshops in storytelling education, and other opportunities to showcase America's stories, storytellers, and rich and varied storytelling traditions.

To find a local festival, conference, or storytelling event, contact your local library or arts council. You may even find an event near you in this extensive listing developed from the resources of the National Association for the Preservation and Perpetuation of Storytelling.

ONGOING

Colorado Storytellers Concert *P.O. Box 588, Monument, CO 80132*

Conferences and Workshops *Phoenix Power and Light Company, Inc., Drawer C, Odenton, MD 21113*

Fifth Sunday Storytelling *Callanwolde Fine Arts Center, 980 Briarcliff Road NE, Atlanta, GA 30306*

Oro City Yarn Spinners Gathering *Colorado Mountain College, Leadville, CO 80461*

Second Sunday Storytelling *Boiserie Coffeehouse, University of Washington, 846 Northeast 98th Street, Seattle, WA 98115*

Spellbinders Storytelling Series for Adults *301 Jacob Street, Seekonk, MA 02771*

Stories After Dark *99 Arlington Street, Brighton, MA 02135*

Storytellers in Concert *P.O. Box 994, Cambridge, MA 02238*

Winter Tales *North Columbia Schoolhouse Cultural Center, 17894 Tyler-Foote Crossing Road, Nevada City, CA 95959*

Young Israel of Hancock Park Jewish Storytelling Extravaganza *321 North Detroit Street, Los Angeles, CA 90036*

JANUARY

Festival of the Moon of the Geese *Order of Storytellers in Mississippi and Louisiana, 1505 61st Court, Meridian, MS 39305*

Mid-Winter Storytelling Conference *Tellers of Tales, 4432 South Paseo Don Juan, Tucson, AZ 85746*

Olde Christmas Storytelling Festival *Callanwolde Fine Arts Center, 980 Briarcliff Road NE, Atlanta, GA 30306*

Wintertales Storytelling Festival *Arts Council of Oklahoma City, 400 West California Avenue, Oklahoma City, OK 73102*

FEBRUARY

Institute on Storytelling Skills for Ministry *Storyfest Productions, 3901 Cathedral Avenue NW, #608, Washington, DC 20016*

Toronto Festival of Storytelling *The Storytellers School of Toronto, 412A College Street, Toronto, Ontario M5T 1T3 Canada*

MARCH

Rocky Mountain Storytellers Conference *University of Colorado at Denver, 1200 Larimer Street, Denver, CO 80204*

Sharing the Fire Storytelling Conference *New England Storytelling Center, Lesley College Graduate School, 49 Washington Avenue, Cambridge, MA 02238*

APRIL

A(ugusta) Baker's Dozen: A Celebration of Stories *Richland County Public Library, 1400 Sumter Street, Columbia, SC 29201*

Bay Area Storytelling Festival *2808 Hillegass Avenue, Berkeley, CA 94705*

Connecticut Storytelling Festival *Department of Education, Connecticut College, New London, CT 06320*

Fremont Storytelling Festival *Baybottom Talespinners, 1448 Valdez Way, Fremont, CA 94539*

Northlands Storytelling Conference and School of Storytelling *Northlands Storytelling Network, P.O. Box 758, Minneapolis, MN 55458*

Sangamon State University Storyfest *Sangamon State University, Shepherd Road, Springfield, IL 62708*

Stone Soup Storytelling Festival *Woodruff Branch Library, East Georgia Street, Woodruff, SC 29388*

Storytelling Festival *Southern Association for the Preservation and Perpetuation of Storytelling, P.O. Box 1154, Fairhope, AL 36532*

Storytelling Festival *Tennessee Association for the Preservation and Perpetuation of Storytelling, East Tennessee State University, Box 21910A, Johnson City, TN 37614*

Storytelling Gathering *1712 Aupuni Street, Honolulu, HI 96817*

Tampa/Hillsborough Storytelling Festival *Tampa/Hillsborough County Public Library, 900 North Ashley Drive, Tampa, FL 33602*

Tapestry of Talent: Student State Storytelling Festival *504 Allen Hall, West Virginia University, Morgantown, WV 26506*

Virginia Storytelling Festival *Route 1, Box 576, Chantilly, VA 22021*

MAY

Biscayne Bay Storytelling Festival *101 West Flagler Street, Miami, FL 33130*

Busch Gardens Storytelling Festival *Busch Gardens, The Old Country, P.O. Drawer F-C, Williamsburg, VA 23187*

Claremont Spring Folk Festival *220 Yale Avenue, Claremont, CA 91711*

Mountain Valley Arts Council Storyteller Festival *P.O. Box 525, Guntersville, AL 35976*

OOPS Storytelling Conference *Ohio Historical Society, 1985 Velma Avenue, Columbus, OH 43211*

Renaissance City Storyfest *585 Manoogian Hall, Wayne State University, Detroit, MI 48202*

St. Louis Storytelling Festival *314 Lucas Hall, University of Missouri–St. Louis, 8001 Natural Bridge Road, St. Louis, MO 63121*

Southern California Storyswapping Festival *19573 Cave Way, Topanga, CA 90290*

Storytellers Special Interest Group of the International Reading Association *East Tennessee State University, Box 21910A, Johnson City, TN 37614*

Storytelling Institute *Palmer School of Library and Information Science, C. W. Post Campus, Long Island University, Brookville, NY 11548*

Storytelling Workshop *University of Washington, Graduate School of Library and Information Science, FM-30, Seattle, WA 98195*

Tapestry of Talent Children's Storytelling Event *38 School Street, Enfield, CT 06082*

Tarheel Storytelling Festival *818 Woodcote Street, Winston-Salem, NC 27107*

Texas Tale Trading and Music Festival *Armand Bayou Nature Center, P.O. Box 58828, Houston, TX 77258*

Washington Storytelling Festival *2631 Kirklyn Street, Falls Church, VA 22043*

Women's Storytelling Intensive *724 Berkley Street, Berkley, MA 02780*

JUNE

Clearwater's Hudson River Revival *112 Market Street, Poughkeepsie, NY 12601*

Great Lakes International Storytelling Festival *250 Martin Street, Birmingham, MI 48011*

Marion Carter Storytelling Festival *168 West 500 N, Salt Lake City, UT 84114*

Michigan Storytellers Festival *Flint Public Library, 1026 East Kearsley Street, Flint, MI 48502*

Missouri River Storytelling Gathering *Midwest Storytelling Theatre, 9100 Cherry Street, Kansas City, MO 64131*

National Congress on Storytelling *National Association for the Preservation and Perpetuation of Storytelling,* P.O. Box 309, Jonesborough, TN 37659

Open Air Storytelling Festival *Finger Lakes Library System, 314 North Cayuga Street, Ithaca, NY 14850*

Storytelling Conference *University of Rochester, 125 Lattimore Hall, Rochester,* NY 14627

SunFest Storytelling Festival *P.O. Box 3705, Bartlesville,* OK 74006

Taking Words, Making Worlds Storytelling Conference *56 Brighton Street, Rochester, NY 14607*

JULY

The Art of Storytelling from the Inside Out *P.O. Box 214, Oak Bluffs,* MA 02557

CONFRATUTE *Conference/Institute on Gifted Education, University of Connecticut, Box U7, Room 28, Storrs Hall, 231 Glenbrook Road, Storrs,* CT 06268

Copper Beech Tree Storytellers Festival *Arlington Heights Memorial Library, 500 North Dunton Avenue, Arlington Heights,* IL 60004

Illinois Storytelling Festival *P.O. Box 1012, Woodstock,* IL 60098

Jewish Storytelling Conference *525 West End Avenue, Apt. 8C, New York,* NY 10024

Long Island Summer Storytelling Festival *Cartoon Opera,* P.O. Box 354, Huntington, NY 11743

Mansfield University Storytelling Workshop *P.O. Box 117, Mansfield,* PA 16933

Sierra Storytelling Festival *North Columbia Schoolhouse Cultural Center, 17894 Tyler-Foote Crossing Road, Nevada City,* CA 95959

Storyfest Ministry Travel Seminar *3901 Cathedral Avenue NW, #608, Washington,* DC 20016

Storytelling in Central Park *New York Public Library, 455 Fifth Avenue, New York,* NY 10012

AUGUST

Chippewa Valley Storytelling Festival *Chippewa Valley Museum,* P.O. Box 1204, Eau Claire, WI 54702

Conference on Jewish Storytelling *525 West End Avenue, Apt. 8C, New York,* NY 10024

Garrett Lakes Arts Storytelling Festival *Garrett Community College, McHenry,* MD 21541

Great Lakes Area Storytellers Symposium *Great Lakes Storytellers, Suite 186, 1043 Robbins Road, Grand Haven,* MI 49417

Hoosier Storytelling Festival *P.O. Box 20743, Indianapolis,* IN 46220

Laura Simms Storytelling Residency *Wellspring Renewal Center, P.O. Box 332, Philo, CA 95466*

Texas Folklife Festival *Institute of Texan Cultures, P.O. Box 1226, San Antonio, TX 78294*

SEPTEMBER

Cedar River Storytellers Festival *Wartburg College, 222 Ninth Street NW, Waverly, IA 50677*

College of Lake County Storytelling Conference *College of Lake County, 19351 West Washington Street, Grayslake, IL 60030*

Corn Island Storytelling Festival *12019 Donohue Avenue, Louisville, KY 40243*

Fall Storytelling Festival *Wake County Public Library System, 4020 Carya Drive, Raleigh, NC 27610*

Fish Story Telling Contest *Cuyahoga County Public Library, 5225 Library Lane, Maple Heights, OH 44137*

Northern Appalachian Storytelling Festival *P.O. Box 117, Mansfield, PA 16933*

Rockford Storytelling Festival *5690 East State Street, Rockford, IL 61108*

September Storytelling at the Stovall House *Callanwolde Fine Arts Center, 980 Briarcliff Road NE, Atlanta, GA 30306*

Three Apples Storytelling Festival *P.O. Box 994, Cambridge, MA 02238*

OCTOBER

Alabama Tale-Tellin' Festival *1103 Selma Avenue, Selma, AL 36701*

Children's Literature and Storytelling Conference *Trenton State College, Forcina Hall 384, Hillwood Lakes, Trenton, NJ 08650*

Family Halloween Storytelling Festival *P.O. Box 101, Blue Mounds, WI 53517*

The Gathering *Kalamazoo Nature Center, 2528 Aberdeen Drive, Kalamazoo, MI 49008*

National Storytelling Festival *National Association for the Preservation and Perpetuation of Storytelling, P.O. Box 309, Jonesborough, TN 37659*

Pumpkin Patch Festival *145 Walnut Street, Englewood, NJ 07631*

Storyfiesta *Storytellers International, 4703 Club House Lane NW, Suite H-5, Albuquerque, NM 87114*

Storytellers on Tour in Colorado *P.O. Box 588, Monument, CO 80132*

Storytelling *2825 Kimberly Street, Ann Arbor, MI 48104*

Storytelling Conference *National College of Education, 2840 Sheridan Road, Evanston, IL 60201*

Storytelling Festival *Caldwell County Public Library, Caldwell Arts Council, 601 College Avenue SW, Lenoir, NC 28645*

Storytelling Institute: University of New Mexico *Storytellers International, 4703 Club House Lane NW, Suite H-5, Albuquerque, NM 87114*

T.A.L.E.S. Storyfest *10523 100 Avenue, Edmonton, Alberta T5J 0A8*

Wisconsin Storytelling Get-Together *7306 23rd Avenue, Kenosha, WI 53140*

NOVEMBER

Cherokee Rose Storytelling Festival *1971 South Highway 16, Carrollton, GA 30117*

Elva Young Van Winkle Storytelling Festival *901 G Street NW, Washington, DC 20001*

Fall Festival of Tales *P.O. Box 6051, Charlottesville, VA 22906*

National Council of Teachers of English *Department of Education, University of Michigan–Flint, Flint, MI 48508*

National Festival of Black Storytelling *P.O. Box 27456, Philadelphia, PA 19118*

Women's Storytelling Intensive *724 Berkley Street, Berkley, MA 02780*

DECEMBER

Tulsey Town Storytelling Festival *3913 East 37th Place, Tulsa, OK 74135*

Winter Solstice Storytelling Celebration *Northampton Center for the Arts, 6 Round Hill Road, Northampton, MA 01060*

Storytelling Education

Colleges and universities, storytelling organizations and centers, and other agencies throughout the United States are offering learning opportunities in the practice, uses, and applications of storytelling. To find a program in storytelling education near you, contact your local college or university, community library, or arts council. Or, a listing of programs offering opportunities in storytelling education has been developed from the resources of the National Association for the Preservation and Perpetuation of Storytelling.

Dominican College: Academy for Personal Development *Education Department, 1520 Grand Avenue, San Rafael, CA 94901*

National Storytelling Institute *National Association for the Preservation and Perpetuation of Storytelling, P.O. Box 309, Jonesborough, TN 37659*

New England Storytelling Center *Lesley College Graduate School, 49 Washington Avenue, Cambridge, MA 02138*

Storytellers School of Toronto *412A College Street, Toronto, Ontario M5T 1T3*

For information and resources on storytelling, contact:

National Association for the
Preservation and Perpetuation of Storytelling
P. O. Box 309
Jonesborough, Tennessee 37659
(615) 753-2171

Glossary

Ballad   A traditional narrative song, usually anonymous, handed down from generation to generation.

Bard   A storyteller who created and told the poetic, oral narratives of Ireland, Wales, Scotland, and parts of Brittany.

Cumulative tale   A story with repetitive lines and rhythm.

Droll   A traditional story about sillies or numbskulls.

Epic   A traditional story about a hero and his adventures.

Fable   An animal tale that teaches a lesson or moral.

Fairy tale   A story with fairies, pixies, leprechauns, or elves.

Folklore   The traditional beliefs, skills, and stories of a people.

Folktale   A traditional story usually portraying ordinary people having extraordinary adventures.

Griot   A person in African cultures who sings the songs, tells the stories, and recounts the history of his or her native land.

Hero tale   A traditional story about an extraordinary person who embodies the ideals of a culture.

Legend   A story, told as if it were true, about a person, place, or event that relates the history of a culture.

Literary tale   A short story written with elements reminiscent of a traditional folktale.

Minstrel   A traveling storyteller and singer of the Middle Ages.

Monologue   A performance, usually theatrical, presented by one person.

Myth   A traditional story used to explain the world and human existence.

Revivalist storyteller   One who tells stories he or she has learned through research and collecting.

Tall tale   Stories about the exaggerated exploits of people or animals.

Traditional story   A story handed down generation after generation.

Traditional storyteller   One who tells stories handed down by those in his or her own culture.